Scholars in Context

Scholars in Context

The Effects of Environments on Learning

Edited by
W. J. CAMPBELL
Professor of Education
University of Queensland

JOHN WILEY & SONS AUSTRALASIA PTY LTD
Sydney   New York   London   Toronto

10 9 8 7 6 5 4 3 2 1

National Library of Australia card service number and Standard Book Number: Cloth 471 13310 8; Paper 471 13311 6

Library of Congress catalog card number: 72-89961

Composition by Smith & Miles Pty Ltd, Sydney

Printed in Hong Kong by Toppan Printing Co., (H.K.) Ltd

THIS book aims to explore the nature, and effects upon school learning, of environments ranging from nation to classroom. The assumption is made that environments are important determiners of learning behaviour, but in no sense do we wish to discount the significance of other variables, such as the unique personalities of learners. These latter are clearly of tremendous importance, but, although they interact with environments, they can be studied more fruitfully and economically within the framework of other learning theories. The decision to focus upon contextual variables was taken because of the relative neglect of these in many educational studies. This neglect has persisted despite the fact that teachers and educational administrators are continually structuring and manipulating environments in the hope that particular behaviours will be elicited in their pupils. As Sir Fred Clarke was moved to write a quarter of a century ago:

> If we conducted our medical and engineering services and our industrial production with the same slipshod carelessness, the same disregard for precision of thought and language, the same wild and reckless play of sentimentality or class prejudice or material interest masquerading as principle, with which we carry on our public discussions about education, most patients would die, most bridges would fall down, and most manufacturing concerns would go bankrupt.
>
> Education has at least as much claim to systematic study as animal husbandry or rural economy or coal mining. . . . Systematic, courageous and uncontaminated thinking about national education touches our national salvation.[1]

It will be obvious to the reader that the task of ascribing learning effects to contextual variables is extremely difficult, for the phenomena are so disparate. Can one really link within a causal chain physical phenomena such as class grouping or size of school, and psychological phenomena such as analytical skills, commitment and flexibility? Leading psychologists such as Lewin[2] and Brunswik,[3] both of whom would be most sympathetic towards the attempt, would answer with a resounding 'No'. On the other hand, Barker[4] and his associates would answer the question with a tentative 'Yes', and they suggest ways of overcoming what they agree is a serious dilemma in handling non-psychological data psychologically.

A second difficulty in undertaking contextual studies lies in the fact that human behaviour, except perhaps in psychological laboratories, can seldom, if ever, be related in a one-to-one fashion with 'input' variables. Rather this behaviour is a response to a *pattern* of interacting variables. It is one thing to acknowledge this and quite another to cope with it in the research studies, for techniques of multivariate analysis are not well advanced.

The book has been divided into six parts which have a funnelling relationship with one another: cultural contexts, community contexts, home contexts, peer-group contexts, institutional contexts, and classroom contexts. Within each of the six parts, too, the funnelling approach has been adopted, for broad survey chapters which identify important issues are followed by research reports related to these issues. The reports are exploratory in the sense that none is claimed to be definitive, and all are best regarded as shafts aimed at tapping the field.

The research studies have a common theoretical orientation but they differ in two main respects. First, they concern different settings within the total environment; thus, for example, some focus upon home issues and others upon institutional ones. Our main interest has been in the environments of institutions and classrooms, but some of the chapters deal with the more inclusive settings, thus enabling a wider picture to be painted however sketchily. Obviously the net could have been thrown further still, but the majority of elements which have importance in a study of learning are likely to be encompassed within national boundaries. The more significant respect in which the studies differ relates to *scope*. According to the view taken here, the field of education extends from things and events in the environment through an intrapersonal region to immediate and long-term achievements by the person. Some of the studies in this book attempt to trace cause and effect relationships along the full lode. Others, following the classical Lewinian tradition, start at the intrapersonal region, and regard the environment, *per se*, as a 'primitive given', or shadowy background, to the investigation. Thereafter, however, they proceed in the same manner as the first group. Some start with ecological facts, such as organization of school grades, omit the intrapersonal region, and concentrate upon correlations with pupil achievements. Finally, some undertake an extensive analysis of particular contexts, and content themselves with speculating about effects upon pupil learning. Taken together the studies are intended to complement one another and to throw further light upon learning from the kindergarten to the university.

I would like to acknowledge the considerable help I have received as editor from my colleagues in the period when the book was in press and I was overseas. Particularly, I would mention Drs R. P. Tisher and D. J. Drinkwater. Thanks are due, too, to Mrs M. Young, who prepared the indices and assisted in numerous other ways.

Notes

[1]Clarke, F., 1943: *The Study of Education in England*. Oxford University Press, London, ii-iv. By permission of the Clarendon Press, Oxford.

[2]Lewin, K., 1935: *A Dynamic Theory of Personality*. McGraw-Hill Book Co., New York.

[3]Brunswik, E., 1955: The conceptual framework of psychology. In *International Encyclopaedia of Unified Science*. Vol. 1, Pt 2, University of Chicago Press, Chicago, Ill., 656-750.

[4]Barker, R. G., 1960: Ecology and motivation. In M. R. Jones (Ed.), *Nebraska Symposium on Motivation*. University of Nebraska Press, Lincoln.

Contributors

R. S. ADAMS, MA, DipEd (N.Z.), PhD (Otago), DipT (Well.)
Associate-Professor, Center for Research in Social Behavior, University of Missouri

B. J. BIDDLE, BA (Antioch), PhD (Michigan)
Director, Center for Research in Social Behavior and Professor of Sociology and Psychology, University of Missouri

E. BOWKER, MA, DipEd (Liv.)
Senior Lecturer in Education, University of Queensland

W. J. CAMPBELL, MA, DipEd (N.Z.), PhD, DipAIE (Lond.)
Professor of Education, University of Queensland

K. F. COLLIS, BA, MEd (Q'ld)
Lecturer in Education, University of Newcastle, N.S.W.

D. J. DRINKWATER, MA (Syd.), MA, PhD (Lond.)
Senior Lecturer in Education, University of Queensland

M. J. DUNKIN, BA (Syd), PhD (Q'ld)
Senior Lecturer in Education, Macquarie University

G. T. EVANS, BSc, BEd, PhD (Q'ld)
Associate-Professor, Ontario Institute for Studies in Education

J. M. GENN, BSc, BA, BEd, PhD (Q'ld)
Senior Lecturer in Education, University of Queensland

DAPHNE M. KEATS, BA, DipEd (Syd.), MEd, PhD (Q'ld)
Staff Tutor, Adult Education, University of Sydney

J. R. LAWRY, BA, BEd (Melb.), PhD (Monash)
Senior Lecturer in Education, Monash University

R. V. McSWEENEY, MA, DipEd (Auck.)
Lecturer in Education, University of Queensland

ANNE SILCOCK, BA, PhD (Q'ld)
Lecturer in Education, University of Queensland

R. P. TISHER, MSc, DipEd (Syd.), BA (New Eng.), PhD (Q'ld)
Senior Lecturer in Education, University of Queensland

BETTY H. WATTS, BA, BEd (Q'ld)
Senior Lecturer in Education, University of Queensland

Contents

Part I
The Cultural Context

1

The Cultural Context

E. Bowker

ONE OF the rewarding yet unconsidered incidental advantages of man's attempts to conquer space has been a liberating effect on the work of cartoonists and creators of jokes. Man's eyes may well have been turned upwards to the heavens, and speculation about the place of mankind in the order of things may have become more widespread; of equal significance is the parallel development of self-consciousness in people, an increasing curiosity about how representatives of other civilizations may see us. Hence, in part at least, the spate of cartoons and jokes involving flying saucers and Martians who are usually to be found in conversation with some kind of machinery and demanding to be taken to see the machine's leader. The possibilities for oblique comment on human society are obvious, based, as the situations are, on a misunderstanding or on an incomplete knowledge of the ramifications of something seen in isolation. Moreover, the device of standing outside a society and making naïve or disingenuous comments can bring a new perspective to our understanding. This awareness, anchored in the fact that we perhaps see other countries and other peoples as odd, and that other peoples will find us equally peculiar, can to a considerable extent be attributed to the growth of interest in our fellow men which has been stimulated by the vast curiosity of the mass media fed by television reports, film documentaries and books of travel, as well as being promoted by ever easier means of communication. Our knowledge of other peoples and their ways of life is continually being enriched by the work of anthropologists; it is often suggested, too, that the desire to know more about ourselves, which is by no means a monopoly of modern times, has been given fresh impetus by the probings of psychologists and, indeed, by work in all the behavioural sciences. It is the task of this chapter to indicate the main broad factors which can have an impact on the attitudes and work of children in the classroom. To do this we shall need our Martian visitors' impartial sense of inquiry, sharpened, yet modified, by the speculations and research of workers in the social sciences.

This is not the place to enter into a detailed discussion of the nature and aims of education itself, but it is necessary, at the outset, to declare the way in which the term is to be employed. For our purpose, it is convenient to use Durkheim's (1956) statement, 'Education is the influence exercised by adult generations on those that are not yet ready for social life. Its object is to arouse and to develop in the child a certain number of physical, intellectual, and moral states which are demanded of him by both the political society as a whole and the special milieu for which he is specifically destined.' (p. 71.*)

For Durkheim, then, education is essentially the socialization of the child. As he expresses it, the child brings its own nature as an individual to the process of education, but each new generation is almost a *tabula rasa* as far as society is concerned. There may well be common features of educational ideals in different countries but, in Durkheim's view, each society produces its own 'ideal of man' and makes this its focal point of education.

One of the tasks of educationists is to consider these ideals of man as they manifest themselves in different societies, and to explore the ways in which each society seeks to produce this ideal in its young people. Such an approach may appear difficult to reconcile with that of the traditional theorists, concentrating, as they usually do, on universal definitions of education. Indeed, Durkheim specifically dismisses definitions which 'assume that there is an ideal, perfect education, which applies to all men indiscriminately; and it is this education, universal and unique, that the theorist tries to define. But first, if history is taken into consideration, one finds in it nothing to confirm such an hypothesis. Education has varied infinitely in time and space.' (p. 64.*)

Mannheim (1940) stresses the dual function of education, and reinforces the points made by Durkheim, 'Sociologists do not regard education solely as a means of realising abstract ideas of culture, such as humanism or technical specialisation, but as part of the process of influencing men and women. Education can only be understood when we know for what society and for what social position the children are being educated.' (p. 271.)

Despite these warnings, however, it is possible to discern a number of what Moehlman (1963) refers to as 'major long-range factors which shape the primary components and characteristics of all educational systems'.

In our constant search for specifics and for the detail it is easy to dwell on differences between societies and to destroy universal claims. But more fundamental than the search for differentiation is the reminder that human societies, in all their diversity, are in every case facing common

*From E. Durkheim, *Education and Sociology* (translation by S. D. Fox), The Free Press, Glencoe, 1956. Copyright 1956 The Macmillan Company and reprinted with their permission.

problems of adjustment to environment, of coming to terms with the basic human experiences of birth, life and death. As Maritain (1960) expresses it, 'Of course the job of education is not to shape the Platonist man-in-himself, but to shape a particular child belonging to a given nation, a given social environment, a given historical age. Yet before being a child of the twentieth century, an American-born or a European-born child, a gifted or a retarded child, this child is a child of man.' (p. 1.)

This common core of humanity enables us to perceive patterns of influence operating in all societies, inevitably in varying degrees and with differing emphases, but none the less important for being unmeasurable.

As their discipline has developed, comparative educationists have been concerned to discuss these patterns of influence, which they usually call factors influencing education. Kandel (1933), for example, in one of the pioneer works, entitles his first two chapters 'Education and Nationalism' and 'Education and National Character'. Under the first heading he discusses such topics as education and social forces; the concept of nationality, in which he raises briefly the issues of a common racial origin, language and religion, and a common culture. Dealing with the distinctiveness of national systems of education, he brings out historical factors, state and church relationships in education, class and social distinctions, racial characteristics, population, social and economic organization, and political theory. Hans (1950) subtitles his work 'A Study of Educational Factors and Traditions', and a glance at the table of contents indicates an approach having much in common with that of Kandel. Part I concerns itself with Natural Factors, in which Hans discusses racial, linguistic, geographic and economic factors. Part II, Religious Factors, explores religious traditions of Europe, then devotes sections to the Catholic, the Anglican and the Puritan traditions. In Part III, Secular Factors, Hans examines Humanism, Socialism, Nationalism, and Democracy and Education. Only in Part IV, Education in Four Democracies, does he discuss in detail education systems, those of England, the U.S.A., France and the U.S.S.R.

Moehlman (1963) concerns himself with 'the selection and depiction of the long-range factors which determine a system of education's orientation, organization and operation—i.e., effectiveness in a culture or nation'. (pp. 8-9.) He lists the long-range factors as follows:

Folk—Ethnic sources, quantity, quality, and age structure of population.

Space—Spatial concepts, territoriality, and natural features.

Time—Temporal concepts, historical development, and evolution of culture.

Language—Symbols, message systems, and communication of conceptual thought.

Art—Aesthetics, search for beauty and play.

Philosophy—Value choices, pursuit of wisdom and the good life.

Religion—Relation of man and the universe, belief systems.

Social Structure—Family, kinship, sex, etiquette, and social classes.

Government—Ordering of human relations, governmental structures and operations.

Economics—Satisfaction of wants, exchange, production, and consumption.

Technology—Use of natural resources through machines, techniques, and power resources.

Science—The sphere of knowledge concerning both natural and human realms.

Health—The condition of physical, mental, and emotional well-being, including functions of living.

Education—The social process of directed learning, both formal and informal.

The impact of these factors, says Moehlman, determines the profile of education. He suggests that this comprehensive list presents a means of evaluating how well an education system responds to major challenges and, significantly enough, he goes on to discuss 'Strategies of Education and National Style'.

Kandel uses the term 'national character', and Moehlman the term 'national style'. This is a field where it is rather dangerous and somewhat unfashionable to tread. Discussion of race and national character (if such a thing exists) easily becomes involved in emotional generalizations and expressions of prejudice rather than in objective conclusions based on valid evidence and reasoning. The claims that some nations are not merely different from, but also superior to, their neighbours by dint of racial inheritance, are recent enough to illustrate the dangers inherent in a discussion of national characteristics or style. Moreover, stress on differences between peoples, rather than on common problems uniting them, often leads to implications of superiority and inferiority. To say this is not to deny that there are, in fact, distinctive national styles which manifest themselves in education. The belief in national differences is strong even though the components of national style may be elusive when we seek to grasp them.

Writing at a time when claims of racial superiority were creating international discord, Huxley, Haddon and Carr-Saunders (1939) examined the concepts of national characteristics and racial qualities, and preferred to use the term 'group-sentiment'. They quote approvingly the following definition: 'A "nation" has been cynically but not inaptly defined as "a society united by a common error as to its origin and a common aversion to its neighbours".' Their discussion of the nature of group sentiment leads them to assert:

Group-sentiment, when submitted to analysis, thus proves to be based on something much broader but less definable than physical kinship. The occupation of a country within definite geographical boundaries, climatic conditions inducing a definite mode of life, traditions that gradually come to be shared in common, social institutions and organizations, common religious practices, even common trades or occupations—these are among the factors which have contributed in greater or less degree to the formation of national sentiment. Of very great importance is a common language, strengthened by belief in a fictitious 'blood-tie'. But among all the sentiments that nurture feelings of group unity, greater even than the imaginary tie of physical or even of historic relationship, is the reaction against outside interference . . . . Pressure from without is probably the largest single factor in the process of national evolution. (pp. 25-6.*)

Many of the factors mentioned here as contributing to the formation of group sentiment can be traced in their educational consequences. The awareness of physical kinship has always been a strong unifying force, particularly when more than one easily identifiable group is living within a single country. Perhaps the most potent factor in encouraging this awareness is the colour of skin. We can see this clearly in countries such as South Africa, the United States of America, and some of the emergent nations like Malaysia and Kenya, where the existence of more than one racial group within a country has had a considerable impact on educational ideals and organization, with a corresponding influence on the problems now being faced by educationists in these countries. In the Republic of South Africa, the policy of apartheid, of separate development for the different racial groups, is essentially an attempt by a white minority to retain the existing power structure which is based on fears that the white group would lose its identity if the black majority ever achieved the position now held by the minority. The segregation of children into different racial groups for schooling, Europeans, 'coloureds', Asiatics and Bantus, existed before the policy of apartheid was officially proclaimed in 1948, and different school systems cater for each ethnic group. Considerable impetus was given to the separate development of negro education by the Bantu Education Act of 1953. Diametrically opposed to the South African view is the decision handed down by the Supreme Court of the United States of America in 1954 (Fellman, 1960). 'We conclude that in the field of public education the doctrine of "separate but equal" has no place. Separate educational facilities are inherently unequal.'

That legal decisions in themselves are not enough to shatter long-held opinions is evident from the slow pace at which school integration has been progressing in the southern states of America since 1954. In many cases, it has been pointed out, segregated schools are essentially the product of segregated housing, and are symptoms of more general problems. Schools operating on the neighbourhood principle are bound to draw their pupils mainly from one race if separate ethnic groups are concentrated in different parts of a city. An indication of a sincere desire to overcome this problem has been the provision of 'bussing' in many American cities, whereby children are driven from their own locality to

*From J. Huxley, A. C. Haddon and A. M. Carr-Saunders, *We Europeans* (2nd edn), Penguin Books, Harmondsworth 1939. Reprinted by permission of A. D. Peters & Co.

schools in other areas in an attempt to obtain racial integration in the schools.

Many of the emergent nations face problems traceable to the inheritance of education systems which evolved for the separate ethnic groups within their borders; in Kenya, for example, there were quite distinct systems for Europeans, Africans, Asians and Arabs. As part of the search for national unity and identity the schools are now integrated, but there are many residual problems. Similarly in Malaysia, there were four branches of the school system, English, Malay, Chinese and Indian, differing, not only in the language used as the medium of instruction, but in organization, curriculum, administration and finance.

The occupation of a country within definite geographical boundaries as a factor in stimulating group sentiment needs little discussion here, though in passing we should note that, as boundaries are often no more than lines arbitrarily drawn on maps, they sometimes cut across tribal or ethnic areas of longer historical standing. In ex-colonial territories, for example, similar peoples sometimes came under different colonial traditions and were therefore exposed to different patterns of education. More specifically, the geographical situation of a country can have a marked effect on the curriculum of schools. It is evident that small countries situated between powerful neighbours will usually find it advantageous both for trade and for political reasons to encourage the learning of the languages of both neighbours. More complex than this are the problems facing a country such as Australia. Originally sharing the cultural heritage of the United Kingdom, and with a population predominantly European in origin, Australia undoubtedly belongs to what is called the Western world; yet geographically she is a Pacific nation. Her peculiar difficulties may be illustrated by the fact that she calls the part of the world lying to the north-west of Australia by the term 'the Far East'. With an ever-increasing sense of national identity, she has a number of curriculum problems to resolve. As a product of Western culture, and having close ties with the United Kingdom, Australia has expected that the schools should teach British and European history, and that school children should learn French or German. From her geographical position, and taking into account her strategic and economic commitments in the area, Australia, it is being urged, should ensure that the schools teach the history of Asian countries, and languages such as Japanese, Chinese or Malay. Clearly, unless the curriculum is to be overloaded, choices must be made.

Another factor in the development of education systems is the influence of climatic conditions. Hans points to the structure of the school system, types and methods of transport to and from school, and the age limits of compulsory attendance as illustrating this influence. Concerning the lower age limit of school entry, for example, Hans contrasts pre-war practices in northern and Mediterranean countries of Europe. The fact that in the northern countries primary education started at age seven or older, one or two years later than in the Mediterranean countries, he attributes to the severity of the northern climate making it unsuitable for children to be out of doors in winter. Moreover, as he points out, open-air schools would not be feasible in Scandinavia but are common in tropical and sub-tropical countries. Here we may also suggest that equipment, syllabus and the range of activities available in school may well be influenced by climatic considerations. Indeed, the very preservation of books, scientific equipment and teaching aids can be a problem in tropical areas. Not unrelated to climatic considerations is the effect that malnutrition and disease can have on a child's performance in school. These health problems are particularly acute in the underdeveloped parts of the world and are in part attributable to difficulties of climate.

Demographic patterns, depending partly on general geographical and climatic factors, have important consequences for educational organization and practice. Where the population is widely scattered or isolated, special arrangements become necessary. Examples of these are the provision of boarding schools, with a corresponding rise in the costs of education, the use of itinerant teachers, and the development of such specialized services as 'Schools of the Air'. There is often, though by no means always, a tendency for countries where the population is very unevenly distributed throughout the land to develop centralized education systems, usually in an attempt to ensure that standards are not markedly different in urban and rural schools. On the other hand, sheer isolation may combine with other factors to produce a decentralized system. Nash (1962), in an article entitled 'Historical versus Geographical Factors in Canadian Education', states as his thesis, 'the outstanding problems of Canadian education stem largely from a conflict between the forces of geography and those of history'.

He points out that, whereas the structure of the school in Canada is typically North American, the curriculum tends to follow a traditional European pattern. Among the historical forces shaping Canadian education he mentions those of pre-Revolutionary, Catholic France, a puritanism stemming from Scotland and Colonial New England, and Anglicanism. Geographically, the vast area of the country, combined with a small population, has produced a decentralized pattern of education and a strong provincialism. The presence of a powerful neighbour to the south, reinforced by the fact that natural lines of communication run north and south rather than east and west, increases the difficulties of establishing a national identity, especially when we take into account what Nash calls the jealous autonomy of the provinces and a desire not to incur the reproach of cultural dependence on Europe.

The impact of historical factors on education systems is of paramount importance. Sir Michael Sadler, writing at the turn of the century, helped to set the pattern for the development of comparative studies in education and gave a salutary piece of advice for educational planners in what has become a much quoted passage (Higginson, 1961):

> In studying foreign systems of Education we should not forget that the things outside the schools matter even more than the things inside the schools, and govern and interpret the things inside. We cannot

wander at pleasure among the educational systems of the world, like a child strolling through a garden and pick off a flower from one bush and some leaves from another, and then expect that if we stick what we have gathered into the soil at home we shall have a living plant. A national system of Education is a living thing, the outcome of forgotten struggles and difficulties and 'of battles of long ago'. It has in it some of the secret workings of national life. It reflects, while seeking to remedy, the failings of national character. (p. 290.)

Following in the Sadler tradition, Ulich, in *The Education of Nations* (1961), defines his intention as to contribute to an understanding of the forces that have moulded the educational ideals and systems of a number of nations, and asserts that we cannot understand the nature of the educational process unless we see it in its historical context. Accordingly, Ulich traces the evolution of educational thought and education systems from the Middle Ages. Two traditions are contrasted: 'In the Greek anthropocentric or autonomous tradition, man reaches up to the Divine, perhaps becoming divine himself; in the Christian tradition, God reaches down to save the sinner who surrenders to his judgment. There is a world of difference between the two.' (Ulich, 1961.)

Despite these fundamental differences, the classical secondary schools of Europe were originally based on the idea that the Christian and the Graeco-Roman traditions were compatible. Almost inevitably, the conflict inherent in these two views increased; on the one hand, we have the Christian ideal of self-negation; on the other hand, the humanist ideal of self-realization. The split, which Ulich sees as still persisting through the whole of Western culture, was to produce that hypocritical solution whereby the Greek tradition led to a curriculum centred round the classics in schools for the privileged, while the Christian tradition led to a curriculum centred round Christianity in the elementary schools designed for the poor. As the author expresses it, the former had to learn how to rule, the latter had to learn patience.

Ulich goes on to examine the impact on education of the Renaissance, the Reformation, the Age of Reason and the Era of Technology. The second part of the book examines individual countries; in the chapter on France, for example, he brings out the strong belief in centralization in French history, the sense of being the trustees of the Roman heritage, the influence of Catholicism and the effects of the Enlightenment as some of the fundamental determinants of the French educational system.

As part of the historical process, the sharing of traditions and the acceptance of certain social institutions not only contribute to the growth of group sentiment but also have their influence in the educational sphere. A fundamental task of the school has always been the preservation and handing on of accepted traditions. Here we may refer to the United States of America and Australia. Both countries share with the United Kingdom a common language—one of the most important unifying factors—and both have much in common with the cultural heritage of the United Kingdom. In the United States, and increasingly in Australia, a coherent and recognizable culture pattern has emerged, markedly different in many ways from the British one, as common experiences have led to the evolution of common traditions. Indeed, the school in America played an important part in the absorption into the American tradition of immigrants from many parts of the world.

The essentially conservative function of the school, the cherishing of a society's values and traditions, is an accepted task of the teacher. Fundamentally different in many respects, however, are the problems facing teachers in many emergent countries. In some cases, independence has meant the re-emergence of a coherent and easily recognizable entity, but often it has signified the creation of one state from many diverse elements. In these circumstances, one of the main problems facing a new nation is the creation of a sense of identity; the inclusion of different tribes in a single political unit brings with it the double necessity of respecting local traditions and yet of stimulating new loyalties. Here the teacher is faced, not merely with the task of preservation, but with the task of creation. In a very real sense, teachers in emergent nations can be regarded as the midwives of a new society.

Few people would disagree that the sharing of common religious practices can act as a unifying force. Later, we shall have to investigate more closely the interrelationship of religion and education, but at this point it may be mentioned that the evolution of secular, state systems of education is rooted in schools established by religious organizations, and in many countries there is a partnership, uneasy at times, between church and state to provide adequate educational facilities.

Religious factors apart, the possession of a common language is felt to be of such importance in the fostering of group sentiment that educational problems are often considered much less in the light of educational needs than in the glare of political expediency. Of course, these needs and expediency may coincide. It is generally agreed that a child should be taught in his mother tongue, at least for some time, when he starts his school career. This can be very difficult to achieve, however, in countries where different groups use different languages; in some countries there are very many languages, often spoken by small numbers and perhaps not even codified in writing. Moreover, the claims of national unity often lead people to urge that one language be selected as the national language and used, from the outset, as the medium of instruction in school. Here, educational and political purposes may clash. To make a child on his entry into school face not only a totally new situation but one in which his linguistic experience is without value is to impose an extra strain on him. The practice of using a language other than the mother tongue in school has been termed an attempt to teach the unknown through the medium of the partly known. In addition, the use of a second language means that the child will use one language in school and another at home, and thus can start a divergence between home and school experience which will isolate him from his family in an increasing number of ways. However, if one of the aims of education is to effect social changes, then this practice may become more acceptable, especially when parents are in any case unable to reinforce the lessons and values taught in school and may, in fact, militate against them. Nevertheless, the difficulties facing the child are obvious. Nor is this all. As new nations emerge, the problem of selecting a national language, normally to be used as the medium of instruction in school, becomes acute. When the emergent nation becomes independent there may well be an emotional reaction against the language of the ex-colonial power, even though this may be a world language offering access to the mainstream of technological development. Yet there may well be, at the same time, no local language sufficiently developed to be of adequate use. Alternatively, there could be a number of languages available, but the choice of any one would be politically dangerous. That such matters are not purely of 'academic' importance is shown by the riots which recur in such disparate countries as India and Belgium.

The situation is particularly complicated in India. Maxwell (1967, pp. 892-4) sets out the problems as follows. Some forty per cent of the population speaks Hindi or a closely related language; there are twelve other main regional languages spoken in the country, none by more than ten per cent of the total population, and over one thousand local languages. At independence, it was envisaged that English would be used as an official language for a period of fifteen years, and would then be replaced by Hindi as the only official language. Opposition to this provision, which was originally written into the constitution, has grown steadily over the years in the non-Hindi speaking parts of India (which are mainly in the south), as it was realized that to make Hindi the only official language was to give an enormous advantage to Hindi speakers in all-India examinations for the civil service. As long as the language for higher education and for civil service entrance is English, so it is argued, chances are more even for people from all parts of India. The argument is exacerbated by claims that, whereas English opens a window onto the world, the use of Hindi would partly close this window; in addition, it is asserted, Hindi is not flexible enough to become an instrument for defining and expressing modern scientific and technological developments. However, it is also pointed out that English has never been spoken by more than one per cent of the Indian population and that standards in English are declining since the British withdrawal. In the face of such facts, arguments in favour of retaining English may seem a little thin. Yet the opposition to Hindi is not without foundation. Alternative solutions are also fraught with difficulties. To use regional languages at all levels of education raises the problems of producing textbooks in the various languages and finding enough teachers and lecturers. More fundamentally, it is claimed that extended use of regional languages would give extra impetus to the drive towards parochialism (which is already evident in the creation of states essentially on a linguistic basis) and a splintering of India into ever more independent states; certainly recruitment to the Union Civil Service would become more difficult if candidates were not able to use the national language, whichever that might be, and therefore could not be transferred from their own state. A solution being proposed by the Central Government is known as the 'three language formula', in which Hindi speakers would learn English and one other Indian language—non-Hindi speakers learning Hindi and English. And what about the children in the middle of all this debate? It is sometimes argued in countries not facing such complicated problems that there are 'non-linguistic' children and that foreign languages are not suitable for all children. What, then, about the Indian child who, perhaps, in addition to his own local language, would be expected to make worthwhile progress in the regional language and two other languages? The ricochet effects of such problems are no less daunting. To have so many languages in the timetable means that there will be less time for other subjects; teachers competent in these languages must be trained; and the medium of instruction at different levels must be determined.

Less complicated, but hardly less intense, are problems manifesting themselves in Belgium. Here, some five million Dutch-speaking Flemings and approximately three and a half million French-speaking Walloons, together with about one and a half million people living in the bilingual area around Brussels, make up the Belgian nation. French, a language of greater international prestige than Dutch, has traditionally been used in political, business and social circles, and there has for some time been resentment by the Flemings of Walloon domination. The old Roman Catholic university at Louvain is a bilingual foundation situated in the Dutch-speaking area of the country. There is considerable agitation for the French language faculties to be transferred to the French-speaking area so that teaching at Louvain would be carried out only in Dutch. In this case, linguistic issues are but symptomatic of deeper troubles, but have led to serious political crises and have a clear effect on education.

When we approach the problems generated by the interaction of politics and education, discussion is made more difficult by the use of ambiguous terms and a vocabulary which is often emotive. At the outset, it may be useful to recall a distinction drawn by Hans (1950) when discussing the word 'democracy'. 'The English-speaking countries, and especially America, understand the term to mean a political democracy based on the English tradition of tolerance and constitutional government by popularly elected representatives. The Soviet Union and the Communists in all countries understand by it a social democracy based on a socialist economy and state monopoly.' (p. 235.)

All states use the formal education system to teach an acceptance of the values considered desirable by the leaders of the country. This can be seen most easily, perhaps, in the educational theories and practices of totalitarian states; one of the most striking examples in recent years of the use of education for political indoctrination was in Nazi Germany. There, the task of education was conceived to be the production of loyal young people whose main concern was to serve the state; changes in the structure of education (only during the period 1933-1945 has there been a centralized, fully-unified education system in Germany) and in the curriculum were not enough. New types of schools, controlled by the Nazi Party, were created; one type of these schools, the *Adolf-Hitler-Schule*, was designed as a six-year secondary school, entry to which depended partly on recommendation by party officials. It was conceived as the first stage of an educational structure completely devoted to serving political ends which would, in time, have produced the second generation of Nazi leaders.

Communist countries are usually explicit in the tasks they expect their education system to perform in the creation of a new society. Thus, for example, Article 41 of the 1949 Common Programme (UNESCO, 1955) which served as a temporary constitution for the People's Republic of China until the formal adoption of a constitution in 1954, declared:

> The culture and education of the People's Republic of China shall be New Democratic—national, scientific, and popular. The main tasks of the People's Government in cultural and educational work shall be the raising of the cultural level of the people, the training of personnel for national construction work, the eradicating of feudal, compradore and Fascist ideology, and the developing of the ideology of service to the people. (pp. 166-7.)

Similarly, the five principal aims of the Soviet school system as listed in the entry on the U.S.S.R. in UNESCO's *World Survey of Education* begin:

> 1. To give the pupil a thorough grounding in the fundamentals of the sciences dealing with nature, society and human intellect and train in him a materialist world out-look.
> 2. To provide the young generation with knowledge and understanding of the fundamentals of socialist production and to train them to link up that knowledge within the practical problems of socialist construction . . . (p. 629).

By contrast, the educational problems facing Western liberal democracies are less clear cut and more complex. They, too, must generate in the young people loyalty to their society, but because the state is not felt to be of such overriding importance the pressures for conformity cannot be so great. Characteristically, in these countries are to be found private schools side by side with a state system of education, since belief in the rights of minorities to choose the schools their children should attend is fundamental to the Western concept of democracy. Educational planning is made more difficult when the claims of the parent have to be balanced delicately against the needs of the state.

Many of the emergent countries face this problem in a particularly agonizing form. On the one hand, they have the responsibility of providing universal primary education as soon as possible: this is held to be a basic human right and one which parents are claiming more and more for their children—especially if education appears to be the highroad to individual advancement. On the other hand, secondary education must be extended urgently, for the development of national prosperity depends on the provision of a sufficient number of secondary school graduates. Moreover, it may be asked, how adequate can a primary school education be, on its own, in providing a sufficient degree of training and skills for the person who has received it to be employable? Yet, on political grounds, to advocate a delay in the introduction of universal primary education so as to develop a more adequate secondary education system could be folly. The wishes of the electorate may dictate one course, the claims of national development may point to a different choice, if choice there must be, when there is not sufficient money to do both simultaneously.

In a liberal democracy, whether well-established or emergent, conflicting political ideologies may well affect the structure of the education system, and plans for educational reform may depend on the electoral fortunes of a particular political party. Indeed, it is easy to sympathize with the West German comment (UNESCO, 1955): 'Great difficulties are experienced in getting State educational legislation passed, owing to constant changes in the parties commanding a majority.'

While it would be a gross oversimplification to call the British Labour Government's decision to introduce a secondary school system consisting of comprehensive schools a party political decision, it is certainly an issue on which opposition has found expression primarily in the ranks of the Conservative Party, and although nearly all local authorities are currently engaged in reorganizing the structure of secondary education, opposition is centred mainly in areas where the local authority is of a different political persuasion from that of the central government. This is an issue which is being determined on more than purely educational grounds since it is claimed that a comprehensive system, in addition to providing better facilities for children, will help to overcome the socially divisive effects of a tripartite secondary school system and lead towards a truer equality of educational opportunity.

Here, we approach the social factors which influence systems of education. As Holmes (1965) expresses it 'Education . . . plays a considerable part in the maintenance or disruption of the power structure of society.'

At this point we might call to mind the rather ambiguous ways in which the term 'social' is used. Durkheim, it will be remembered, distinguished between 'the political society as a whole' and 'the special milieu' for which a child was destined in society. 'Social', then, in its general sense, can be taken to mean 'pertaining to society', that is, to a nation or a political entity. The values and skills to be inculcated in children will be determined, in part at least, by the type of society that is desired. Hall and Lauwerys (1956) point out, 'It is a truism that all societies have an adequate educational system, for if they did not they would vanish. All cultures teach a language which, however primitive in form or restricted in vocabulary, is adequate for immediate needs. All transmit the essential secrets of sex and reproduction, as well as the knowledge needed to survive.' (p. 2.)

Precisely what place the school is to take alongside other agencies of education in this process of socialization will depend partly on the complexity of the social structure and partly on the function assigned to the school by members of the society.

Very commonly, we take the term 'social' to mean 'relating to the class structure of society'. In this sense, one of the main tasks of the school is envisaged to be the provision of an education suitable to the particular social background of the child. Here, concepts of social mobility and equality of opportunity become relevant. In most European countries the development of national systems of education was determined by the class structure of society. Side by side there grew two almost completely separate education routes; for the privileged, the progression was from preparatory schools to classical secondary schools and on to universities. For the less fortunate, elementary education was for long considered all that was necessary. As the systems evolved, post-primary schools provided the next stage of education from which pupils from poorer classes could pass on to vocational or technical schools, but very rarely to universities. And again, many nations retain features reflecting the class structure of society even when attempts have been made to rationalize the structure of education and provide a single education ladder. In England, for example, despite the successful introduction of secondary education for all (this is still an empty slogan in many parts of the world), inequalities persist, and the decision to bring in a system of secondary comprehensive schools has been taken as much on social as on educational grounds. Pedley (1963) likens the separate educational routes 'to the lanes in which the 400 metres is run, with one vital exception: there is no staggered start to ensure an equal chance for all competitors'.

Route one is typically for children whose parents can afford to pay large fees; starting at a private kindergarten, the child progresses to a preparatory school, then to a 'public' or independent school and on to Oxford or Cambridge University. Route two, much more determined by ability, goes from primary school to grammar school or a comprehensive school and on to a provincial university. Route three, for the majority, caters mainly for those who fail to enter a selective school at the age of eleven. As Pedley points out, this is an oversimplified picture and there are escape channels from one route to another, but it is an accurate enough representation of the education system in England before recent plans for reorganization. Even now, Pedley's comment remains appropriate, that discussion is centred mainly round the desirability of removing the line between the middle and the outside lanes. In other words, the role played by selective schools in maintaining elitist patterns of education is complicated by the problem which is posed by the existence of private schools, a problem unsolved in many Western countries. On the one hand, democracies wish to preserve minority rights—one of which can be the freedom to maintain private schools. These schools may become exclusive and exercise a disproportionate influence in the power structure of society. On the other hand, it may be argued, the school should be a place where all children are given an equal opportunity to develop their abilities to a maximum, and the provision of private schools will be seen as the provision of unequal chances in education. Yet, where education is regarded as a commodity, the claim is often made that parents should be able to buy as good an education as possible for their own children and that they have the right to choose the type of education they desire. All countries, however, are realizing more and more that to assist in the drive for national prosperity they need to make the most of the talents of all their young people. Ability, rather than birth or wealth, is increasingly becoming the passport to success, and national education systems are being overhauled to tap this ability. As a consequence, it is often pointed out, the school can be the most important vehicle for social mobility.

Not unrelated to the problem of social class in education, and certainly a social factor influencing the structure and content of education throughout the world, are the varying attitudes towards the relationships of men and women. Erikson (1963) brings out the issue in general terms: 'Youth shares with other groups, such as women and old people, the fact that the role assigned to it by nature has been elaborated by cultures as a set of differences from some standard human being, the norm, of course, being usually the normal adult male.'

In almost every country, provision for the education of girls has lagged behind that for boys, and in many parts of the world there are still inequalities based on a social attitude to the place of women in society rather than on actual sex differences. To underline this point it is necessary only to point to books and articles concerned in some way or other with the education of girls and women. It would be unusual to meet works calling similar attention to the education of boys and men. In traditional societies women are often assigned an ambivalent but basically inferior role; this can carry over into unequal provisions for education, especially where the social pattern demands early marriage and domesticity for women, so that a girl who completes a full education may be considered at a disadvantage in her matrimonial prospects. Many modern societies, too, retain such inequalities; the Robbins Report on Higher Education (1963) reveals that only a quarter of students in British universities are women. This figure would not be untypical for most countries; the percentage will depend to a very large extent on the prevailing attitude to the role of women in society.

There can be little doubt that women are being called upon to play an increasingly important part in the industrial and commercial life of most nations. The entry of females into spheres of activity previously reserved for males, while undoubtedly made possible by evolving and changing social attitudes, must also be viewed as having an underlying economic motive. As already mentioned, modern nations need to harness the talents of as many of their members as possible to help ensure economic growth and prosperity in a competitive world. Hence, the relationship between economics and education is of fundamental importance, particularly because the whole educational process becomes more and more expensive as a nation seeks to improve or maintain its position in relation to other countries.

It is obvious that economic factors must exercise considerable influence on a country's education system; this influence is easily seen at a material level, where the relative wealth or poverty of a country will help to determine such factors as the adequacy or inadequacy of school buildings and equipment, teachers' salaries and size of class. Even here, of course, economic pressures are by no means the sole determining factor; the general attitude to the importance of education will also help to determine these standards. Education must take its place in the queue for financial grants. Its claims must be considered in relation to the claims of national defence, health and medical services, communications, economic development plans and countless other needs. Concerning this point, however, it has been stated that the ability, or at any rate the desire, to spend increasing sums on education and to give a high priority to educational expenditure, is the hallmark of a vigorous nation confident of its future prosperity. The increasingly complex structure of modern societies normally leads to a general agreement that the state should accept much more responsibility for national planning than in the past. But this is happening at a time when the demand for education is rising dramatically, and when the needs of society for people qualified in a very wide range of skills are becoming ever more urgent. Education, moreover, is such a costly business nowadays that only the state has the full financial resources capable of ensuring an adequate education for all. At an earlier period, when the provision of schools was left to religious and private agencies, the costs were met either by fees or in such a way that the state was not involved. It was the advent of mass education that made it necessary to raise from taxation enough money to provide a full education system.

Countries such as the United Kingdom and the United States of America, with their tradition of decentralized, strong local government, for long have raised much of the money needed by local taxation through rates. This, one can argue, is likely to help in stimulating widespread interest in education, but it may also lead to variations in standards of educational provision, depending on the ability and willingness of the local community to pay for an adequate service. Almost inevitably, therefore, a steadily rising share of the financial burden has, in recent years, been taken over in many countries by the central government using national taxation as the means of raising the money required. It has been suggested, however, that local interest in and support for education might diminish in countries where the central authority increases its control of educational finance. However, as Hall and Lauwerys point out, it seems likely, where money is provided from central funds, that there will be a larger proportion of the national revenue spent on education than when the money is raised locally.

One problem generated by this dilemma has led to important consequences. Increased financial contributions by the central authority may well lead to increased central control of a country's education system, and, as a result, the state may feel itself entitled to stress social needs rather than individual desires in education, and therefore to extend the ramifications of educational planning. All education systems need careful planning and integration into overall plans for national development, but the extent and direction of the planning will be influenced by the structure of society and its prevailing attitude to the amount of individual freedom which is compatible with social needs. Blaug and Lauwerys, in their General Introduction to *The World Year Book of Education, 1967,* which took educational planning as its theme, distinguish three main approaches to their topic, the first being the 'social-demand' approach—where consumer choice is taken greatly into account partly because of difficulties in forcing young people to study subjects which do not interest them and partly because it is not easy to forecast what kinds of training will be needed in a country with a rapidly changing economy. As the authors comment 'It is evident that this approach commends itself to those who favour a permissive social climate, who are attached to traditional cultural values and who work in societies where public opinion has great influence.' (p. 5.)

The second approach, which stresses the employment aspects of education, is called the 'manpower-requirements' approach where 'the fundamental idea is that total production should grow as fast as possible, even if this involves some limitation on personal choice'. (p. 5.) This method of procedure carries with it the danger of inflexibility and a considerable narrowing in the aims of education.

The third approach is the 'cost-benefit' approach—where the costs of different types of education are worked out and compared with their returns to the individual and society in terms of productivity and earnings. These calculations give some guide as to which sectors of education 'pay off' best and should therefore be given some priority.

The three approaches considered raise fundamental questions about the aims and objectives of education, and the type of schooling provided will certainly be influenced by decisions taken by education planners. Economic factors have become crucial in resolving educational issues since investment in education is seen to be a means of ensuring national prosperity. Economic considerations have been made particularly urgent by what has been termed the 'Education Explosion', which was the theme of *The World Year Book of Education, 1965.* This explosion is seen as having three components. The first, an explosion of population, especially in the underdeveloped parts of the world, has given rise to grave problems at all levels; the tasks of increasing food production and of industrial development involving the full exploitation of natural resources must be seen against a pattern of rapidly increasing urbanization and mobility of population. The implications for education are apparent; merely in terms of numbers, the provision of enough schools and teachers is stretching the resources of most countries. The difficulties are compounded when we start to consider the second component, the explosion of expectation. Not merely are there more children to be educated; people are demanding more and better education in the belief that education is a basic human right, not as previously a privilege, and is the key to personal advancement as well as to national prosperity. Pressure for equality of opportunity is one of the factors leading to educational reform and the movement away from selective systems of education. In some ways, however, the most intractable problems are those caused by the third component, the explosion of knowledge. The spectacular increases during the present century in the amount of knowledge, especially in the sciences and technology, provide a challenge to educationists affecting not only the structure of schools and the nature of teacher training, but many aspects of the curriculum. New fields of study lead to a shifting emphasis both in the content of courses and the method of teaching. Old problems given a new urgency include decisions on the most desirable balance between scientific and literary studies, the most appropriate time to begin specialized courses and the apparent clash between general and vocational education. Cros, in a chapter of *The World Year Book of Education, 1965,* entitled 'The Demand for General Education in France', discusses the relationship between general education and subsequent vocational or specialized training. As he declares, 'There is now no trade, however modest, of which the practice is not linked with study and theory which are constantly changing; there is no trade in which one must not continually adapt oneself to new ideas, practise methods which were unknown when one began. Practical skill is now an extension of theoretical knowledge.' (p. 268.)

In other words, there is today a need for more general education than formerly; indeed, Cros points out, the French national economy feels the need for technical and specialized knowledge less than the need for more general and basic qualities and skills, and he observes:

> It is still expected that general education shall provide children with a fund of information, but about methods rather than results; a training is expected from it, but one conceived more as a training in thought and judgment, in research and methods of communication, in expression and creation in all its forms—oral and written, technical and artistic. Henceforward imagination and new ideas are most in demand. Much more than formerly, to be educated means to learn how to learn. (p. 269.)

How quickly national education systems adapt themselves to these changing demands depends, to a large degree, on the strength of professional conservatism which varies markedly from country to country. National systems of education in Western countries are essentially products of the nineteenth century and were profoundly influenced by the course of the Industrial Revolution. But the demands of a modern economy, and indeed the very pace and character of modern society, make necessary a constant reappraisal of the school's structure and function. McLuhan (1967), on this point, roundly asserts:

> There is a world of difference between the modern home environment of integrated electric information and the classroom. Today's television child is attuned to up-to-the-minute 'adult' news—inflation, rioting, war, taxes, crime, bathing beauties—and is bewildered when

he enters the nineteenth-century environment that still characterizes the educational establishment where information is scarce but ordered and structured by fragmented, classified patterns, subjects, and schedules. It is naturally an environment much like any factory set-up with its inventories and assembly lines. (p. 18.*)

The education explosion, reinforced by the steadily increasing costs of providing an adequate school system, has had a marked effect in the sphere of private education and has given fresh impetus to discussion of church and state relations in education. Here we approach in one sense the religious factors, mentioned previously, which exert an influence on education systems. Bereday and Lauwerys, in the Editors' Introduction to *The World Year Book of Education, 1966,* which took as its theme Church and State in education, declare:

> Broadly speaking, church-state relations in education turn nowadays upon two chief issues:
> 1. Should religion be taught in state schools? And if so, may the state interfere with the teaching?
> 2. In countries where separate schools, under church control exist, should they have a share of public funds?

The second of these two issues assumes fresh urgency when well-established religiously-based private school systems are faced by rapidly increasing costs. Ideological considerations become, in a way, irrelevant, especially where such private schools cater for a significant proportion of the school population and thus relieve the state of certain financial burdens in providing an adequate educational system. In France, for example, some fifteen per cent of elementary school children are educated in Roman Catholic schools, and approximately double that percentage of secondary school pupils.

The often uneasy partnership between church and state in education, especially in Christian parts of the world, reflects, to an extent, the swaying fortunes in the struggle for power between religious and secular authorities. In most parts of the world, formalized education in the sense of school institutions sprang from religious needs and was provided by ecclesiastical bodies. In Europe, during the Middle Ages, schools were established by the church to help in the provision of an educated body of people who would find their career in the church. In fact, as Goodings and Lauwerys (1966, p. 1) point out, only the church at that time had the money, knowledge and the organization necessary for the development of an educational service. Even the Reformation, which led to an alliance between the religious and the secular powers in matters of education, left basic control in the hands of the church. Lutheranism, with its stress on the necessity for individual Bible study, generated in parts of Germany the need for something approaching a universal system of elementary education, and this led, in partnership with the secular authority, to an early provision of schooling, but essentially the control of the curriculum and provision of teachers was acknowledged to be a responsibility of the church. Not until the emergence of the modern nation-state in the nineteenth century, with the Industrial Revolution creating a demand for training, did the secular power find the need to make extensive financial provision for schools and thus find it possible to assert claims for control of the structure and content of education itself. Such a situation led often, though not inevitably, to clashes between the church and the state. The basic issue, as Lauwerys and Hans (1951) expressed it, is simply 'Those who control the schools determine what shall be taught and how: it is they who ultimately decide what the new generations shall believe, and who mould their attitude to existing institutions.'

The church, as the original provider of schools but now unable to continue this role without financial assistance from the state, has often been forced into compromise in order to retain its influence, but essentially it must believe that education should be religiously based, and it usually claims to be the best equipped body to deal with moral as well as spiritual issues in education. Lauwerys and Hans (1951) declare 'In a word, the desire of the Church is to call the tune, while leaving the state to pay the piper—the justification being that the latter has no musical tradition of its own and is largely tone-deaf.'

Of course, a church-based system of education is likely to become the national one only in countries where a single religion or denomination is accepted by the state and the people. In countries where several religious bodies claim the right to provide schooling, the resultant patterns can be both wasteful and incomplete. Roucek (1966, p. 256) draws our attention to the difficulties experienced in the early days of Australian educational development where the leading denominations provided full and competing educational facilities at both elementary and secondary school level in the urban areas, but neglected the needs of rural communities; this situation, he points out, led eventually to the provision of a state-controlled education system. Many of the newer countries in Africa have had to face not dissimilar problems, stemming from the mission-type schools which first provided formal education during the period of colonial rule. These mission schools, avowedly evangelical in nature, offered the basis for educational expansion and still exert considerable influence at the present time. Nwosu (1966, p. 190), for example, points out that in many of the recently independent countries of Africa over one half of the primary schools, the secondary schools, and the teacher training institutions are in the hands of mission authorities. Such a situation is particularly delicate when the government is pledged to develop education at all levels and sees the education system as a main instrument of national development. The problem is further complicated since, as Goodings and Lauwerys (1966) remind us, the Christians represent only a small minority without much political power. The mission schools, moreover, had in the course of time become 'instruments of modernization which changed the attitudes of the native peoples and taught them new skills and new knowledge. They became agencies of acculturation. Even now, in the last third of the twentieth century, mission schools are still in many countries the best, most up-to-date, most progressive schools available.'

To this extent, they are still very important elements in many countries' general education systems since they operate in parts of the world with great shortages both in quantity and quality of education, and relieve poor countries of some of their financial burden. Yet by the same token these schools may be felt to be relics of foreign domination and difficult to integrate into a national system.

The varying relations between church and state within the framework of Western Christianity are grouped into three patterns by Goodings and Lauwerys, who bring out the educational implications in the following terms. First are distinguished countries with one dominant religion, such as Italy, Sweden and Eire, where lack of opposition will tend to mean that the state will include religious education in the schools with an attendant conscience clause for parents who object. The second group of countries is characterized as having one dominant religion with strong opposition to it. Examples given are France and Belgium; most of the countries concerned are identified as being Roman Catholic and Latin in culture. The strong opposition is provided, not by members of other churches, but by a significant proportion of non-believers who are usually anti-clerical in sentiment. Here, typically, there exist both a state and a church education system, often with political battles over the question of state aid to church schools. The third category, multi-denominational countries such as England and the U.S.A., show very little sign of anti-clericalism. Denominational schools may or may not come under some degree of state control, depending partly, it is suggested, on the degree of concentration of denominations within particular parts of a country. Where compact groups occur, the state often meets at least part of the costs of the schools; where denominations are more thinly spread, state aid is less common.

The problems posed for education by church and state relations in Western Christian countries are undoubtedly caused, to a large extent, by the peculiar evolution of the nation-state in those parts of the world involved, but basically similar problems are faced in all countries of the world. The great religions are concerned less with practical skills and material well-being than with the inculcation of correct attitudes, and religiously-based education may devote less time to secular activities than the state would wish. Indeed, the whole concept of secular education has by no means gained universal acceptance. Tibawi, writing on 'Philosophy of Muslim Education' in *The Year Book of Education, 1957*, which concerned itself with Education and Philosophy, declares 'Islam has always stood for one universal spiritual community of believers which transcends the limitations of race and geography. Hence the national state, and more particularly secular education, is alien to its philosophy and system.'

We can see how such a viewpoint affects education in a specific country in the assertion made by Abdur Rauf (1966) 'It need hardly be emphasized that the materialistic concepts and philosophies of education current in the West, which are mostly based on a divorce between education and religion, have not the least chance of acceptance in Pakistan.'

The profound influence of a religious tradition, focused through the efforts of a single person, can be seen in the Indian concept of basic education, which owes so much to Gandhi's teaching and philosophy; his stress on character building and moral training was fundamental to his educational ideas. This mention of the part which may be played by an individual in determining the characteristics of an education system could lead us into the controversial question of the role played by individuals in influencing historical development. Here, we may suggest that in the sphere of organization, curriculum and method the impact of individuals may be felt. Napoleon's administrative measures in France, Dewey's substantial effect on American education, the influence of such figures as Pestalozzi, Herbart and Froebel, not merely in their own country, could well be considered. Sir Cyril Burt, for example, writing on 'The Impact of Psychology on Education' in *The Year Book of Education, 1957*, mentions Herbart's doctrine of apperception, and goes on:

> From it he deduced his celebrated five 'Formal Steps' in classroom instruction—preparation, presentation, association, generalization, application. And in the light of it he pleaded for a specific study of the teaching methods appropriate to each particular subject of the curriculum. The practical outcome was to emphasize, in every process of learning, the supreme importance of interest. In this and many other ways his psychological doctrine exerted a far-reaching influence on educational practice. (p. 166.)

Moreover, in their introduction to the section in which Sir Cyril Burt's chapter appears, the editors point out that he, himself, through his own life's work, has made a significant contribution to educational policy, at least in England.

The effect of individuals such as those mentioned above often spreads beyond the frontiers of one nation. There are almost always foreign influences working on education systems, and it seems likely that such influences will continue to grow in importance as education becomes more international in character and content. Schneider (1961), in fact, sees foreign influences as one of the basic formative factors in education. This influence is, of course, particularly obvious in the emergent countries which were for a significant period of time under colonial rule; but, generally speaking, plans for educational reform are increasingly being made only after consideration of foreign patterns and practices. As Schneider mentions, with the rise of world trade and the development of international exchange not merely through books, periodicals and newspapers, but through radio and television, international organizations and congresses, and the activities of UNO and UNESCO, all countries of the world are increasingly becoming neighbours in the sphere of education. As he says, it is neither possible nor desirable for a country to develop its educational theory and practice without foreign contact, though, at times, there may be a conscious rejection of foreign influences. Three ways are distinguished in which these influences may operate; there can be a slavish imitation, without regard to whether or not the 'pure import' is suitable to a people's character, culture and sociological structure; there can be an acceptance, after careful consideration and with more or less modification, of only those aspects which are felt to be valuable and appropriate; and third, contact with foreign influences may stimulate creative sources and lead to the solution of an identical or similar problem without taking over anything specific.

Before concluding this brief survey of factors helping to determine the nature of education systems, mention must be made of a formative influence propounded by Schneider, and different in essence from those already touched on. All the factors we have so far discussed may exert an influence which could be described as exogenous in that they are external to the process of education. To these factors Schneider would add endogenous factors stemming from within education itself. Taking the development of plants, animals and human beings as an analogy, he suggests that, in addition to being influenced by external factors, education has its own laws of structure and development.

Much work remains to be done in this field although there have been some stimulating contributions. Beeby (1966) stresses the need to develop a theory of growth in education which can be used to balance economic theories in the important area of educational planning. Part of his argument is that an education system, if it is to achieve high quality, must pass through certain distinct stages which may perhaps be shortened but which cannot be skipped. In putting forward this hypothesis of stages of development Beeby tentatively suggests four stages in the growth of a primary school system.

First comes the Dame School Stage, where the teachers are both ill-educated and untrained. Here, characteristically, the syllabus is vague and skimpy, there is a very narrow subject content with little but mechanical drill in the three R's and most of the time being spent on memorizing relatively meaningless symbols. The teacher's confusion and uncertainty spreads to the children and eventually all but the very brightest pupils cease to make much progress. Second comes the Stage of Formalism, where the teachers, although ill-educated, receive some training. Now, by contrast to the first stage, everything is highly organized; there is a rigid syllabus, an emphasis on the three R's, where the symbols have limited meaning, and a heavy stress on memorization. Typically, there are rigid methods—there is 'one best way' with one textbook. Examinations are external and there is a rigorous system of inspection. Discipline is tight and external. Third, we have the Stage of Transition; here, the teachers, in addition to being trained, are themselves better educated and have probably received some secondary education. Since the gap between what they know and what their pupils know is greater than in previous stages, teachers feel more secure and may allow children more latitude in asking questions, although they are unlikely to go out of their way to stimulate the pupils to do so. The goals are roughly the same as for the previous stage but are more efficiently achieved. There is more stress on meaning, but in a rather formal way, and although both syllabus and textbooks are less restrictive, teachers hesitate to use their greater freedom. Final leaving examinations often restrict experimentation, and at this level there is little in the classroom which caters for the child's emotional and creative life. Lastly, we reach the Stage of Meaning. This, it is pointed out, is more difficult to describe than the earlier stages for we become involved in disputes over the nature of a good modern education. At this stage the teachers are both well-educated and well-trained. There is an emphasis on meaning and understanding, with a wider curriculum and a variety both in content and in method. Attention is paid to individual differences; activity methods are employed with a stress on problem solving and creativity. Tests are held internally; there is a relaxed and positive discipline with provision made for a child's emotional and aesthetic life, as well as for his intellectual needs. There are now closer relations with the community, and at this stage better buildings and equipment are essential.

Beeby is careful to stress that his hypothesis is purely an exploratory one which might provide a starting point for a body of genuine educational theory. As he warns 'In the dividing of a process of continuous growth into arbitrary stages, distinctions that should shade off into greys become glaringly black and white.'

The Dame School Stage, for example, may not form an essential part in the life history of every mass education system. More fundamentally, he points to the dangers of assuming that all parts of a school system are at exactly the same stage. Indeed, if we take into account the achievements of individual pupils, teachers and grades, we can see that a national system may straddle two or even three stages of development. Nevertheless, Beeby's work indicates a most important field of investigation.

Schneider, too, suggests many fruitful lines of investigation. Pursuing the biological analogy referred to earlier, he mentions the concept of polarity which could have relevance to the evolution of education. This immanent evolution, revealed in an inner causality, could be said to show itself, for example, in education as in all manifestations of life by the fact that the development of everything living proceeds in phases. Progress is followed by a pause during which the progress is consolidated and new strength is collected for further steps forward. Thus, for example, a period of extensive absorption of foreign ideas and institutions in education will be followed by a phase when attention is concentrated on one's own traditions and ideals. Similarly, the work of creative, highly gifted individuals will be followed by a generation of educationists who, lacking such outstanding qualities, will concern themselves with mastering the new contributions in order to make them their own, to elaborate and make use of them, and to hand them on. Educational theory and practice may also be considered as factors contributing to and deriving from this inner causality, for educational developments depend, to an extent, on the relationship between theory and practice. Just as theory, by providing norms and setting aims, influences methods of education and instruction, so educational practice can give an impetus to progress in educational theory.

The factors which have been set out above all help to determine the profile of an education system and the work that goes on in the schools. A word of warning is necessary. The very attempt to isolate factors is dangerous since it may easily lead to assumptions that education systems are the sum total of a number of factors which vary in proportion and importance from country to country, or indeed that these strands can fully be disentangled and mounted for exhibition. Lytton Strachey, describing the character of Francis Bacon, declared that his subject was no striped frieze; he was shot silk. The same is true for systems of education. Moreover, we must always guard against assigning too much significance to what goes on in schools, or to the fundamental importance of plans for educational reform. As King (1967) says, 'Those who set up and administer school systems tend to suppose that by fiddling about with them (and leaving everything else alone) they can alter the world. They can indeed, but not always in a constructive and rounded way. Education and civilization are no more matters only for the school than health is a matter only for the clinic. The school is simply the instrument that society (that is, people) selects and perfects for a particular job in particular circumstances.' (p. 321.)

What the particular job may be is determined by a variety of circumstances, and often seems not to have been determined at all. The school used to be a place of instruction; increasingly, it is an extension of general welfare services and the place where real or imagined defects of other social institutions, such as the family or the church, are remedied. Thus, our Martian visitors, armed with a check-list of factors influencing education and possessing a sensitive time machine, may become better informed tourists of the scholastic scene than they would have been without these aids. But they would still provide rich material for jokes and cartoons unless they extended considerably beyond the school the scope of their investigations. It is often said that the school mirrors society, or is a microcosm of society. How far, and in what ways this is true, would be interesting to learn from our planetary cousins. If only they would make a concerted landing in each country of the world and, by accident or design, choose school playgrounds as their landing sites! Returning to Mars after observing a school day, what report would they give of life on earth and its social organization? How would they explain single-sex schools? What significance would they attach to separatist school systems? The list of questions could be a very long one; the opportunities for wit and humour are obvious; the replies could well be illuminating.

References

Beeby, C. E., 1966: *The Quality of Education in Developing Countries.* Harvard University Press, Cambridge, Mass.

Bereday, George Z. F. and Lauwerys, J. A., 1966: Editors' Introduction. In *The World Year Book of Education, 1966.* Evans Brothers, London.

Blaug, M. and Lauwerys, J. A., 1967: General Introduction. In *The World Year Book of Education, 1967.* Evans Brothers, London.

Burt, Sir Cyril, 1957: The impact of psychology on education. In *The Year Book of Education, 1957.* Evans Brothers, London.

Cros, L. 1965: The demand for general education in France. In *The World Year Book of Education, 1965.* Evans Brothers, London.

Durkheim, E., 1956: *Education and Sociology* (translation by S. D. Fox). The Free Press, Glencoe, Ill.

Erikson, E. H. (Ed.), 1963: *Youth: Change and Challenge* (2nd edn). Basic Books, Inc., New York & London.

Fellman, D. (Ed.), 1960: *The Supreme Court and Education.* Bureau of Publications, Teachers College, Columbia University, New York.

Goodings, R. F. and Lauwerys, J. A., 1966: General Introduction. In *The World Year Book of Education, 1966.* Evans Brothers, London.

Hall, R. K. and Lauwerys, J. A., 1956: Editors' Introduction. In *The Year Book of Education, 1956.* Evans Brothers, London.

Hans, N., 1950: *Comparative Education* (2nd edn). Routledge and Kegan Paul, London.

Holmes, B., 1965: *Problems in Education.* Routledge and Kegan Paul, London.

Huxley, J., Haddon, A. C. and Carr-Saunders, A. M., 1939: *We Europeans* (2nd edn). Penguin Books, Harmondsworth.

Kandel, I. L., 1933: *Studies in Comparative Education.* George G. Harrap and Co. Ltd, London.

King, E. J., 1967: *Other Schools and Ours* (3rd edn). Holt, Rinehart and Winston, Inc., New York.

Lauwerys, J. A. and Hans, N., 1951: Education and morals. In *The Year Book of Education, 1951.* Evans Brothers, London.

McLuhan, M., and Fiore, Q., 1967: *The Medium is the Massage.* Penguin Books, Harmondsworth.

Mannheim, K., 1940: *Man and Society.* Kegan Paul, Trench, Trubner and Co., London.

Maritain, J., 1960: *Education at the Crossroads* (2nd edn). York University Press, New Haven, Conn.

Maxwell, N., 1967: India and language. *New Society,* 10, 273, 892-894.

Moehlman, A. H., 1963: *Comparative Education Systems.* The Center for Applied Research in Education, Inc., New York.

Nash, P., 1962: Historical versus geographical factors in Canadian education. *International Review of Education,* Vol. VIII, 13-21.

Nwosu, S. N., 1966: Mission schools in Africa. In *The World Year Book of Education, 1966.* Evans Brothers, London.

Pedley, R., 1963: *The Comprehensive School.* Penguin Books, Harmondsworth.

Rauf, A., 1966: The role of denominational institutions in the educational development of Pakistan. In *The World Year Book of Education, 1966.* Evans Brothers, London.

Roucek, J. S., 1966: The churches and the control of the curriculum with special reference to the United States. In *The World Year Book of Education, 1966*. Evans Brothers, London.

Sadler, M. quoted in J. H. Higginson, 1961-2: The centenary of an English pioneer of comparative education, Sir Michael Sadler (1861-1943). *International Review of Education*, Vol. VII, 286-298.

Schneider, F., 1961: *Vergleichende Erziehungswissenschaft*. Quelle und Meyer, Heidelberg.

Tibawi, A. L., 1957: Philosophy of Muslim education. in *The Year Book of Education, 1957*. Evans Brothers, London.

Ulich, R., 1961: *The Education of Nations*. Harvard University Press, Cambridge, Mass.

UNESCO, 1955: *World Survey of Education*. UNESCO, France.

2

The Wider Context: Early
Parliamentary Discussions
about Education in Queensland

J. R. Lawry

EXPEDIENCY and economic necessity, rather than educational principles, have played a prominent part in the development of education the world over. For example, the earliest academies in Scotland were founded by municipalities because town councillors, who tended also to be prominent local business men, wanted a supply of recruits trained in the 'new subjects' such as modern languages and the sciences, rather than in the subjects of the traditional grammar school—Latin grammar and rhetoric. 'Enlightened' employers of the late eighteenth and early nineteenth centuries set up their factory schools mainly to improve the abilities of their young workers in reading and counting, skills increasingly in demand because of the new manufacturing and commercial techniques that were being introduced into the factories. Modern equivalents might be the Industrial Training Act passed in the United Kingdom in 1964, and the postponement for two years of the raising of the school leaving age to sixteen.

The example explored in this chapter is the shaping of the educational provision in the State of Queensland where there is a highly centralized system, and, therefore, no local political level which might conceivably blur the connection between state parliamentary policies and their appearance in educational practice. (An example of such a 'blurring' is to be found in the United Kingdom Labour Government's attempts to have secondary education reorganized on comprehensive lines. In 1966, local education authorities were requested to submit their plans for such a reorganization, but, in the face of slow progress and the raising of numerous difficulties, the government has now decided to legislate for the change, so making it mandatory.)

Debates and decisions about education in Queensland during the period

1860 to 1904 are examined for their significance in laying the foundations of the centralized system which exists almost unaltered to this day. Whether these debates reflected the thinking of even a substantial proportion of the electorate, or only of the more vocal and influential sections of it, is a moot question. Seemingly, education has seldom been the kind of issue which makes or breaks governments. Yet, because the quantity and quality of the provision is determined largely by the size of the funds voted by parliament, the policies approved there, over the years, merit examination. They provide the framework in which administrators and teachers must work whether they like it or not. And once a system has taken on a certain shape it is extremely difficult for radical changes to be made in it. What seems to happen is that modifications are made to it here and there as the occasion demands, but the basic shape and the relationships of the different parts remain unaltered.

The thesis is argued in this chapter with particular reference to (a) the role of the state and (b) the nature of the curriculums proposed.

The Role of the State (1860-1904)

State aid to denominational education ceased in 1860 with the establishment of a central Board of General Education, and from that time the state assumed the role of providing primary education to all who wished to avail themselves of it irrespective of station in life and geographical location.[1] Religious instruction was a matter for the home, Sunday school and church, but secular instruction was the responsibility of the state.

Most candidates for election to the first parliament favoured the national system of education,[2] and the Education Act of 1860 was based on the version of this system then operating in New South Wales. Under this system education was provided, without regard to denominational differences, in two types of schools, both of which followed the curriculum of what was considered to be a sound English elementary education. *Vested* schools were established by the Queensland Board of General Education with a local contribution for building and maintenance, and the school property and control were vested in the Board. *Non-vested* schools were conducted in buildings under the control usually of various churches, and received only the teacher's salary and a supply of books from the Board. Secular instruction and general or non-sectarian religious instruction were given in both types of school during normal school hours by the teachers, but at other times special or sectarian religious instruction could be given by clergy of the denominations represented in the schools. The national system aimed to extend the benefits of a sound education to all parts of the colony, and to promote toleration and harmony among people of different religious beliefs. Control of education was constitutionally the responsibility of parliament and administratively the task of the Board of General Education.

The national system was supported consistently by the government, despite repeated attempts to secure aid for denominational schools by the

Church of England Bishop Tufnell and the Roman Catholic Bishop Quinn.

By 1867 free education was being foreshadowed because a fall in school fees was interpreted by the Board as indicating 'a growing idea that the education in the Primary Schools ought to be obtained, as a matter of right, without payment at all'.[3]

The Board was committed to a policy of expansion, of providing schools where justified by attendances and by local contributions toward building and maintenance costs. But growth accentuated the difficulties of administering a system catering for an expanding population in a vast colony with only limited resources. The abolition of school fees from the beginning of 1870 marked the first extension of state responsibility in education.

In theory, at least, the state knew nothing of social distinctions in its schools where the education was supposed to be 'the best possible in quality and universally available'.[4] In fact, however, the Board accepted lower qualifications for teachers in *provisional* schools, which were established as a cheap substitute for vested ones in settlements unable or unwilling to subscribe for a vested school.

Dependence on the state was increasing by 1873, when voluntary contributions for new schools declined following proposed legislation which created the impression that the entire cost of education would ultimately be borne by the state.[5] The government's insistence on economic and efficient administration, and the predominant view of the state as a monolithic entity separated from the church and confined to the secular sphere, although not necessarily anti-religious, set the future pattern for the control of education. There was general support for the Board in 1873 when it stopped teachers in state-supported schools from giving special religious instruction. The restriction of instruction to secular subjects was viewed as carrying out the spirit of national education adopted in 1860, and as being in the best interests of the state. The causes of secular education and of greater parliamentary control to ensure the universal provision of education, as proposed in the Education Bills of 1873, 1874 and 1875, gained general public backing. Members of the Church of England and the Presbyterian Church supported non-sectarian instruction as consistent with national education. The Congregational Union, Baptists and the Jewish community favoured secular education, and Methodists wanted to end state aid for denominational schools through the non-vested schools.

Earlier moves had failed to involve the state in a completely free system from primary school to university, with compulsory attendance from six to twelve years of age and education under the control of a responsible minister and a department of the public service, when Lilley introduced an Education Bill in 1873.[6] The Bill asserted the child's right to be educated, as it was to the state's advantage to educate its children. At the economic level, it was necessary for the state to secure the benefits certain to come from the establishment of industrial, technological and scientific schools. The less radical, liberal politician, Griffith, accepted free state secular primary education and no state aid for the propagation of religion, but he rejected the notion that further education beyond the primary school should be entirely free. His own Education Bill of 1874 to abolish aid to non-vested schools was based on the right of the state to provide education in a unified system which excluded religious instruction. Griffith's narrow view of the state's responsibility meant that the state did not provide every part of education, but limited itself to instruction which all citizens could equally enjoy[7] and which was necessary to enable every child to become a good member of society.[8]

These two Bills failed because they were unrelated to issues which attracted general political attention. An issue of the latter kind attracted the attention of the government in 1874. Changes in the system were contemplated because the education question was becoming too large for the Board of Education to handle, especially as expenditure was nearly £100,000 a year and rising.[9] The needs for administrative reform and for the establishment of an exclusive state system with free and secular instruction were widely discussed during the 1873 Royal Commission 'to inquire into the management and working' of schools maintained at public expense. The Report of the Royal Commission accepted that the intention of the Education Act of 1860 was 'to lay the foundation of a truly national system', and that free education was beneficial to the colony. Dogmatic religious instruction was not the business of the state but of the churches, and aid to any sect 'would be a violation of the non-sectarian principles on which the Constitution' was founded.[10] The Commission favoured retaining the system of local contributions for new schools as evidence of good faith.

The main work of reorganizing the administration of state primary education came with the Education Bill of 1875. The only Royal Commission recommendations incorporated in the Bill were those administratively feasible and politically acceptable suggestions, which fitted the narrow view of state education advocated by Griffith. He believed that secondary education was of limited value and not so necessary or highly advantageous to the welfare of the whole community as primary education. The state could offer elementary instruction, but if primary schools were to give technical instruction it had to be 'limited to elementary instruction in mechanical science'.[11] Griffith proposed to continue the narrow type of primary education offered by the Board since 1860, and he endorsed the low attainments insisted upon in the training of primary school teachers. He approved of grammatical instruction as the means of training pupils to think accurately, but eliminated instruction in higher subjects which had been available up to 1875.

The Education Act of 1875 created a Department of Public Instruction under a responsible minister, thus establishing new administrative arrangements for the control of education. The Act was justified on the grounds of a lack of direct government control over the Board, which was insisting on its superior rights over the government through the provisions of the Education Act of 1860. The problem was not for the Board 'to obtain from Parliament more money for the schools, but, on the part of the

Executive, to keep the Board of Education within reasonable limits as regards to calls upon the public purse'.[12]

During the debate on the Education Bill Griffith reiterated the axiomatic nature of free education at the primary level. In justifying the basis of secular instruction he appealed to the principles 'that the majority must govern', and that in schools vested in the state 'the education imparted . . . at the expense of the State should be uniform and should be secular'.[13] Non-vested schools were redundant as the giving of denominational religious instruction as part of the normal school routine, which seemed to be their main justification in 1875, had not received state approval since 1860. Expediency was the final test applied by Griffith in dealing with any differences between the Royal Commission recommendations and the Bill. Free secondary education was inexpedient because only a small number of children could take advantage of it. The establishment of a university was also 'merely . . . a question of time and expedience'. The limitations imposed by expediency, and the narrow view of the state's responsibility, resulted in the plan for education being 'not by any means so grand or comprehensive a scheme as many gentlemen in the colony would like to see brought in . . . but it is the best we can at present afford'.[14] The final expedient was to make the primary curriculum narrower than previously to avoid clashes between the free primary schools and the fee-charging grammar schools.

After debate in which many points of view were expressed, the Bill passed in the Legislative Council when several members switched their votes rather than leave 'over the whole question of education for another year' or lose 'the Bill by further resistance'.[15] The governor was surprised by the passing of the Act, which was 'contrary to what was expected by either ministry or opposition'.[16]

State control of education was accepted by some members of parliament because of the need for social homogeneity in a democratic state, and because education was a weapon against ignorance and disorder. The contemporary faith in the liberal, democratic and secular state was basic to the predominant views that the will of the majority must prevail and that schools vested in the state must be secular. Those politicians who supported 'the-majority-must-prevail' view based their position on the belief either that the state had no responsibility to provide funds for sectarian religious instruction, or that, if aid to non-vested schools ceased, these schools would no longer function and all children would be educated in the state system. Other views expressed during the debates on the Education Bill were not as widely held as those advanced in favour of secular education and social homogeneity.

In 1875, the view that only the state could provide education when required and wherever the population settled was accepted by a majority of politicians as it had been in 1860. The fact that both Acts restricted state assistance to secular instruction only, and permitted religious instruction out of normal school hours, emphasizes that the extension of legislative control over the rapidly growing and increasingly expensive administrative and school structure under the Board was the key feature of the Education Act of 1875. Secularism in 1875, however, did not permit the General (Religious) Lesson included in the normal curriculum in 1860.

Control of education by a responsible minister through a Department of Public Instruction enabled the state to play a more direct role than previously under the Board. Just as the view that the state could support only secular education gained acceptance gradually through experience with the non-vested schools, so opposition to ministerial control was eliminated as the wide powers of the Board and its resistance to enforced economies became known during the debates from 1873 to 1875. The role of the state was modified by the creation of the Department and by arguments about the type of education to be offered in state schools. Thus, the adoption of a curriculum limited to rudimentary subjects at an elementary level left no doubt about the extent of state responsibility.

The ideas, problems, and excuses used to justify the Education Act of 1875 were related to a liberalism which held the state and not the church responsible for secular education which the state alone could support, to the expediency of avoiding illiteracy in a political democracy, and to meeting the demands of a growing population for education and of economy in public administration. Despite their importance, some of these arguments were peripheral to the final political outcome. The determination to curb an irresponsible Board and to place a ceiling on expenditure and, during the final stages of debate in the Legislative Council, to settle the education question once and for all time, provided the crucial reasons for accepting the Education Act. The only educational consequence was a narrowing of the curriculum by the exclusion of advanced subjects such as languages and Euclid.

The essential feature of the period from 1876 to 1904 was the continuity of the existing system as far as was possible in the changing conditions of an expanding colony. Methods of instruction, teacher training and organization of schools scarcely varied. The policy of the administrators was to extend the number of schools and teachers only to meet requirements, subject always to the availability of finance. Continuity was checked only by economic difficulties and politically influential criticism after 1892. Griffith, the first Minister in control of the Department of Public Instruction from 1876, set the pattern of administration from which few deviations occurred except in response to political direction, problems of growth and economy, and experience gained in the practical operation of the Department.

The continuity of the educational task from the Board to the Department encouraged the senior professional officers, subjected as they were to hierarchical authority within the civil service, to see their roles as perpetuators of the system. They did not emerge as innovators with a personal responsibility for educational development. The pressure of routine work absorbed their time and energies and prevented them from keeping up to date with even those innovations and methods which were occurring in the other Australian colonies. By the time they were forced to become better informed about conditions elsewhere after the Civil Service Royal Commission of 1888, their capacity to advise was impaired by adherence to long-established practices and 'the traditions of the Department'. Responsibility for the education system rested with the Minister and the development of future policy was a political matter beyond the control of the Minister's professional advisers, who merely had to see that the system was conducted according to the Act and the Regulations.[17]

The work of establishing the Department of Public Instruction consisted mainly of modifying the existing structure of the Board to make it more amenable to ministerial control. Neither in this, nor in the subsequent operation of the Department, was there any change in the role of the state in providing education in state and provisional schools. The limited curriculum and the need for economy were both explicit in the administration of the Department from 1876 to 1888 which was a period of expansion without administrative change. The ordinariness of the system was determined by the curriculum and the low standard of teachers' qualifications, and the restrictiveness of the system was enforced by regulations and supervision, which virtually prohibited initiative and deviation from instructions.[18]

Concern was expressed repeatedly about the failure to reach high standards in grammar and mathematics as these formal subjects were the basis of the 'mental culture' which, the administrators believed, it was the task of the school to cultivate. But educational excellence was never a general political objective, and Griffith was more easily satisfied with the Department's achievements since the provisions of the Education Act were observed, the best schools were built for the money subscribed, and the best teachers available were appointed.[19] In reply to other attacks on the high and inappropriate standard of state education, Griffith asserted that the standards were as low as possible and designed only to make a youth a good handicraftsman or a girl a good domestic servant or the good wife of an artisan.[20] Primary education was not allowed to go much beyond the limits of the three R's, which was regarded as the appropriate level for free education.

Although the curriculum escaped further criticism for some years, the administration of the Department was subjected to a scathing attack for inefficiency and waste of public funds in the Report of the Civil Service Royal Commission of 1888. The full force of the criticism was avoided by the ministers accepting responsibility for the actions of their senior officers in a period of expanding activity, and asserting that the system of education was working satisfactorily.[21] No basic changes in the administration of the system, or in the role of the state, could be made without the assent of the government, and for some years no change was considered politically necessary. The economic depression of the 1890s changed the situation. Strong political pressure for extra financial aid to provisional schools, which had been established in districts with too small a school population to support a state school, and for the extension of the curriculum to include higher subjects in the fifth and sixth classes, forced the government to accept slight changes in the system between 1895 and 1899. The government would not abolish local contributions for new schools, despite improving conditions, as the Act provided that only the cost of instruction should be met by the government. An increasingly popular view was that 'if a school is needed it should be provided by the State'.[22] This was opposed by the Brisbane *Courier* in an editorial favouring 'a severe limitation of the free system',[23] which indicated support for *limiting* the role of the state at a time when other pressures were being applied for a radical redefinition of the curriculum, and for the state to assume an enlarged or total responsibility for costs. The unusual phenomenon of members of parliament asserting control over government policy resulted from the hardships of depression retrenchment and economies, active representations from school committees and teachers' associations, and the flexibility of political groupings at a time of uneasy coalition government.

Curricula (1860-1904)

Curriculum developments from 1860 to 1904, which have been touched upon briefly in the preceding section, provide another measure of attitudes and values which influenced the provision of state-supported primary education. The curriculum under the Board included reading, writing, arithmetic, grammar, geography, object lessons and general religious instruction. These were the elements of an English education adopted as consistent with state-supported primary education in 1860. Teachers were expected to train their pupils in habits of punctuality, regularity, cleanliness and orderly behaviour. Some few schools offered instruction in Latin, Euclid and algebra.

Virtually no changes were made to the curriculum and textbooks from 1860 to 1875, but the number of schools providing instruction in the higher subjects was reduced, especially as results proved unsatisfactory. Teachers were advised 'to devote their energies to rendering their schools what they were designed to be—efficient primary schools'.[24] The problem was that only a minority of pupils remained at school long enough to learn to read, write and cipher. The Board did not seek innovation and stressed the high degree of continuity in methods and in school supplies. By the early 1870s the narrow view of the state's obligation to provide nothing but primary education gained ascendancy over the earlier official view that classes in higher subjects could be conducted provided the other subjects suffered no neglect.[25] The higher subjects were excluded from the curriculum after 1875 until political pressure forced them back in 1897.

The nature of the educational task was defined, in the 1876 report, as the development of 'mental culture', but this definition was appropriate from 1860 to 1904, and beyond. Schools were to provide the minimal foundation upon which life and further education could be built by all classes of the community.[26] It was impossible for the primary school to include any scientific or technical education because, it was claimed, the pupils lacked the mental maturity and training to make such instruction profitable. (The new schedule of 1904 stated again that the curriculum was the means of imparting mental culture, but some concessions were made by including practical instruction in cooking, woodwork and needle-work.)[27] With technical education regarded as the parent's responsibility, and further education limited by the colony's demand for manual labour, it is not surprising to find that the official view of the primary school's task from 1860 to 1904 and beyond was 'to teach the usual elementary subjects'.[28]

The results of instruction obtained up to 1880 contributed to some slight amendments to the curriculum. Laws of Health and Domestic Economy were substituted for mechanics in the case of girls in the fourth and fifth classes, and the needlework course was modified. No attention was given to the difficulties encountered in the intellectual subjects or to the suggestions that, instead of preparing pupils for clerical positions, technical and agricultural education should be fostered, and cookery instruction given to girls to fit them as 'domestic servants or wives of the working people'.[29] Most of the school work was based on memory, rote and mechanical learning, and only gradually did it make demands on the higher mental abilities.[30] The tendency for the standard of work to suit the average child continued more rigidly with the clear definition of work provided in 1885, and testing under very tough standards.[31] Very few concessions were made to the high value placed on the disciplinary restraints of the intellectual subjects in the upper classes of the schools. Lessons on agriculture were included to give some practical relevance to lessons dealing with everyday objects, and drill was prized as a means of securing habits of prompt obedience, and later as a contribution to national defence. Drawing was accepted gradually as a subject which should be taught for its usefulness in technical education.[32]

By 1890, the narrow three R's curriculum, designed to produce literate citizens who could look to their civic duties and any further education themselves, after the primary school, was under attack from several directions. There was increasing concern about curriculum revision, technical education, child development through the kindergarten method, and growing awareness of the national importance of education. Developments in all these areas were checked by the economic depression of the 1890s, but the criticism continued, drawing support to an increasing degree from emerging teachers' associations and a few members of parliament who took an active interest in education.

Curriculum changes in 1892 were minor, but re-enforced the utilitarian rather than ornamental programme offered in the schools for all classes of the community. Most of the school time was devoted to the basic subjects of reading, writing, arithmetic and grammar.[33] The concept of utility involved in the curriculum at this time was the provision of the minimal preparation for life, rather than vocational or practical education. The official reply to proposed curriculum changes in 1895 was based on a defence of the *status quo*, because, in the opinion of the Department, there would always be only a few children whose circumstances permitted them to continue their formal education beyond the primary school.[34] Mounting pressure for a redefinition of primary education was ignored officially although it was supported by overseas and Australian experience and, more embarrassingly for the Department, by some local headteachers and school committees in towns without a grammar school, where the demand for wider educational opportunity was strong enough to gain enthusiastic political action. A forceful attempt to establish state superior schools for instruction in the higher subjects, as was done in New South Wales where these schools offered instruction in languages, mathematics, science and English literature, was brushed aside when an Education Bill was debated in 1895.

Basic differences about the function of schools and the nature of the curriculum in the case of the higher subjects, in particular, emerged before an amendment of the Education Act was forced on the government by a majority of members of parliament in 1897. There was a clear demand for more than mere elementary education, but the big questions were whether the state had any responsibility for providing for the gifted few who desired a higher education than the primary schools offered, and whether higher education should prepare students for work in the trades, professions, and scientific and industrial pursuits, or provide the more traditional, non-vocational courses in mathematics and the classics.[35] The government attitude was that parents, not the state, should pay for secondary education, but a majority of members disagreed in 1895. The government promised further consideration of an amending Bill, but this was not given until the Legislative Assembly forced the presentation of reports by the Under-Secretary and the General Inspector on the advisability of amending the Education Act to incorporate the superior school provisions of the New South Wales Public Instruction Act of 1880. These reports grudgingly conceded the desirability of going beyond the existing primary course by including mathematics, higher English, science and drawing for the few children who reached the highest class in state schools.[36] This limited extension of the curriculum was followed by an almost total refusal to make further amendments, and so the attempts to resolve the issues of the function of schools and content of the curriculum were frustrated, as neither the government nor the Department wanted the changes. The Department was content to push on with the existing system as far as means would allow under existing conditions.[37] The system was maintained, for all practical purposes, without modification, despite the movements in other countries which had introduced great changes in technical, agricultural and secondary education. By the end of the 1890s, there was such pressing disquiet about the future capacity of primary education to meet the demands for trained ability, that inquiries were instituted and special reports prepared in most of the Australian educational systems. Queensland did virtually nothing to develop a satisfactory link between primary and secondary education, or to cope with the inadequacies of technical education, until after 1904, when some innovations in content and method were incorporated in the primary curriculum.

Concessions to vocational training came in 1902 when commercial subjects, commercial correspondence and office routine, and shorthand, were added to the course for the fifth and sixth classes as alternatives to the science subjects.[38] By 1904, no definitive answer was provided to the curriculum confusion, although non-vocational subjects were more prominent than vocational ones. Neither secondary nor technical education experienced the great transformation and critical appraisal evident in Great Britain and in other Australian states. Lack of innovation resulted, in part, from the belief 'that they had a wonderfully perfect system' which could not be improved.[39] Teachers' associations tended to support the Department's conservatism in keeping the curriculum within the narrow traditional lines of the previous years, especially in their hostility to the higher subjects in which teachers received no training. The outcome was that the new curriculum produced in 1904, was remarkably like that of 1876, with only slight changes in nomenclature and in the expressed intention of meeting demands for practicality. This new curriculum was drawn up when the Minister, bowing to political pressure, convened a conference of teachers, inspectors and senior administrators from whom great changes were expected. However, items considered by the conference as involving any radical scheme of reform were quietly put aside. Subjects regarded as the 'means of imparting mental culture' were endorsed, and old courses were updated with new books and revisions based on experience. Once the conference endorsed general principles, the work of revision was done by the senior administrators without further consultation. The only concessions to practicality were cooking, woodwork, and needlework, although correlation of subjects, the self-activity of the pupil, and the school's contribution to the social development of the child were paid lip service.[40]

Aftermath

The only criterion of educational achievement applied by the state from 1876 to 1904 was that 'the department was doing the best it possibly could with the means at its command'.[41] The means provided by various governments for the Department to supply elementary education appear to have responded to the two main variables of economic prosperity or depression, and the growth of population, particularly the size of school population. Increases in the number of children in the higher classes, and a rise in the average daily attendances, reflected a tendency of children to stay longer and attend school more regularly in 1904 than in 1876. Increased costs were involved also in the reduction of the staff-pupil ratio, the growing proportion of classified to unclassified teachers, and the rising costs associated with provisional schools, which were all features of the system up to 1904. Since then factors of growth and increased expenditure have continued to dominate the provision of education by the state and to influence political decisions about educational developments. Politicians sometimes overlook the fact that increased expenditure on education represents mainly factors associated with the size and distribution of the school population, especially in the more costly areas of higher education, rather than improvements in the quality of education (Karmel, 1966). The dominance of political control of education, largely in the absence of professional advice, resulted in the administration of the system, up to 1904, responding to the main influence of practical and economic problems in providing primary education for an ever-increasing school population. Little attention was given to theoretical policies, and innovations in practical school management and the curriculum rarely intruded into the realm of practical political decisions. Extensions of the role of the state in education came very slowly because governments were unwilling or unable to finance the educational advances demanded by social, industrial and commercial developments. The existing system could not meet the demand for trained ability, but only slowly did the state move towards an articulated system of education, which had been the aim of Lilley as far back as 1873, by taking over control of technical education in 1908, opening the University of Queensland in 1911, and establishing state high schools and secondary departments in 1912. These changes lagged well behind perceived needs for innovations in the structure and content of state education, but they came at a time when the state was forced to extend its role in social welfare and industrial legislation because of 'the sheer inefficiency of the previous range of services' (Tierney, 1965). The changes in secondary and technical education and revisions of the primary school curriculum were also more or less faithful imitations of innovations accepted in the other Australian states. Some allowance must be made for the adoption of innovations just to keep up appearances of modernity, but even this factor is one of political expediency.

Practical administrative and economic problems and questions of political expediency still dominated the state's role in education in 1964 and confirm the essential continuity of the system from 1860 to the present. The main practical problems were concerned with providing for an increasing number of children seeking primary and secondary education, and with meeting new demands for technical and tertiary education. These questions are illustrated in debates on the education Estimates and the Education Bill in 1964, in which it was acknowledged that developments in education resulted from the increased number of children, the interest taken in education by parents, and the government's policy of extending secondary education in country areas. Technical education had not advanced at the same rate as demand because resources were limited and the government could not afford to lag behind other parts of the world or of Australia in providing tertiary education.[42] Education Minister Pizzey admitted that the state was still a long way from doing all the things the community would like it to do in education, but progress had been made, especially as secondary education was regarded as a right for all and no longer merely a privilege for a few. In fact, however, the state was trailing behind demand for education at all stages. Although the politicians said that education was very important, they did not have any vital political reason for changing the system, with the result that the Education Bill merely tidied up a few administrative loose ends, and introduced a few changes of no great importance. The only speaker during the debates who paid any attention to educational aims discussed the function of all levels of education in terms associated with the state primary education in 1860. The state's obligation was to educate people to read, write and acquire the necessary knowledge to continue their education, and 'to acquire a character that will enable them to be generous, charitable and tolerant, and to be motivated by considerations of good will'.[43] Other members contributed to the debates at the level of justifying past political action or inaction, and by particularizing the material needs of their electorates. In the debate on the Education Bill, which was only the seventh amendment of the Education Act of 1875, it soon became clear that members had exhausted the subject of education during the previous Estimates debate. There was much self-adulatory congratulation during the first reading, and much repetitious and irrelevant discussion about school uniforms and pastoral colleges during the second reading which lasted one hundred and fifty eight minutes. The committee stage passed without debate, except for a foreshadowed amendment which was moved and briefly supported. The main purpose of the Bill was clearly to bring the law 'up to date with practices which had developed over the preceding years'[44] as a result of practical administrative decisions.

These debates provide evidence that political interest in education was still the pragmatic criterion of doing the best with available resources. Free education still involved only free instruction, and parents and citizens' associations were required to provide much needed facilities for schools by fund raising activities. Parliamentary discussion of education was still unrelated to the best contemporary theory, practice and research findings, but decisions based upon these discussions place inescapable constraints on each school, class, teacher and pupil.

The area of state responsibility has been enlarged from the limited primary instruction provided in 1860 to include the primary, secondary, technical and tertiary levels in one system of formal education. Moreover, adjustments have been made to cope with the established fact of secondary education for all children at the end of primary school, and with demands for more technical education which could not be ignored any longer in view of industrial and technological developments in Queensland. There is, however, no sign of any fundamental change in the role of the state in providing education, or in the method of determining the structure and content of education.

Notes

[1]*Moreton Bay Courier*, 30.7.1859, 7.9.1859 (hereafter referred to as *Courier*).
[2]*Courier*, 11.2.1860, 28.2.1860.
[3]*Report of the Board of Education*, 1867, p. 4.

[4]ibid., 1870, p. 12.
[5]ibid., 1873, p. 2.
[6]*Queensland Parliamentary Debates*, 1873, Vol. 15, pp. 35-224 (hereafter referred to as *Q.P.D.*).
[7]*Q.P.D.*, 1874, Vol. 16, pp. 395-396.
[8]*Q.P.D.*, 1874, Vol. 17, pp. 582-853.
[9]ibid.
[10]*Royal Commission Report*, 1874, pp. 29-43.
[11]ibid.
[12]Governor's Despatches (*QSA*), Vol. v, No. 33, 19.4.1875.
[13]*Q.P.D.*, 1875, Vol. 18, pp. 527-530.
[14]ibid.
[15]*Q.P.D.*, 1875, Vol. 19, p. 1292.
[16]Governor's Confidential Despatches (*QSA*), Vol. i, 10.9.1875, pp. 86-87.
[17]*Report of the Department*, 1893, p. 55.
[18]ibid., 1876, pp. 19-1889.
[19]*Q.P.D.*, 1878, Vol. 26, p. 896.
[20]*Q.P.D.*, 1880, Vol. 33, pp. 805-807.
[21]*Q.P.D.*, 1889, Vol. 57, p. 575.
[22]*Q.P.D.*, 1895, Vol. 73.
[23]*Courier*, 18.9.1895.
[24]*Report of the Board of Education*, 1869, p. 14.
[25]ibid., 1871, p. 4.
[26]*Report of the Department*, 1892, p. 56.
[27]ibid., 1904, pp. 23-25.
[28]ibid., 1899, p. 53.
[29]*Q.P.D.*, 1880, Vol. 33, pp. 805-807.
[30]*Report of the Department*, 1881, p. 47.
[31]ibid., 1885, pp. 3, 68.
[32]*Q.P.D.*, 1880, Vol. 33, pp. 805-807.
[33]*Report of the Department*, 1892, p. 56.
[34]ibid., 1895, p. 6.
[35]*Q.P.D.*, 1895, Vol. 74.
[36]*Journal of Legislative Council, Queensland*, 1896, Vol. 46, Pt II, pp. 1063-1079.
[37]*Courier*, 8.12.1902.
[38]*Queensland Government Gazette*, 19.7.1902, p. 170.
[39]*Q.P.D.*, 1896, Vol. 76, p. 1509.
[40]*Queensland Parliamentary Papers*, 1904, pp. 289-290.
[41]*Q.P.D.*, 1902, Vol. 90, p. 1566.
[42]*Q.P.D.*, 1964, pp. 1429-2255.
[43]ibid.
[44]ibid.

References

Karmel, P. H., 1967: Some arithmetic of education. In E. French (Ed.), *Melbourne Studies in Education, 1966*. Melbourne University Press, Melbourne.
Tierney, L., 1965: The pattern of social welfare. In A. F. Davies and S. Encel (Eds), *Australian Society*. Cheshire, Melbourne.

Part II

The Community Context

3

The Community Context

W. J. Campbell

Introduction

THE TERM 'community' has several different meanings, but here it is being used in the everyday sense of a geographic location within which a group of persons, possessing at least some common beliefs and ways of behaving, share in a common set of facilities. Even within this definition enormously wide variations exist. At one extreme are primitive tribal groups, such as the Santal of India, or tightly-knit religious units such as the Amish of Pennsylvania; at the other are the somewhat ill-defined suburbs of a giant metropolis such as London or Los Angeles.

Linked with the problems of conceptualization and identification is the difficulty of ascribing any effects to the community, *per se*. As long ago as 1941, Angell wrote:

> In earlier, simpler societies, the local community was equally as impor-
> tant as the family and religious institutions in supplying the individual
> with a sense of basic common values. And it was much more important
> than the larger society itself which, because communication was poor,
> could foster such values only in the most general and abstract way . . .
> This type of local community has practically vanished in America. One
> may find it exemplified perhaps in a few isolated villages, but the great
> bulk of our citizens come under its influence no longer. . . . We are
> justified in regarding the local community as morally vestigial. (p. 11.*)

The recent growth in communication systems and urbanization throughout the world may have strengthened Angell's case, but his dismissal of the
community has not passed unchallenged. In 1965, Arensberg and Kimball
took a very different view: 'We believe the community to be . . . a master
institution or master social system; a key to society; and a model, indeed
perhaps the most important model, of culture. We are convinced that the
community has shown itself, in the research of recent years, to be a main

*Reprinted from *The Integration of American Society* by R. C. Angell. Copyright
1941, McGraw-Hill Book Company. By courtesy of McGraw-Hill Book Company.

link, perhaps a major determinant, in the connections between culture and society.' (p. IX.) Some of the apparent discrepancies between the views, of Angell and Arensberg could stem from slightly different definitions or emphases, but it is possible, too, that, as Arensberg states, the recent research has given a new appreciation of the significance of communities. Presumably this significance, as it concerns us, could arise in two main ways: (a) indirectly, through the fostering or inhibition of personality characteristics that have educational significance; and (b), more directly, through the nature and quality of the schools and education that specific communities provide. This chapter discusses both of these, but before this is done an attempt is made to identify some of the current and developing characteristics of modern-day communities.

Some Potentially-Significant Characteristics of Modern Communities

Among world-wide trends in community development there are four that appear to possess special significance for education:

An Increase in Urbanization: Writing in 1968, Mack states that if the present rate of urbanization continues soon all but a few of the world's population will live in cities of twenty thousand or more. Other prophets, being less concerned with urbanization and more concerned with population increase, have forecast that in the space of a few generations, unless there is a change in current trends, the human race will be so plentiful that individuals will be fighting for standing room! Certainly some of the increase in urbanization can be related to the more general phenomenon of population increase, but this is not the whole story; there is a *differential* rate of growth in favour of urban areas.

To those who obtain their ideas of Australia from overseas films, or from her folklore and literature, it may be a shock to learn that this country is probably the most urbanized in the whole world. This emerges most clearly if one accepts Davis' index (Broom & Selznick, 1958) in which greater weight is assigned to large cities than to smaller ones. 'On this basis the index of urbanization for Australia is 68 compared with . . . 65.9 for Great Britain, 42.3 for U.S.A. and 8.8 for India.' (Brennan, 1965.) On the rather cruder definition of urbanization used for census purposes Australia's index remains the same but is exceeded by those from Great Britain, Israel, Netherlands, West Germany and Hawaii. The existing concentration of population in Australia is likely to go even further. As Brennan (1966) reminds us, 'Rapid though Canberra's growth is, Sydney adds a Canberra-sized population to itself every year, and even a score of new Canberras away from the main centres of population would not slow down the growing giants of Sydney and Melbourne enough to alter the main pattern.'

Urbanization is a convenient 'marker' variable which comprises a number of features. Among the more important of these which have implications for school learning are *large populations* and *large institutions*. These will be discussed later in this chapter.

Increase in Outer-City Growth: So far we have been discussing urbanization as though cities continued to grow with a single identity. This, however, rarely happens: rather, somewhat like a eucalyptus tree whose central stem has been damaged, any number of offshoots spring from the outer layers. This complex of a central city area with more vigorous suburbs falling unhappily between functioning units of the larger whole and satellite towns, is variously described as a 'polynucleated centre', 'megalopolis', or, more poetically, 'galaxy of urban solar systems'! Cities such as Chicago and Sydney spring readily to mind, but this structural phenomenon occurs almost everywhere, and may be seen also in the emerging countries of Africa, as Biobaku (1967) makes clear:

> Lagos began as a fishing island with a few thousand people, some of whom were migrants from Benin. After the advent of the Europeans it was effectively linked with the Nigerian mainland and a suburb rapidly developed at Ebute Metta. As Lagos grew and became the seat of Government, commerce and the National Railway Administration, a satellite settlement was established at Ikeja as a European reservation, and Yaba developed as an extension of Ebute Metta, and later Apapa, to serve growing port and industrial needs. As business, commercial and governmental, expanded, more people came in and the suburbs further extended into the hinterland so that Mushin and Ikeja, some sixteen miles from the centre of the Island, provide dormitories for Lagos workers. At Ikeja also stand the Lagos Airport and another suburban settlement accommodating modern residences and industrial development. The population of Greater Lagos is well over a million and a half . . . (p. 454).

The differential development of inner and outer areas, as referred to above, is also revealed in the fact that between 1950 and 1960 the population of 'central city' regions in the U.S.A. increased only 1.5 per cent while that of outer regions increased 62 per cent (Havighurst, 1968).

Cultural Segregation: In some cases the progression towards a 'dead heart' in the central city regions has been effectively arrested by urban renewal programmes, and, in others, the place of the upwardly-mobile indigenous inhabitants has been taken by newly-arrived migrants. Thus King writes (1967):

> In so far as indigenous British inhabitants tended to move out to suburban areas with the improvement in their economic purchasing power and their rising social expectation, there has been a recognizable but still small tendency for some areas in Britain to be populated either by the first post-war wave of immigrants (Czechs and Poles in some cases and in others Italians), or more recently by immigrants from the Commonwealth. Consequently some London areas appear to have a majority of West Indians, or Indian-Pakistani inhabitants. . . . The areas most likely to be affected in this way are certain London inner suburbs, parts of Birmingham or large seaports, and manufacturing

towns in the North or Midlands like Bradford or Bedford. (p. 444.)

With the passage of time, most suburbs in the megalopolis (and not only the central region) become decreasingly like standard samples of the whole as they differentiate on socioeconomic and sociocultural bases. Havighurst (1961) writes:

> As the total population of a megalopolis grows, the slum belt around the central business district becomes thicker. This is a result not only of the growth in total population but also of the concentration of lower-class people in areas of poorest housing, which are usually in the oldest parts of the city. Those who can afford to do so move away from the inner city as their economic circumstances improve. In general, working-class people whose income permits it move out of the slum district and take up residence farther from the center of the city, while people in middle-class districts of the central city move out to middle-class suburbs. Thus the ever-growing total population divides itself into a lower-class conglomerate at the center, with successively higher socioeconomic groups at greater distances and the upper-middle class and the upper class largely in the suburbs. While this process goes on in the central city, the suburbs themselves become stratified into communities . . . (p. 252).

The large and older Australian cities illustrate this development into segregated suburbs. After writing of an inner ring, within Sydney, where 'about a quarter of a million people live in conditions which are almost intolerable', Connell (1957) goes on to describe outer rings culminating in 'the North Shore line and middle and upper class homes, where at election time the Labor Party sometimes does not even bother to enter a candidate. . . . These bands can ultimately be traced, even if not quite concentric and clear, from the decaying slums in the centre to the ample homes of the urban fringe.' A decade ago the situation was not quite as clear in the middle-level cities, such as Brisbane, but considerable segregation has occurred within recent years, and, although geographically separated by only eight or nine miles, the youngsters in Petrie Terrace and those in Kenmore and Brookfield live in very different social and cultural worlds.

What is the educational significance of living in the sordid slums of Woolloomooloo or Surry Hills, or in the spacious areas of 'gracious living' with their attractive water and sylvan views such as Killarney Heights or St Ives? This is a further issue to which we shall return later.

Static Rural Communities: Although there are difficulties in making comparisons of rural populations across time and countries, it is clear that the rural growth, if any, is consistently below that of urban areas. For example, in terms of absolute numbers, Australia's rural population has been constant at around 1.8 million since 1954, and the rural percentage of total population has, of course, dropped steadily. The United States' rural population has, as the following table shows, varied little from 1900 (Robinson, 1965).

Non-metropolitan Rural Population: Coterminous U.S.A.

Year	Population
1900	40,469,951
1910	43,292,334
1920	43,208,727
1930	43,162,152
1940	44,256,303
1950	43,070,119
1960	41,191,226

A clear illustration of the differential growth pattern is revealed in the following figures from Denmark (Goldstein, 1965).

Average Annual Rate (Per 1,000 Population) of Increase in Capital, Capital Suburban, and Rural Districts: Denmark, 1951-1960

	Births	Deaths	Natural Increase	In Migration	Out Migration	Net Migration	Population Change
Capital City	12.9	10.6	2.3	70.7	78.3	–7.6	–5.3
Suburbs of Capital	22.6	5.6	17.0	138.6	101.4	37.2	54.2
Rural (other than Built-up)	18.1	8.5	9.6	129.5	138.5	–9.0	0.6

Goldstein comments '. . . the Danes are getting worried that, before long, they will be left with a huge sprawling capital and a deserted countryside. Although the rate of metropolitanization in Denmark may be higher than that of some other western countries, the basic pattern is quite similar.'

Small, scattered rural districts give rise to educational issues related to: *effects of living in small communities, correspondence lessons, direction of teachers,* and *consolidation of schools.* These issues will be discussed in the next section.

The preceding survey of some community characteristics provides us with a list of variables that could have importance for school learning. These may be summarized as follows: (a) size of community; (b) size of school; (c) consolidation of schools; (d) direction of teachers to rural areas; (e) correspondence lessons; (f) differential development within metropolitan communities; (g) cultural segregation of communities. Although these overlap somewhat, the intention is to discuss each in turn.

The Educational Significance of Community Characteristics

Size of Community: During a large and careful study of child life in small (town) and large (city) communities, Wright (1961) was told:

'Town kids have more of a chance to participate in many activities.'

'All of them get to use their talents.' 'They enjoy more freedom and more independence.' 'They know more people and have more friends, especially intimate friends.' 'You can trust them in the hands of the community.' 'They're never lost, and they seem to be more at peace with themselves.'

However:

'City has more constructive activities for children than a small place like town.' 'There is lots more culture in every direction.' 'All a child can do in a small town is to watch Mickey Mouse on TV or go to the drugstore and get a coke.' 'There's too much gossip in a small town and this leaves its mark on people, children included.'

Wright's study of twenty communities ranging in size from a population of 421 to 10,784 (town 421–1,548; city 4,095–10,784) gave some support to some of these prejudices! He reports that children in large cities, in comparison with those from small towns, enter a wider range of 'settings' (such as drugstore, dance hall, etc.), but have fewer positions of importance, re-enter the settings less often, spend less time in community settings, and are generally less familiar with objects and persons in their neighbourhoods.

Barker's study (Barker & Gump, 1964) of adolescents in communities ranging from a population of 450 to that of 101,155 gave similar results:

(a) student adolescents in the smaller town were employed more frequently, attended and took an active part in church activities more frequently, and, generally, were much more active in community activities;

(b) more settings were made available to adolescents in the smaller towns, and these young persons were more 'functionally important' in 'behavior settings that were rich in people and rich in behavior'.

The findings from the Barker and the Wright studies are unequivocal, but one wonders: (a) to what extent the differences noted would apply in other cultures; and (b) about the educational significance of the differences. Neither query is satisfactorily answered by the research literature. However, in a cross-cultural study of two small towns, one in Yorkshire, England, and the other in Kansas, U.S.A., Barker (1960) found some striking differences suggesting the overriding importance of the broader culture within England. English adolescents and children, for example, held responsible community positions to only one-quarter of the extent of their American counterparts, and they experienced more than twice as many behaviour-setting exclusions on account of age. Barker comments:

The Midwest [Kansas] and Yoredale [Yorkshire] systems for educating children are congruent with these facts about the settings of the communities. According to the Midwest theory of education, children are prepared for adulthood by participating to the maximum of their abilities in the regular behavior settings of the town along with adults;

it is of particular value to children to undertake important and responsible roles even before they can discharge them with complete adequacy. . . . School behavior settings are considered important in the Midwest education, but they are thought to function best along with regular community settings.

According to the Yoredale theory of education, children are prepared for adulthood by removing them from the community settings and placing them in special, reserved school settings under the direction of experts who, over a period of time, are able to prepare children for entrance to the normal life of the town's behavior settings. School settings are the unique and almost complete means of educating children, and it is one of their particular values that when they are in school behavior settings, children do not disturb community settings until the requisite skills and responsibilities have been imparted to them so they can take their parts smoothly. (p. 46.*)

The question of the educational significance of greater community participation still remains, and will be left unanswered here. The best that one can do is to trace effects through to personalities and then speculate on the implications of these. Mangus (1948) gave the Elementary Series of the California Inventory to 573 school children in Ohio towns under 2,000 in population, and to 285 comparable children in an Ohio city of 16,000. The town children outscored the city children in self-reliance, sense of personal freedom, sense of belonging, sense of personal worth, social skills, good school relations and good community relations. These findings *seem* to be consistent with the differences in community experience likely (on the basis of the Barker and the Wright data) to have been encountered by the two groups of children. They would also seem (but here one is treading on even thinner ice) to be the qualities likely to assist with school achievement.

One of the most direct effects of living in a large, rather than a small community, is the opportunity to choose among schools. Instead of having to make do with the one school which happens to be within access, students (or their parents) may have a choice among state schools, private, denominational schools and private, non-denominational schools. There may also be opportunities for selection within each of these broad types, and it is not unknown for parents in Brisbane to queue all night in an attempt to enrol their children in a particular state high school. However, when 'zoning' exists, as it frequently does in cities, the opportunities disappear. Moreover, under the present system of standardized curriculums and standardized textbooks, the effect of exercising choice, when this exists, might be slight. Probably the opportunities are worth most when, for various reasons, the pupil cannot profit maximally from normal curriculums and methods, but requires a 'special' education programme. Despite

*Barker, R. G., Ecology and Motivation. In M. R. Jones (Ed.), *Nebraska Symposium on Motivation.* Copyright 1960, University of Nebraska Press, and reproduced with their permission.

the commendable efforts of most educational authorities to provide equal opportunities for all pupils, irrespective of location, those closest to the major centres of population and administrative headquarters are likely to fare best. At considerable sacrifice to their own careers, many country parents of handicapped children move to towns and cities in search of the best facilities that the nation provides.

This wider opportunity *might* be offset to some extent by the fact that while most pupils in the cities are likely to live within almost walking distance of the school, most teachers are likely to commute from other suburban communities. One effect of this phenomenon is that the urban teacher seldom knows the parents or the backgrounds of his pupils, and seldom participates in parent-school associations. With reference to schools in Papua and New Guinea, Richardson and van der Veur, for example, write (1968):

> The teachers themselves expressed the opinion that the degree to which school and teacher were an integral part of the community was one of the chief differences between teaching in the town and in a village. When teaching in his own village a teacher is automatically a part of village activities. Even when he comes from a different district the villagers feel some responsibility for his accommodation and food and there is personal contact in the course of the everyday activities of gardening, hunting or fishing. These traditional media of contact do not exist in the towns where there is a money economy and where the teacher does not necessarily live in the area in which he is teaching.
>
> Opportunities for teacher-parent contact are more formal in the towns than in the village. Participation in the community life of the town depends to a large extent on the interest and initiative of individuals rather than any traditional pattern, obligation or responsibility. Furthermore, many of the possible channels of contact have a sectional appeal. (p. 92.)

Size of School: If we assume that small communities are likely to have small schools, if any, and that large communities are likely to have large schools, the effects of these institutions upon their inhabitants can legitimately be discussed here.

By invoking arguments on scale, some educationists see the large system as inevitably more efficient than small ones; this, however, is doubtful. The argument appears to rest upon the assumption of a direct positive relationship between the properties of schools and the experiences and behaviours of their pupils, e.g., a rich curriculum means rich experiences for students, or a comprehensive programme of extracurricular activities means strong individual involvement. Obviously good facilities provide good experiences only if they are used. The educational process is a subtle and delicate one about which we know little; but it surely thrives upon participation, enthusiasm and responsibility. Without participation, education cannot occur however excellent the arrangements may be. All of the research findings (Larson, 1949; Dawe, 1934; Anderson, Ladd & Smith, 1954; Barker & Gump, 1964) reveal a negative relation between school size and individual student participation. As Barker says:

> To an outside observer, a school with many students is impressive; its imposing physical dimensions, its seemingly endless halls and number-less rooms, its hundreds of microscopes, its vast auditorium and great audiences, its sweeping tides of students, all carry the message of power, movement, vitality, purpose, achievement, certainty. In contrast, a small school with its commonplace building, its few microscopes, its dual-purpose gym-auditorium half-filled with students who assemble and depart, not in tides but in a tangle of separate channels, is not impressive. The members of the field-work team never ceased to marvel that the directly experienced differences between large and small schools were, in these respects, so compelling, like the differences between a towering mountain and an ordinary hill, between a mighty river and a meandering brook. But to an inside participant the view is different. When the field workers were able to participate in the functioning behavior settings of schools, they saw the small schools as in some respects more coercive and dominating than the large schools. ... There is, indeed, an inside-outside perceptual paradox, a school size illusion. (p. 62.)

The Kansas studies of school size, under the direction of Barker (1964), provide the best evidence on this issue, and this may be briefly summarized as follows:

> The large school offers its pupils a larger number of, and more varied, activities. However, pupils from the smaller school *participate* in more activities and in a greater range of these; moreover their participation levels are higher (more often key personnel and less frequently onlookers). In line with the higher participations, pupils from the small schools report more satisfactions related to the development of competence, sense of challenge, and engagement in worthwhile pursuits.

The Barker studies are important and challenging; however, they have not been pushed to the point where a direct relationship between school size and school learning has been established.

Consolidation of Schools: Closely linked with the issue of school size is that of *consolidation*—the transportation of pupils outside their own small communities to a larger school within another community. This issue has given rise to considerable controversy. On the one hand, the supporters of school consolidation claim that: (a) pupils benefit through: better and more varied curriculums; better classification into school grades; better facilities, especially in such subjects as science and music; contact with better teachers; opportunities to participate in better and more varied extra-curricular activities; wider social opportunities and experiences; more regular attendance at school; (b) parents benefit through: reduced expenditure on education; (c) the community benefits through: the creation of closer ties with neighbouring communities. On the other hand, the opponents of consolidation claim that: (a) pupils lose through: increased breaks in their education; loss of contact with teachers who know the local community and families well; spending time on commuting which might be spent with greater profit on other activities; (b) parents lose through: being denied opportunities to participate in the control of their school; (c) the community loses through: being denied the facilities of an active school which could serve as a cultural and educational centre; the breakdown of community cohesion and participation, especially in youth activities.

Few systematic attempts, however, have been made to examine the above assertions empirically (Parkyn, 1952; Skrabanek, 1956; Campbell, 1964). On the basis of personal observations, interviews, tests and questionnaires, Parkyn concluded, with reference to New Zealand:

> In the main it would seem possible to provide very well for the educational needs of the younger children in the small country school, so long as there are enough of them to ensure a certain amount of companionship and social activity and to give the school some stability over the years, and so long as the teachers are not at the same time faced with the problem of giving an adequate schooling to older children . . . (p. 139).

> But the small school as such cannot be made suitable for the older children (11+); it cannot give the cultural breadth needed by them. Nor can it reach such high standards of work in the broader subjects, for such standards are dependent on a moderate degree of specialization of interest and ability on the part of the teachers. Nor can it provide a variety of optional classes and clubs, based on differences in the children's own interests and abilities, which can play a valuable and important part in fostering cultural activities. (p. 140.)

Parkyn is aware of the distinction between qualities that are inherent in the small local school, and those that might be termed fortuitous, but his conclusion which is quoted above appears to be unduly influenced by the situation as it existed, and not as it could be. Among these fortuitous factors, which have considerable educational significance in their own right, is that of teacher experience and quality, to which reference is made immediately below.

Direction of Teachers to Rural Areas: Although some exceptions exist, most teachers aspire to a position in a large urban centre—and most are sent, on initial appointment, to less attractive (which, to the young, often means more remote) communities. As Havighurst says (Havighurst & Neugarten, 1957): 'Although teachers move from one place to another for a variety of reasons—to leave or to return to their families, to gain new experience, and so on—the most typical direction of movement has been from the smaller to larger communities. In general, with added academic training and added years of experience, teachers tend to go from an orbit of small towns to small cities to large cities; such moves are usually accompanied by increased salary, increased security, or increased prestige in the profession.' (p. 437.*)

Some countries, such as New Zealand, attempt to equalize school opportunities by offering incentives (usually cheap housing and higher salaries) in order to attract teachers to remote communities, but many do not, and 'country service' becomes something of an occupational hazard, to be escaped if possible, otherwise to be borne stoically. Probably, the effect of a teacher upon his pupils will depend more upon his reaction to the country posting than upon his measure of experience. Certainly, although many rural teachers may be young and inexperienced, some are strongly dedicated and able, as the following delightful passage from McRae (1963) suggests:

> We had reached the district headquarters, Albury [N.S.W., Australia], at the end of January, just as a two-year drought was finishing with a flourish. For a month the temperature was rarely below 100 degrees, day or night, and mostly it was well above. For a couple of weeks I sweated through the day over teachers' applications for water, and a score of other academic problems no one had thought to mention. At night it was almost impossible to sleep, because in that dry heat our city-bred furniture kept splitting its sides wide open with crackling laughter.
>
> When it was time to go out into the field, I selected as first victim an ex-student on probation who had been brought up in Bondi, within sight and sound of the surf he loved. He had been appointed to a remote one-teacher school . . .
>
> The day of my visit was comparatively cool, 108 degrees inside the building. Every few minutes the school was smacked by a 50-mile-an-hour gale, laden with dust from the parched plains. It seemed that every fly in Christendom had come in out of the wind. At 12.30, we gnawed at a few dry sandwiches, washed down by a little of the water which the children had brought with them, the school tank being dry . . .
>
> Now it is unquestionably true that there are other Australians who do their daily toil in an environment even less congenial than that hot, dusty, unpainted school. What I beg leave to doubt is whether those others do their job as well as that young teacher was doing his. With unshaken enthusiasm he was bringing joy and interest into the lives of thirteen young Australians as he handed on to them the torch of knowledge. (p. 210.)

Education authorities are likely to justify the direction of young teachers to remote rural areas on the grounds that it enables the new graduate to find his professional feet in relatively calm and shallow water. There could be some merit in this argument, and yet in many respects teaching in a remote area is a difficult assignment for which little prepara-

*From Robert J. Havighurst and Bernice L. Neugarten, *Society and Education*, p. 437. © Copyright 1957 by Allyn and Bacon, Inc., Boston.

tion is given. Courses are given in how to instruct, how to nurture, how to transmit the culture, how (to a lesser extent) to clarify the culture, how to discipline, how to evaluate, how to supervise, how to fill in forms, how to behave in parents and citizens' meetings, and so on, but seldom do teacher trainees receive guidance and instruction in how to provide *educational* leadership within communities in rural areas. In some instances, the rural teachers, like the bank clerks, live as fringe dwellers owing allegiance to an authority far beyond the community; in other instances, especially among the young, they immerse themselves completely in the activities and value systems of the community, and, in doing so, appear to forfeit their rights and obligations to provide effective educational leadership on a community basis. In either case, the education of the community's children is likely to be less effective than it could be.

Correspondence Lessons: An extreme example of the effects of sparse population upon school learning occurs where the number of pupils is so small that no school is provided. In such cases, depending mainly upon the stage of development reached by the country's education system as a whole, schooling may be completely non-existent, or may proceed by means of governesses (often unqualified as teachers) within the home-steads, correspondence lessons, radio or television. Although there are no evaluative studies of these practices in such circumstances, educationists and others frequently write eloquently on their merits. Thus, Shilliday (1955, p. 1) writes of correspondence lessons:

> As a child I thought it a rather wonderful system of instruction; even the growth of adult status and the realization that the materials and methods of the Primary Correspondence School are far from perfect have not dimmed my admiration for the work done by administrators and teachers in this branch of education. The scholars and critics may find flaws in a system but if the pupils are contented and enjoy the course it must have many worthwhile features. Perhaps in my own case a satisfactory and well-rounded home life compensated for the elements found lacking in the actual school work. My mother taught my sister and me; she had been a trained teacher before her marriage. Many others might not have had the benefit of a competent home supervisor.

Probably the practices listed above cannot be evaluated in simple terms; as Shilliday appreciates, much will depend upon the *total* context within which they occur. Perhaps the best that can be done is to demonstrate feasibility, and this has been done on numerous occasions and in numerous countries. In addition, however, evidence is available on such issues as 'greater participation in discussions' as a result of membership of 'Schools of the Air'. (Since these schools are not found in all parts of the world, it should be explained that they involve two-way radio communication between pupils and teacher, and, by providing opportunities for 'feed-back' as well as more general social encounters, they inject something of the atmosphere of normal classrooms into 'outback' education in countries such as Australia.)

Differential Development within Metropolitan Communities: One of the main effects of the uneven and changing growth within urban areas is a lag in facilities in some communities and a surplus of unusable ones in others. Thus, when small rural schools on the outskirts of rapidly-growing cities are suddenly inundated with hundreds of new pupils at the beginning of a school year, facilities (such as buildings and playgrounds) soon become hopelessly inadequate, and often the inadequacies cannot be overcome on the existing site. To take only one example: although Kenmore school in Brisbane was established about 1900, it remained, until 1958, a one-teacher school serving a rural community on the western outskirts of the city. Then, in the space of six years, enrolments rose to over 600, and although the education authorities manfully added classrooms, etc., by the time new schools could be built within the area the existing facilities were grossly 'over-manned'. By way of contrast, there must be few large cities in the world which do not have surplus schools and classrooms in their inner areas.

Again, of course, one might ask, 'So what, in terms of effects upon school learning?' The answer depends upon knowledge related to the subtle effects of overcrowding, and to the more direct effects of inadequacies in such things as libraries, playing fields, creative facilities and so on, and, while most educationists would agree in claiming that these characteristics inhibit school learning, it must be confessed that the scientific evidence is just not available. This point will be discussed more fully below.

Cultural Segregation of Communities: Numerous studies in all parts of the world have established relationships between economic and sociocultural indices of communities, on the one hand, and various measures of school performance, on the other. On the basis of this evidence, Rogoff (1961) concludes:

> . . . let it be granted that the various social classes are not randomly distributed among the diverse sizes and types of communities in the United States today . . . . It follows that each of the social classes will be more heavily concentrated in some kinds of community environments than in others, and that communities will vary in the predominant or average social-class affiliation of their residents. Such structural differences may set in motion both formal arrangements—such as school, library, and general cultural facilities in the community—and informal mechanisms, such as normative climates or modal levels of social aspiration, which are likely to affect *all* members of the community to some extent—parents and children, upper, middle, and working classes. (pp. 242-3.*)

Rogoff's thesis is a plausible one; nevertheless, it must be admitted that

*Reprinted from N. Rogoff, Local social structure and educational selection. In A. H. Halsey, J. Floud and C. A. Anderson (Eds), *Education, Economy and Society*. The Free Press, Glencoe, 1961. Copyright 1961 The Macmillan Company, and reprinted with their permission.

his own data, and those of others frequently quoted in support, do not provide conclusive evidence of an effect that can be ascribed to the *community,* and not to home or personality variables. The difficulty is that these variables co-exist; a low economic district is likely to contain low economic families whose members are, for example, low in ability and motivation. Probably the most sophisticated study bearing on this issue is that reported by Sewell and Armer (1966) in which the educational aspirations of metropolitan Milwaukee youth were examined. The authors conclude:

> The zero-order correlation (r) of neighbourhood status with college plans is +0.299. The multiple correlation (R) of sex, [family] socio-economic status, and intelligence with college plans is +0.479 and the coefficient of determination (R^2) is 0.229, which means that these three background factors account for 22.9 per cent. of the variance in college plans. The addition of neighborhood status as a predictor variable increases the multiple correlation (R) to +0.497 and the coefficient of determination (R^2) to 0.247. Thus, neighborhood status results in an absolute increase of 1.8 per cent. in the explained variance of college plans beyond the effects of sex, [family] socioeconomic status, and intelligence. Consequently, it may be concluded that although neighborhood context makes some contribution to the explained variance in college plans over and above that made by the traditional variables, its added contribution is indeed small. (p. 167.*)

Although this conclusion has been strongly attacked (Turner, 1966; Michael, 1966; Boyle, 1966), it is difficult to refute, and the best that one can do is to take refuge in the argument that the multiple-correlation analysis masks the importance of the community effect in special cases—as, for example, slums, affluent communities where the families are prepared to combine their resources to provide better school facilities, and communities cut off from the main stream of culture.

One of the ways in which the environment of slums can affect the aspirations of youth is revealed in this verbatim report contained in a survey of a Spanish Harlem 'fortress' (Hammer, 1964):

> In Scarsdale, the first things the kids learn are how to read and write; that's taken for granted. In my neighborhood, the first things the kids learn are how to fight and steal, and not take any crap from anyone . . .
>
> Man, when I was a kid, I used to have dreams that maybe I'd be a scientist and discover all kinds of things. But they were only dreams; when I woke up there wasn't anything real about them, there couldn't be anything real about them; there aren't any scientists, or anyone else who has a big job, on my block so I haven't got the least idea of what they're like. It's hard to even picture them mentally. These things are so far above us they aren't real. They're like a cloud that looks solid

*From W. H. Sewell and J. M. Armer, Neighborhood context and college plans. *American Sociological Review,* 31(1966), 2, 159-168. Reprinted with permission of the American Sociological Association.

until you grab into it and find it falls apart in your hands.*

The tragedy of this 18-year old, intelligent boy lay in the fact that the sordid environment of the neighbourhood provided no leavening to an impoverished home life. As Conant (1965) has so forcefully said, even when the family has aspirations, 'The unemployed floaters on the street are walking evidence to all the youth that nothing can be accomplished through education, that the door of the neighborhood schoolhouse indeed opens on a dead-end street.' Here Conant is referring to Negro youth, but what he has to say applies with equal force to disadvantaged groups everywhere, including communities of Aborigines in Australia. It is precisely these kinds of depressing and explosive situations that Havighurst and other educationists interested in the educational effects of urbanization hope to ameliorate through vigorous programmes of urban renewal. Havighurst (1961) argues for the maintenance of a community 'status ratio' (calculated from the formula $(2(U + UM) + LM) \div (UL + 2LL)$, where U = upper class, M = middle class, and L = lower class) above a critical point of .6, for the evidence suggests that, once the ratio becomes lower than this, middle-class families tumble over one another in their attempts to leave, and soon only a solid mass of lower-class families remains.

Some educationists attempt to overcome the harmful effects of segregation of underprivileged families by reversing the current trend of 'zoning' and transporting pupils across community boundaries. However, neither the maintenance of an appropriate status ratio nor 'bussing' is any guarantee that beneficial effects will accrue from the interaction of pupils from different socioeconomic classes. Indeed, as one of Havighurst's own students (Neugarten, 1946) has shown, neither practice will guarantee even interaction. Havighurst's contention that, 'If lower-class boys and girls are in classes where a third or more of the pupils are from a middle-class family, they will be stimulated to keep up with the middle-class children in school-work, and they will also be in a position to form friendships and thus learn some of the social behavior and social values of middle-class children' (Havighurst, 1961, p. 255) could be little more than a pious hope unless the schools capitalize upon the opportunities in organization, curriculum, and methods of instruction.

Among the more tangible educational handicaps of low socioeconomic communities are: inability to attract or retain the highest quality teachers, inability to provide the best school facilities, and an absence of libraries and other cultural aids. With reference to the United States, Cunningham (1968) writes: 'Few laymen and only a relatively small number of professional educators are aware of the extensive variation that marks the American educational system. Moreover, few persons raise important questions about the meaning of such variation . . . . Although the correla-

*From R. Hammer, Report from a Spanish Harlem 'Fortress.' In *The New York Times Magazine*, January 5, 1964. Copyright © 1964 by The New York Times Company. Reprinted by permission.

tion between expenditures per pupil and educational quality is less than perfect, the preponderance of evidence suggests that the more money spent on schooling the better the educational product.' (p. 94.)

To end this section on 'slums' on a more cheerful note: in most parts of the world, state and federal governments are increasingly assisting depressed communities to overcome their educational inequalities. The United States Elementary and Secondary Education Act of 1965 is a good illustration of this. *Title I* of this Act provides for financial assistance to local educational agencies with high concentrations of children of low-income families, to: (a) arrange and finance field trips for cultural and educational development; (b) schedule concerts, dramas, lectures, and visits of mobile art exhibits and libraries; (c) purchase musical recordings of a classical nature and recordings of poems and addresses; and (d) provide enrichment programmes on Saturdays. *Title II* of the Act provides financial aid for school library resources and other instructional materials. As most educationists realize, it is not merely a question of raising the facilities of disadvantaged communities to those of the advantaged but of raising them above as a compensation for other handicaps. Equality of educational opportunity should often mean inequality of educational provisions.

At the other end of the scale from the disadvantaged communities are those where the residents are affluent, achievement-oriented, and school-minded. Under these favourable conditions, 'light-house schools', serving as beacons of educational progress, have developed. Perhaps the most outstanding examples of these are to be found in countries where so much depends upon the willingness of local citizens to tax themselves for educational purposes. However, they are not unknown in countries like Australia and New Zealand, where most of the money for educational purposes comes from central coffers, for the policy in these countries is essentially one of 'bread for all, and jam or cake for those who show a willingness and ability to pay for such luxuries'. This policy is seen clearly in the way that most central educational authorities will ensure that a teacher with minimum qualifications is placed in a classroom adequately equipped with chalk and blackboard. If additional teaching aids are desired by the parents, a subsidy can often be attracted after the local school has taken the initiative in raising some (usually half) funds. Thus, while some Australian parents and citizens' associations struggle along with a membership of three and a budget around $30 per annum, others count their members in hundreds and spend in excess of $10,000 on 'extras' per annum. Affluent communities may equip their schools with swimming pools, sophisticated musical instruments and instruction, creative art centres, well-stocked and parent-staffed libraries, additional scientific equipment, television sets, and the latest in curriculum innovations. Inevitably, some of this equipment will not be used to full advantage, but the discrepancy between schools of this kind and those in depressed areas is so great that, even in the absence of scientific evidence, one cannot help but be impressed by the great educational advantage enjoyed by pupils in schools such as

those described above. 'To him who hath shall be given' is the operating
principle as good homes combine their resources to provide enriched
school and community experiences for their children.

Along a somewhat different dimension from that which we have been
discussing (namely depressed/advantaged) are communities which have
elected, often on religious or ethnic grounds, to separate themselves from
the mainstream of the national culture. Examples are to be found in most
countries—the Amish of Pennsylvania and the Sikhs living in Australia,
are but two. Writing of the 'Amish Folk', Gehman (1965) states: 'When
I was a boy in Lancaster County, Pennsylvania, my parents used to take
me to visit my great-grandparents in their old white frame farmhouse near
Beartown, in the heart of the Pennsylvania Dutch country. . . . It seemed
to me then that the Amish lived in another world, and so it still seems.'

Special concessions have been made to the Amish as far as education is
concerned: they may withdraw their children from school at the age of
fourteen years except for attendance of three hours per week. They run
their own schools and season the curriculum liberally with religious
subject matter in the hope that the *kinder* will be strengthened to resist
the siren calls of the 'gay' people.

Communities such as those set up by the Amish and Sikhs are usually
exceptionally cohesive and single minded, and they provide a cocoon-like
existence for the young. Education for the kind of life chosen appears to
be highly effective, for communities, homes, schools and churches provide
unusually strong reinforcement for each other. The educational criterion of
'preparation for life in a rapidly changing and complex world' is hardly
applicable, for as an Old Order Amishman said (Gehman, 1965), 'Elec-
tricity is not in the Bible, and so we have not the use of it.'

Conclusion

Probably the outstanding conclusion from this survey is that definitive
knowledge related to the effects of communities *upon school learning* is
lacking. This, however, does not make an exception of communities, for,
as other writers in this book have emphasized, little is known, too, about
the effects upon learning of the wider culture, peer groups, homes,
institutions and classrooms. This could be interpreted as a deficiency in
the research, and, certainly, more research is needed, but one cannot
reasonably expect to establish a firm link between such a broad contextual
element as a community and specific learning achievements. For one
thing, there are too many other influences operating and some of these
could conflict. For a second, and this is the more important, there is not
an immediate line between communities and achievement—intervening
variables such as peer-group values, teacher personality and skill, and
curriculums all interrupt the flow of events. The most that one could expect
to show are relationships between community characteristics, on the one
hand, and pupil personalities and educational provisions, on the other.

There is a substantial body of knowledge to suggest that particular communities predispose towards the development of particular personality characteristics. Thus, small communities, by exerting greater 'claim' upon their youth, foster qualities of self-reliance, responsibility and achievement, while depressed communities inhibit achievement striving and promote disillusionment. Again, there is a substantial body of knowledge to suggest that particular communities predispose towards the development of particular educational provisions. Thus, large communities tend to contain large schools, and affluent communities can, and often do, provide facilities well beyond the dreams of less fortunate neighbourhoods.

Evidence surveyed in this chapter does not provide convincing support for Arensberg's claim that the community is the main link between culture and society, but it is sufficient to reject Angell's judgment of moral vestigiality. The community does not, and cannot, have a profound effect upon the specific learning that occurs within classrooms, but, through its influence upon personality and educational provisions, it is a *context* of considerable significance.

References

Anderson, K. E., Ladd, G. E. and Smith, H. A., 1954: A study of 2500 Kansas high school graduates. *Kansas Studies in Education*, University of Kansas, 4.

Angell, R. C., 1941: *The Integration of American Society*. McGraw-Hill Book Co., New York.

Arensberg, C. M. and Kimball, S. T., 1965: *Culture and Community*. Harcourt, Brace & World, New York.

Barker, R. G., 1960: Ecology and motivation. In M. R. Jones (Ed.), *Nebraska Symposium on Motivation*. University of Nebraska Press, Lincoln.

Barker, R. G. and Gump, P. V. (Eds), 1964: *Big School, Small School*. Stanford University Press, Stanford, Calif.

Biobaku, S., 1967: The effects of urbanization on education in Africa: The Nigerian experience. *International Review of Education*, XIII, 451-452.

Boyle, R. P., 1966: On neighborhood context and college plans. *American Sociological Review*, 31, 5, 706-707.

Brennan, T., 1965: Urban communities. In A. F. Davies and S. Encel (Eds), *Australian Society*. Cheshire, Melbourne.

Brennan, T., 1966: *Urbanization—Implications for Social Welfare*. Seminar paper, Council of Social Services of Queensland.

Broom, L. and Selznick, P., 1958: *Sociology: A Text With Adapted Readings*. Row, Peterson and Co., New York.

Campbell, W. J., 1964: Some effects of high school consolidation. In R. G. Barker and P. V. Gump (Eds), *Big School, Small School*. Stanford University Press, Stanford, Calif.

Conant, J. B., 1965: Social dynamite in our large cities: Unemployed out-of-school youth. In A. Kerber and B. Bommarito (Eds), *The Schools and the Urban Crisis*. Holt, Rinehart and Winston, Inc., New York.

Connell, W. F., *et al.*, 1957: *Growing Up in an Australian City*. Australian Council for Educational Research, Melbourne.

Cunningham, L. L., 1968: Organization of education in metropolitan areas. In R. J. Havighurst (Ed.), *Metropolitanism: Its Challenge to Education. NSSE Yearbook*, LXVII, Pt I, University of Chicago Press, Chicago, Ill.

Dawe, H. C., 1934: The influence of size of kindergarten group upon performance. *Child Development*, 5, 295-303.

Gehman, R., 1965: Amish folk. *National Geographic*, 128, 2, 227-253.

Goldstein, S., 1965: Rural-suburban-urban population redistribution in Denmark. *Rural Sociology*, 30, September, 267-277.

Hammer, R., 1964: Report from a Spanish Harlem 'fortress'. *The New York Times Magazine*, January 5.

Havighurst, R. J., 1961: Metropolitan development and the educational system. *School Review*, 69, 3, 251-267.

Havighurst, R. J. (Ed.), 1968: Introduction. In *Metropolitanism: Its Challenge to Education. NSSE Yearbook*, LXVII, Pt I, University of Chicago, Chicago, Ill.

Havighurst, R. J. and Neugarten, B. L., 1957: *Society and Education*. Allyn & Bacon, Boston, Mass.

King, E. J., 1967: Urbanisation and education in Britain. *International Review of Education*, XIII, 4, 431-433.

Larson, C. M., 1949: School-size as a factor in the adjustment of high school seniors. *Bulletin No. 511, Youth Series*, No. 6, State College of Washington, Washington, D.C.

Mack, R. W., 1968: Suburb, central city and education. In R. J. Havighurst (Ed.), *Metropolitanism: Its Challenge to Education. NSSE Yearbook*, LXVII, Pt I, University of Chicago Press, Chicago, Ill.

McRae, C. R., 1963: Teachers are the salt of the earth. *Australian Journal of Education*, 7, 3, 207-212.

Mangus, A. R., 1948: Personality adjustments of rural and urban children. *American Sociological Review*, 13, 566-575.

Michael, J. A., 1966: On neighborhood context and college plans. *American Sociological Review*, 31, 5, 702-706.

Neugarten, B. L., 1946: Social class and friendship among school children. *American Journal of Sociology*, 51, 305-313.

Parkyn, G. W., 1952: *The Consolidation of Rural Schools*. NZCER, Wellington, New Zealand.

Richardson, P. and van der Veur, K., 1968: Community-school relations in urban areas of the territory of Papua and New Guinea. *Australian Journal of Education*, 12, 1, 90-101.

Robinson, W. C., 1965: Changes in the rural population of the United States by metropolitan and nonmetropolitan status, 1900 to 1960. *Rural Sociology*, 30, June, 166-183.

Rogoff, N., 1961: Local social structure and educational selection. In A. H. Halsey, J. Floud and C. A. Anderson (Eds), *Education, Economy and Society*, The Free Press, Glencoe, Ill.

Sewell, W. H. and Armer, J. M., 1966: Neighborhood context and college plans. *American Sociological Review*, 31, 2, 159-168.

Shilliday, J., 1955: Primary correspondence in Queensland. Unpublished MS, University of Queensland.

Skrabanek, R. L., 1956: The effect of commuting to school upon the performance of high-school students. *Rural Sociology*, 21, 171-174.

Turner, R. H., 1966: On neighborhood context and college plans. *American*

Sociological Review, 31, 5, 698-702.

Wright, H. F., 1961: *The City-Town Project*. Mimeographed report, University of Kansas.

4

*Some Effects of Secondary School Consolidation on the Experiences of Pupils**

W. J. Campbell

AT ONE extreme are large schools struggling with problems of organization, and at the other are very small ones struggling to survive against the wave of consolidation. The study reported in this chapter was undertaken to assess the effects of school consolidation upon the daily experiences of the pupils concerned. In design and methodology it is similar to the one concerned with school size and organization (Chapter 10), and the reader who wishes to know more details about the theory and questionnaires used should refer to pages 175-9. However, the issues involved in the two studies are quite different and the investigations were carried out in different countries. Moreover, the scope of this study is greater than that of the other.

'Consolidation' is variously defined, but, as used in this study, it signifies the transportation of secondary school pupils from their local communities to a school in a neighbouring community. The essential elements are: (a) commuting; and (b) attendance at a school which is larger than that which had previously existed, or could exist, in the local community.

Scope and Sample

The investigation was focused upon the out-of-class experiences of the students and can be divided into four sections: (a) nature of the forces which led to participation in extracurricular behaviour settings; (b) the

*First published in R. G. Barker and P. V. Gump (Eds), *Big School, Small School: High School Size and Student Behavior*. Stanford University Press, Stanford, Calif.

extent and level of participation in these settings; (c) the satisfactions gained from these participations; and (d) a daily-round-of-life survey. Answers were sought to questions such as the following:

Are pupils in consolidated schools under more or less pressure to participate in school activities?

Does the nature of the pressures differ?

Do pupils in consolidated schools participate to a greater or lesser extent in school activities?

Do they miss out or gain in particular kinds of activity?

Do pupils in consolidated schools report more or less satisfaction with school activities?

How does consolidation affect the daily rounds of life of the pupils involved?

Does consolidation affect community participations by pupils?

The state of Kansas, in 1962, provided an excellent field laboratory for the study of questions such as these. In many districts consolidation at the secondary school level had already taken place, and schools which were formerly used for secondary pupils were being used for grade pupils or were standing idle. On the other hand there was no dearth of small local secondary schools that were still functioning actively.

For purposes of the study three groups of students were selected:

Group 1: Small-local—those in attendance at small rural secondary schools within the boundaries of their own communities. There were two schools involved here and each had a pupil population of 53. Each, too, was situated within a small town of about 200 persons.

Group 2: Consolidated—those who came from communities which were similar in size to those of Group 1, but who were transported daily by bus to a county secondary school, with a roll of 370 pupils, within a larger district. These pupils, like the previous ones, came from two different communities, each of which contributed 41 pupils.

Group 3: Larger-local—those in attendance at the larger county secondary school referred to above, but who came from the community within which the school was situated. There were 84 pupils in this group, and the total population of the community was 551 persons.

As a first step in obtaining a study sample, a combined list of the 82 consolidated pupils was drawn up, and then attempts were made to match each student on the list with one from each of the small-local and larger-local groups yielding a matched three. This matching was undertaken on the basis of sex, class in school, and percentile rank on the Differential Aptitude Test. By maintaining fairly rigorous standards in the percentile rank matching, it was possible to form 61 matched threes (30 girls and 31 boys).

The study was designed to isolate the effects of the two variables listed earlier, namely, commuting and size of school, but it was impossible to avoid the inclusion of a third variable—size of community. Thus, the small-local pupils came from small communities and attended small-local schools; consolidated pupils came from small communities and attended what was for them a larger consolidated school; and the larger-local pupils came from a medium-sized community and attended what was for them a larger-local school.

It seems likely that the three variables, and perhaps others, interact in a complex manner, so that to treat them as distinguishable causal elements is to do less than justice to the complexity of relationships. Nevertheless, it seems reasonable to assume that:

1. No differences between any two of the groups would suggest that the effects of consolidation in the areas studied are negligible.
2. A difference between small-local students, on the one hand, and consolidated and larger-local ones, on the other, would suggest the influence of some school factor.
3. A difference between consolidated students, on the one hand, and small-local and larger-local ones, on the other, would suggest the influence of commuting.
4. A difference between larger-local students, on the one hand, and small-local and consolidated ones, on the other, would suggest the influence of community size.

Forces to Participate

As in the study of school size and organization (Chapter 10), data on forces were obtained from a questionnaire designed by Willems (1963). The settings used in this study were: Home Basketball Game, Homecoming Dance, Christmas Music Program, Magazine Sale, and Pep Rally. These were chosen because of their occurrence in each of the schools during the current school year.

Students in all three groups reported the existence of a considerable number of forces associated with entry into the settings: a mean of 10.48 per setting for small-local, 9.60 for consolidated, and 9.67 for larger-local. Overall differences here were not significant. The three groups did not differ either with respect to the relative potency of the forces; No 11—'I like to be active and do things', No 13—'I knew this activity needed people', and No 9—'I like this activity' were consistently at the top of the lists, while No 14—'It gave me a chance to be someone special', No 10—'I saw that everyone else was going, and it's not fun to be left out', and No 15—'This activity is required for students like me' were invariably given few affirmative markings.

An analysis in terms of *own* and *foreign* forces revealed no overall or subgroup differences in the number of own forces, but small-local pupils reported more foreign forces than did those from the other two groups.* F values were: Groups 1 and 2—8.894 (.01); Groups 1 and 3—11.293 (.01); Groups 2 and 3—ns.

---

*Unless otherwise stated, an F value based on the formula for the matched-pair design has been used to assess significance levels.

In an attempt to examine the broad difference in greater detail further subdivisions were made as follows:

1. Items suggesting intellectual attraction.
2. Items suggesting external pressures.
3. Items suggesting anticipated enjoyment.
4. Items suggesting social attractions.
5. Items suggesting personal responsibility.
6. Items suggesting opportunity to acquire primary status.

Significant intergroup differences were found with respect only to external pressures and personal responsibilities, and in each case the small-local pupils scored higher (.01 level) than those from the other two groups.

From this examination of entry forces two conclusions can be drawn. (a) Pupils attending small-local schools are more aware than others of claims associated with wishes, expectations, demands and requirements of other persons, and they also mention more frequently claims associated with personal responsibilities which they hold or perceive themselves as holding. (b) The differences noted clearly appear to be associated with school size.

Extent and Levels of Participation

To assess the extent and level of pupil participation in the extracurricular behaviour settings of the schools, a survey of all settings which had occurred from September 1961 to March 1962 was made, and then students were asked to complete a questionnaire in which they indicated: (a) whether or not they attended the settings at least once during the period under review, and (b) exactly what they did in those settings which they attended. The statements given in the second part of this questionnaire were then used to determine levels of penetration (Chapter 10, p. 181).

As a first step in the analysis of the data each student's *grand total* score of participation was considered. This revealed the following means:

Small-local   33.43
Consolidated   36.79
Larger-local   39.31

F values were: Groups 1 and 2—6.011 ($< .05$); Groups 1 and 3—14.606 ($< .01$); Groups 2 and 3—ns.

Thus, on first glance, pupils attending the larger school appear to record greater participation than do those from the smaller ones. However, a breakdown of the grand total score into *entries* (levels 1 and 2) and *performances* (levels 3 and 4) shows that the apparent superiority of the larger school arises from the many more *entry* participations which its students experience. Group means for this category were:

Small-local   21.29
Consolidated   29.41
Larger-local   30.75

F values: Groups 1 and 2—53.746 (< .01); Groups 1 and 3—66.653 (< .01); Groups 2 and 3—ns.

Performance scores, on the other hand, suggested the superiority of the small schools for group means were:

    Small-local   12.14
    Consolidated   7.38
    Larger-local   8.56

F values: Groups 1 and 2—5.085 (< .05); Groups 1 and 3—7.862 (< .01); Groups 2 and 3—ns.

Although, as we have seen, pupils from the larger school had a higher grand total score than did those from the small schools, the reverse was true for *scope* score—that is, pupils from the smaller schools participated in a broader range of activities (super-varieties). Mean scores were: small-local, 7.00; consolidated, 6.49; and larger-local, 6.39. If only these super-varieties in which performance scores were recorded are taken into consideration, the small-local students are found to widen the distance between themselves and the others. Thus, from a total of 10 super-varieties, mean scope performance scores were:

    Small-local   4.49
    Consolidated   3.06
    Larger-local   3.18

F values were: Groups 1 and 2—26.762 (< .01); Groups 1 and 3—27.978 (< .01); Groups 2 and 3—ns.

These findings on extracurricular behaviour suggest that:

(a) pupils in attendance at larger schools are likely to report more entry participations;

(b) pupils in attendance at small schools are likely to report more performance participations;

(c) pupils in attendance at small schools are likely to report participation in a broader range of super-variety settings.

Satisfactions from Participation

After reporting participations in extracurricular settings, the pupils were asked: (a) to record those settings that were for them especially good, satisfying and worthwhile; and (b) to indicate alongside each selected setting precisely what made it especially good, satisfying and worthwhile.

The first finding is that the small-local students were inclined to list more settings as especially worthwhile than were students from either of the other two groups. Mean numbers were: small-local—3.86, consolidated —2.67, and larger-local—2.92. *F* values were: Groups 1 and 2—21.161 (< .01); Groups 1 and 3—13.560 (< .01); Groups 2 and 3—ns.

In the first-level analysis of the values data, use was made of the code devised by Gump and Friesen (1964). It was not anticipated that many of the forty categories would yield significant intergroup differences, but, on the basis of both theory and previous research, differences were predicted within a small number of super-categories. For this reason, a special examination was made of *competence, general learning, novelty, large entity affiliation, big action and test* and *vicarious enjoyment,* and the findings showed that the study groups did not differ significantly with respect to the first four of these, but that the small-local pupils were more inclined to mention values denoting *big action and test* and *vicarious enjoyment* (both at the .05 level) than were the other two groups. This super-category analysis tends to be mainly descriptive in nature and tells little about the dynamics of behaviour. For this reason it was decided in this consolidation study to proceed to a second-level analysis in which use was made of the developmental-task concept. It was assumed that: (a) in the process of growing up, adolescents (as well as children and adults) are faced with a series of developmental tasks, and (b) they will tend to seek out and report as most worthwhile those settings which contribute to the achievement of these developmental tasks. Accordingly, the value categories were further grouped into ten clusters on the basis of inferences made about the nature of the developmental tasks being satisfied. These clusters were:

Physical health, care and use of the body. Included here were such responses as 'It helped to keep me fit', 'I learned how to play football better', and 'I improved my skill at shooting baskets'.

Getting along with others. In this cluster were placed such responses as 'I learned how to get along with girls (or boys)', 'I learned a lot about people', 'I liked being with the other students', and 'It was fun being with the other boys'.

Acquiring knowledge and developing intellectual interests. Included here were all those values concerned with learning new cognitive elements, acquiring items of information which would aid one in future educational and vocational choices, and experiencing novel events, new and interesting situations. Thus, 'I learned a lot about science from it', 'It was very educational', 'I gained a lot of knowledge from the visit', and 'I liked seeing the new exhibits'.

Developing social responsibility and group loyalties. Here we included those unit values in which reference was made to satisfactions gained from helping others—'I was able to help the team', 'It was a good cause', 'I helped the school in a small way'—as well as from knowing that the goals of the group were being fostered—'I liked this immensely because it improved school tone', 'It brings the different groups of students closer together'.

Acquiring a philosophy of life and ethical code. Included here were such comments as 'It made me into a better person', 'I saw more clearly what the right behaviour was', and 'It helped me to set good standards for myself'.

Developing a self-concept. Included in this cluster were those responses concerned with challenges, competitions, and success. Thus, 'I liked the hard work', 'It helped me to find out my strengths and weaknesses', and

'I knew that I was improving'. These all seemed to suggest satisfactions arising from the emergence of an acceptable self-concept.

Achieving primary status. In some respects this cluster resembles the previous one, but here the emphasis is more upon recognition and appreciation by others. Thus, 'It showed others that there was something I could do well', 'I enjoyed it because I had the leading part', 'It gave me an opportunity to display my talents'.

Achieving derived status. In the cluster above, students were making reference to feelings of satisfaction and security gained as a result of recognition by others, but here the same feelings stem from support of others. Included here were such comments as 'I liked being so closely associated with the principal', 'I felt like a member of one real large group', and 'I liked being part of the crowd'.

Ability to express oneself adequately. This is a mixed bag of categories which appear, nevertheless, to possess a common element of psychological expression. Thus, 'It taught me to have more confidence in myself', 'I felt greatly relieved as a result of taking part', 'It was a change from the frustrations of home and school', 'It gave me a chance to do something', and 'I had a chance to say what I really thought'.

Developing a zest for living. Included here were all those responses which suggest exhilaration and plain enjoyment: 'I like doing these things', 'I just love to dance', 'I am mad on watching football', and 'It was tremendous fun'.

After arranging the value categories into these developmental-task clusters we considered: (a) the number of pupils from each study group who recorded at least one value that has been assigned to a particular cluster; and (b) the number of mentions recorded by these pupils.

The pupils did not differ with respect to their responses associated with *responsibility, a philosophy of life, primary status, derived status* and *self-expression.* However: (a) more pupils from the small-local group than from the others mentioned values concerned with *physical well-being* and the development of a *self-concept,* and the number of times that these were mentioned by small-local pupils was correspondingly higher; (b) while the number of small-local pupils who mentioned values associated with *knowledge* and *zest for living* was not very much higher than the number of pupils in the other two groups, the former group tended to mention these values more frequently; and (c) while the number of pupils mentioning *social values* did not differ from one group to another, the small-local and consolidated pupils made use of this cluster more frequently than did those from the larger community.

What do these findings tell us about the schools, commuting, and communities? Presumably, any differences might point to differences in the significance of the task, differences in the provisions for the satisfaction of these, or a mixture of both. The study was not designed to unravel these factors, but the community difference associated with social values would appear to reflect either a paucity of *social* experiences within a small community and hence a greater need to seek out such experiences elsewhere, or a stronger demand from smaller communities for the development of social competence. On the other hand, differences in values associated with *physical well-being, knowledge, self-concepts* and *zest for living* appear to be related to the factor of school size. A small school would appear to provide, within its extracurricular settings, more opportunities for the satisfaction of these particular personality needs.

Daily Round of Life

In order to obtain data on the effects of school consolidation upon the pupils' daily rounds of life, diary record forms were prepared and given to those students from the matched samples who were at school on the chosen day. These records sought information on: (a) time of getting up in the morning; (b) out-of-class activities engaged in during the day; (c) the places where these activities were undertaken; (d) the persons who were present when the activities were undertaken; (e) the amount of time spent on each activity; and (f) time of going to bed.

A total of 165 records were returned by the pupils on the following day, and none of these was facetious or grossly incomplete. This represented a return of just over 90 per cent (95 per cent from the small-local, 90 per cent from the larger-local, and 85 per cent from the consolidated) and accounted for more than 95 per cent of those who had been at school on the previous day. Unfortunately, but not unexpectedly, the 18 absentees did not form six groups of matched threes, but rather were scattered differently throughout the lists. Since only complete threes have been used in subsequent analyses, the total number of records used has dropped to 138, i.e., 46 matched threes.

The amount of out-of-class time available to the students was found by calculating the total time available between getting up in the morning and going to bed at night, and then subtracting from this time spent in school classes. The mean number of minutes were: small-local—509; consolidated —527; larger-local—517.

The amount of time unaccounted for was very small; 102 of the 138 pupils accounted for every minute available to them (indeed a small proportion of these over-estimated slightly), and the remaining 36 failed to account for an average of 30 minutes each. This unaccounted-for time was only 1.5 per cent of the total available time. Since the diaries which could not be used in the analyses because of absentees among the threes did not differ from the others in the matter of accounting for time we can summarize the position by stating that 90 per cent of the pupils in the samples accounted for 98.5 per cent of their out-of-class time.

How accurate are the data recorded by the students? It is possible that the 1.5 per cent of unaccounted-for time was spent on activities which the students did not wish to disclose, but a certain proportion of this probably resulted simply from under-estimations. It is possible, too, that some of the students 'cooked up' the information given, but checks concerned with meals, personal activities, travel and the like, suggested that the records were completed carefully and accurately. Estimations of time are, of course, subject to personal errors—30 minutes spent 'talking with the girl friend' might seem like only 5, whereas the same time spent on 'homework' might seem like 90.

In the analysis of the data, the daily stream of life was first broken into *situations*, which are compounds of activities, places and social groups. Thus 'watching television, in the living room, with mother and father' is one situation, and 'eating lunch, in the cafeteria, with school friends' is another. Any change in one or more of the components results in a changed situation. Thus 'doing homework, in the living room, with mother and father' is a different situation from 'watching television' in the same place with the same persons, and 'eating lunch, in the local cafe, with school friends' is different from 'lunch in the school cafeteria'. Finally, 'watching television, in the living room, with mother and father', is different from engaging in the same activity, in the same place, but with friends instead of parents.

A consideration of the total number of different situations experienced showed that small-local pupils averaged 14.1, consolidated pupils 13.1, and larger-local 14.7. The difference between the last two groups was significant beyond the .01 level. A classification of the situations according to locale (home, school, community and trafficways) revealed that (a) the larger-local group entered more *trafficway* situations than did the other two groups; (b) both the small-local and the larger-local groups entered more *community* situations than did the consolidated group; and (c) no statistically significant differences were found with respect to *home* situations or *school* ones.

The analysis based on situations was followed by one according to *activities* engaged in. A preliminary reading of the records suggested that these activities could be classified as follows:

1. *Meals*   breakfast, lunch, supper, snacks.
2. *Personal*   washing, dressing, changing clothes, getting ready for bed, etc.
3. *Chores*   cleaning up the house, milking the cows, setting the table, doing the dishes, bathing younger siblings, etc.
4. *Travel*   (a) to school; (b) other.
5. *Talking*   mainly face to face, but some telephone conversations as well.
6. *Studying*   school work done at home, or at school before classes began or in the noon hour.
7. *Television*   watching.
8. *Sports*   (a) competitive; (b) spectator; (c) playing. (These were originally classified separately, but the amounts of time were so small that they were finally grouped together.)
9. *Reading*
10. *Dancing*
11. *Radio*
12. *Miscellaneous*   (a) clubs; (b) religion; (c) music; (d) hobbies; (e) resting; (f) entertaining; (g) excursions; (h) writing letters;

(i) movies; (j) shopping; (k) waiting for the bus. (Each of these was originally classified separately, but the counts were so small that they were finally grouped together in this catch-all category.)

We can discuss some of those activities fairly quickly, since, while they occupied a large amount of time, they tended to be favoured equally by students in the three groups. Thus, *watching television* was, overall, the activity which accounted for more time than any other (mean times were 69, 78, and 85 minutes*), and differences within groups were very much greater than those between groups. The same was true for *chores* (mean numbers of minutes were 69, 57, and 73), *meals* (mean times were 58, 65, and 65), *personal activities* (58, 63, and 60), and *talking* (35, 33, and 45). Another group of activities can be dismissed equally easily since they appeared to be of minor importance, and, like the former set, revealed no intergroup differences. These included *reading* (most students did not mention this activity and mean times were 10, 7, and 4 minutes), *dancing* (seldom mentioned, and mean times were 4, 2, and 4), and *radio* (5, 3, and 1 minutes).

Among the remaining five activities *travel to school* and *studying* revealed the largest intergroup differences. It is not surprising, of course, that differences were found in the former of these. It is common knowledge that the removal of students from their own communities is likely to increase the amount of time which they spend travelling to school. In this study, consolidated pupils were found to spend, on an average, 79 minutes commuting to and from school, whereas those in the small-local group spent 40, and those in the larger-local, 27. Highly significant differences were found between each pair. These findings show the importance of consolidation in increasing travel time, but, in addition, they suggest that in a small community some pupils are inevitably faced with a considerable amount of travelling whereas in a community with a greater population a higher proportion of students are likely to be within almost walking distance of the school. (Median distances from school were: small-local—2¼ miles; consolidated—7 miles; larger-local—1½ miles.) Indeed, as one would suspect, some of the pupils attending the small-local school spent more time on travelling than did some of those who commuted from other communities.

In the case of travel to school, both consolidation and size of community appeared to be important. When we turn to examine *studying* it is immediately obvious that some school variable is affecting the amount of time given to this for both study groups from the larger school (consolidated and larger-local) recorded almost identical times (80 and 81 minutes) whereas students from the small-local schools recorded a mean figure which differed greatly (49 minutes). Commuting and size of community do not appear to be influential in this case. In terms of our assumptions we should infer that size of school is the important variable, but this does not seem particularly plausible. It is more likely that the

*Throughout the remainder of this chapter the results for 'small-local' are given first, 'consolidated' second, and 'larger-local' third.

difference between the larger school and the small-local ones with respect to study practices is associated with school policy rather than with school size.

Other travel, sport and *miscellaneous activities* appeared on a considerable proportion of the records, but, since in each case there were many instances in which they did not occur, it was decided to use a nonparametric technique (chi square) in testing for significant differences. When this was done in the case of *other travel*, small-local pupils were found to differ from those in both the other groups by including a significantly greater number who reported at least some *other travel*. Again, this finding does not seem to be clearly associated with school size. Rather, the smaller number of pupils from the larger-local group reporting *other travel* arises from the fact that a greater number of them reside in the town section and, as a result, do not need to travel for shopping, etc. On the other hand, the smaller number from the consolidated group reporting *other travel* arises from the fact that they do not participate in those activities which require travelling. Thus, in one case, size of community appears to be important, and, in the other, commuting seems to be at least a contributing factor.

In some respects *sport* differences resemble study ones, although here a school difference is found in favour of the small-local schools. More students from these participated in sport activities, and the numbers from both Groups 2 and 3 were identical, and yet size of school may not be the only factor. Rather, one suspects a difference in school policy on participation in non-league sporting events (and this is where the pupils from the small-local group scored). On the other hand, size is certainly a contributing factor, especially since, as we have already seen, this influences entry and penetration into extracurricular activities.

Pupils in the small-local group reported significantly greater participation in *miscellaneous activities* than did those who were commuting, but other intergroup differences were not statistically significant. This suggests that commuting limits the range of activities, and a comparison of the consolidated and larger-local groups, where differences were just below the .05 level of significance, supports this. The daily round of life for the consolidated pupils appears to be more highly structured with a greater concentration upon the big seven activities: study, travel to school, television, meals, personal activities, chores and talking. They have less time for leisurely participation in excursions, hobbies, entertainment, music and the like. A somewhat similar picture emerged when a *scope* score for all activities was calculated although in this case there was clearly no difference between consolidated and larger-local students. Mean scores were: small-local, 8.5, consolidated, 7.9, and larger-local, 7.9. F values were: Groups 1 and 2—4.555 ($<$ .05); Groups 1 and 3—25.184 ($<$ .01); Groups 2 and 3—ns.

The out-of-class activities were distributed over seven distinct areas:

1. Own house: bedroom, bathroom, kitchen, dining-room, etc.
2. Own yard or farm: backyard, farmyard, barn, front gate, etc.

3. Other houses or yards: homes of friends, relatives, etc.
4. Transportation: bus, car, truck, etc.
5. School: gymnasium, hall, teenroom, restroom, entrance, etc.
6. Own neighbourhood: local streets, shops, roads, halls, etc.
7. Other neighbourhoods: streets, shops, roads, halls, etc.

As the earlier discussion of *situations* would suggest, *own house* was the place in which the pupils spent most of their out-of-class time. Differences between groups with respect to this locale were not statistically significant (mean times were 288, 312, and 319 minutes), and the same applied to *yard or farm* (39, 25, and 32 minutes), *school* (91, 78, and 100 minutes), *other houses* or *yards* (10, 3, and 3 minutes) and *other neighbourhoods* (1, 11, and 0 minutes).

As we have seen, time spent in various forms of transportation is not identical with time spent travelling to school, but in the case of consolidated and larger-local pupils it is nearly so. Thus, it is to be expected that the three groups will once again show marked differences, with larger-local pupils reporting the least amount, and consolidated the greatest (mean number of minutes were 49, 82, and 29).

Lastly, as far as time spent in places is concerned, the consolidated pupils were found to spend less time in their *own neighbourhoods* than either of the two local groups.

The final analysis that has been made in this study has been based upon the social groups involved in the situations. There were four main ones— or perhaps it is more accurate to say there were three, plus a state of aloneness.

1. Other family members: mother, father, siblings.
2. Friends.
3. Family members plus friends or other adults.
4. Alone.

Other family members featured prominently on the diary records of all pupils (mean times were 214, 191, and 233 minutes) although in the case of consolidated and larger-local groups a statistically significant difference appeared. The most plausible explanation here is probably associated with commuting, and the difference between small-local and consolidated pupils, while not significant, provides some support.

Time spent with *friends* was also universally high (mean times were 149, 162, and 129 minutes), and, although the consolidated pupils had the highest average, differences were not statistically significant. Consolidated pupils also spent more time *alone* than did those in the other two groups (mean numbers of minutes were 118, 160, and 132), and in this case the difference between small-local and consolidated pupils was statistically significant. No differences were found with respect to time spent with *family and friends or other adults*.

Many of the experiential items surveyed in this round of life appear to be unaffected by consolidation. In this category are: home situations, school situations; time spent on meals, personal chores, talking, watching television, reading, dancing, listening to the radio; time spent in own house, at school, in own yard or farm, in other houses and other neighbourhoods; time spent with friends, and with family and friends together.

On the other hand, statistically significant differences were found among groups with respect to: total situations, traffic situations, and community situations; school travel, other travel, sports, study and miscellaneous activities; time spent in transportation, and own neighbourhood; time spent with family and alone.

For at least three reasons these findings ought to be taken as tentative and subject to confirmation: the time interval was short, the number of subjects was small, and among the experiences studied there were many in which no intergroup differences appeared. However, the evidence consistently supports two hypotheses: (1) Consolidation leads to a decrease in neighbourhood and community participations; and (2) Consolidation leads to a reduction in the variety of situations and activities.

Summary and Implications

This study of consolidation effects suggests that if the small-local pupils were transferred to a county secondary school they would probably undergo the following changes in experiences:
A *decrease* in:

1. External pressures aimed at increasing their participations in extracurricular activities. (Size of school effect.)
2. Sense of personal responsibility associated with extracurricular activities. (Size of school effect.)
3. The number of school settings penetrated to the performance level. (Size of school effect.)
4. The range of super-variety settings penetrated. (Size of school effect.)
5. The number of school settings judged to be most worthwhile. (Size of school effect.)
6. Satisfactions associated with physical well-being, acquiring knowledge and developing intellectual interests, developing a self-concept, and zest for living. (Size of school effect.)
7. Neighbourhood and community participations. (Commuting effect.)
8. The range of out-of-class situations and activities. (Commuting effect.)

An *increase* in:

1. The number of school settings penetrated to the entry level.

This is quite an impressive list of changes, but how important are they? Several of the differences in experiences would lead one to hypothesize that the small-local pupils would display greater maturity in various aspects of development than would other pupils. The increased external forces to participate, the higher level participations, and the greater versatility, are likely to be important causative factors in this matter. It is, therefore, not surprising to find that, on the measures of maturity used in this study, the small-local pupils *do* rate higher. They show a greater sense of responsibility towards school activities and their satisfactions indicate a stronger concern with personal growth. This combination of theoretical expectations and supporting empirical data, however limited, suggests that the findings do have implications for child development. What, then, are the implications for those responsible for organizing secondary education?

In the first place, consolidation ought not to be embarked upon lightly and indiscriminately and, when it does occur, special efforts are demanded from both the school and the local community. Through its structural organization, its instructional procedures and its extracurricular activities, the larger school, upon which consolidation has occurred, needs to ensure that *all* its students participate actively and acquire a genuine sense of attachment and contribution to group goals. There is a temptation in a larger school to concentrate upon extracurricular goals and standards which can be achieved by only the most talented pupils at the expense of the rest. Similarly, the local community from which the pupils are drawn must take special pains to so arrange its recreational programmes and community tasks that its young members are appropriately challenged and stimulated. Once consolidation has taken place there is a temptation for the community to discard some of its obligations to its children and adolescents, whereas the data presented here suggest the need for a still more determined effort to meet those obligations.

In the second place, if, as the research evidence suggests, the negative relationship between school size and individual participation is deeply based, and difficult, if not impossible, to avoid, it may be easier to bring specialized and varied behaviour settings to small schools than to raise the level of individual participation in large ones. In Australia this is already done to some extent in such fields as guidance, music, physical education, etc., but it could be extended very considerably. The use of more itinerant specialists, the appointment of bright, enthusiastic teachers to positions of area advisors, and the encouragement of greater interschool cooperation, through the transporting of teachers and equipment, rather than students, are some suggestions aimed at ensuring that our pupils enjoy the best of both worlds. Certainly, many of our very small schools are dreary and impoverished educational centres as they now stand, but these characteristics are not inevitabilities of small size.

It may well be, also, that some of the innovations which are cautiously being introduced into the educational system will enrich the small schools. Self-teaching machines, taped school courses, television classes, wired television linking separate schools, new conceptions of the contributions of the community to educational objectives, and new materials and standards for school construction, could all mean that the specialization and variety that are available to, but seldom able to be capitalized upon by, the large-school pupil, would be within the grasp of the small-school pupil under conditions of maximum opportunity.

Schools are specialized environments, established and manipulated in order to produce certain educational opportunities and effects. We are in need of more investigations, employing new concepts and methods, in order to determine the nature and consequences of these environments.

References

Gump, P. V. and Friesen, W. V., 1964: Satisfactions derived from nonclass settings. In R. G. Barker and P. V. Gump (Eds), *Big School, Small School.* Stanford University Press, Stanford, Calif.

Willems, E. P., 1963: Forces toward participation in behavior settings of large and small institutions: A field experiment. Unpublished MA thesis, University of Kansas.

Part III
The Home Context

5

The Home Context

Betty H. Watts

WHILE the specific direction of the learning process is largely a function of the teacher's manipulation of the classroom setting, during both the years of infancy and the out-of-school hours of the school child the home is an active force helping to shape the child's abilities and attitudes. The importance of the home as a factor influencing school learning is emphasized by studies such as the Manchester Survey. Wiseman (1967), reporting on this survey, which set out to investigate the relationship between the educational attainment of primary children and environmental factors, summarized the results as follows: 'The most important of our findings, perhaps, is the demonstration that the major forces associated with educational attainment are to be found within the home circumstances of the children. These "home" variables have, *pro rata*, nearly twice the weight of "neighbourhood" and "school" variables put together.'

The characteristics the child has developed by the time he enters school, and those that he develops thereafter, cannot, of course, be attributed in entirety to the influence of the home environment—due account must be taken, for one, of the child's own genetic potentials. However, the embryo is endowed with an immense variety of potentials for development, and a proportion, only, of these potentials will be developed. The degree of actualization is, in the first instance, a function of the early home environment.

A weakness in the current research picture related to the topic of this chapter is occasioned by the existence of only a few studies which have traced the full lode—from home antecedents of attitudes and aptitudes through to the effect of these characteristics on school learning. At times, therefore, while it is possible to cite research findings to show the influence of the home upon *development*, it is not possible to demonstrate firmly and directly the influence of the home upon *school learning*.

The plan of this chapter is to begin with a discussion of the effects of the home upon significant affective qualities of children, and then to focus, with a greater measure of confidence, upon family interactions which shape intellectual and cognitive development.

The Development of Significant Affective Qualities

Some General Qualities: Several attempts have been made to define the significant dimensions of the psychological environment of the home. For example, Baldwin, Kalhorn and Breese (1945) working at the Fels Institute, determined three main clusters of parent behaviours: democracy in the home, acceptance of the child, and indulgence. Schaefer (1961) suggested that two dimensions, love-hostility and control-autonomy, could account for the many variables of maternal behaviour. Recently, Stott (1967) has claimed that important variables in family interaction may be subsumed under four headings: interpersonal attitudes and feelings, emotional climate of the home, mutuality of interests and activities, and parental guidance; there are some twenty-two component variables of these four areas.

It is considered that these psychological characteristics of homes influence the development of such child qualities as dependence-independence, passivity, hostility, aggressiveness, friendliness, creativity, originality of thought, and that these, in turn, exert an influence on the child's relationships with others and on his performance in school. However, because of the complexity of the issues, it is not easy to demonstrate the chain of events conclusively. For example, while it is possible to study the association between a particular personality characteristic and a specific dimension of parental behaviour, the child's personality is the result, in part, of his own potentialities and idiosyncratic reactions to parents, and, in part, of his response to the *total* psychological environment of the home. The task of analysing the impact of the home is made all the more difficult by the existence of the complex interrelationships and interplay among the component variables.

The determination of a causal relationship between personality characteristics and school learning is equally difficult because of the many intervening variables, both child characteristics (e.g., cognitive functioning and readiness for the learning experience), and school variables. Classrooms and schools exhibit their own characteristics; differences between teachers are as pronounced as differences between children. Learning, particularly in the early years, is partly a function of the 'match' between teacher personality and child personality, and partly a function of the degree of congruence between the child's characteristics and the demands of the classroom.

The research in this area of home antecedents of personality characteristics is so extensive that no attempt can be made here to summarize the evidence. Excellent reviews are available in *Review of Educational Research*, December 1967, and *NSSE Yearbook*, Part I, 1963. Here it will suffice to make brief comments on the self concept, and on behavioural consequences of democracy, permissiveness and restrictiveness.

Self concept: The child initially builds his concept of himself and makes his associated self-evaluations and self-judgements on the basis of reflected appraisals from his parents who, in the early years, are the main 'significant others' in his world. Parental reactions to his attempts at the developmental tasks of infancy and early childhood determine whether he sees himself as capable and successful, or inept and clumsy. He brings these self-judgements to the new tasks set up by the school and, accordingly, faces up to the school demands with confidence, or assumes a doubtful, hesitant role as school learner.

The child who, in the home, is loved for himself and accepted as he is, has a secure foundation on which to build and a confidence in his encounters with the peer group and teachers. The child who, through parental rejection or over-protection, has had to strive for primary status, will have less relaxed relationships with the new social situation, and this may well have repercussions on his school performance.

Shirley (1942) emphasized the importance of the influence of the home on the child's security:

> . . . a child's level of adjustment depends little upon the extrinsic features of the day, and little even upon his health. It depends much more upon the wholesomeness of his upbringing in the home, and the security and confidence and affection given him by his parents. A secure and wholesomely loved child goes forth to meet new experience in a spirit of adventure and comes out triumphant in his encounters with new places, new materials, and new friends, young and old. A child that is over-sheltered and underloved goes forth from home with misgivings and doubts, and gives an impression of inadequacy and immaturity in his encounter with new experiences that makes him unwelcome either in the society of adults or children. (p. 77.)

There have been repeated demonstrations of the relationship between a child's concept of his own ability and his level of school achievement. One typical illustrative study is that of Brookover, Thomas and Patterson (1964). In a study of 1,050 seventh-grade students these researchers found a significant and positive relationship between self concept and performance in the academic world; this relationship was substantial even when measured IQ was controlled.

Behavioural correlates of democracy, permissiveness and restrictiveness: These dimensions of mother-child interaction have been widely studied in relation to behaviours among children. Few researchers have directly traced the causal chain from maternal restrictiveness/permissiveness through child characteristics to performance in school. However, many of the characteristics which are associated with degree of strictness of parental control are likely to be significant in affecting the child's relations with his peers and teachers and the way he attacks problems, and hence the efficiency of his school learning.

Earlier researchers distinguished between authoritarian and democratic parental control of children and studied characteristics of children in the two types of homes. Baumrind (1966) refined the concept of adult control and distinguished three types of control: permissive (where the child is allowed to regulate his own activities as much as possible), authoritarian (where punitive measures are used to enforce right conduct) and authoritative (where there is firm control but also a valuing of autonomous self-will and disciplined conformity). She concluded: 'The body of findings on effects of disciplinary practices as reviewed and interpreted here give provisional support to the position that authoritative control can achieve responsible conformity with group standards without loss of individual autonomy or self-assertiveness.' (Baumrind, 1966.) It seems likely that school learning would be fostered when both parents and teachers exert authoritative control (as defined by Baumrind).

Watson (1957) made an intensive study of the effects of strictness and permissiveness of parental control on boys aged five to twelve years. All the homes in his sample were 'good', but whereas in one group there was strict discipline, in the other there prevailed an extraordinary degree of permissiveness. He found a difference between the two groups of boys in relation particularly to persistence. Boys from the strict homes were more apt to be either unusually persistent or very easily discouraged. The boys from the permissive homes exhibited a more moderate persistence, and these children maintained a better quality of intellectual activity under difficulty than did the boys from the strict homes. In respect to other consequences of the degree of strictness of parental discipline, Watson found that 'Greater freedom for the child is clearly associated with (a) more initiative and independence (except perhaps at school tasks), (b) better socialization and co-operation, (c) less inner hostility and more friendly feelings towards others, and (d) a higher level of spontaneity, originality and creativity.' Again, one would expect characteristics such as these to play a significant part in a child's adjustment to the learning situation, to teachers and to peers.

The development of achievement motivation has received particular attention from researchers during the last decade, and, since this quality would seem to have special significance for school learning, it is treated separately in the section below.

Achievement Motivation: Other chapters in this book will deal with situational factors in the *school* and *classroom* that arouse and sustain motivation for school learning. However, the home, too, plays a vital role. Within the home is created an intellectual climate which, at the one extreme, fosters favourable attitudes to learning, develops in children a commitment to striving and learning and leads to a high value being placed on school success; at the other extreme, school learning is held in low or negative regard and there is an absence of parental reinforcement for the academic endeavours of the child.

Douglas (1964), in his study of 5,362 children from every type of home

in England and Wales, found a cumulative effect of parental encouragement on school achievement. He concluded that:

> The attitude of children to their school work is deeply affected by the
> degree of encouragement their parents give them and by their own level
> of emotional stability. The children who show few symptoms of
> emotional instability and whose parents are ambitious for their
> academic success have an increasing advantage during the years they
> are at primary school, largely because they pursue their studies with
> greater vigour and concentration than the less favoured children are
> prepared or able to do. (pp. 67-8.*)

Analysis of the data of the 1964 National Survey of Parental Attitudes
and Circumstances Related to School and Pupil Characteristics (Plowden
Report) also provides evidence on the importance of the home in shaping
the child's attitude to and success in school.

> Before the inquiry, it was plain, as a matter of common-sense and
> common observation, that parental encouragement and support could
> take the child some way. What the inquiry has shown is that 'some
> way' can reasonably be interpreted as 'a long way' and that the varia-
> tion in parental encouragement and support has much greater effect
> (on school progress) than either the variation in home circumstances or
> the variation in schools. . . . If the least co-operative parents rose to
> the level of the most co-operative the effect would be much larger than
> if the worst schools rose to the level of the best or the least prosperous
> parents to the level of the most prosperous, because the effect of the
> range in co-operation is much greater than the effect of the range in
> parental prosperity or that of the range in schooling. (Appendix 4,
> Para. 4.)

The survey showed that the relative importance of the parental attitudes
increases as the children grow older. The Manchester Survey of ten-year
old children revealed this same emphasis on the intellectual climate of the
home. Wiseman (1967) concluded that what matters is the degree of
literacy within the home and the attitude of parents towards books and
towards school; these characteristics are seen as more important than mere
membership of a social class, and he makes the point that there are many
'good' homes in the working class and many 'bad' homes in the middle
class.

A similar emphasis on this role of the home can be found in the
American research literature. Dave (1963) was concerned to identify and
measure environmental process variables related to educational achievement. He identified the following home variables: (a) achievement press,
(b) language models in the home, (c) academic guidance provided in the
home, (d) stimulation provided in the home to explore various aspects of
the larger environment, (e) the intellectual interests and activities of the

*From J. W. B. Douglas, *The Home and the School*. MacGibbon & Kee Ltd,
London, 1964. Reprinted with permission of Granada Publishing Limited.

home, and (f) the work habits emphasized in the home. Measurement of these variables led to the determination of an overall index of the home environment, and the correlation between this index and children's total score on an achievement battery was + .80. Bloom, *et al.* (1965), in commenting on Dave's study, point out that this correlation is much higher than that usually obtained between school achievement and other indices of the home environment such as socioeconomic status or parental education. They echo Wiseman's finding: 'It is what the parents do in the home rather than their status characteristics which are most influential on the achievement of their children.'

The attitudes parents exhibit towards education and the consequential degree of encouragement they offer their children in school activities are, in part, a reflection of the value they place on education and an indication of their perception of the relevance of educational achievement to their own life purposes and to their aspirations for their children.

Hess and Shipman (1965) asked each of the mothers in their study sample what she would tell her child on the eve of his enrolment in school, how she would prepare him for school. One replied:

> First of all I would remind her that she was going to school to learn, that her teacher would take my place, and that she would be expected to follow instructions. Also that her time was to be spent mostly in the classroom with other children, and that any questions or any problems that she might have she could consult with her teacher for assistance.

A second mother replied:

> Well, John, it's time to go to school now. You must know how to behave. The first day at school you should be a good boy and should do just what the teacher tells you to do.

In the first case cited we see the mother as having a view of school as a place where learning is the important activity; the second mother was concerned with her child's behaviour rather than with his learning.

Researchers interested in the home antecedents of motivation for school learning have concentrated their interests on the specific motive for learning—the need for achievement (N Ach). McClelland, one of the major workers in this field, has defined achievement motivation as follows:

> Now what about achievement? What adaptation levels or expectations distinguish this motive from others? Clearly the expectations are built out of universal experiences with problem-solving—with learning to walk, talk, hunt or read, write, sew, perform chores and so forth. The expectations also involve standards of excellence with respect to such tasks . . . . The child must begin to *perceive performance in terms of standards of excellence* so that discrepancies of various sorts from this perceptual frame of reference . . . can produce positive or negative affect. The surest sign of such a frame of reference is *evaluation* of a performance in one of our T.A.T. stories . . . . What then becomes

crucial in scoring stories for achievement motivation is detecting *affect in connection with evaluation.* (McClelland, *et al.*, 1953, pp. 78-9.*)

Research into the development of this motive has led to two major conclusions: (a) subcultural values determine the orientation taken by the achievement motive; (b) the antecedents of the strength of the achievement motive are to be found in parental child-rearing practices.

Rosen (1959) is one of the investigators who has explored the relevance of subcultural values for achievement striving. He writes:

Achievement motivation is one part of the achievement syndrome; an equally important component is the achievement value orientation. Value orientations are defined as meaningful and affectively charged modes of organizing behavior . . . . They establish criteria which influence the individual's preferences and goals. Achievement values and achievement motivation, while related, represent genuinely different components of the achievement syndrome, not only conceptually but also in their origins and, as we have shown elsewhere, in their social correlates. Value orientations, because of their conceptual content, are probably acquired in that stage of the child's cultural training when verbal communication of a fairly complex nature is possible. Achievement motivation or the need to excel, on the other hand, has its origins in parent-child interaction beginning early in the child's life when many of these relations are likely to be emotional and unverbalized. Analytically, then, the learning of achievement oriented values can be independent of the acquisition of the achievement motive, although empirically they often occur together. (p. 51.)

In his research, Rosen explored the achievement motivation, values and aspirations of members of six racial and ethnic groups; the values examined were activistic-passivistic orientation, individualistic-collectivistic orientation and present-future orientation. Activistic, individualistic and future orientations were associated with achievement and social mobility.

This issue of motivational values is taken up in the chapter which follows this one. Accordingly, the main focus here is on child-rearing practices.

Studies since 1953 have demonstrated an association between strength of achievement motive and socialization practices concerned with the age and severity of achievement and independence training, the affective interactions between parent and child, and the levels of aspiration parents hold for their children. Excellent critical reviews of the major researches conducted are available in Crandall (1963) and Heckhausen (1967). In this chapter only a brief description of research results will be made.

Katkovsky, Preston and Crandall (1964) showed that parents' orientations towards their own achievements may influence their behaviours with

*From D. McClelland, J. Atkinson, R. Clark and E. Lowell. *The Achievement Motive.* Copyright 1953, Appleton-Century-Crofts, Educational Division, Meredith Corporation, and reprinted with their permission.

their children. 'The greater the value both mothers and fathers placed on intellectual achievement for themselves, the more they valued intellectual achievement for their offspring.'

Rosen and D'Andrade (1959) explored the relation between achievement motivation and child-training practices by observing parents' behaviour as their sons engaged in solving problems. The tasks were so constructed as to make the boys relatively dependent upon their parents for aid. The authors maintained an important distinction between *achievement* training (the child is trained to do things 'well'), stressing competition in situations involving standards of excellence, and *independence* training (the child is trained to do things 'by himself') involving putting the child on his own. Forty boys matched on age, race, IQ and social class were used in the study; half of the boys had high *n* achievement scores, half had low scores. The conclusions arising from the study are worth quoting in full.

> To begin with, the observers' subjective impressions are that the parents of high n achievement boys tend to be more competitive, show more involvement and take more pleasure in the problem-solving experiments. They appear to be more interested and concerned with their son's performance; they tend to give him more things to manipulate rather than fewer; on the average they put out more affective acts. More objective data show that the parents of a boy with high n achievement tend to have higher aspirations for him to do well at any given task, and they seem to have a higher regard for his competence at problem solving. They set up standards of excellence for the boy even when none is given, or if a standard is given will expect him to do 'better than average'. As he progresses they tend to react to his performance with warmth and approval or, in the case of the mothers especially, with disapproval if he performs poorly. (Rosen & D'Andrade, 1959, p. 215.)

Rosen and D'Andrade point out that while mothers and fathers both provide achievement training and independence training, fathers stress the latter while mothers stress the former.

Research emphasizes the early origins of the strength of the achievement motive. It seems that if strong achievement motivation has not developed by the age of eleven years it is not likely to develop at a later date. Strodtbeck's analysis (1958) of the internalization of standards of excellence perhaps accounts for the stability of strength of this motive.

> When the mother-child relationship is warm and the required acts of independence are slightly beyond the son's level of easy performance, then the child is exposed to the complicated system of rewards which requires him to withdraw from the intimate circle of his mother's activities in order to win the affection which is contingent upon his achievement. The strain of this relationship in which affection has become conditioned upon more mature performance has two effects. First, the more mature achievement behaviors which are rewarded are

accepted into the response repertoire with a strength and resistance to extinction. . . . Second, this substitute for direct interpersonal gratification creates a relatively greater sense of personal isolation. These tendencies combined result in behavioral dispositions which are captured as expression of n achievement in projective productions and as a disposition to substitute achievement gratifications for interpersonal gratifications in later career crises. (p. 184.*)

Ausubel (1968) suggests that achievement motivation in school settings has three components: a cognitive drive which is task-oriented—the need to know; an ego-enhancing component, concerned with achievement as a source of primary or earned status; and an affiliative component, oriented towards achievement as a way of ensuring continued derived status through the approval of a superordinate with whom a child identifies.

> Varying proportions of the cognitive, ego-enhancement and affiliative components are normally represented in achievement motivation, depending on such factors as age, sex, culture, social class membership, ethnic origin and personality structure. Affiliative drive is most prominent during early childhood when children largely seek and enjoy a derived status based on dependent identification with, and intrinsic acceptance by, their parents. During this period they strive for academic achievement as one way of meeting their parents' expectations and, hence, of retaining the approval they desire. However, children who are not accepted and intrinsically valued by their parents, and who therefore cannot enjoy any derived status, are compensatorily motivated to seek an inordinate amount of earned status through academic achievement. Thus high levels of achievement motivation typically represent low affiliative drive that is more than compensated for by high ego-enhancement drive. (p. 376.†)

Research indicates that, although the strength of the achievement motive lies in child-rearing practices and its orientation is due to subcultural values, the *arousal of the motive* is a function of situational factors in the classroom. Campbell's research (Chapter 20 of this book) for example, shows that warmth and challenge on the part of the teachers are prerequisites for the arousal of the achievement motive. Accordingly, one would not necessarily expect to find a high correlation between child-rearing practices associated with a high level of achievement motivation and actual performance in school.

Indeed, the research results in this area are somewhat conflicting. For example, Heckhausen (1967, p. 151) reports research conducted by himself and Kemmler in which it was found that, 'mothers of beginners who

*From *Talent and Society* by David C. McClelland, *et al.*, Copyright © 1958 by Litton Educational Publishing, Inc.

†From *Educational Psychology, A Cognitive View* by D. P. Ausubel. Copyright © 1968 by Holt, Rinehart and Winston, Inc. Reprinted by permission of Holt, Rinehart and Winston, Inc.

were mentally and socially ready for school expected and desired independence and freedom of choice earlier in their sons than did mothers whose sons were not yet mentally and socially ready for school'. However, he points out that, 'A massive, premature pressure for achievement on the part of the parents indicates rather a cold rejection of the child's needs which is not intended to further the child's self-reliance for its own sake. It appears not to further but rather to prejudice achievement motivation . . .'. Kurtz and Swenson (1951) conducted a study of home backgrounds of forty underachievers and forty overachievers. It was found that pride, confidence, affection and interest of parents in their children were in greater evidence for overachievers than for underachievers. d'Heurle, *et al.* (1959) investigated the relations among independent behaviour, achievement motivation and efficient intellectual performance in a group of seventy-six gifted children. They found, within even this restricted range of intelligence, that children who scored high on tests of school achievement were less dependent and more competitive in their overt behaviour than children who scored low on these tests.

On the other hand, however, Crandall, *et al.* (1964) found that, 'Girls who were competent readers had both less affectionate and less nurturant mothers than did the girls who demonstrated less proficiency in that academic area.'

Ausubel (1968), in exploring the actual effect of motivation on school achievement, concludes that:

   (i) although high ego-enhancing drive *generally* leads to higher levels of aspiration, the school performance of these children is not necessarily superior to that of intrinsically accepted pupils of comparable academic ability;

  (ii) some individuals with high achievement motivation lack the personality traits necessary for implementing high aspirations;

 (iii) a disabling high level of anxiety may interfere with the facilitating effect of high ego-enhancement drive;

 (iv) cultural influences mediated through age and sex role expectations are important determining factors. (pp. 400-1.*)

Merville Shaw (1967) in his review of motivation in human learning is led to the conclusion: 'Some fairly specific information is becoming available on the relationship between certain parent attitudes and both motivation to learn and learning outcome, but causality cannot be assumed, and studies designed to determine causality seem desirable at this point.'

Family Interactions Which Shape Intellectual and Cognitive Development

The concern in this section will be to examine current findings on the influence of interactions within the family setting upon the developing child—in particular, upon his cognitive and language development. Research attention to these interactions is a relatively recent phenomenon. In studying the literature over the past several decades one can discern a funnelling movement: from concern with broad environmental influences, through more detailed definition of aspects of the environment significant for cognitive development, to, finally, an examination of the processes of interaction between the environment and the child. As Jensen (1967) has said:

> The trend has been away from rather crude socio-economic variables toward more subtle intra-family and inter-personal psychological variables. This shift in emphasis is given cogency by the fact that crude socio-economic variables do not correlate as highly with intelligence and educability as do ratings of more psychological variables. . . . Most variables that index socio-economic status are better thought of as incidental correlates of I.Q. rather than as causal factors. The quality of the parent-child relationship, on the other hand, may be thought of as causal correlation . . . (pp. 10-11).

Although they recognized that environment had some part to play in regulating intellectual development, early researchers (e.g., Goddard, 1912) emphasized that it contributed a far smaller proportion of the variance of intelligence test scores than did heredity. It was Hebb (1949) who cogently directed the attention of psychologists to environment as an active force shaping a child's intellectual development. He argued that it was pointless to ask which of the two forces—heredity or environment—was the more influential, since both were necessary: the inborn neural mechanism (Intelligence A), and the stimulating environment to actualize and develop the potential and to result in a level of functioning intelligence (Intelligence B).

This viewpoint has wide support today. For example, Murphy (1963) writes: 'Intelligence is a potentiality to be achieved. The genetic capacities are released, guided and developed by environmental—especially social—challenge and stimulation.'

During the 'forties, a number of correlational studies confirmed a relationship between environmental forces and level of cognitive functioning, but, in the main, only broad environmental factors were considered; these included aspects such as social class, urban-rural location, and size of family.

The 1950s saw the beginning of the attempt to specify, in a more detailed way, the influence of the environment. Nisbet's study (1953) serves as a good example of this trend. Earlier, the Scottish Mental Survey (1949) had established that there was a negative correlation between the intelligence test scores of children and the size of the family to which they belonged. Nisbet, taking the view that there is an intimate connection between language development and the efficiency of abstract thought, hypothesized that the environment of the large family which depressed the environmental component of a child's test score operated through the limited amount of contact between parent and child, and the consequential restriction of the normal language growth of the child.

The degree of contact a child has with his parents, the quality of the language model they provide for him, and their reinforcement of his speech activities are important determinants of his language and cognitive development. Children who have a high degree of contact with their parents show marked language development. Research has shown that homes differ considerably in the number of opportunities they offer for such contact. In the typical middle-class home, settings for verbal interchange are created and utilized—at meal times conversation is fostered; family discussions on topics of interest are common; rewards and punishments tend to be verbal rather than physical; stories are told and books read to children as a part of the daily pattern of life.

By contrast, lower social class and culturally-deprived children tend to live in a much more impoverished verbal environment, and, as a consequence, exhibit verbal and cognitive retardation. Deutsch (1965) reported that in such homes there is a paucity of organized family activities, and, consequently, less conversation (for example, at meals, since meals are less likely to be regularly scheduled family affairs). He believes that the finding that fifth-grade children from fatherless homes have significantly lower IQ scores than children from intact homes is a consequence, not so much of the absence of the father, as of the diminution of organized family activity. Milner (1951), in a study of forty-two first-grade children who were identified as high and low scorers on reading readiness tests, was led, through interviews with the children and their mothers, to conclude that high scorers had a much richer verbal environment than low scorers. She commented:

> There appears to be a radically different atmosphere around the meal table from the child's point of view for the high scorers than for the low scorers. More frequently for the high scorers meal time at home, particularly the first meal of the day, serves as a focus for total family interaction. Further, this interaction seems to be positive and permissive in emotional tone for these children and has a high verbal content —that is, the child is talked to by adults with mature speech patterns, and in turn he talks to them. The opposite situation apparently exists for the low scorers. There was, in fact, indication from the responses of some of these mothers that they actively discourage or prohibit their children's 'chatter' and refuse to engage in conversation with them during meals; this prohibition is based on a belief that talking during meals is a 'bad' practice. (p. 109.*)

Vera John (1963), who was also concerned with the influence of the early social environment upon the patterning of intellectual skills in young

*From E. Milner, A study of the relationships between reading readiness in grade one school children and patterns of parent-child interactions. *Child Development,* 22, 95-112. Copyright 1951, The Society for Research in Child Development, Inc., and reprinted with their permission.

children, drew attention to the fact that 'the corrective feedback offered to a much-listened-to child gives him an opportunity to experiment with strategies of language behavior'. This feedback is absent in the case of the lower-class child whose environment is much less responsive to his speech.

Hunt (1964a), in his investigations into intellectual development, also emphasized the role of parent-child verbal interaction particularly during the second and third years of the child's life. He believed that during these years crowded home conditions which so often accompany poverty hamper the child's development. '... late in his second or early in his third year, after he has developed a number of pseudo-words and achieved the "learning set" that "things have names", the child in a crowded, poverty-stricken family probably meets another obstacle: his questions too seldom bring suitable answers, and too often bring punishment that inhibits further questioning.' (p. 88.) This leads to a diminution of question-asking activiᴛy, with disadvantageous effects on later problem-solving activity. Hunt (1964b) emphasizes throughout his writings the tremendous significance for cognitive development of the early years of a child's life. 'It was commonly believed before World War II that early experience was important for emotional development and for the development of personality characteristics, but unimportant for the development of intellect or intelligence. . . . It looks now as though early experience may be even more important for the perceptual, cognitive and intellective functions than it is for the emotional and temperamental functions.' (p. 222.)

However, *frequency* of verbal contact is not the major factor in cognitive development. Of more significance, according to the current research picture, is the nature of the language *code* used by the home. As Jensen (1967) writes, 'The characteristics of the language habits that are being acquired and the kinds of functions the language serves in the child's experiences, actually shape his intellectual development, especially the development of the ability for abstraction and conceptual learning. Poor development of this ability places a low ceiling on educational attainment.' (p. 14.)

Bernstein (1961a and b), taking a sociological view of language, argued that, 'Forms of spoken language induce in their learning, orientations to particular orders of learning and condition different dimensions of relevance.' He differentiated between the cognitive styles of lower and middle-class families. In the former, characterized by a public or restricted language code, language is used in a way that discourages the speaker from verbally elaborating subjective intent, and progressively orients him to descriptive rather than analytic concepts; it is a vehicle for expressing and receiving relationships organized within a relatively low level of conceptualization. This restricted language code includes characteristics such as: short, grammatically simple sentences with a poor syntactical form stressing active voice; simple and repetitive use of conjunctions; little use of subordinate clauses; inability to hold a formal subject through a speech sequence; rigid and limited use of adjectives and adverbs; frequent use of statements where the reason and conclusion are confounded to produce a categoric statement. It is a language of *implicit* meaning. Middle-class families, on the other hand, while having access to this restricted code have access also to a formal or elaborated language code, in which the formal possibilities for sentence organization are used to clarify meaning and make it *explicit*; it is a language use which points to the possibilities inherent in a complex conceptual hierarchy for the organizing of experience.

Bernstein sees the restricted language code as a major cause of educational difficulty for lower-class children. Within the home itself the system of social relationships which is reflected by the language code produces a specific order of learning—one in which, in the lower class, language is not used to explore relationships, one in which categoric statements by the mother shut off curiosity and confirm her (the mother's) authority. By contrast, in the middle class, language and verbal reasoning between the mother and child enhance a quite different sort of learning.

> The implications (of public or restricted language) are logical, social and psychological. It is suggested that a correlate of this linguistic form is a relatively low level of conceptualization, an orientation to a low order of causality, a disinterest in processes, a preference to be aroused by, and to respond to, that which is immediately given, rather than to the implications of a matrix of relationships; and that this partly conditions the intensity and extent of curiosity as well as the mode of establishing relationships. These logical considerations affect what is learned and how it is learned, and so affect future learning. (Bernstein, 1961*b*, p. 302.*)

The child who has incorporated these restricted syntactical structures will, when he encounters the elaborate language code of the middle-class school, be unable to respond to the language, unable to communicate, less able to learn, and will become frustrated and defeated. Deutsch (1965), in his study of Negro and white lower and middle-class children (first and fifth-graders), found that as the complexity of levels of language usage increased the negative effects of social disadvantages were enhanced. Siller (1957) reached similar conclusions working with white sixth-grade children of high and low status: he found social-class differences on all tests of conceptual ability, particularly those involving verbal material. Bereiter and Engelmann (1966) summarize the verbal disadvantage from which the lower-class children suffer: 'But what is lacking, by comparison, is the use of language to explain, to describe, to instruct, to inquire, to hypothesize, to analyse, to compare, to deduce and to test. And these are the uses that are necessary for academic success.'

Jensen (1967) made reference to the importance not only of the charac-

*From B. Bernstein, Social class and linguistic development: A theory of social learning. In A. A. Halsey, J. Floud and C. A. Anderson (Eds), *Education, Economy and Society*. The Free Press, Glencoe, 1961. Copyright 1961, The Macmillan Company, and reprinted with their permission.

teristics of the language habits that are acquired but also of the kinds of functions the language serves in the child's experience. Bernstein, throughout his work, has emphasized that the two language codes he has described serve and reinforce different social relationships. This emphasis on the influence of the matrix of social relationships in the home on the development of language codes, and on the nature of the verbal interactions within the home appears also in the work of Strodtbeck (1964) and Hess and Shipman (1965). Strodtbeck examined the social structure of the middle-class home and concluded that the structure itself requires elaborate conversation; the power play is conducted through language, and 'the conditions which facilitate the development of verbal ability in children relate to power differentials and organizational considerations'. He saw the mother and father as holding relatively equal power positions and observed that this created a situation in which careful use of language and recognition of subtle differences are necessary for the attainment of personal goals.

Hess and Shipman (1965) explored with a sample of 163 Negro mothers and their four-year old children from four social-status levels, an hypothesis that the 'central quality involved in the effects of cultural deprivation is a lack of cognitive meaning in the mother-child communication system'. They distinguished between the control systems that operate in middle-class and in deprived families; the former are oriented towards *persons*, the latter towards control by *status* appeal.

> In this paper we will argue that the structure of the social system and the structure of the family shape communication and language and that language shapes thought and cognitive styles of problem-solving. In the deprived family context this means that the nature of the control system which relates parent to child restricts the number and kind of alternatives for action and thought that are opened to the child; such constriction precludes a tendency for the child to reflect, to consider and choose among alternatives for speech and action. It develops modes for dealing with stimuli and with problems which are impulsive rather than reflective, which deal with the immediate rather than the future, and which are disconnected rather than sequential. (Hess & Shipman, 1965, pp. 870-1.*)

They highlight the major difference between the two systems of control: in status or position-oriented families, behaviour is regulated in terms of role expectations, norms of behaviour are stressed by means of imperatives; in a person-oriented control system, the characteristics of the child modify the demands made, and decisions are individualized and behaviour justified in terms of personal and unique reactions. The latter demand an elaborated linguistic code.

*From R. D. Hess and V. C. Shipman, Early experience and the socialization of cognitive modes in children. *Child Development*, 39, 869-886. Copyright 1965, The Society for Research in Child Development, Inc., and reprinted with their permission.

Hess and Shipman (1965), as an example to illustrate the contrast between the two cognitive styles, use the situation where a child is playing noisily in the kitchen when the phone rings. In the one home, the mother says 'Be quiet!' or 'Shut up!'; in the second home, the mother says 'Would you keep quiet a moment? I want to talk on the phone.' The authors pose the question, 'What inner response is elicited in the child, what is the effect upon his developing cognitive network of concepts and meaning in each of these two situations?' They continue,

> In one instance the child is asked for a simple mental response. He is asked to attend to an uncomplicated message and to make a conditioned response (to comply); he is not called upon to reflect or to make mental discrimination. In the other example the child is required to follow two or three ideas. He is asked to relate his behavior to a time dimension; he must think of his behavior in relation to its effect upon another person. He must perform a more complicated task to follow the communication of his mother in that his relationship to her is mediated in part through concepts and shared ideas; his mind is stimulated or exercised (in an elementary fashion) by a more elaborate and complex verbal communication initiated by the mother. As objects of these two divergent communication styles, repeated in various ways in situations and circumstances during the pre-school years, these two imaginary children would be expected to develop significantly different verbal facility and cognitive equipment by the time they enter the public school system. (p. 872.*)

Early experiences with these codes not only have an effect on cognitive structure but also establish potential patterns of relation with the external world. The children bring to the school situation already established modes of relating to others; if these modes are incongruent with the school demands, then learning is likely to suffer.

Hess and Shipman provided further information on mother-child interactions through their analysis of maternal teaching styles. This information helps us to see more clearly how mother-child interaction shapes the child's cognitive development, and how it establishes within him expectations regarding the demands made by, and the type of support likely to be forthcoming from, other teachers. Each mother in the sample was taught three simple tasks and then was asked to teach these tasks to her child. One task concerned teaching the child how to group or sort a small number of toys. Hess and Shipman's description of the teaching carried out by the mothers follows:

The *first mother* who gives explicit information about the task and what is expected of the child, and who offers support and help says:

*From R. D. Hess and V. C. Shipman, Early experience and the socialization of cognitive modes in children. *Child Development*, 39, 869-886. Copyright 1965, The Society for Research in Child Development, Inc., and reprinted with their permission.

'All right, Susan, this board is the place where we put the little toys; first of all you're supposed to learn how to place them according to color. Can you do that? The things that are all the same color you put in one section; in the second section you put another group of colors, and in the third section you put the last group of colors. Can you do that or would you like to see me do it first?'

Child: 'I want to do it.'

The *second mother*, whose style is less clear and precise, who relies on non-verbal communication, does not define the task and who does not provide the child with ideas or information, says in introducing the same task:

'Now, I'll take them all off the board; now you put them all back on the board. What are these?'

Child: 'A truck.'

'All right, just put them right here; put the other one right here; all right put the other one there.'

The *third mother* is even less explicit:

'I've got some chairs and cars, do you want to play the game?'

Child does not respond. Mother continues: 'O.K. what's this?'

Mother: 'Hm?'

Child: 'A wagon?'

Mother: 'This is not a wagon. What's this?'

Predictably, the testing of the children showed that the lower-class children both performed the tasks less accurately and were less able to verbalize the principle on which the grouping was made than were the middle-class children.

To this point, there has been a concentration on verbal interactions as important determinants of cognitive development. Affective interactions between parent and child have also been studied, and have been shown to be significant antecedents of general cognitive development. Furthermore, certain child-rearing practices seem to be associated with particular patternings of cognitive abilities.

Bing (1963) was concerned to determine whether home conditions which favoured the development of verbal ability might militate against the development of non-verbal skills such as numerical and spatial ability. Her sample consisted of sixty mothers of fifth-grade children who had discrepant cognitive abilities (that is, high verbal and low spatial or number ability, or low verbal and high spatial or number ability). Data on the mothers were gathered from a questionnaire, an interview and from observation of a mother-child interaction situation. Bing's own summary of her results is presented:

In accordance with predictions, high verbal group mothers (whose children were low in either spatial or number ability) gave their children more verbal stimulation during infancy and early childhood, remembered a greater number of their children's early accomplishments, let their children participate more in meal conversations, punished them less for poor speech, bought more story books for them, and criticized them more for poor academic achievement, used anxiety arousal more in cautiousness training, showed less permissiveness with object experimentation, had more restrictions, and perceived their husbands as stricter than themselves.

With respect to the interaction section, as predicted, high verbal group mothers were found to be higher than low verbal mothers in all categories of helping behaviour, in pressure for improvement, in giving help after request by child, in asking the observer more questions, in giving more physical help and in giving such help sooner. Contrary to the prediction, high verbal mothers were also higher on withholding help and disapproval than the low verbal mothers.

The findings led to the general conclusion that discrepant verbal ability is fostered by a close relationship with a demanding and somewhat intrusive mother, while discrepant non-verbal abilities are enhanced by allowing the child a considerable degree of freedom to experiment on his own. (Bing, 1963, p. 647.*)

Research by Levy (1943) and Haggard (1957) had also established a relationship between parent-child relationships and verbal ability. Levy found an association between over-protective mother-child relations and high performance in the area of language skills. Haggard found that children of high intelligence who were high achievers in reading and spelling tended to have dependent relations with their parents.

Differences in expressive styles—that is, between an abstract and a concrete mode of approaching problems—have been linked by Miller and Swanson (1960) with social-class differences in child-rearing practices, particularly modes of discipline. Typically, in the middle-class families, characterized by maternal self control, use is made of psychological discipline and symbolic reward, and the child tends to develop a conceptual style. Again typically (but not inevitably) in the lower class, where the mother exhibits limited self control, use is made in child rearing of physical discipline and tangible rewards, and the child develops a motoric style. Goldberg (1963) sums up the characteristics of these two styles: 'In general, the expressive style of the lower-class child can be described as more often motoric, concrete, "thing-oriented" and non-verbal. The middle-class child, on the other hand, is more often conceptual, abstract-symbolic, "idea-oriented" and verbal in his style of expression.' The expressive style of the middle-class child is much more likely to lead to efficient learning in the traditional schools of the day. As Riessman (1965) has said, ' . . . the school does not emphasize the physical style. I think that low socio-economic youngsters very often learn in what I call a physical style. They have to do something physically in order to learn

*From E. Bing, Effect of child rearing practices on development of differential cognitive abilities. *Child Development*, 34, 631-648. Copyright 1963, The Society for Research in Child Development, Inc., and reprinted with their permission.

about it. They can't simply talk about it. They are quite able to conceptualize. But essentially they learn through physical things, through touching, through moving, through gestures and the school doesn't particularly reward this pattern.' (p. 47.)

The research which has been surveyed in this section indicates quite clearly that cognitive development is highly dependent upon the verbal and effective interactions between parent (especially mother) and child. The particular patterning of cognitive abilities which the child has developed is a direct function of his home environment, and it will, in its turn, help determine his academic future.

Conclusion

This review has shown how the homes of children help determine cognitive and affective characteristics which influence progress in school. The extent of home influence is emphasized by a recent American report (Coleman, et al., 1966):

> Taking all these results together, one implication stands out above all: That schools bring little influence to bear on a child's achievement that is independent of his background and general social context; and that this very lack of an independent effect means that inequalities imposed on children by their home, neighborhood and peer environment are carried along to become the inequalities with which they confront adult life at the end of school. For equality of educational opportunity through the schools must imply a strong effect of schools that is independent of the child's immediate social environment, and that strong independent effect is not present in American schools. (p. 325.)

One must ask, 'Need this be so?' Can schools, through modification of their programmes and methods, foster the educational development of children from all backgrounds? Can they help children from emotionally-deprived and culturally-deprived homes as well as children from warm, nurturant and stimulating homes? Recognition and understanding of the characteristics and life situation of children from varying backgrounds must come first; goals must be clearly determined; only then can adequate methods and programmes be devised.

With regard to the culturally deprived, many educationists believe that the early years are so vital that intervention with compensatory programmes should begin at the preschool level. The 1964 Research Conference on Education and Cultural Deprivation recommended that special nursery schools and kindergartens should provide for:

- a. Stimulation of children to perceive aspects of the world about them and to fix these aspects by the use of language.
- b. Development of more extended and accurate language.
- c. Development of a sense of mastery over aspects of the immediate environment and an enthusiasm for learning for its own sake.
- d. Development of thinking and reasoning and the ability to make new insights and discoveries for oneself.

    e. Development of purposive learning activity and the ability to attend for longer periods of time. (Bloom, Davis & Hess, 1965, pp. 17-18.*)

Reports on experimental programmes are very encouraging; Gray and Klaus (1965) reporting on the Early-Training Project, indicate that their experimental children, on a battery of preschool screening tests, performed much better than control children.

It is interesting to note that intervention is possible at an even earlier age. Levenstein and Sunley (1968) report a small experiment in which meaningful verbal interaction was encouraged between mothers and two-year old disadvantaged children in their own homes. Social workers visited the mothers fifteen times over a four-month period taking with them toys and books to demonstrate to the mothers and children together. The materials were then left in the home. Experimental children showed a significantly greater increase in IQ than did controls—a mean IQ gain of 13.7 points as compared with a mean loss of .4 points.

Will intervention at preschool level alone be sufficient? Riessman (1967) sounds a note of caution. 'To my mind this notion that the pre-school is the only approach is really a very dangerous one, because for the most part, the gains that have been achieved in the pre-school do not remain if the school is not changed to back up the new motivations or improvements in the children.' (p. 129.)

Compensatory education is, of course, being attempted at the primary and secondary school levels. A variety of approaches is being used. *(See, for example, United States Department of Health Education and Welfare, National Conference on Education of the Disadvantaged, Washington, July 1966).* Gordon (1965) distinguishes eight main approaches: reading and language development programmes; attempts to individualize instruction; extracurricular innovations, including study centres, cultural activities, hobby clubs; increase of parental involvement; community involvement; teacher recruitment and training; guidance; use of special personnel.

The tendency for compensatory programmes to aim at increased parental involvement seems worthy of special comment, since while children are in school, parents play a continuing and vital role in their education. On the one hand, increased teacher-parent contact should lead to an increase in teachers' understanding of their pupils. On the other hand, if parents can be helped to see the aim of the school programme and come to a clearer appreciation of their role in their children's education, one would expect to see better academic results for the children in school (as a result of the breaking down of the barrier between home and school) and, furthermore, younger children in these families could be expected to benefit from changed parental attitudes. One attempt to involve parents in the elementary school programme in Michigan is described by Smith and Brahce (1963). Their experimental programme was designated 'School and Home: Focus on Achievement'. They describe their programme as

*From *Compensatory Education for Cultural Deprivation* by B. S. Bloom, A. Davis and R. Hess. Copyright © 1964 by Holt, Rinehart and Winston, Inc. Reprinted by permission of Holt, Rinehart and Winston, Inc.

follows: 'Parents were: (a) impressed that they must do more than tell their children that they need to achieve in school. They were frequently reminded that they must *show* their children that their schoolwork is important: (b) given suggestions of activities and behavior which would provide at home a climate conducive to academic achievement.' (p. 317.) The children in the experimental schools, compared with controls, showed greater gains in reading, improved work habits and attitudes toward schoolwork. The parents considered that the programme had helped the children and that they would like to have it continued.

In the field of the education of culturally-deprived children, educators must be clear on their goals. Riessman (1967) considers this problem:

> There are two different goals that are generally considered. The first goal relates to the idea of having these youngsters become middle-class citizens exactly like us; to become, in a sense, carbon copies of us; to be people just like us in their goals, in their methods, in their learning, in their academic motivation and the like. I submit that this is a very difficult thing to achieve and we are not going to be successful in doing it most of the time. We can be very successful in having these youngsters learn and become part of the mainstream of our society in the schools provided we want to get something from them as well as give something to them. (p. 133.*)

Olsen (1965), too, doubts whether a goal of changing lower-class ways of behaving to a middle-class pattern of life is desirable or realistic:

> Lower class values have grown out of a firm matrix of economic and cultural patterns. These values are transmitted from the parent to the child. Unless we are prepared to change the way in which the family socializes the child—a power only dictatorships have—we cannot expect to convert most of the culturally different to a middle class way of life.
>
> It seems much more reasonable to reduce the social distance between the school and its students by finding out what the content of lower class culture is and then modifying or changing some of what we teach or how we teach it. (p. 82.)

Olsen, like Riessman, would advocate that educational programmes make use of the strengths of the culturally disadvantaged. Riessman (1962) has drawn up a balance sheet of the strengths and weaknesses of the under-privileged. On the liability side, he puts: 'narrowness of traditionalism, pragmatism and anti-intellectualism; limited development of individualism, self-expression and creativity; frustrations of alienation; political apathy; suggestibility and naivete; boring occupational tasks; broken, over-crowded homes.' On the asset side, he puts: 'the cooperativeness and mutual aid that mark the extended family; avoidance of the strain accompanying

---

*From Frank Riessman, Blueprint for an educational revolution. In William C. Kvaraceus, John S. Gibson and Thomas J. Curtain, *Poverty, Education and Race Relations: Studies and Proposals*, p. 133. © Copyright by Allyn and Bacon, Inc., Boston.

competitiveness and individualism; equalitarianism, informality, and warm humor; freedom from self-blame and parental over-protection; the children's enjoyment of each other's company, and lessened sibling rivalry; the security found in the extended family and in a traditional outlook.' What is needed, then, is imagination and enterprise on the part of educators to build school programmes which will capitalize on the existing strengths of the deprived, and, concomitantly, overcome the liabilities which militate against their successful academic progress.

Our earlier survey suggested that some children are disadvantaged in school because of the inadequacies in the emotional climate of their homes, these inadequacies stemming from the personality characteristics of their parents. We must turn to school and community mental health programmes to effect a change here. The schools have many functions to serve, not the least of which is the fostering of healthy personalities; if, in the academic programme itself, the teachers and the counsellors can promote the mental health of children where necessary by undertaking a remedial role, these children, when they become parents, are more likely to establish satisfactory relationships with their own children and create within the home a climate conducive to cognitive and personality development.

Finally, important for its long-term effects, the schools and colleges must accept a responsibility for widening their curriculums to include the study of child growth and development. Bloom (1964) has stated: 'What is being suggested here is that more desirable child rearing environmental conditions can be identified and implemented in the twentieth century.' He continues to say, 'Perhaps in the future we will find the task of being a mother or father requires far more training and preparation than has been commonly recognized.' If children of the future are to profit from knowledge about the impact of environment on development and about the antecedents of child characteristics, then parents of the future must share this knowledge.

References

Ausubel, D. P., 1968: *Educational Psychology, A Cognitive View*. Holt, Rinehart and Winston, Inc., New York.

Baldwin, A. L., Kalhorn, J. and Breese, F. H., 1945: Patterns of parent behavior. *Psychological Monographs*, 58, number 3, 1-73.

Baumrind, D., 1966: Effects of authoritative parental control on child behavior. *Child Development*, 37, 887-907.

Bereiter, C. and Engelmann, S., 1966: *Teaching Disadvantaged Children in The Preschool*. Prentice-Hall, Inc., Englewood Cliffs, N.J.

Bernstein, B., 1961a: Social structure, language and learning. *Educational Research*, 3, 3, 163-176.

Bernstein, B., 1961b: Social class and linguistic development: A theory of social learning. In A. A. Halsey, J. Floud and C. A. Anderson (Eds), *Education, Economy and Society: A Reader in the Sociology of Education*. The Free Press, Glencoe, Ill.

Bing, E., 1963: Effect of child rearing practices on development of differential cognitive abilities. *Child Development*, 34, 631-648.

Bloom, B. S., 1964: *Stability and Change in Human Characteristics*. John Wiley & Sons, Inc., New York.

Bloom, B. S., Davis, A. and Hess, R., 1965: *Compensatory Education for Cultural Deprivation*. Holt, Rinehart and Winston, Inc., New York.

Brookover, W. B., Thomas, S. and Patterson, A., 1964: Self concept of ability and school achievement. *Sociology of Education*, 37, 271-278.

Coleman, J. S., Campbell, E. Q., Hobson, C. J., McPartland, J., Mood, A. M., Weinfeld, F. D. and York, R. L., 1966: *Equality of Educational Opportunity*. U.S. Government Printing Office, Washington, D.C.

Crandall, V. J., 1963: Achievement. In H. W. Stevenson (Ed.), *Child Psychology. NSSE Yearbook*, LXII, Pt I, University of Chicago Press, Chicago, Ill.

Crandall, V. J., Dewey, R., Katkovsky, W. and Preston, A., 1964: Parents' attitudes and behaviors and grade school children's academic achievements. *Journal of Genetic Psychology*, 104, 53-66.

Dave, R. H., 1963: The identification and measurement of environmental process variables that are related to educational achievement. Unpublished doctoral dissertation, University of Chicago.

Deutsch, M., 1965: The role of social class in language development and cognition. *American Journal of Orthopsychiatry*, 35, 1, 78-88.

d'Heurle, A., Mellinger, J. C. and Haggard, E. A., 1959: Personality, intellectual and achievement patterns in gifted children. *Psychological Monographs*, 73, 13, 1-28.

Douglas, J. W. B., 1964: *The Home and The School. A Study of Ability and Attainment in the Primary Schools*. MacGibbon & Kee, London.

Goddard, H. H., 1912: *The Kallikak Family: A Study in the Heredity of Feeble-Mindedness*. Macmillan & Co., New York.

Goldberg, M., 1963: Factors affecting educational attainment in depressed urban areas. In A. H. Passow (Ed.), *Education in Depressed Areas*. Teachers College Press, New York.

Gordon, E. W., 1965: A review of programs of compensatory education. *American Journal of Orthopsychiatry*, 35, 4, 640-651.

Gray, Susan W. and Klaus, R. A., 1965: An experimental preschool program for culturally deprived children. *Child Development*, 36, 887-898.

Haggard, E. A., 1957: Socialization, personality and academic achievement in gifted children, *School Review*, 55, 388-414.

Hebb, D. O., 1949: *The Organization of Behavior*. John Wiley & Sons, Inc., New York.

Heckhausen, H., 1967: *The Anatomy of Achievement Motivation*. Academic Press, Inc., New York and London.

Hess, R. D. and Shipman, V. C., 1965: Early experience and the socialization of cognitive modes in children. *Child Development*, 39, 869-886.

HMSO, 1967: *Children and Their Primary Schools. A Report of the Central Advisory Council for Education (England)*. Vol. II, Research and Surveys, Appendix 2.

Hunt, McVicker, 1964a: The implications of how children develop intellectually. *Children*, 11, 3, 83-91.

Hunt, McVicker, 1964b: The psychological basis for using pre-school enrichment as an antidote for cultural deprivation. *Merrill-Palmer Quarterly*, 10, 209-248.

108 · The Home Context

Jensen, A. R., 1967: The culturally disadvantaged: Psychological and educational aspects. *Educational Research*, 10, 1, 4-20.

John, V., 1963: The intellectual development of slum children: Some preliminary findings. *American Journal of Orthopsychiatry*, 33, 4, 813-822.

Katkovsky, W., Preston, A. and Crandall, V., 1964: Parent attitudes toward their personal achievements and toward the achievement behaviors of their children. *Journal of Genetic Psychology*, 104, 67-82.

Kurtz, J. J. and Swenson, E. G., 1951: Factors related to over-achievement and under-achievement in school. *School Review*, 59, 472-480.

Levenstein, P. and Sunley, R., 1968: Stimulation of verbal interaction between disadvantaged mothers and children. *American Journal of Orthopsychiatry*, 38, 1, 116-121.

Levy, D. M., 1943: *Maternal Over-Protection*. Columbia University Press, New York.

McClelland, D., Atkinson, J., Clark, R. and Lowell, E., 1953: *The Achievement Motive*. Appleton-Century-Crofts, New York.

Miller, D. R. and Swanson, G. E., 1960: *Inner Conflict and Defence*. Holt, Rinehart and Winston, Inc., New York.

Milner, E., 1951: A study of the relationship between reading readiness in grade one school children and patterns of parent-child interactions. *Child Development*, 22, 95-112.

Murphy, Gardner, 1963: Freeing intelligence. *Childhood Education*, 39, 363.

Nisbet, J., 1953: Family environment and intelligence. *Eugenics Review*, XLV, 31-42.

Olsen, J., 1965: Challenge of the poor to the schools. *Phi Delta Kappan*, 47, 2, 79-84.

Riessman, F., 1962: *The Culturally Deprived Child*. Harper & Row, New York.

Riessman, F., 1965: Low income culture, the adolescent and the school. *Bulletin of the National Association of Secondary School Principals*, 49, 45-49.

Riessman, F., 1967: Blueprint for an educational revolution. In W. C. Kvaraceus, J. S. Gibson and T. J. Curtin (Eds), *Poverty, Education and Race Relations: Studies and Proposals*, Allyn & Bacon, Boston, Mass.

Rosen, B., 1959: Race, ethnicity and the achievement syndrome. *American Sociological Review*, 24, 47-60.

Rosen, B. and D'Andrade, R., 1959: The psychosocial origins of achievement motivation. *Sociometry*, 22, 185-218.

Schaefer, E. S., 1961: Converging conceptual models for maternal behavior and for child behavior. In J. C. Glidewell (Ed.), *Parental Attitudes and Child Behavior*. Charles C. Thomas, Springfield, Ill.

Scottish Mental Survey, 1949: *The Trend of Scottish Intelligence*. University of London Press, London.

Shaw, M. C., 1967: Motivation in human learning. *Review of Educational Research*, 37, 5, 563-582.

Shirley, M. M., 1942: Children's adjustment to a strange situation. *Journal of Abn. and Soc. Psychol.*, 37, 201-217.

Siller, J., 1957: Socio-economic status and conceptual thinking. *Journal of Abn. and Soc. Psychol.*, 55, 365-371.

Smith, Mildred B. and Brahce, C. I., 1963: When school and home focus on achievement. *Educational Leadership*, 20, 314-318.

Stott, L. H., 1967: *Child Development: An Individual Longitudinal Approach*. Holt, Rinehart and Winston, Inc., New York.

Strodtbeck, F. L., 1958: Family integration, values and achievement. In D. C. McClelland, *et al., Talent and Society.* D. Van Nostrand & Co. Inc., Princeton, N.J.

Strodtbeck, F. L., 1964: The hidden curriculum of the middle class home. In C. W. Hunnicutt (Ed.), *Urban Education and Cultural Deprivation.* Syracuse University Press, New York.

Watson, Goodwin, 1957: Some personality differences in children related to strict or permissive parental discipline. *Journal of Psychology,* 44, 227-249.

Wiseman, S., 1967: The Manchester Survey. In *Children and Their Primary Schools. A Report of the Central Advisory Council for Education (England).* Vol. II, Research and Surveys, Appendix 9. HMSO.

6

Achievement-Related Values in Two Australian Ethnic Groups

Betty H. Watts

Introduction

THE STUDY reported here is part of a larger project (Watts, 1969) designed to explore the antecedents of achievement motivation in girls selected from four Queensland districts—two government Aboriginal 'communities', a white rural district, and a white metropolitan suburb.

Concern has been expressed throughout Australia about:

(a) the low social mobility and the below average living standards of significant numbers of Aborigines;

(b) the unsatisfactory educational standards reached by many Aborigine children and their failure to proceed in anything like proportionate numbers to the upper grades of secondary schooling;

(c) the low levels of achievement motivation displayed.

Can this lack of social mobility, lack of success as measured in Australian economic and educational terms, and lack of striving, be attributed, in part at least, to the value orientations of the people? Do the Aborigines underemphasize achievement-related values, as described by Rosen (1959), and Strodtbeck (1958)? This study attempts to identify the major value orientations of Aborigine mothers and daughters, and to determine the extent to which they differ from those of white Australians.

Following Kluckhohn and Strodtbeck (1961), value orientations are defined as patterned principles, combining cognitive, affective and directive elements, which influence human behaviour. The four explored in this study were: the relation of man to nature (man-nature); the temporal focus of human life (time); the emphasis given to activity (activity); and the relationship of man to other men (relational). Kluckhohn and Strodtbeck assume that these are cultural universals, and, moreover, that there is everywhere only a limited number of 'solutions' which might be adopted.

Thus:

(i) *man-nature* subjugation-to-nature (a fatalism and an acceptance of the inevitable)

harmony-with-nature (no real separation of man, nature and supernature)

mastery-over-nature (man's duty is to overcome natural forces and put them to use)

(ii) *time* future

present

past

(iii) *activity* doing (demand for activity which results in accomplishments measurable by standards external to the individual)

being (preference for activity which is a spontaneous expression of what is 'given' in human personality)

(iv) *relational* individualism (individual goals have primacy and the individual has autonomy)

collaterality (goals and welfare of the laterally extended group have primacy)

lineality (group goals have primacy; continuity of the group through time and ordered positional succession within the group are crucial issues).

One would expect that the values held by a group of people would be influenced by a variety of factors including basic temperamental characteristics, prior life histories, traditional norms and patterns of behaviour, and current life experiences (Getzels & Guba, 1957). No evidence was available on the first two of these (i.e., the ideographic group), but the social anthropologists (particularly Berndt & Berndt, 1964, and Elkin, 1954) have presented valuable data on the last two (i.e., the nomothetic group). Before presenting some of these data as they relate to the specific values being investigated, two general statements seem justified.

First, traditionally the Aborigines had their own form of tribal and social organization, their own values and philosophy. Over the last two centuries their way of life, and possibly their underlying values, have been subject to change as they encountered the European settlers who were to become the dominant group in the Australian setting.

Second, the Aborigines studied here grew up on government communities under rather special circumstances. The communities were cut off from the mainstream of white Australian life; in the case of Aboriginal community 1 there was a marked geographical separation from towns and cities. Some of the Aborigines participated in the economic life of the surrounding countryside, but many were employed on the community itself. Also, the people were subject to special legislation—The Aborigines and Torres Strait Islanders Preservation and Protection Acts 1939. This legislation, as the name signifies, was highly protective and, in some instances, restrictive of personal freedoms and decision making. Some Aborigines sought exemptions from this Act and left the communities to settle in towns and cities. However, those included in this study had elected to remain on the communities and hence were subject to the provisions of the Act as interpreted and applied by community officials. A new Act was promulgated in 1965, but the immediate past had been dominated by the old one.

Man-Nature: In traditional times, the Aborigines are likely to have adopted a harmony-with-nature orientation. Commenting on totemism Berndt and Berndt (1964), for example, write: 'Very broadly it has to do with a view of the world in which man is an integral part of nature, not sharply distinct or differing in quality from other natural species, but sharing with them the same life essence.' In similar vein, Elkin (1954) writes: 'Man and natural species are brought into one social and ceremonial whole and are believed to share a common life.'

The 'welfare state' condition which prevailed under the legislation was unlikely to be conducive to the development of an activistic approach to the environment. Rather, it was likely to reinforce the traditional value by fostering a passive expectant relationship; when needs are met by a beneficent authority, striving and personal effort might well atrophy.

Time: With regard to the time value, traditionally the Aborigine's emphasis was on the past. Berndt and Berndt (1964) write: '. . . these Aboriginal societies are, or were, tradition-oriented. They stress the value of keeping to the forms laid down in the past, rather than building on them with a view to creating something new or different.' And, again, 'The pattern or blueprint of behaviour is everywhere in traditional Aboriginal Australia framed in terms of the past.'

Again, the current life situation of the Aborigines with its protective legislation and practices is unlikely to promote an overwhelming concern for the future; security is provided rather than earned. However, one would expect some exceptions to occur among families, and, particularly when the Aborigine's past culture is not valued highly by the Australian society at large, there could be a shifting of values, if not to the future, at least to the present.

Activity: The items used to measure activity orientation presented, in the main, a choice between working and achieving, or being with friends. It is difficult to guess at the traditional preferred choice for Aborigine women, although the importance of kinship relationships in the tribal societies might predispose one towards a judgement of 'being'-rather than 'doing'-oriented. With regard to the present situation, the secure and protected government community is unlikely to arouse achievement needs. Furthermore, when, for a variety of reasons, vocational opportunities are limited there is little point in striving to excel. In at least one of the two Aboriginal communities there are examples of bright adolescents working at semi-skilled occupations after having attended secondary school within the white man's system. It is likely, therefore, that the Aborigines included in this study would be oriented towards being, rather than doing.

Relational: While traditional Aboriginal society allowed of some individual initiative, this was limited. The major characteristic was the prominence and salience of the kinship system. Elkin (1954) writes: '... relationship is the basis of behaviour; indeed it is the anatomy and physiology of Aboriginal society and must be understood if the behaviour of the Aborigines as social beings is to be understood'. Group goals and the welfare of the group had primacy; collaterality would have occupied a favoured position in the value hierarchy. Lineality, too, was likely to be preferred to individualism, for, as in many primitive societies, the aged retained many powers of decision (Berndt & Berndt, 1964).

In current Aboriginal society, collaterality is still stressed. Indeed, it is frequently argued that this emphasis upon fulfilling obligations to kin is one of the prime hindrances to social mobility. The phenomenon has been noted even in the case of Aborigines who, like Namatjira, have achieved national fame for outstanding attainments.

The brief statements presented above do not rank as hypotheses, or even as serious predictions; they are more in the nature of hunches based upon generalized snippets of information taken from regions that are likely to have significance in the determination of value systems.

Scope of the Study

The Value Instrument: The instrument used consists of a modification (Hausfeld, 1966) of the Kluckhohn-Strodtbeck schedule. Five items measuring each of the four orientations, referred to earlier, were included. These tapped areas of behaviour as follows:

Man-Nature		*Time*	
MN1	Children dying	T1	Child training
MN2	Facing conditions	T2	Expectations about change
MN3	Care of gardens	T3	Philosophy of life
MN4	Belief in control	T4	Ceremonial innovation
MN5	Length of life	T5	Selection for job training

Activity		*Relational*	
A1	Job choice	R1	Decision to move elsewhere
A2	Ways of living	R2	Help in family problems
A3	Care of boats	R3	Choice of delegate
A4	Housework	R4	Livestock inheritance
A5	Non-working time	R5	Job conditions

An illustrative item from each area is reproduced below. In each case, the respondent was asked to indicate (a) 'Which one do you think had the right idea?' (b) 'Which of the other two do you think was most right?'

Man-Nature

   MN2   Three people were talking about man and nature.

Dominance over	A	The first said: If people learn more, they can make things work out the way they want them to, and they do not need to worry about nature.
Harmony with	B	The second said: If people work along with nature, things usually work out best.
Subjugation to	C	The third said: It does not matter how hard people work or what they try to do, nature can spoil everything.

Time

   T3   Three people were talking about what to expect in life.

Present	A	The first said: I believe it's best just to think about what is happening now. The past is finished and no one can be sure of the future.
Past	B	The second said: I believe things were better in the past. The more things change the worse they get. It's best to try to keep things the way they used to be.
Future	C	The third said: I believe things get better all the time. If we work hard now the future will be better than the present.

Activity

   A2   Two people were talking about the way they liked to live.

Doing	A	The first said: I like doing things. I feel good when I have done something as well or better than other people. I like to see some results for my work.
Being	B	The second said: I like best to be left alone to live the way that suits me. I do not worry if I do not get much done as long as I can enjoy life day by day.

Relational

   R1   A man had a chance to take his wife and children away to live a good life in another place. Three people were talking about what he ought to do.

Lineality	A	The first said: He should ask the most important people he knows and do what they say.
Collaterality	B	The second said: He should talk it over with his relations and friends and do what they say.

Individualism   C   The third said: He should think about it himself and do whatever he thinks is best.

The instrument was administered orally in an individual situation, and
the preferences marked by the researcher.

The Sample

The populations from which random samples within each district were
drawn were—
  (a) girls born 1957-1958
  (b) girls born 1953-1954
The adolescent girls (born 1953-1954) completed the value schedule,
as did their mothers and the mothers of the younger girls. The total
sample comprised 97 adolescents and 190 mothers distributed as follows:

TABLE 6.1

The Sample

	Adolescents	Mothers
Metropolitan	23	48
Rural	25	50
Aboriginal Community 1	25	46
Aboriginal Community 2	24	46

The metropolitan samples were drawn from a middle to upper-middle-
class suburb in Brisbane; the rural district, on the outskirts of Brisbane,
contained farmers and townspeople; the first Aboriginal community was
distant from Brisbane and was effectively isolated; the second Aboriginal
community was also distant from Brisbane, but the inhabitants had greater
contact with neighbouring white communities. In the Aboriginal communities, the adolescent girls were the totals of the age group, but in the
white districts the numbers were greater and samples were drawn by
means of random numbers after lists had been compiled. These lists were
obtained from one primary school and one state high school in the
metropolitan case, and, in the rural district, the rolls of all schools in the
districts. While a small percentage of girls were probably being educated in
schools elsewhere, no serious distortion of the samples is likely to have
occurred. The cooperation of both the girls and their mothers was sought
before the study began, and this was given in ninety-eight per cent of cases.

Results

The results can be conveniently considered under two headings: orders
of preference, and, particularly when the orders do not differ, degrees of
preference.

Orders of Preference: Table 6.2 shows the preferences, based on a binomial
analysis, within each group for each of the value orientations. The results

TABLE 6.2

(i) Man-Nature

	Item MN1	Item MN2	Item MN3	Item MN4	Item MN5	Average
Mothers						
Metropolitan	S>D>H	H>D>S	D>H>S	S>D>H	D>S≥H	D≥S≥H*
Rural	S>D≥H	H>S≥D	D>H>S	S>D>H	∅D≥H≥S	∅S≥D=H
Community 1	H≥D>S	H≥D>S	H≥D>S	S≥H>D	H≥D>S	H>D>S
Community 2	∅H≥D≥S	∅H≥D≥S	H≥D>S	S>H≥D	∅No pattern	∅H≥S≥D
Adolescents						
Metropolitan	S>D≥H	H>D>S	D≥H>S	S>D≥H	∅H≥S≥D	∅H≥D≥S
Rural	S>H≥D	H>D≥S	D>H>S	S>H=D	S≥H>D	H=S>D
Community 1	∅No pattern	H≥D≥S	D≥H>S	S>D≥H	∅H≥D≥S	∅H≥D≥S
Community 2	∅H>D=S	H>D≥S	D=H>S	S≥H≥D*	∅H≥D=S	∅H≥S≥D

(ii) Time

	Item T1	Item T2	Item T3	Item T4	Item T5	Average
Mothers						
Metropolitan	F>Pr>P	F>Pr>P	F>Pr>P	F≥P>Pr	F>P≥Pr	F>Pr>P
Rural	F>Pr>P	F>Pr>P	F>Pr>P	F≥Pr>P	F>P≥Pr	F>Pr>P
Community 1	F>Pr≥P	F>Pr>P	F>Pr≥P	Pr≥P>F*	F>Pr≥P	F>Pr≥P
Community 2	F>Pr>P	F>Pr≥P	F>Pr>P	Pr>P≥F	F≥Pr≥P*	F>Pr>P
Adolescents						
Metropolitan	F>Pr>P	F>Pr>P	F>Pr>P	∅F≥Pr≥P	F>P>Pr	F>Pr>P
Rural	F≥Pr>P	F>Pr>P	F>Pr>P	∅F≥P≥Pr	F>P≥Pr	F>Pr>P
Community 1	F>Pr≥P	F>Pr=P	F≥P>Pr*	Pr>P>F	F>Pr≥P	F>Pr≥P
Community 2	F>Pr=P	F>Pr≥P	∅F≥Pr≥P	∅Pr≥P≥F*	F≥P*≥Pr	F>Pr≥P

(iii) Activity

	Item A1	Item A2	Item A3	Item A4	Item A5	Average
Mothers						
Metropolitan	D>B	D>B	B>D	B>D	B>D	B≥D
Rural	D>B	D>B	B≥D	B≥D	D≥B	D≥B
Community 1	D≥B	D>B	D≥B	D>B	D>B	D>B
Community 2	D≥B	D≥B	D≥B	D>B	D>B	D>B
Adolescents						
Metropolitan	D>B	D>B	D≥B	B>D	B≥D	B≥D
Rural	D≥B	D>B	D≥B	B≥D	B≥D	D≥B
Community 1	D≥B	D>B	D≥B	D≥B	D>B	D>B
Community 2	D=B	D≥B	D≥B	D>B	D>B	D>B

(iv) Relational

	Item R1	Item R2	Item R3	Item R4	Item R5	Average
Mothers						
Metropolitan	I>L≥C	I>C>L	I>C>L	C≥I>L	I>C=L	I>C>L
Rural	I>C≥L	I>C>L	I>C>L	I>C>L	I≥L≥C*	I>C>L
Community 1	I>L≥C	I≥L>C	∅I>L≥C	C>I≥L	I≥L>C	I>L≥C
Community 2	I>L≥C	I>C≥L	I>C≥L	C≥I>L	L>I≥C	I>C=L
Adolescents						
Metropolitan	I>C>L	I≥C>L	I>C>L	C≥I>L	C>I≥L	I≥C>L
Rural	I>C>L	I≥C>L	I>C>L	C≥I>L	∅C≥L≥I	I≥C>L
Community 1	I>L≥C	I>C≥L	I>C≥L	C>I≥L	∅L≥C≥I	I>C>L
Community 2	I>C≥L	∅I≥C≥L	I>C≥L	C≥I>L	∅L≥C≥I	I>C≥L

for each item are shown separately, and in the final column of the table the patterning of preferences which sums up the culture is shown.

The symbolic notation which is used is as follows:

A>B>C : all preferences are significant at the .05 level or better.

A≥B>C : only the preferences A over C and B over C are significant although A is preferred to B.

A>B≥C : only the preferences A over B and A over C are significant although B is preferred to C.

A≥B*≥C: only the preference A over B reaches the .05 level of significance.

A≥B≥C*: only the preference A over C reaches the .05 level of significance.

A≥B≥C : none of the preference frequencies within the pairs reaches the .05 level of significance.

= : conventional usage.

It will be noted that, in the table, certain patterns are marked φ. This signifies that there was a lack of concensus in the sample; the null hypothesis, that there were no preferences for some ranking patterns rather than for others could not, in these cases, be rejected.

Perhaps the two most striking findings in Table 6.2 are the similar ordering of values across communities and between the age groups, and the lack of support given to the hunches presented in the Introduction section of this chapter. With reference to the latter, the Aborigines, both mothers and daughters, preferred future (*not* past), doing (*not* being), individuality (*not* collaterality), and there was no clear evidence of a strong preference for harmony over subjection or dominance. However, it is possible to have similar orderings, but significantly different emphases within these, and it is to a consideration of this issue that we now turn.

Degrees of Preference

Between-culture similarities and differences were determined by using a one-way analysis of variance technique. Cultures are placed on ten dimensions to carry out the analyses of variance. Each dimension involves two positions from each of the value orientations; for example, for the relational orientation, the cultures are placed on an individualism-collaterality continuum, on an individualism-lineality continuum, and a collaterality-lineality continuum. The basic data for the analyses of variance are the mean preferences over all items for one position as against the other in a value orientation for each culture. The one-way analysis of variance is followed by the application of Tukey's test of the gaps among a group of means to determine significant differences.

(i) Man-Nature

Mothers: Figure 6.1 shows the results of the analysis of variance.

Both the dominance-harmony and harmony-subjection dimensions distinguish clearly between the white and Aboriginal groups. The metropolitan and rural communities group together showing a moderate preference for dominance; the Aboriginal communities group together showing a moderate preference for harmony. On the harmony-subjection dimension, Aboriginal community 1 shows a preference for harmony significantly greater than that of Aboriginal community 2, while the metropolitan and rural groups cluster together to show a slight preference for subjection.

On the dominance-subjection dimension, the position is less clear, all groups showing only a slight preference for one dimension as against the other. Reading from the dominance end of the dimension the groups are ordered: Aboriginal community 1, metropolitan, Aboriginal community 2, rural, with a *t* test showing a significant difference (.01) between the two Aboriginal communities.

FIGURE 6.1

MAN-NATURE
The Dominance-Harmony Dimension

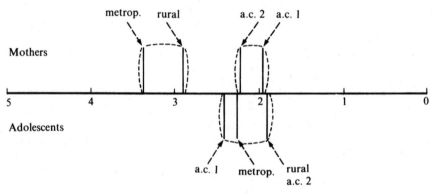

The Dominance-Subjection Dimension

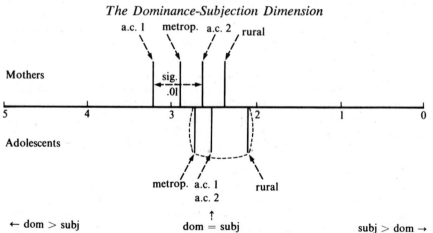

The Harmony-Subjection Dimension

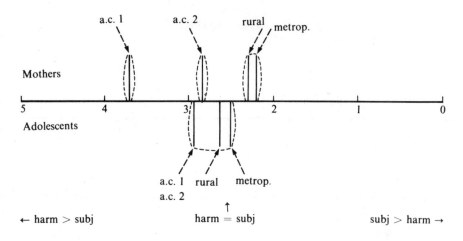

Adolescents: As Figure 6.1 shows, there are no significant differences between groups on any of the dimensions in this value orientation. The dimensions, dominance-harmony and dominance-subjection, show no ethnic ordering, but on the harmony-subjection dimension the two Aboriginal groups are very close together and show themselves (not significantly) as having a slightly greater preference than the white adolescents for harmony.

(ii) Time

Mothers: Figure 6.2 shows all four groups preferring future over present; the only significant difference here is a difference (.05) between the metropolitan group and the two Aboriginal groups. While all four groups prefer future over past, this preference is significantly more marked in the case of the two- white groups than in the Aboriginal cases; furthermore, there is a significant difference between the two Aboriginal groups, with Aboriginal community 2 showing the least marked preference for future over past. On the present-past dimension, the white groups show a more marked preference for present over past, although the only significant difference is that between the two white groups (which occupy the same position) and Aboriginal community 2.

Adolescents: On the future-present dimension there is no significant difference between the groups, although the two white groups show a slightly greater preference for future over present than do the Aboriginal groups.

On the other two dimensions, the Aboriginal adolescents are significantly different from the two white groups, in being less positively attracted to the future over past, and to the present over past.

FIGURE 6.2

TIME

The Future-Present Dimension

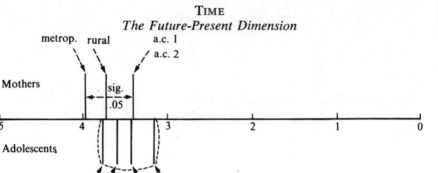

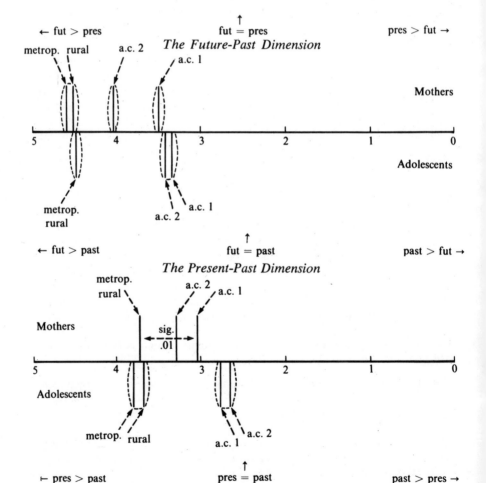

The Future-Past Dimension

The Present-Past Dimension

(iii) *Activity Orientation*

Mothers: On the doing-being dimension (Figure 6.3) the Aboriginal groups show themselves as more doing oriented than the white groups; the difference between Aboriginal community 2 and the metropolitan group is significant at the .01 level.

This was a somewhat surprising result. Perhaps the Aboriginal mothers give what they believe to be the more socially desirable response; perhaps they feel more conscious of pressures to work and achieve, while the white mothers feel more confident in their social situation and are conscious of the need for relaxation as well as for work. As can be seen below, this same pattern is repeated with the adolescent girls.

FIGURE 6.3

ACTIVITY

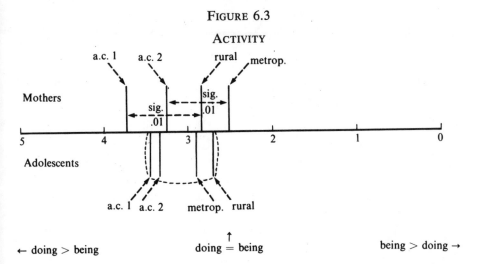

Adolescents: The adolescents repeat the pattern of the mothers on this dimension, with a more marked preference of doing over being shown by Aboriginal community 1, followed by Aboriginal community 2, metropolitan group and rural group. The differences, however, are not significant.

(iv) *Relational Orientation*

Mothers: Table 6.2 showed that both white groups emerge as clearly preferring individualism over collaterality over lineality. Aboriginal community 2, while selecting individualism as its first alternative, ranks collaterality and lineality equally; Aboriginal community 1, also selects individuality as its first alternative, but shows a not significant preference for lineality as a second rank over collaterality.

The analysis of variance (Figure 6.4) shows significant differences on each dimension between the two ethnic groups, with the white groups having a significantly stronger preference for individualism over collaterality, individualism over lineality (a significant difference obtaining

FIGURE 6.4

RELATIONAL
The Individualism-Collaterality Dimension

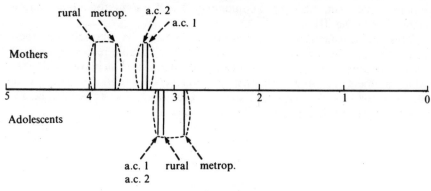

← ind > coll   ind = coll   coll > ind →

The Individualism-Lineality Dimension

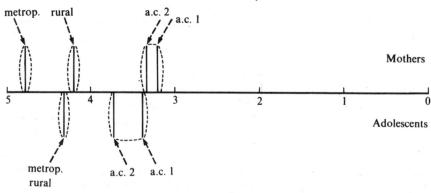

← ind > lin   ind = lin   lin > ind →

The Collaterality-Lineality Dimension

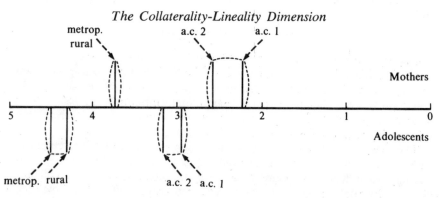

← coll > lin   coll = lin   lin > coll →

between the two white groups) and collaterality over lineality.

Adolescents: Figure 6.4 shows that, on the individualism-collaterality dimension the two Aboriginal groups are slightly, but not significantly, more attracted to individualism. Although all four groups favour individualism over lineality there are significant ethnic groupings, with the white adolescents showing a higher mean individualism score. On the collaterality-lineality dimension, the Aboriginal groups show a slight preference for collaterality; this preference is much more strongly marked in the case of the two white groups.

Comparison of Mothers and Adolescents

It was thought profitable to analyse the responses of the adolescents and their mothers to discern whether there were any significant differences between the two age groups in each sample. One might expect to find greater differences between the generations in a culture contact situation than one would find in the general community. In particular, the Aboriginal adolescents have had a longer exposure to education than had their mothers, and this longer exposure to white Australian values, as promulgated by the school curriculum and the school staff, might have modified the adolescents' values in the direction of those of the majority group.

Out of the forty comparisons, however, across all four groups, significant differences are noted in only eleven cases; on the whole, the adolescents, both white and Aborigine, show a remarkable similarity to their mothers in their value orientations.

The most consistent difference is on the collaterality-lineality dimension, with each group of mothers showing a less marked preference for collaterality than the adolescents.

The following are the dimensions where significant differences were discovered:

Aboriginal Community 1
Dominance-Subjection The mothers prefer dominance, the adolescents show an equal preference for both positions.
Collaterality-Lineality The adolescents prefer collaterality while the mothers prefer lineality.

Aboriginal Community 2
Present-Past Both mothers and adolescents show a preference for the present over the past, but this preference is more strongly marked in the case of the mothers.
Collaterality-Lineality As is the case in Aboriginal community 1, the adolescents prefer collaterality while the mothers prefer lineality.

Rural Community
Dominance-Harmony The mothers show a slight preference for dominance while the adolescents show a somewhat more marked preference for harmony.

Individualism-Collaterality The mothers show a very marked preference for individualism; this preference is less marked in the case of the
adolescents.
Collaterality-Lineality The adolescents show a more marked preference for collaterality than do the mothers.

Metropolitan Community
Dominance-Harmony The mothers prefer dominance while the adolescents prefer, though less strongly, harmony.
Individualism-Collaterality As in the rural community the mothers
show a much stronger preference for individualism than do the
adolescents.
Collaterality-Lineality The adolescents show a stronger preference for
collaterality than do the mothers.

Discussion

At the beginning of this chapter, we raised the query as to whether the low
social mobility, lack of success and lack of striving of the Aboriginal
people, as a group, could be attributed, in part at least, to an under-
emphasis on achievement-related values. As Rosen (1959) has said,
'Achievement values affect social mobility in that they focus the individual's attention on status improvement and help to shape his behavior
so that achievement motivation can be translated into successful action.'
Kluckhohn (1961) saw the middle-class American culture as emphasizing
mastery-over-nature, the future, doing and individualism. We suggested
earlier that in the traditional past the dominant preferences of the
Aborigines were likely to have been: harmony-with-nature, the past, being
and collaterality. If these were the preferences in pre-contact days one
would, by examining the value orientations of contemporary groups of
Aborigines, be able to gauge the extent to which acculturation, *as
measured by verbal statements of conscious belief systems*, has taken
place. One would ask two questions:

  (a) Have the Aborigines adopted the same ordering of alternatives
      within these value orientations as the white Australians?
  (b) Do the Aborigines show as marked a preference as do the white
      Australians for one position as against another on each of the
      orientations?

On the *time* orientation, the data on the summary statements (that is,
the average of all items) show identical orderings for all four groups in
the case of both the mothers and the adolescent girls. The ordering for all
groups is future over present over past. The only item on which the two
ethnic groups differ significantly is the item on ceremonial innovation.
Both white groups prefer change, but the Aborigines appear to be resis-
tant to change in this area; their dominant preference is for the present
(leaving the ceremonies as they are now) followed by past (keeping the
ceremonies the way they have always been). The answer to the second

question is given by the analysis of variance: the Aborigines exhibit a less marked preference for future over present, for future over past and for present over past. On this orientation, therefore, there is evidence of acculturation, but in terms of degree of preference for these positions, there are differences between the two ethnic groups.

Again, on the *relational* orientation, there is a close similarity between the two ethnic groups on the ordering of the two alternatives. In the case of the mothers in the two white groups and in the two Aboriginal groups, the dominant preference is for individualism; the white groups select collaterality in the second position, while Aboriginal community 2 gives equal second preference to collaterality and lineality, and in Aboriginal community 1 lineality occupies the second order preference although it is not significantly preferred over collaterality. For the four groups of adolescents, the ordering is individualism over collaterality over lineality. Two items on this orientation are worth a brief comment. On item R4 (livestock inheritance) all groups, adult and adolescent, with the exception of the rural mothers, prefer collaterality over individualism over lineality. Item R5 pertains to job conditions. The respondents were given three situations: working on one's own and deciding for oneself the best way to do the job (individualism); working with others who all have a say in how to do the job and help each other (collaterality); working for a boss where one just had to do as one is told (lineality). The mothers in Aboriginal community 2 and both groups of Aborigine adolescents choose as their dominant preference lineality, that is, working for a boss. The mothers in Aboriginal community 1 show a not significant preference for individualism over lineality—while twenty-four of the forty-six mothers select individualism as their first choice, a sizeable proportion (seventeen) select lineality first. By contrast with the Aboriginal groups, only seven of the forty-nine metropolitan mothers select lineality as their first choice. Individual autonomy in the job sphere is thus not seen by the Aborigines as being important; perhaps this can be partly accounted for by their past history in which they have been, in the main, unskilled and semi-skilled employees. One could speculate that until sufficient numbers aspire to undertake personal responsibility for job decisions, mobility will be limited.

The analyses of variance show that the Aborigines exhibit a significantly less marked preference for individualism over collaterality, for individualism over lineality and for collaterality over lineality than do the white groups. Thus, although the Aborigines have tended to select the same ordering of alternatives as the white groups, their degree of commitment to the dominant positions is less marked.

Regarding the *activity* orientation, we have already commented on the surprising difference between the white and Aboriginal groups, with the latter showing an unexpected preference for doing over being. Possible reasons for this have already been suggested. A somewhat parallel situation was discovered by Kahl and Hamblin (1961); they found a curvilinear relationship between occupational primacy values and occupation and tried to account for this as follows:

> Successful men probably take their success somewhat for granted and
> turn their attention to the 'higher things of life'. Automatically assum-
> ing that their sons will have good positions, the fathers advise the
> sons to learn to play the piano or enjoy tennis and not concentrate
> all their attention on preparation for their careers. This does not mean
> that upper-status men disapprove of business success; rather it means
> they do not have to think about it all the time. But men who have
> achieved less success in a society which puts great emphasis on it are
> inclined to keep pushing both for themselves and their sons. (p. 680.*)

Whether this verbal emphasis on doing is likely to lead to action depends,
of course, on the total life situation of the people; unless the latter is
perceived as demanding action, the verbal statements will remain
untranslated into behaviour. This would seem to be the case with many
of the Aborigines.

On the *man-nature* orientation, a somewhat confused picture emerges,
but clearly there are marked differences between the two ethnic groups,
particularly among the mothers. The adolescents show a similar first-order
preference, on the average, for harmony-with-nature and the analyses of
variance fail to separate the four groups on any of the dimensions.

The average picture for the mothers shows the Aborigines selecting
harmony-with-nature as their first-order preference, while the metropolitan
mothers choose dominance-over-nature (not significantly greater than
harmony-with-nature) and the rural mothers choose subjugation-to-nature
(not significantly greater than dominance-over-nature). Clear differences
between the ethnic groups are shown on the items MN1, MN3, MN4
(second-order preference) and MN5. The analyses of variance quite
definitely separate the two ethnic groups on the dominance-harmony and
harmony-subjugation dimensions; in each case both groups of Aboriginal
mothers show a preference for the harmony position.

On this orientation, then, the Aboriginal mothers have not adopted the
dominant orientations of the white mothers. Other researchers (Kahl &
Davis, 1955; Strodtbeck, 1958; Rosen, 1956; Cox, 1964) have concerned
themselves with activism or mastery as a part of the achievement-
orientation syndrome. It might be argued that a concern with individualism,
the future and doing needs to be accompanied by a belief that one can
control nature, that one, through one's own actions, can control one's
destiny, if effort and striving are to characterize one's behaviour and if
social status and occupational mobility are to be achieved. Berndt and
Berndt (1964) discussing the culture contact situation, wrote of the
Aborigines, 'In coping with these circumstances the Aborigines made use
of the approach which had served them so well in their traditional
environment. They did not try to change their surroundings, human and

*From J. A. Kahl and R. W. Hamblin, Socioeconomic status and ideological
attitudes: A non linear pattern. Quoted in J. A. Kahl, Some measurements of
achievement orientation. *American Journal of Sociology*, 70, 669-681. Copyright
© The University of Chicago Press and reprinted with their permission.

otherwise; instead they tried to exploit them, to adapt to them while deriving from them all the benefits they could.' (p. 440.) Such an approach is in marked contrast to the achievement-related value, dominance-over-nature, where man is seen as dominant over, and able to change, natural forces.

In summary then, these research data would suggest that there is evidence of acculturation of the Aborigines in regard to certain value orientations, but that they have not reached the stage yet where positions on these orientations are as strongly held as they are by the dominant white group. Perhaps this relatively less-marked preference for achievement-related values helps to explain their lack of social mobility.

In seeking to explain social mobility, one's concern does not rest solely, however, with such values. As Rosen (1959) has pointed out, there are three components of the achievement syndrome: a psychological factor, achievement motivation, and the two cultural factors of certain value orientations and culturally influenced educational-vocational aspiration levels. The research on which the author is engaged has revealed low levels of achievement motivation among the Aboriginal girls and it is intended to seek the origins of this in the child-rearing practices of the mothers. An examination, too, will be made of the educational-vocational aspirations the mothers hold for their daughters and the daughters' own aspirations.

References

Berndt, R. M. and Berndt, C. H., 1964: *The World of the First Australians.* Ure Smith Pty Ltd, Sydney.

Cox, H., 1964: Study of social class variation in value orientations in selected areas of mother-child behavior. Unpublished doctoral dissertation, Washington University, St Louis.

Elkin, A. P., 1954: *The Australian Aborigines* (3rd edn). Angus & Robertson Ltd, Sydney.

Getzels, J. W. and Guba, E. L., 1957: Social behaviour and the administrative process. *School Review*, 65, 423-441.

Hausfeld, R., 1966: Unpublished modification of Kluckhohn-Strodtbeck Value Orientation Schedule, University of Sydney.

Kahl, J. A. and Davis, J. A., 1955: A comparison of indexes of socio-economic status. *American Sociological Review*, 20, 317-325.

Kahl, J. A. and Hamblin, R. W., 1961: Socio-economic status and ideological attitudes: A non-linear pattern. Referred to in J. A. Kahl, Some measurements of achievement orientation. *American Journal of Sociology*, 70, 669-681.

Kluckhohn, F. R. and Strodtbeck, F. L., 1961: *Variations in Value Orientations.* Row, Peterson and Co., New York.

Rosen, B. C., 1956: The achievement syndrome: A psychocultural dimension of social stratification. *American Sociological Review*, 21, 203-211.

Rosen, B. C., 1959: Race, ethnicity and the achievement syndrome. *American Sociological Review*, 24, 47-60.

Strodtbeck, F. L., 1958: Family integration, values and achievement. In D. C.

McClelland, *et al.*, *Talent and Society*. D. Van Nostrand & Co. Inc., Princeton, N.J.

Watts, B. H., 1969: The family antecedents of achievement motivation among white and Aboriginal Australians. Unpublished PhD thesis, University of Queensland.

Part IV
The Peer-Group Context

7

The Peer-Group Context

W. J. Campbell and R. V. McSweeney

TO MANY, the concept of peer group may conjure up an image of long-haired youths with distinctive speech and dress, an insatiable appetite for loud pop music and lengthy telephone conversations, and with such a degree of irresponsibility that they openly reject the standards of judgement and value held by their elders and betters. However, the concept itself is innocent of such connotations. It merely means a more or less enduring association of individuals who enjoy parity of status and at least some common motives and interests. Obviously, such groups may be of many different kinds ranging in structure from the simple and informal set of neighbourhood playmates to the complex and highly formal society, such as Rotary or The Australian College of Education, and, in size, from the clique of two or three close friends to the school crowd. Peer groups, too, may be unisexual or bisexual, located in back alleys or in the Hilton Hotel. Running through these variations, however, are common characteristics: all peer groups possess their own code or rules, all provide opportunities for members to interact in order to achieve the goals of the group, and all evoke from their members feelings of loyalty. Because of these common characteristics, one may speak of them in a collective way as 'the peer group' in much the same way as one speaks of 'the child' or 'the school'.

It follows from what has been said above that peer groups are not distinctively youth phenomena; they occur among all age groups. However, for purposes of this chapter, which focuses upon the effects of peer groups on school learning, most attention will be given to children and adolescents. The chapter begins with a brief statement on the structure and developmental functions of peer groups. Then are discussed in turn: the significance of peer groups relative to parents and teachers, the notion of a distinctive peer culture, the significance for education of particular peer orientations, and, finally, implications for teachers and school authorities.

Structure and Developmental Functions of Peer Groups

Evidence suggests that pre-adolescent peer groups are typically unisexual in composition, but that, as the members move into adolescence, hetero-sexual cliques and crowds, with more clearly defined status boundaries, develop. In late adolescence more loosely associated groups of couples appear and mark the beginning of the end for this type of peer group. Dunphy's study (1963) of Sydney adolescents provides one of the clearest demonstrations of this progression.*

FIGURE 7.1

Stages of Group Development in Adolescence
(Dunphy, 1963, p. 236)

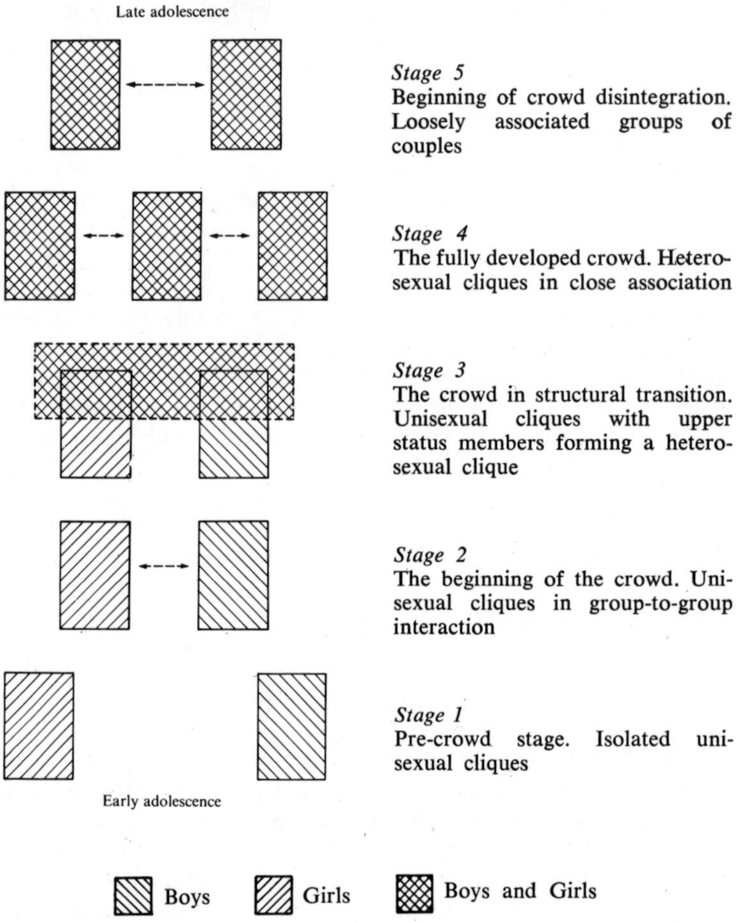

Late adolescence

Stage 5
Beginning of crowd disintegration. Loosely associated groups of couples

Stage 4
The fully developed crowd. Hetero-sexual cliques in close association

Stage 3
The crowd in structural transition. Unisexual cliques with upper status members forming a hetero-sexual clique

Stage 2
The beginning of the crowd. Uni-sexual cliques in group-to-group interaction

Stage 1
Pre-crowd stage. Isolated uni-sexual cliques

Early adolescence

Boys   Girls   Boys and Girls

*From D. C. Dunphy, The social structure of adolescent peer groups. Sociometry, 26(1963), 230-246. Reprinted by permission of the American Sociological Association.

The prevalence of peer groups (Connell, *et al.*, 1957, report adolescent membership as 70 per cent for boys, and 82 per cent for girls), and the substantial proportion of waking time that is spent in them (Campbell, 1962*a*, gives this as 32 per cent), suggests that the youth find them satisfying and worthwhile. Ausubel (1958, pp. 460-1) identifies their contributions to development in the following terms:

1. Depending on the prevailing degree of cultural discontinuity between child and adult roles, the peer group furnishes a little to a goodly portion of the child's primary status. In any case, it is the only cultural institution in which his position is not marginal, in which he is offered primary status and a social identity among a group of equals, and in which his own activities and concerns reign supreme . . .

2. The peer group is also a subsidiary source of derived status for the satellizer during childhood. . . . This 'we-feeling' furnishes security and belongingness and is a powerful ego support and basis of loyalty to group norms.

3. By providing primary and derived status, a new source of values and standards, and experience in behaving as a sovereign person, the peer group devalues parents, transfers part of the child's loyalties from them to itself (resatellization), and hence promotes desatellization. As a result of the support the child receives from his peer group, he gains the courage to weaken the bonds of emotional anchorage to parents. . . . By creating precedents and then appealing to the prevailing group standards, the peer culture operates as a pressure group, obtains important concessions for individual members with restrictive parents, and emancipates itself from adult and institutional controls.

4. Like home and school, the peer group is an important socializing, enculturative and training institution. . . . Through the peer group children also pick up knowledge, misinformation and folklore regarding science, sex, sports, religion, etc.

5. Finally, the peer group provides a particularized social identity for the child insofar as it permits him to play roles that are most compatible with his personality orientation toward group experience.

It is clear that the peer group is an important educative agency in its own right; it is a highly effective teacher for, in contrast to more formal agencies, the culture that it transmits, and the manner of transmission, are attractive to the learners. The group does, of course, exert pressure on its members to conform, but the techniques are subtle (threat of ostracism rather than of the cane) and the rewards high.

Relative Significance of Peer Groups

There is general agreement in the research literature that peer groups are next to parents, and distinctly ahead of teachers, in the influence which they exert upon children and adolescents. In the Coleman study (1961), for example, students responded to the following question, 'Which one of these things would be hardest for you to take—your parents' disapproval, your teacher's disapproval, or breaking with your friend?' by nominating 'parents' disapproval' slightly ahead of 'breaking with friend'. 'Teacher's disapproval' received scarcely any votes—3.5 per cent from boys and 2.7 per cent from girls. In case it is felt that Coleman is biasing his results when he contrasts *'breaking with* friends' with *'disapproval of* parents and teachers', it is useful to turn to Epperson's findings (1964) in response to the question: 'Which one of these things would make you most unhappy? (a) If my parents did not like what I did. (b) If my (favourite) teacher did not like what I did. (c) If my best friend did not like what I did.' With this wording, parents rated significantly higher than best friend (81 per cent of both boys and girls choosing parents, as against 16 per cent of boys, and 18 per cent of girls choosing best friend), but the rating of teachers did not improve.

The hierarchy of *parents, peers, teachers* occurs, too, in an Australian study by Campbell (1962*b*) in which adolescents were asked to indicate how they would act in a number of situations structured so as to involve conflict between the expectations of various social systems, including home, school, peer group and church. From the responses, an 'index of significance' was derived. The relative indices were: *home*: 100; *peers*: 75; *school*: 67; *church*: 50.

As a final source of evidence concerning the influence of peer groups relative to other persons or groups, reference can be made to the Sydney study undertaken by Connell, *et al.* (1957). In this, adolescents were asked to nominate the two persons who had most influence upon them, and the responses were:

TABLE 7.1

	Percentages			
	13 years		17 years	
Influential Person	*Boys*	*Girls*	*Boys*	*Girls*
Mother	60	70	52	70
Father	49	50	42	39
Girl-friend	10	13	21	13
Boy-friend	9	10	12	22
Teacher	9	8	4	4
All others	11	13	19	24

Parents who carry the scars of recent battles with their teenage offspring might be surprised at the high level of influence which they are accorded, but teachers are unlikely to doubt the validity of *their* relatively low rating. Perhaps the reasons for this latter lie in the image of the teaching profession and in the personalities of the individuals attracted to it; perhaps the low esteem accorded to teachers is an inevitable concomitant of the relationship of teacher to student. For example, Waller (1932) claimed that the classroom was in a 'state of perilous equilibrium', and he attributed this, in part, to the nature of the teaching/learning situation, which charges teachers with the responsibility of transmitting a traditional culture to youth who accept it only with reluctance.

Peer-Group Culture

The significance of the data presented above lies in the degree of similarity between the cultures of homes, peer groups and schools, and in the nature of the regions where differences occur. If homes and schools are in essential agreement with peer groups, or if they differ in regions that have no relevance for school learning, little concern need be expressed at the relative devaluation of teachers. On the other hand, if the cultures differ in regions associated with school learning, the issue could be more serious.

Somewhat in the manner of a grand sociologist, and without the embarrassment of empirical data, Parsons (1942) deplores the alienation of youth from the general culture:

> By contrast with the emphasis on responsibility in this 'the adult male' role, the orientation of the youth culture is more or less specifically irresponsible. One of its dominant notes is 'having a good time' . . . there is a strong tendency to repudiate interest in adult things and to feel a certain recalcitrance to the pressure of adult expectations and discipline . . . [and] to develop in directions which are either on the borderline of parental approval or beyond the pale, in such matters as sex behavior, drinking and various forms of frivolous and irresponsible behavior. (pp. 606-8.*)

In similar vein, but from a background of empirical research, Coleman writes (1960):

> Industrial society has spawned a peculiar phenomenon, most evident in America, but emerging also in other Western societies: adolescent subcultures, with values and activities quite distinct from those of the adult society—subcultures whose members have most of their important associations within [themselves] and few with adult society.

Coleman bases his conclusions upon extensive data concerned with: qualities needed to gain entry to 'élite' groups, qualities of popular heroes and leaders, interests, attitudes and values of peer-group members, and the nature of achievements that attract rewards and punishments from peers. The data, however, do not unequivocally support the existence of a distinctive subculture, and Coleman, himself, is forced to admit (1961): 'Thus, even the rewards a child gains from his parents may help reinforce the values of the adolescent culture', but he goes on to add, '. . . not because his parents hold those same values, but because parents want their children to be successful and esteemed by their peers'.

The majority of other researchers in this area of peer culture (for

*From T. Parsons, Age and sex in the social structure of the United States. *American Sociological Review*, 7(1942), 5, 604-616. Reprinted by permission of the American Sociological Association.

example, Elkin & Westley, 1955, Bealer & Willits, 1961, Gordon, 1963, Epperson, 1964, Jahoda & Warren, 1965 and Lehrman, 1966, from the United States; Morris, 1958 and Musgrove, 1965, from Great Britain; Connell, 1957 and Campbell, 1962, from Australia) find that, *in general*, the youth values are similar to adult ones.

Within the wider context of changing social values, Spindler (1963) gathered data from college students over a period of eight years in an attempt to identify those aspects of social character considered to be of most worth. Using simple, value-projective techniques, he was able to delineate the characteristics of the 'ideal American boy' as: sociable, popular, well-rounded (able to do many things without being an expert at any), athletic, ambitious (within limited areas), considerate of others, Christian (moral and respectful), patriotic and of *average* academic ability. Characteristics mentioned only infrequently were: leadership, independence, high ability and individuality. Spindler concluded that the most desired character type could be described as balanced, outward-oriented, sociable and conforming. Creativity, deviancy and introspective behaviour were definitely not highly valued.

As suggested above, Spindler attributes these values to a generalized 'emergent' culture, rather than to a distinctive youth one, although he would agree that they are likely to prevail among the young rather than the old. His concepts of emergent and traditional values have been developed by Getzels (1958). The following is a summary of these contrasting values.

The Spindler-Getzels Dichotomization of Secular Values

Traditional	*Emergent*
1 *Puritan Morality*, consisting of the marks of 'common decency', such as: thrift, self-denial, sexual restraint; commitment to unchanging moral or ethical standards.	1 *Moral Relativism*. Absoluteness in right and wrong is not acceptable as a principle of conduct; the group sets the standard of morality; emphasis on *shame*, rather than guilt; lack of commitment to standards; values are in a constant state of flux.
2 *Work-Success Ethic,* which endorses the value of hard work as the key to success ('work is good'); everyone has an obligation to strive for success and to value achievement and self-improvement.	2 *Sociability*, which entails getting along well with others. Affability and successful interpersonal relations are more important than hard work.
3 *Independence (The Autonomous Self)*. The self is sacred and is of more consequence	3 *Conformity*. The antithesis of the autonomous self. Everything is relative to the group;

than the group. Self-activity and originality are sanctioned; self-determination and self-perfection are the criteria of personal worth.

4 *Future-Time Orientation.* The future is more important than the present or the past; present gratifications should be deferred in favour of future rewards.

self-goals must be subordinated to group goals; compliance to group wishes and demands is to be sought after.

4 *Present-Time Orientation.* Instead of looking to, and providing for the future, we should live for the 'here and now'. As the future cannot be predicted, a hedonistic outlook is sanctioned.

In shifting the issue from adults versus youth to traditional versus emergent societal values, Spindler appears to have made a significant contribution to our understanding of peer groups. His stand—and the one which is adopted in this chapter—is that youth peer groups do not possess a distinctive subculture, but they are more likely than groups of adults, such as parents and teachers, to hold values which reflect the emergent culture.

Consistent with the viewpoint taken above is the conclusion reached by almost all researchers that peer groups place a low value upon academic achievement. Spindler's study among college students, as we have seen, showed that while possession of *average* ability could be something of a help in acquiring status, high ability could be a distinct handicap. Coleman's study (1961) confirms these findings among high school students. To be accepted in the leading crowds, or élites, boys needed personality, reputation and athletic ability, while girls needed personality, reputation and friendliness. High scholastic achievement was rated low by both sex groups. Although Coleman found some variation among and within schools, the more striking finding was that in *all* schools academic achievement did not count for much within the peer groups.

Sanford (1959), Hughes, Becker and Geer (1962) and Ringness (1967) report similar findings, and before one dismisses these as distinctive, and widely-recognized American phenomena, reference might be made to two, among several, Australian studies. In the first of these, Wheeler (1961) found that among West Australian youth, school achievement rated below sporting ability, sociability, good physical appearance, and 'altocentric' personality traits. In the second study, Campbell (1968) presented Brisbane adolescent girls with hypothetical situations involving excelling at sports, excelling in school achievement, achieving a position of responsibility (captain) within the school, and being voted the most popular girl, and asked them to indicate which of a variety of actions, parents, teachers, special friends and peers would advise them to adopt. Thus the first situation, which involved excelling at sports and school achievement, read as follows:

You have a 45 per cent chance of coming top of the class in the annual examination, and also a 45 per cent chance of winning the sports championship. The following alternatives are open to you:

(a) Give more time to both study and sports.
(b) Give more time to study and keep to the present schedule with your sports.
(c) Give more time to sports and keep to the present study schedule.
(d) Re-allocate your present time by giving more time to study and less to sports.
(e) Re-allocate your present time by giving more time to sports and less to study.
(f) Keep to the present time allocations.
   What would the following people advise you to do?
   Mother:
   Father:
   Teacher:
   Special Friends:
   Other Pupils:

From the 'advice' recorded by each adolescent girl ($n = 100$, ages 12-16 years), Campbell calculated a hierarchy of values for each reference group, and these are shown below.

TABLE 7.2

Value Hierarchy

Rank Ascribed by Adolescents to:

Value	Mothers	Fathers	Teachers	Special Friends	Peers
Excelling at school	1	1	1	3	4
Attaining school responsibility	2	3	2	4	2
Excelling at sport	4	2	3	1	1
Excelling at popularity	3	4	4	2	3

In this study, doing well in school work was, at least in the eyes of the respondents, not highly rated by peers although it was by teachers and parents.

An interesting American study (Tannenbaum, 1960) suggests that brilliance in academic achievement is not an insuperable handicap to peer group acceptance—but studiousness could be. In this study, Tannenbaum examined the attitudes of 615 students towards fictitious others who were brilliant versus average, studious versus non-studious, and athletic versus non-athletic. The three dichotomized characteristics appeared in every possible combination, producing descriptions of eight stimulus characters. Respondents were asked to assign various desirable and undesirable traits to these, and, on the basis of ascribed traits, Tannenbaum calculated a mean acceptability rating. The eight characters were ranked as follows:

1. Brilliant non-studious athlete.
2. Average non-studious athlete.
3. Average studious athlete.
4. Brilliant studious athlete.
5. Brilliant non-studious non-athlete.
6. Average non-studious non-athlete.
7. Average studious non-athlete.
8. Brilliant studious non-athlete.

These results show very clearly the high prestige of athletic ability and the strong reaction against studiousness. Brilliance is tolerated in a non-studious athlete but not in a studious non-athlete!

Educational Significance of Peer Orientations

There seems little doubt that, in general, peer groups do not give strong support to school authorities and academic learning.

It is one thing to identify this phenomenon and another to trace its effects through to actual scholastic achievements. Some educationists appear to accept a causal relationship between values and achievements as a self-evident truth, while others content themselves with showing that a relationship of some kind exists between these variables. Most, however, are scientific to the point of establishing the relationship, and then proceed to interpret this as a causal one from values to achievements. Thus, in a study of elementary-school students, Fox, Lippitt and Schmuck (1964) found that peer-group sociometric diffuseness, interpersonal support for the individual pupil, attitudes towards self and school, and academic productivity vary together in a systematic fashion, and they conclude: 'The results of this study point to the significant impact of the immediate class-room milieu for a pupil's utilization of intelligence. Social-emotional aspects of both peer-group relations and teacher relationships appear to take precedence over the extra-school influences of the family in shaping a pupil's motivation to learn and his consequent academic performance.' (p. 137.)

At the secondary-school level, Sugarman's study (1967) showed that London boys who were deeply involved in teenage culture may be expected to perform at an academic level below their potential and to have poor conduct records at school. Sugarman refers to strong teenage identification as fulfilling the function of a 'social opiate'. Ringness (1967) writes in similar vein from the United States of America.

Finally, at the college level, Sanford (1959), Hughes, Becker and Geer (1962), Gottlieb and Hodgkins (1963), and Wallace (1966) are among those who establish a positive relationship between peer-group membership and low academic grades. Gottlieb and Hodgkins, for example, found that the 'non-conformist' group of students had the best academic records, and the 'collegiate' group the poorest. Wallace reports: 'At the very start of their college careers, freshmen's attitudes towards grades and toward social integration with their peers were *positively* related, but rapidly became *negatively* related, and this change came about as a result of a precipitous decline in grades orientation among students who were strongly desirous of social integration, rather than as a result of any increase in grades orientation among those less desirous of such integration.' (p. 47.)

Granted that the relationship so consistently reported by the researchers *does* exist, the explanation could lie in such a simple fact as limited resources. Like everyone else, students are unable to satisfy all the demands that the environment places upon them, and if they devote a large amount of energy to peer activities, they have less available for scholastic ones. If this is a part explanation, the specific values of the peer group might be unimportant, and it would be expected that students who spend correspondingly large amounts of time on highly reputable activities, such as campaigning for improvements for Aborigines or Negroes, could also have depressed academic grades. A second possible explanation is that students who encounter failure in their scholastic work turn to other sources of satisfaction, and among these might be peer groups, religious associations, and a variety of 'good causes'. These two explanations which are not mutually exclusive, and others like them, are not rejected by the researchers, but the findings are more frequently interpreted in terms of 'seduction of the innocent'—the anti-intellectual values of the peer groups are seen as deterrents to academic achievement, and the rewards of peer membership are so high that students dare not risk exclusion by failure to adopt the norms. Braham (1965), for example, writes:

> ... when intelligence is just beginning to function as a coordinated structure, and requires the most nurturing circumstances, the adolescent meets a major deterrent to its development, that of the intellectually negating adolescent peer-group structure. . . . This represents the adolescent's predominant social environment within the high school, where intellectual activities should be a major concern. By demanding of its members a high degree of conformity to its own non-intellectual standards, the [peer group] manages to suppress intellectual interest and motivation in all but the deviates. (p. 252.)

Implications for Teachers and Others

If it is true, as the weight of evidence suggests, that the peer-group culture merely reflects society's emergent values, if these values are somewhat harmful to academic achievement and if high academic achievement is a matter of considerable importance to individuals and nations the task confronting teachers and others is indeed a mammoth one. In their attack upon this task, our educational leaders start with a number of handicaps.

In the first place, the stereotypic image of the successful teacher (Anderson, 1966) is of one who: (a) possesses a body of knowledge to impart; (b) is sufficiently firm and dignified to maintain discipline and hold the respect of his pupils; (c) is skilled at record-keeping and stock-taking; (d) is an exemplary adult, offering an attractive but conventional model to the pupils in his charge. With an image of this kind it is not surprising that the teaching profession does not attract the most dynamic members of each succeeding generation. Indeed, all of the studies show that, in comparison with recruits to other professions, teacher trainees are lacking in sparkle. Gillis (1964) writes:

> It is their strong dependency needs which most sharply differentiate future teachers from the general college population . . . future teachers are more willing to minimize their own personal worth, repress aggression, and defer to the authority of others. They also express a particularly strong need for a highly structured environment with well defined interpersonal relationships. Cognitive activities must also be carefully organized. (p. 597.)

There is some consolation in the evidence that Australian teachers have weaker needs for deference, order and abasement than have American ones (Dunkin, 1966).

Second, the teaching profession tends to call forth, and to reward, patterns of orderliness, conformity, deference and authoritarianism. Dunkin, for example, has shown clearly that expectations of low warmth and dominance are typically ascribed by classroom teachers to superiors such as headteachers and inspectors (see Chapter 17). The combination of personality needs and occupational *press*, predisposing teachers towards dependency and deference, and *not* towards originality, flexibility and divergent thinking, militates against highly effective work with peer groups.

A third challenge lies in the low standards of scholarship and the anti-academic orientation of many teachers themselves. In the recent large survey of teachers in Australia undertaken by the Australian College of Education (1966), almost one-third of teachers were found to be unmatriculated (and many of these were teaching matriculation classes), twenty-two per cent had reached a bare matriculation standard, twenty-eight per cent had some post-matriculation, but sub-graduate qualifications, and only nineteen per cent had graduated from a university. This is a sorry record of scholarship for an occupational group charged with the responsibility of developing scholarship in youth. Here, and in the two issues discussed above, teaching is caught up in a vicious circle which could have disastrous effects. As Coleman (1961) has said, bright students who seek the highest rewards will turn away from teaching and those who are seen as the guardians of intellectualism will not really be those of highest intelligence, but persons who are willing to work hard at a relatively unrewarded activity. A long-term effect of this is that the adult society becomes increasingly diluted, in its leadership and professional levels, by persons of mediocre ability. If our society is serious in this matter of improving intellectual standards, it must offer much higher rewards to the members of the teaching profession.

The key which will open the way to overcoming the deleterious effects of some elements in the emergent culture lies in staffing our schools and colleges with individuals who possess attractive personalities and are themselves strongly committed to intellectual endeavours. If this is not done, all other measures are likely to be ineffective gimmicks; if it *is* done other measures will arise naturally and will no longer be gimmicks. Among changes that one would hope to see is the bestowing of school rewards upon the scholastically able. At the moment these rewards are few and are not always of the best kind, but even in bestowing those that exist, many high schools appear to make the position of the scholars more untenable. As an extreme example, in one high school the group of eighty boys from which eight prefects were to be chosen contained six students who won both national Commonwealth scholarships and gained the highest possible grades in all subjects in the first public examination, four who won scholarships and who also achieved well in the examination (but did not get a full hand of top grades), and two who did not win scholarships but who achieved throughout the examination at the highest possible level. To the extent that the Commonwealth scholarships were given to boys of outstanding intellectual *capacity*, and top grades in the public examination indicated outstanding academic *achievement*, these twelve students could be regarded as the most academically able in the group of eighty, and one might have expected that, even on a chance basis, some would be nominated by the teachers for the prefect positions—but not one was!

The more discriminating bestowal of individual rewards could be a step in the right direction, although Coleman (1960) is probably right when he makes a strong plea for the creation of *school* rewards for intellectual achievement, with which all the students can identify.

> The theory and practice of education remains focused on *individuals*; teachers exhort individuals to concentrate their energies in scholarly directions, while the community of adolescents diverts these energies into other channels. The pressure of the present research is that, if educational goals are to be realized in modern society, a fundamentally different approach to secondary education is necessary. Adults are in control of the institutions they have established for secondary education; traditionally, these institutions have been used to mold children as individuals toward ends which adults dictate. The fundamental change which must occur is to shift the focus: to mold social communities as communities, so that the norms of the communities themselves reinforce educational goals rather than inhibit them, as is at present the case. (p. 338.*)

Coleman goes on to suggest the wider introduction of interschool scholastic competitions, and those who are sceptical of the effects of these should visit one of the schools in the United States which have their scholastic teams competing in national competitions through the television medium.

*From J. S. Coleman, The adolescent subculture and academic achievement. *American Journal of Sociology*, 65(1960), 4, 337-347. Copyright © The University of Chicago Press and reprinted with their permission.

This harnessing of peer-group energies for educational ends represents one of the major challenges facing teachers today, and its solution is less dependent upon increased expenditure than upon the sympathy, ingenuity and wisdom of those to whom society has entrusted this task.

References

Anderson, R. H., 1966: *Teaching in a World of Change*. Harcourt, Brace & World, New York.

Australian College of Education, 1966: *Teachers in Australia*. Cheshire, Melbourne.

Ausubel, David P., 1958: *Theory and Problems of Child Development*. Grune and Stratton, Inc., New York.

Bealer, R. C. and Willits, F. K., 1961: Rural youth: A case study in the rebelliousness of adolescents. *Annals of the American Academy of Political and Social Science*, 338, 63-69.

Braham, M., 1965: Peer group deterrents to intellectual development during adolescence. *Educational Theory*, 15, 248-258.

Campbell, W. J., 1962a: *Television and the Australian Adolescent*. Angus & Robertson Ltd., Sydney.

Campbell, W. J., 1962b: *Growing Up in Karribee*. Australian Council for Educational Research, Melbourne.

Campbell, W. J., 1968: Adolescent values towards academic achievement. Unpublished MS, University of Queensland.

Coleman, J. S., 1960: The adolescent subculture and academic achievement. *American Journal of Sociology*, 65, 337-347.

Coleman, J. S., 1961: *The Adolescent Society*. The Free Press, New York.

Connell, W. F., *et al.*, 1957: *Growing Up In An Australian City*. Australian Council for Educational Research, Melbourne.

Dunkin, M. J., 1966: Some determinants of teacher warmth and directiveness. Unpublished PhD thesis, University of Queensland.

Dunphy, D. C., 1963: The social structure of adolescent peer groups. *Sociometry*, 26, 230-246.

Elkin, F. and Westley, W. A., 1955: The myth of adolescent culture. *American Sociological Review*, 20, 680-684.

Epperson, D. C., 1964: A re-assessment of indices of parental influence in the adolescent society. *American Sociological Review*, 29, 93-96.

Fox, R. S., Lippitt, R. O. and Schmuck, R. A., 1964: *Pupil-Teacher Adjustment and Mutual Adaptation in Creating Classroom Learning Environments*. Institute for Social Research, The University of Michigan, Ann Arbour, Mich.

Getzels, J. W., 1958: The acquisition of values in school and society. In F. S. Chase and H. A. Anderson (Eds), *The High School in a New Era*. University of Chicago Press, Chicago, Ill.

Gillis, J., 1964: Personality needs of future teachers. *Educational and Psychological Measurement*, 24, 3, 589-600.

Gordon, C. W., 1963: Essay review: James Coleman on 'The Adolescent Society'. *School Review*, 71, 377-385.

Gottlieb, D. and Hodgkins, B., 1963: College student subcultures: Their structure and characteristics in relation to student attitude change. *School Review*, 71, 266-289.

Hughes, E. C., Becker, H. S. and Geer, B., 1962: Student culture and academic effort. In N. Sanford (Ed.), *The American College*. John Wiley & Sons, Inc., New York.

Jahoda, M. and Warren, N., 1965: The myths of youth. *Sociology of Education*, 38, 138-149.

Lehrman, P., 1966: Issues in subcultural delinquency. Unpublished doctoral dissertation, Columbia University.

Morris, J. F., 1958: The development of adolescent value judgments. *British Journal of Educational Psychology*, 28, 1-14.

Musgrove, F., 1965: *Youth and Social Order*. Indiana University Press, Bloomington, Ind.

Parsons, T., 1942: Age and sex in the social structure of the United States. *American Sociological Review*, 7, 604-616.

Ringness, T. A., 1967: Identification patterns, motivation, and school achievement of bright junior high school boys. *Journal of Educational Psychology*, 58, 93-102.

Sanford, N., 1959: Motivation of high achievers. In O. D. David (Ed.), *The Education of Women*. American Council on Education, Washington, D.C.

Spindler, G. D., 1963: *Education and Culture*. Holt, Rinehart and Winston, Inc., New York.

Sugarman, B., 1967: Involvement in youth culture, academic achievement, and conformity in school. *British Journal of Sociology*, 18, 151-164.

Tannenbaum, A. J., 1960: Adolescents' attitudes towards academic brilliance. Unpublished PhD thesis, New York University.

Wallace, W. L., 1966: *Student Culture*. Aldine Publishing Co., Chicago, Ill.

Waller, W., 1932: *The Sociology of Teaching*. John Wiley & Sons Inc., New York.

Wheeler, D. K., 1961: Popularity among adolescents in Western Australia and in the United States of America. *School Review*, 69, 67-81.

8

The Nature and Correlates of Adolescent Values

R. V. McSweeney

THIS study is closely linked with issues raised in the previous chapter—in particular, with the issue of a 'distinctive subculture' raised by Coleman (1961) but disputed by Pressey and Jones (1955), Epperson (1964) and others. It draws attention to the pervasive nature of the student's value system which is, in the words of Dressel and Mayhew (1954), 'irretrievably interwoven into the thinking he does and the solutions that he reaches'.

The aims of the study were:

(a) to identify the secular values held by a group of adolescents in attendance at non-state (independent) secondary schools;

(b) to relate these values to those ascribed by the adolescents to various reference groups;

(c) to inquire into a possible relationship between values and certain personal, home, school and cultural variables; and

(d) to relate values to academic achievement.

Data were obtained by means of a modified Differential Values Inventory (Prince, 1958) which is based on the concept of traditional-emergent values outlined by Spindler (1955), and applied by Prince (1957), Anderson (1961), Thompson (1961), Lehmann (1963) and Bidwell, *et al.* (1963). One premise of the Differential Values Inventory is that: '. . . under the necessity of reorganizing our social structure to meet the demands of a new technology and of a spatial mobility unparalleled in modern history, our inherited system of status and roles is breaking down, while a new system compatible with the actual conditions of modern life has not yet emerged' (Prince, 1957, p. 40).

Prince's questionnaire consists of sixty-four pairs of items, each containing a traditional and an emergent value statement, and preceded by the words 'I ought to . . .'. The sixty-four pairs represent eight from each of the eight value regions (four traditional and four emergent—Chapter 7, page 128). Prince determined test validity by means of judges and by a graphic analysis that took into consideration both item difficulty and discrimination. A factor analysis of 1,790 responses identified eight factors corresponding to the value regions.

Several modifications of the basic instrument were made for purposes of the present investigation. First, the prescriptive element was removed by deletion of the introductory words, 'I ought to'. Second, the scope was enlarged by asking the adolescents to identify, in addition to their own values, those held by: mothers, fathers, teachers, best friends, 'most in class', 'adults generally', and 'teenagers generally'. Third, instead of pitting values against one another, respondents were asked to express measures of agreement or disagreement towards each on a five-point scale. Fourth, in order to reduce tedium arising out of the enlarged scope, the 128 items in the original instrument were reduced to forty. *Finally,* pre-tests indicated that some changes in terminology were needed to make the items completely comprehensible to the Australian respondents. Reliability coefficients, calculated on the basis of both split-half and test-retest procedures, ranged from $+.69$ to $+.80$.

Some indication of the final instrument can be gained from the following items, for each of which adolescents were asked to indicate the extent of their agreement or disagreement using a five-point scale:

1. The important thing is to get as much pleasure as possible out of life.
19. We should live for the present, and let the future look after itself.
23. Hard work is the key to success.
33. One should aim at getting as many thrills and new experiences as possible out of life.

The population, from which a sample of 1,249 students was drawn, comprised pupils in the eighth, ninth, and eleventh grades at independent secondary schools in Queensland. The sample was a stratified one based upon the following variables: sex, type of school (denominational/non-denominational), location of school (metropolitan/other urban/rural), and size of school (large/medium/small). Fifteen schools featured in the study, and of these all but one were single-sex, eight were controlled by the Catholic Church, five by other churches, and two were non-denominational. Five catered for day students only, and the other ten had facilities for both residential and day students.

A breakdown of students according to grade, age and sex is shown in Table 8.1.

All responses were made anonymously by students, but the various school and class groups were assigned code numbers for purposes of later identification.

As a first step in the analysis, mean values and t tests of significance were calculated for each of the eight reference groups (including as one of these the respondents themselves on each of the four value regions (morality, time, autonomy and achievement) and on the totals of these. Some relevant data are shown in the graphical representations of Figure 8.1(a), (b), (c), (d) and (e).

TABLE 8.1

Composition of Sample

(n = 1,249)

Grade	Modal Age (Years)	Males	Females	Total
8	13	281	201	482
9	14	262	201	463
11	16	180	124	204
Total		723	526	1,249

In the most general terms (Figure 8.1(e)), *teachers* are seen by these adolescents to be the most traditionally oriented of the eight groups, and teenagers the least. Neither placement is surprising; as surrogates of the culture, teachers might be expected to place emphasis on traditional values, and, for various reasons (perhaps 'natural' rebelliousness against authority, perhaps the different culture to which they have been exposed), adolescents are likely to place emphasis on emergent values. As in most other studies

FIGURE 8.1

Mean Value Scores — Self and Significant Others

(S = Self; M = Mother; F = Father; Tc = Teachers; B = Best friend; C = Most in class; Tg = Teenagers; A = Adults.)
All differences are significant (at least at the .05 level), except where marked, e.g., M/F.

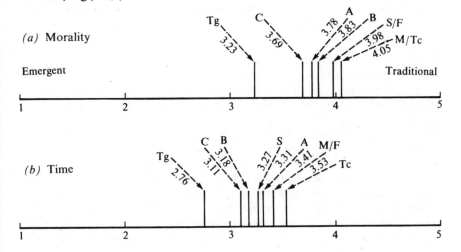

FIGURE 8.1 *(continued)*

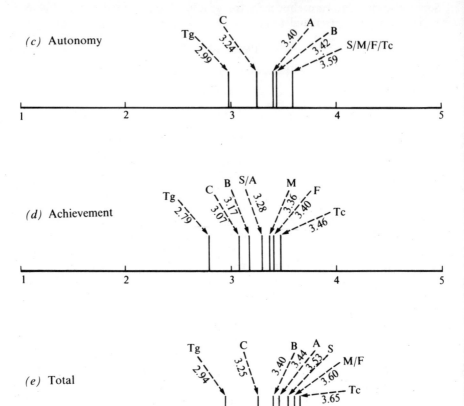

of this kind, the respondents have placed themselves in a compromise position between best friends and parents. It might be that a 'pious bias' is operating here, and that a more accurate placement of 'self' would coincide with that of 'best friend' or of 'most in class'. The picture that emerges from this study is one of adolescents who are distinctly tradition-ally oriented in all four regions; indeed, even the 'teenagers generally' are seen by these respondents to adhere fairly closely to a point midway between extreme emergent and extreme traditional orientations.

At this stage, the careful reader will be saying, 'Ah, but he is working with a grossly biased sample'. This is correct. The sample is, essentially, a middle-class one, and one would have liked to extend the social-class range to include more adolescents from lower-class and upper-class homes. Most of the former, however, are likely to be in attendance at state secondary schools, and the educational authorities declined permission to undertake the study within these schools. According to overseas investigators (for example, Havighurst, 1961), lower-class adolescents tend to be more present oriented than are middle-class ones, and they are less willing than are the latter to sacrifice present gains for possible future ones. In terms of the Spindler concept, then, they are likely to be oriented towards emergent values. The upper class on the other hand, is seen by Havighurst (1961) as 'idiosyncratic, combining a traditional conservatism with a high degree of individual variability'.

Granted that the truncated sample was not a result of deliberate choice, can it be seen in retrospect to possess any special merits? Perhaps it does, for the middle-class adolescents may well be the future leaders of social change. According to Riesman (1961), it is the middle class that '. . . first perceives social change of a noncataclysmic sort: it constitutes the nervous system of society, vulnerable to news and to what is new. The middle class mans the communications and research industries including teaching . . .' That the middle class in society acts as a nerve centre is an apt analogy; it suggests that because of its relations to the whole framework of society, the middle class is especially susceptible ('vulnerable') to change, and should be the most rewarding spot in the organism to test for vitality.

Examination of Variables

The data were analysed to enable an examination to be made of the relationship to value orientations of a number of personal, home and school variables, which included:

> sex and age of adolescents,
> location of home, and
> type of school attended.

Sex: With respect to the sex variable, only on the time dimension were boys significantly more traditional than girls. On both the morality and the achievement subscales girls *tended* to be more traditional than boys, while on the dimension of autonomy the former were *significantly* more traditional than the latter (Table 8.2). In the study made by Thompson (1961) of students in central Californian high schools, differences were not significant on mean total traditional-value scores between boys and girls, but the former were significantly higher (at the .05 level) in work success than the latter. Other researchers appear to have given little attention to an examination of the sex variable.

Table 8.2 also indicates that girls considered that their teachers and their best friends were more traditionally oriented than did boys. This difference was particularly noticeable on the achievement and autonomy dimensions. On the time subscale boys saw most referents having a more traditional-value orientation than did girls.

Age: A review of the data on the age variable reveals an overall trend of increasing traditional orientation with advance in age from twelve to

TABLE 8.2

Comparison of Mean Value Scores for Boys and Girls
(n (boys) = 721; (girls) = 526)

		Self	Mother	Father	Teachers	Adults	Best Friends	Most in Class	Teenagers
Morality	B	3.96	4.04	3.99	4.02	3.79	3.79	3.67	3.22
	G	4.02	4.08	4.01	4.06	3.78	3.90	3.73	3.27
	t	1.67	1.78	0.73	1.58	0.13	4.22‡	2.00*	1.45
Time	B	3.32	3.48	3.46	3.58	3.36	3.20	3.13	2.77
	G	3.21	3.33	3.36	3.48	3.25	3.16	3.08	2.77
	t	3.43‡	5.19‡	3.59‡	3.38‡	4.08‡	1.43	2.07†	0.17
Autonomy	B	3.55	3.56	3.57	3.54	3.38	3.38	3.21	2.96
	G	3.64	3.64	3.65	3.74	3.45	3.49	3.29	3.05
	t	3.29†	3.03†	3.04†	4.06‡	3.11	4.26‡	3.45‡	3.46‡
Achievement	B	3.28	3.34	3.38	3.43	3.25	3.15	3.07	2.79
	G	3.32	3.40	3.44	3.52	3.31	3.22	3.08	2.81
	t	1.70	2.73†	2.95†	4.05‡	2.83†	3.21†	0.70	0.76
Totals	B	3.51	3.60	3.59	3.62	3.44	3.38	3.27	2.93
	G	3.56	3.61	3.62	3.68	3.45	3.44	3.29	2.97
	t	2.04*	0.85	1.54	2.16*		3.79‡	1.52	1.91

* significant at .05 level   † significant at .01 level   ‡ significant at .001 level

sixteen years. Significant differences appear at the .01 level of confidence, as shown in Table 8.3. Two subscales, namely 'morality' and 'achievement' reveal no significant value changes, though the directional trend is still from less to more traditional. There would seem to be evidence here to support the contention that *morality* values are relatively stable by the time the child reaches secondary school. That a similar possibility exists for *achievement* merits further investigation, as its implications for primary school curricula and methods are far reaching.

In a comparable study, Thompson (1961) observed differences in

TABLE 8.3

Age Variable: Mean Value Scores and Significant t Ratios

		12 years (n = 137)	13 years (n = 425)	14 years (n = 307)	15 years (n = 157)	16 years (n = 191)
Morality	$\overline{X}$	4.03	3.97	3.94	3.90	4.01
	S.D.	0.44	0.48	0.52	0.51	0.51
	t	←		ns		→
Time	$\overline{X}$	3.19	3.25	3.22	3.32	3.38
	S.D.	0.53	0.51	0.50	0.54	0.59
	t	←		2.74†		→
Autonomy	$\overline{X}$	3.44	3.50	3.55	3.69	3.80
	S.D.	0.45	0.48	0.50	0.52	0.51
	t	←		6.53‡		→
Achievement	$\overline{X}$	3.25	3.31	3.29	3.25	3.32
	S.D.	0.45	0.39	0.42	0.45	0.46
	t	←		ns		→
Totals	$\overline{X}$	3.48	3.51	3.49	3.52	3.63
	S.D.	0.29	0.31	0.33	0.33	0.36
	t	←		3.96‡		→

† $P < .01$ ‡ $P < .001$

traditional values between freshmen and seniors, but found that these differences were not large enough to be significant at the .05 level.

When the inquiry on the age variable was extended to the respondents' reference groups, a relationship appeared between the value orientations of significant others and of the adolescents in the sample. These relationships become apparent when the results are summarized as in Table 8.4.

A concept of 'balance' may be posited here to account for the occurrence of differences in self-values between the age groups on some dimensions but not on others. Possibly the direction of movement from traditional to emergent in the case of father and adults on the morality subscale (Table 8.4) is balanced by the movement of teachers in the opposite direction. A similar explanation may hold for the lack of self values on the achievement subscale: general adult values are counteracted by teacher values. On the time and autonomy dimensions the preponderance of weight on the side of traditional values is evident; because of the lack of counteracting forces it would be surprising if there were not a progressive increase in self traditional values with advancing age from twelve to sixteen years.

TABLE 8.4

Relationship between Changes in Value Orientations of Self and Significant Others, From 11+ to 17+ Years

	Self	Mother	Father	Teachers	Best Friends	Most in Class	Teen-agers	Adults
Morality								
Significant difference	—	—	*	*	—	—	—	*
Direction of change	—	—	T ◊ E	E ◊ T				T ◊ E
Time								
Significant difference	*	*	*	*	*	*	—	—
Direction of change	E ◊ T	E ◊ T	E ◊ T	E ◊ T	E ◊ T	E ◊ T		
Autonomy								
Significant difference	*	*	*	*	*	*	*	—
Direction of change	E ◊ T	E ◊ T	E ◊ T	E ◊ T	E ◊ T	E ◊ T	E ◊ T	
Achievement								
Significant difference	—	—	—	*	—	—	—	*
Direction of change	—	—	—	E ◊ T	—	—	—	T ◊ E
Totals								
Significant difference	*	*	*	*	*	—	—	—
Direction of change	E ◊ T	E ◊ T	E ◊ T	E ◊ T	E ◊ T			

E: emergent; T: Traditional
* difference is significant at least at the .05 level

Location: Results on the home-location variable revealed no significant differences between metropolitan, other urban, and rural respondents on the total value-orientation dimension or on any of the subscales. This conclusion is in accord with the result obtained by Thompson (1961), who, comparing rural with urban residents, found that value patterns of students were not affected by place of residence.

Type of School: When types of schools were compared the only significant difference that appeared between pupil value orientations was on the morality dimension. On this subscale Catholic pupils were the most traditional, with a mean score of 4.00, followed by other-denominational pupils

(3.80), and non-denominational pupils (3.75). The differences between scores for Catholic and other-denominational students, and between Catholic and non-denominational students were each significant at the .01 level of confidence. No significant difference occurred between scores of other-denominational and non-denominational students on the morality or any other dimension.

Thompson (1965), too, found that scale comparisons among schools revealed that parochial school students had significantly higher scores (1 per cent level) in the traditional value of morality—as well as in time orientation, autonomy and achievement—than students attending other schools. Thompson went on to demonstrate what had been inferred by Prince (1957), and Lehmann (1963), namely, that there is a relationship between frequency of church attendance and the degree of traditional orientation of personal values. No attempt was made in the present study to inquire into students' participation in religious activities.

When the analysis of the 'type of school' variable was extended to the type of primary school attended, significant differences between adolescents appeared on the time dimension as well as on the morality subscale. Six categories were used in this analysis (abbreviations used are shown after each category):

1. State school, urban   Su
2. State school, rural   Sr
3. Catholic school, urban   Cu
4. Catholic school, rural   Cr
5. Other-independent school, urban   Ou
6. Other-independent school, rural   Or

Mean scores on the morality scale showed that the most traditional pupils had attended Catholic schools (rural) for their primary education, and that the least traditional had received their primary schooling at urban state and 'other-independent' schools. The relative positions of all categories are shown in Figure 8.2.

FIGURE 8.2

Relationship between Type of Primary School Attended
and the Morality Dimension

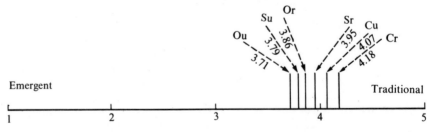

On the time subscale significant differences appeared only between urban Catholic and urban state schools, and between urban Catholic and other-independent rural schools. On this dimension pupils from Catholic urban primary schools were the most traditional, and pupils who had attended other-independent rural schools were the least so.

Values and Academic Achievement

Prince (1957), employing the traditional-emergent (T-E) concept, noted the tendency of high achieving students to have high traditional values (the strength of which declined 'dramatically' with lower grades), and the low achieving students to manifest emergent values. This relationship was found, too, by Thompson (1961) who, using grades earned by students as the criterion of achievement, found that the differences in traditional values among the achievement levels were too large to be considered the result of chance alone.

Where grades are awarded by class teachers it is not surprising that those students whose value orientations are similar to those of their teachers should tend to fare better than their companions who are at cross-purposes with teachers. Furthermore, where academic achievement is gauged largely on diligence and application, one might expect the T-E inventory, with its built-in measures of independence, work success, and future-time orientation to be an effective instrument in separating high achievers from low achievers. Accordingly, the hypothesis tested here was that high achieving students have higher traditional values than low achieving students.

In the Queensland schools that formed the sample, some classes consisted of two or more divisions, the basis of division generally being performance in the previous class, though recourse was also had, by some headteachers, to the results of intelligence tests. Where there were more than two divisions of a class, the group of highest achievers was compared, for purposes of this study, with the lowest achieving group. A total of 202 students was involved: 109 low achievers and 93 high achievers.

A comparison of the traditional-emergent scores obtained by the two groups is shown in Table 8.5.

TABLE 8.5

Comparison of T-E Scores Obtained by High and Low Achieving Students

		Mean	S.D.	t	Significance
Morality	High	3.95	0.53		
	Low	3.83	0.45	1.75	ns
Achievement	High	3.43	0.48		
	Low	3.17	0.52	3.64	.001
Time	High	3.53	0.50		
	Low	3.38	0.50	2.18	.05
Autonomy	High	3.26	0.36		
	Low	3.25	0.41	0.07	ns
Total	High	3.54	0.03		
	Low	3.41	0.03	3.03	.01

The high achievers were found to be significantly more traditionally oriented than were the low achievers, but, as Table 8.5 shows, this was due mainly to the differences on the achievement (work success-sociability) and time (future-present) dimensions.

While this study gives general support to others that have established a relationship between T-E scores and achievement, it does not indicate clearly the explanation for the relationship. Several explanations suggest themselves:

1. Values (particularly those related to achievement and time) affect school achievement directly through greater commitment on the part of 'traditional' students to school learning.
2. Traditionally-oriented students are more in tune with their teachers who reward them in a variety of achievement promoting ways.
3. High achieving students attract different behaviours from their teachers and, as a result, come to adopt the values of their teachers.

These and other 'explanations' could all be supported by psychological theory and empirical research, but there is a need for sophisticated studies to establish the complex interrelationships among the variables.

Conclusion

The teenagers examined in this study are primarily traditional in value commitment, resembling closely the values of their best friends, and occupying a position on a continuum intermediate between an emergent-value orientation of the teenage culture on the one hand, and the highly traditional figures of parents and teachers on the other.

The findings support the Spindler theory of the reflection in the adolescent culture of adult values, and they do *not* support the Parsons concept of alienation of youth from the general culture, or the Coleman theory of the 'spawning' of an adolescent subculture that is antithetic to the ideals and values of the adult society—at least in a traditional-oriented context.

Further speculation on the traditional-value commitment of the sample studied would lead one inevitably to see a possible explanation in the highly authoritarian nature of the Australian independent primary and secondary schools, and of Australian culture in general, with an emphasis on traditional moral values, dedication to the production of 'successful' (in the examination sense) young men and women, and promotion of the future-time ethic.

Lacking previous measures of traditional-emergent orientation in the Australian setting, it is not possible to pronounce upon any *movement* in values among the adult population, or teenagers generally, or even the adolescents attending Queensland independent schools in particular. However, using the present research as a starting point, the study of values may profitably be extended in several directions to include:

(a) longitudinal studies with proper controls, to estimate the influence of the school in changing values;

(b) studies of government-school pupils, to allow for an objective assessment of the contribution of both the independent and the state schools towards the formation of student values;

(c) studies of other reference groups, such as clergymen and youth leaders, for the purpose of examining the ambit of their influence on youth values; and

(d) studies of values at the primary and at the tertiary level of education, that may provide useful insights into the cognitive and the affective development of students at these levels.

Both the present study and the follow-up studies suggested above are based on the proposition that adolescent values warrant the attention of educators. If we subscribe to this proposition we are led to attach importance to the discovery of the sources of values, the means by which they are transmitted, and the methods by which their learning can be most effectively promoted. There are challenges here for the investigator in the field of pure research, as well as for the administrator, the teacher and the parent.

References

Anderson, C. C., 1961: Response of adolescents to American tests of value and character. *Canadian Education and Research Digest*, 1, 4, 71-77.

Bidwell, C. E., King, S. H., Finnie, B. and Scarr, H. A., 1963: Undergraduate careers: Alternatives and determinates. *School Review*, 17, 299-316.

Coleman, J. S., 1961: *The Adolescent Society*. The Free Press, Glencoe, Ill.

Dressel, P. L. and Mayhew, L. B., 1954: *General Education, Exploration in Evaluation*. American Council in Education, Washington, D.C.

Epperson, David C., 1964: A re-assessment of indices of parental influence in the Adolescent Society. *American Sociological Review*, 29, 93-96.

Havighurst, Robert J., 1961: Social class influences on American education. In N. B. Henry (Ed.), *Social Forces Influencing American Education*. *NSSE Yearbook*, LX, Pt II, University of Chicago Press, Chicago, Ill.

Lehmann, I. J., 1963: Some socio-cultural differences in attitudes and values. *Journal of Educational Sociology*, 36, 1, 1-10.

Pressey, S. L. and Jones, A. W., 1955: 1923-1953 and 20-60 age changes in moral codes, anxieties and interests. *Journal of Psychology*, 39, 485-502.

Prince, R. H., 1957: A study of the relationship between individual values and administrative effectiveness in the school situation. Unpublished doctoral dissertation, University of Chicago.

Prince, R. H., 1958: Values study questions: Booklet instructions. University of Chicago, Chicago, Ill.

Riesman, David, 1961: The psychological effects of social change. *Journal of Social Issues*, quoted in N. B. Henry (Ed.), *Social Forces Influencing American Education*. *NSSE Yearbook*, LX, Pt II, University of Chicago Press, Chicago, Ill.

Thompson, O. E., 1961: Student values—traditional or emergent. *California Journal of Educational Research*, 12, 3, 132-143.

Thompson, O. E., 1965: High school students and their values. *California Journal of Educational Research*, 16, 5, 217-227.

Part V
The Institutional Context

9

The Institutional Context

Bruce J. Biddle

SLIGHTLY more than a decade ago, Neal Gross (1956) observed that a systematic study of the school as an organization had yet to be made. Although this observation is no longer true, there are still very few studies of the organizational properties of schools. Often we must make decisions about the organization of education without adequate, empirically-based knowledge about the effects of our decisions. How will the size of our schools affect the interaction of pupils or the professional life of teachers? What difference does it make when a school is organized into academic departments, or when a curricular innovation is introduced? What changes are introduced when interschool athletics are emphasized or de-emphasized? More crucially, how does the organization of education affect the learning of pupils? Until very recently such questions were decided by administrative fiat. Now we are beginning to believe that it is possible to conceptualize and study the properties of schools as organizations—and ultimately to plan for schools that will optimize both learning and other desired goals of education.

This chapter considers the problems of conceptualizing the school as an organization and of studying the effects of its characteristics on desired goals of education. It is broken into two broad sections. The first of these considers the school as an organization—the concept of organization, peculiar properties of schools, tasks of the school, and the school as a social system. The second is concerned with conceptualizing properties that may vary from school to school, and with the effects of these properties on pupil learning and other goals. Of necessity, this latter section must be speculative, since studies of the effects of school properties on learning are difficult to find. The chapter concludes with observations about the need for research.

The School as an Organization

We do not always think of the school as an organization. Indeed, a simple, one-room school exhibits few characteristics in common with other forms of organization such as factories, offices, or political parties. However, most pupils today are educated in larger schools, and larger schools certainly exhibit many features in common with other types of organization—features such as a bureaucratic structure, job specialization, and frequent committee meetings. Thus, it is useful to begin by considering the general characteristics of organizations and by discussing their applications to schools.

Organizational Characteristics

The study of organizations may be said to have begun with the pioneering work of Weber (1922), but many writers have added insights into the nature of the complex phenomena represented by modern organizations (for example, Barnard, 1938; Parsons, 1951; March & Simon, 1958; Bakke, 1959; Cyert & March, 1959; Hopkins, 1961, and Etzioni, 1961). Finding a consensus of specifications for organizational characteristics is therefore difficult. Let us take, however, two example definitions from recent studies of the school as an organization.

> Simply stated an organization consists of deliberate arrangements among groups for doing things. . . . (1) arrangements for coordinating the activities of (2) coalitions of groups that have a collective identity for (3) the purpose of accomplishing certain tasks. (Fraser, 1967.)
> An organization can be defined as: (1) stable patterns of interaction (2) among coalitions of groups having a collective identity (e.g., a name and a location), (3) pursuing interests and accomplishing given tasks, and (4) coordinated through a system of authority. (Corwin, 1966.)

These two definitions are reasonably similar and allow us to identify a number of characteristics presumed to appear within organizations. Let us look at these.

Collective Identity: The organization has a collective identity that is recognized by both its members and by others. Unlike social classes, which may or may not be recognized by their members, we presume that organizations have a corporate identity that is recognized by all. P.S. 91 may have somewhat 'less' of an identity than a Groton, Eton, or Geelong Grammar, but it is still very much of a 'thing' to its pupils, teachers, and community constituents.

Coalitions of Groups: Organizations are made up of more than a single, interacting group, and those groups form into coalitions within the organization. In most organizations, the coalitions are given titles which serve to separate personnel into a series of disjoint positions or *offices*. In schools, for example, 'pupils' are distinct from 'teachers', who may also be distinct from the 'headmaster', the 'psychologist', the 'dietician', and so forth. Groups forming within organizations may be composed of repretatives of one or more offices. Within the classroom, for example, one normally finds a teacher and many pupils. Within the staff meeting both teachers and the headmaster are found. Within the teachers' lounge, however, are usually found only teachers.

Tasks: Organizations are operated for the purpose of accomplishing certain tasks, generally tasks that are understood by all. Whether or not the tasks now performed by organizational activity were intended by the founders or not, certain collective ends may be observed to result from organizational activity. As used in this context, organizational tasks are corporate accomplishments and distinct from individual motivations. Corporate tasks such as the socialization of pupils are characteristic of all schools, whether or not, for example, the individual teacher is motivated by kindness or sadism. Organizations that lose their tasks may persist because of the individual needs of their members, but it is more likely that the organization will either seek out an alternate task or will cease to function. Of course, organizations must accommodate to some extent the needs of their members in addition to tasks they perform. How the organization accommodates both tasks and individual needs we shall see below.

Coordination System: Activities within the organization are to some extent coordinated through a system of rules, and usually by an authority structure. Organizations are thus similar to games in that persons who enter them agree to abide by a set of rules which specify rights and duties for office holders. Moreover, organizations and games are also similar in that the rules are presumed to be conveniences only—ways of doing things that are accepted for the moment but which may be changed in the future if conditions warrant. (In this they are different from families, communities or societies, for which the rules of culture are generally sacred and are not subject to rational debate and change.) In many organizations, too, activities are coordinated through a hierarchical structure with occupants of certain offices not only generally able to dictate what others should do, but also more able to adjust the rules of the system. Within the school, for instance, teachers stand above pupils, department chairmen above teachers, headmasters above chairmen—and within the school system, superintendents above headmasters, and so on. Of necessity, rules specify the hierarchical powers and responsibilities of each office in the organization. They also generally spell out the activities related to task accomplishment and individual needs. Thus, in the typical organization, rules are stated concerning *authority, task accomplishment* and *individual needs*. (Teachers have specific but limited authority over pupils; teachers must perform instructional duties; teachers may stay at home when ill.)

Stable Interaction: Organizations are also presumed to exhibit stable patterns of interaction among their members. In the school, for example, classroom behaviour is reasonably orderly and deferential whereas pupil interaction outside the classroom tends to be boisterous; patterns of friendship appear and persist; a given school exhibits predictability in its stating and enforcing of regulations. Some forms of interaction are, in fact, specified by rules, but some are independent of rules, while others exist in violation of rules. Lesson activity within classrooms usually starts promptly at the appointed hour, but most high schools exhibit a peer culture among their pupils that is unanticipated in its rules, and in some schools teachers sneak off to a private location in the cellar to smoke in violation of rules prohibiting it. Organizational interaction, thus, may also be analysed in terms of *authority, task accomplishment* and *individual needs*—and if we make this analysis we find that some interactions are prescribed by rules, others exist without rules, and still others violate rules.

In summary, *an organization can be conceived as a corporate entity composed of a set of offices whose members are tied together by both rules and stable forms of interaction, these latter reflecting the tasks of the organization, the authority structure tying offices together, and the needs of individuals making up the offices.*

Tasks of the School

It is clear, then, that schools—particularly large ones—are similar in some respects to other forms of organization. They are also distinct, however, and it is now useful to consider some of the ways in which they are different from medical, religious or product-producing organizations. The first of the differences we shall consider is the set of tasks that characterize schools.

Pupil Socialization: The first order of business of schools is the education of pupils; indeed, pupil socialization is normally considered to be the raison d'être of education. Once upon a time the socialization of pupils was the only task of education. This task is, in fact, so central that it has been used as a criterion by which the educational institution is defined (Wilson, forthcoming).

The task of pupil socialization includes, of course, more than simply 'pumping facts into pupils'. Many schools accept within this task the goals of inculcating values, beliefs and norms felt necessary for citizenship or for the accomplishment of adult roles. Thus, 'education transmits a common cultural fund to the next generation and in the process helps to bring hordes of young barbarians to adult ways that are continuous with the past' (Clark, 1962).

The task of socializing the young is, of course, shared by the school with another social institution—the family. It may be wondered why schools were first developed to supplement the earlier forms of socialization that were probably carried on exclusively within a family context. Even today there exist primitive societies in which no schools have yet appeared. The usual explanation given is that with the development of a greater fund of knowledge to be learned, and with the appearance of occupational specializations which took parents away from the home, parents were no longer competent, nor did they have the time, to socialize their own children adequately.

This task is a conservative one in several senses of the word. The school acts so as to conserve the traditions of the society, to constrain the pace of social change, to produce adults of the next generation who have learned to value the traditions of the past. As we shall see below, this conservative task sometimes generates conflicts with other radical tasks schools are also called on to perform.

Pupil Allocation: 'Every society must make some provision for deciding which of its members shall occupy the various positions in the society and perform the roles necessary for its continuation and development' (Goslin, 1965). In contemporary societies, this task is usually assigned to the school, although other institutions may provide supplementary services such as testing agencies, counselling bureaux, and university admissions boards.

In more traditional societies, various ascribed or inherited characteristics have been used in allocating individuals to positions. Family background or title, race, religion, birth-order and sex have all been used to determine occupation, or access to desired social experiences—including higher education. However, these arbitrary criteria are less than ideally suited to the needs of contemporary society where it is important not only to select the right man for each job, but also where many years of training must be given to those who will perform these complex jobs.

Thus, the school is given not only the task of general socialization, but also the more complex task of culling through its pupil population, differentiating those with varying abilities and interests, and providing training that is appropriate to each group. This complex task is accomplished differently in various societies. In some countries (such as England until very recently) competitive examinations are used to separate pupils into educational groups who are then sent to separate schools for different adult occupations. Thus, the English 'grammar school' prepared pupils for university entrance, while the 'secondary modern school' trained for commercial occupations. In other countries (such as the United States) a single, large high school will attempt to offer *all* curricular streams under one roof.*

The Control of Knowledge: Given the transcendent task of instructing the next generation in the knowledge of the past, it is not unreasonable that schools have also been called upon to conserve and develop knowledge for its own sake. This tendency can be seen most clearly within the university where both libraries and research laboratories abound, but it is also becoming true for larger secondary schools whose library and research equipment sometimes exceeds those of impoverished universities.

---

*The author is tempted to observe that whereas the older English system appeared to be inequitous because of its inflexibility and social-class bias, the American system tends to lead towards ever increasing, gigantic secondary schools. In some countries, such as France and Australia, this dilemma appears to be 'resolved' by restricting upper-level secondary education to only those select few who have a chance for university admission.

Although a library may be used for the conservation of the past, the development of new knowledge inevitably challenges existing ways. Thus, the task of controlling knowledge is a radical one which is difficult to reconcile with the conservative task of pupil socialization. The conflict between 'teaching and research' appears in a number of guises. Since research is more highly valued in contemporary society, university staff are sometimes encouraged to devote their energies to its accomplishment and to relegate teaching to the status of a necessary evil. Citizens' groups are sometimes offended when their children are taught to think for themselves rather than to honour age-long verities. As is true for the other tasks undertaken by contemporary schools, the discovery of knowledge is not restricted to education, nor has it always appeared within educational institutions. However, when it does so appear, it tends to complicate the structure of schools and to make life more complex for teachers.

Other Tasks: The three tasks already reviewed are traditional for schools. For many years, schools in Western countries have socialized pupils, engaged in pupil allocation and controlled knowledge. Recently, however, a number of other tasks have begun to appear within schools. One of these is simply the task of *baby-sitting*. As more and more mothers have acquired professional educations, as women's rights for entry into various occupational fields have been confirmed, more mothers have wanted to work and have sought to unload their children into schools that would make this possible. One effect of this pressure has been to reduce the age of school entrance. A kindergarten year is nearly universal in American public schools now, whereas, a generation ago, public education generally began at grade 1. Slum children in the United States are now being given an even earlier year of education in 'Head Start' programmes, and middle-class mothers are now pressuring for funds to establish such programmes universally. Interestingly, educators have (tortuously) recognized that they were, in fact, providing baby-sitting services by institutionalizing a kindergarten dogma that delayed formal instruction until the child demonstrated 'readiness'.

A related task, which might be termed *time-occupancy*, is beginning to appear in urban settings, where it is desired to keep pupils in school as long as possible so as to delay their entry into the job market. The problem is that in an automated society there are few jobs for unskilled hands. Pupils who drop out of school, thus, have few opportunities for employment and are often found on street corners, merely 'hanging around' or engaged in illegal behaviour. If a way can be found to keep them in education, then their time too can be occupied with acceptable activity. Thus, schools are urged to provide a curriculum that is attractive enough to compete with the lures of idleness and recreation.

Quite a different problem is faced by the school in a small community which is often called upon to serve tasks of *public entertainment* and *community identification*. The community high school provides a variety of entertainment spectacles, ranging from football games and other sporting events to music and the theatre. It is also, often in smaller communities, the only institution which truly brings together the community, and its building and social events are a major source of community identification and pride. This is strikingly evident when one studies the consolidation of rural schools in America. Smaller towns in the Midwest which lose their schools tend to die; those lucky enough to acquire the consolidated high school tend to prosper.

'The school also plays an important part in the courtship process by providing a setting in which boys and girls can interact informally and participate in a variety of social activities under the supervision of adults' (Goslin, 1965). In serving the task of *courtship*, the school has begun to take over functions that were performed in an earlier age by church and family. Many social events are now programmed within the typical high school, ranging from dances to parties, which appear to have little relevance to the traditional tasks of pupil socialization, pupil allocation and the control of knowledge. And yet, busy parents would rather have the courtship of their children carried out under school supervision than leave this task to adolescents themselves.

It should be clear that the added tasks we have been discussing—those of baby-sitting, time-occupancy, public entertainment, community identification, and courtship—are likely to interfere to some extent with the traditional, academically-relevant tasks of the school. When funds and staff effort are committed to these expanded goals, less effort and fewer funds are available for instruction, allocation and research. Understandably, then, these added tasks are sometimes attacked as being 'frills'. This attack is most likely to come from educational traditionalists, from those committed to classical subjects, single-sex schools, or those most concerned with preparing our brightest youngsters for university entrance. However, it seems reasonable that if we are to provide universal education for *all* pupils, including the less able, we must also provide curricular experiences for them that are attractive and meaningful at all levels. And if schools are to take over tasks that are abandoned by churches, families and other related institutions, we must also make the necessary effort to see that they are adequately supported and staffed.

Also, additional tasks are sometimes imposed on schools, although neither of these is ever seen as a 'frill'. Some schools are called upon to *maintain subgroup traditions*. This is characteristically true of parochial schools operated by religious denominations such as those sponsored by Roman Catholics, Anglicans, or Friends. It is also true, in addition, for privately-financed schools that represent a particular social class or occupational community and even tends to appear within urban schools that serve a community dominated by an ethnic minority. Schools attempting such a task will often provide not only informal socialization into accent, manners and interests appropriate to membership in the subgroup but, in addition, unique curricula not found in other schools. Thus, one is likely to find 'moral philosophy' taught in Catholic schools and 'African history' taught in Negro ghetto schools. Societies which accept the existence of privately-financed schools that represent subgroup interests face a constant dilemma—how much control will they enforce on these private schools and how much separatism will they tolerate? Too much control leads to resentment and open conflict; too little to pluralistic standards of knowledge and conduct.

Finally, schools are also sometimes seen as agents of *social reform*. A major example of this in America is the socialization to American ways of generations of immigrant children representing many other languages and cultures. Today, American schools are being called on to 'solve' the problems of Negro pupils and to prepare the children—many of whom come from impoverished or broken homes, all of whom face problems of discrimination and prejudice—for adequate adjustments as adults and job-holders. This call comes in many forms; schools are asked to accept pupils from another school district who are to be transported to their doors by buses, curricular innovations are to be attempted, citizens are to be allowed to have something to say about standards and techniques, and so on. Whether or not schools can in fact accomplish the reforms that are laid upon them is moot; however, many educators are idealists, and schools can usually be counted upon to 'try'.

The School as a Social System

Another way in which schools are distinct from other types of organizations is in the complement of social positions, or offices, of which they are made up. Although many of these positions are familiar to the reader, at least in theory, let us see what kinds of investigations have been made of them.

Pupils: The majority position within all schools is that of pupils, who constitute better than ninety-five per cent of the personnel of the school in most cases. Several things characterize the pupil position which makes it different from other positions of the school and many other positions found in organizations. For one thing, pupils are not members of the staff of the organization; they are, rather, *clients* who are to be processed by the organization. Most of the tasks previously discussed for the school are stated as changes to be induced in pupils by school activities. In this sense, then, the school is a person-processing organization, as is the hospital or army training camp. Person-processing organizations may be contrasted with product-producing organizations (*see* Rhea, 1964) in several ways. For one thing, since clients are more complex than physical products, and since they normally do not spend more than a fraction of their time within the organization, the organization's control over clients is usually less secure than over products. For another, changes in clients are harder to measure than changes in products. Again, organizations processing clients are less efficient since they must, of necessity, spend parts of their energy on consummatory activities—keeping their customers happy—and must keep task-relevant effort within acceptable bounds.

Pupils are not only clients, however. They are also minors, and their attendance within the school is usually mandatory. As minors, they are both presumed to be immature in their judgements and capabilities and are protected by laws and customs that do not generally apply to adults. Since their attendance at school is mandatory, staff members of the school cannot count on appropriate pupil motivations for learning at all times. These facts constrain both the rules of the school and staff-pupil interaction into forms that would not normally appear among positions within other organizations. For example, pupils are 'not allowed' into the halls of the school without a pass, teachers must not physically touch a pupil of the opposite sex, elaborate strategies are employed for attracting the attention and motivating recalcitrant pupils, and so on.

Given the vast number of pupils in schools, it is surprising that so little research has been done on the pupils' role. The two major studies reported to date (those of Gordon, 1957 and Coleman, 1961) were both concerned with secondary pupils.* Gordon's research was carried out within a medium-sized, public high school in Indiana and used techniques of participant observation, focused interview and questionnaire. Gordon discovered that students' dominant interests were in nonacademic sectors of school activity; however, as grade level advanced so did students' conformity to academic expectations. For boys, athletics was the major status-determiner, combined with conformity to peer norms bearing on social behaviour. Status among the girls was determined by dress, school service and 'personality'. However, teachers were able to influence status by appropriate use of the grading system. Thus, the picture presented by Gordon is one of a strong pupil peer culture that interprets, moulds, and sometimes defeats the official policies of the school and the behaviours of school staff members.

Gordon's study was, of course, limited to a single school. Coleman, in contrast, studied pupils in ten different high schools, including one Catholic parochial school. Coleman's data were obtained from questionnaires administered to pupils, teachers and parents from each school. In general, Coleman's data support theses advanced by Gordon. For boys, common themes of value-orientation included athletic prowess, dating success and resources for 'fun'. Girls were concerned about good looks, clothes, personality and extracurricular activity. Both boys and girls were self-segregated into cliques that were clearly segregated within sex and school-class categories, and pupils within each clique were more homogeneous in their values than were pupils as a whole. Interestingly, Coleman attributed much of the weakness of academic peer values to the peculiar position of interschool competition in athletics. His argument was bolstered by data from two additional schools which lacked strong athletic programmes. In these schools academic values were more salient for both boys and girls. Unfortunately, Coleman's hypotheses have not been tested outside of the American school population, nor have adequate studies been carried out of the differences in pupils' role between coeducational schools and sex-segregated schools.

---

*However, Barker, *et al.* (1961) present comparative data on the classroom behaviour of American and British primary pupils (*see also* Barker & Barker, 1963).

Teachers: Teachers constitute the second most numerous social position within the school. However, in contrast with pupils, teachers are of course staff members. They are, in fact, the workers whose efforts within the school correspond roughly with the assembly-line employee, the pick-and-shovel miner, and others who are at the bottom of the organizational status-hierarchy and who do most of the real 'work' around the place. Teachers are thus called upon to have relationships with two contrasting groups. Within the classroom the teacher holds a position of high status and authority, for hers is the responsibility for accomplishing many of the tasks of the school through instructional efforts with her pupils. Outside of the classroom, however, she finds herself among a group of professional peers who share the lowest status within a staff hierarchy. Depending on how the school is organized, she may have to 'take orders' from a principal (or headmaster), his assistant, a departmental chairman, a subject matter specialist, an inspector, directives issued from higher authorities, and such specialists as psychologists.

Teachers constitute the largest professional group within Western societies. In the United States, for instance, there are over a million primary and secondary teachers, and more are needed every year to staff schools for the expanding population. The enormous size of the teacher profession has produced several effects. Teachers everywhere are in short supply and are generally paid less than other professionals with comparable training. Again, teaching has tended to attract to its ranks persons whose ability lies in the middle range—and in the United States, and to a lesser extent elsewhere, more women than men. And again, within all countries special training colleges or institutions have been set up for the preparation of teachers whose curricula are suspect in the minds of scholars representing traditional disciplines within the universities. These factors have caused some analysts to wonder whether teaching is, in fact, a profession or not. In some Western countries, for example, teachers are collectively represented by militant teachers' unions rather than professional organizations. However, the spread of unionism among teachers has been retarded in the United States by Balkanization of school districts into more than 20,000 autonomous units and the predominance of women in the field.

It is difficult to overestimate the degree to which the activity of schools depends on the teacher. In contrast with other organizations, even with other person-processing organizations such as hospitals, education is strongly labour-intensive. By far the major costs of education are teacher salaries, and to date few devices have been invented that will reliably substitute for the omnipresent classroom instructor. Yet it is a paradox that few systems have been devised for either improving or evaluating the success of classroom instruction by the teacher. Indeed, since little objective research has been done on classroom processes to date, little is yet known about the ingredients of successful teaching (*see* Chapter 14). As a result, teacher-training has come to be based more upon the inspiration of teacher-trainees, and the provision of information for them that will presumably facilitate their future activities, than upon clear knowledge of teaching strategies that work. In addition, in most schools the teacher's classroom is a sacrosanctum in which the mystic arts of instruction are conducted with only occasional intrusion from other teachers, the head-master, an inspector or (thankfully rarely) parents.

A good deal of research has now been conducted on the role of the teacher. In general, this research may be summed up under three headings. First, several studies have been published dealing with the professional careers of teachers. Waller's (1932) pioneering work presumably falls into this category, as does the early work of Donovan (1938). Probably more representative of this work, however, are the thoughtful researches of Becker (1962) and Peterson (1964) who have studied career lines, pro-blems and rewards of being a teacher. A summary exposition may be found in Stiles (1957).

Second, by now several hundred studies have been published dealing with norms and expectations held for teachers by teachers themselves, parents, pupils, school administrators and others. A general summary of this field is provided by Biddle (1969) who describes several stereotypes reported about teachers in a number of studies. Among other things: 'Teachers generally felt that their position is held in low esteem by members of the com-munity at large and that they do not receive appropriate rewards for their efforts. . . . Teachers were generally felt by others to be non-aggressive, acquiescent, and to sin primarily by omission rather than commission. In addition, both teachers and other subjects expressed concern over the fact that in many (especially smaller) communities teachers are expected to maintain their professional roles during off-duty hours and in settings outside of the school.' Whether or not these stereotypes hold for other societies than the United States is not yet known, although it is noteworthy that the vast bulk of the studies reviewed by Biddle were of American origin. However, studies of norms held for British teachers are reported by Musgrove (1961) and Taylor (1962), and a major comparative study of the teacher's role in Australia, Britain, New Zealand and the United States is just now being completed (Biddle, et al., 1968).

Third, a number of studies have now been published in which the behaviour of the teachers has actually been observed. Most, if not all of these studies, have been conducted in the classroom, so little information is presently available concerning teacher-teacher, teacher-principal or teacher-parent interaction. General reviews of this field are provided by Adams (Chapter 14) and Biddle (1967) who note several general charac-teristics of teacher behaviour, among them being teacher domination of classroom communication, lack of overt displays of affectivity, the high rate of teacher-pupil exchange, the generally boring character of classroom interaction, and teacher focus on pupils who occupy the centre of the classroom. Again, however, the bulk of this research has been carried on within American schools, and it seems likely that British infant schools, Australian schools making use of corporal punishment, or New Zealand primary schools where men teachers can be found at the early grades would exhibit somewhat different patterns (Flanders, 1964; Nuthall & Lawrence, 1965).

Headmasters: If we begin with the very smallest of schools, and then consider schools of larger and larger sizes, we discover administrative hierarchies of ever-increasing complexity. Within the smallest schools (those having but a single teacher) no hierarchy is possible. Schools having fewer teachers than the number of grades taught generally exhibit but a partial hierarchy in which one teacher is 'in charge', though she also carries teaching duties. Only the school which has a full complement of teachers —one for each grade or specialty needed—can afford to employ a separate headmaster or principal, and in some countries it is assumed that headmasters of even large schools will continue to instruct on a reduced schedule. In larger schools yet, particularly in secondary schools, another level appears in the hierarchy, with the appointment of departmental chairmen who are responsible for teachers having common curricular or grade level responsibilities. And, finally, the largest schools may even exhibit a line-and-staff organization with the appointment of an assistant principal, administrative assistants, or secretaries who assist the headmaster in the performance of his administrative duties.

In general, then, most schools exhibit a simple line-type organization with most workers (teachers) involved directly in teaching. The typical primary school involves an 'assembly line' arrangement whereby pupils, collected into grades defined rigidly by age, are passed along from one teacher to another until they pass out of the school. At the secondary level, however, the 'assembly line' is more complex; teachers are responsible for curricular specialties rather than grade levels, and pupils are allowed to choose among a number of curricular offerings although their choices may be constrained by university entrance requirements or other goal regions. Neither system involves many non-teaching personnel. However, as the school grows in size and complexity, as new educative devices are developed, and as expanded tasks are accepted by the school, it tends both towards the additional blurring of 'assembly line' procedures and the introduction of non-teaching specialists. Curricular specialists appear at the primary level, such as music, art and physical education instructors. Primary pupils are offered curricular choices, such as alternative foreign languages. Several levels of instruction are offered within a given subject to suit different pupil abilities. Non-teaching specialists appear, including psychologists, dieticians, health personnel and operators of teaching machines or educational television.

The role of the headmaster, then, shifts radically when one moves from small to larger schools and is being modified today as we move away from 'assembly line' education to more complex models. At a minimum, the principal is responsible for organizing the efforts of a few teachers, setting and maintaining curricular standards, pupil discipline and morale, and contacts between the school and its supporting educational bureaucracy and community. At a maximum, the principal's job is one of great complexity, involving a staff of more than 100 persons and a pupil population of more than 2,000, several levels of administrative hierarchy, a physical plant worth more than a million dollars, a curriculum as complex as that of a small university, and staff members representing a variety of both teaching and non-teaching jobs. Interestingly, in most Western countries there are no formal training procedures for preparing headmasters for their positions. Most headmasters are former teachers who have 'come up from the ranks', and the majority are men. Only in the United States are formal training procedures for school administrators well established. In America, the headmaster must usually earn a doctorate in educational administration before being considered for responsibility in a larger school. However, there is as little empirically-based information concerning the actual details of the headmaster's job as there is available concerning teaching. Thus, in reviewing the available evidence, Erickson (1969) concludes that there is little evidence that administrators do a better job after receiving training for their professions!

But little research has yet been performed on the role of principal. Perhaps the best single study completed is that of Gross and his associates (Gross & Herriott, 1965) although a few smaller studies have also been conducted as doctoral theses. Once again, still less research has been done on the headmaster's role outside of the United States. Two characteristics of the headmaster's role are worth noting, however. For one thing, whether or not teaching is to be considered a profession, headmasters clearly consider themselves professional. It is common to find headmasters formed into professional associations which have a regional or national affiliation. Moreover, these associations commonly attempt to restrict entrance into the profession by requiring applicants to demonstrate job-related competencies of one kind or another. For another, the headmaster suffers from an ambivalence common to all 'regional managers'—local interests versus those of the home office. In the case of the principal, local interests are those of the school and the community it serves, and success in his job means involvement in the many problems of day-to-day school management. However, most headmasters also have a 'home office' in the form of an external bureaucracy to which the headmaster must relate if he is to hope for promotion. If he spends too much time within his school he will be passed over, no matter how brilliant his efforts; but if he orients himself too closely with those from the central bureaucracy, his 'success' may be built on but shallow accomplishments. In time, of course, many headmasters become 'company men', tending to identify with the system rather than with either the school or with the teaching profession, although a few school-identifying principals can be found in stronger schools.

Other School Personnel: As previously indicated, smaller schools may not in fact exhibit any staff members who do not teach. However, most medium-sized schools have at least a janitor, and if the school boasts a lunch programme it will also have food handlers. Within the modern larger school one finds a variety of non-teaching specialists including psychologists and counsellors, sub-professional teacher aids, equipment specialists and administrative personnel. With the exception of a few of these specializations—notably counselling and school psychology—most of these occupations are neither standardized nor as yet professionalized. An excellent study of the role of school psychologist is available however (Runkel, 1962), and a study of the role of the teacher aid will shortly be published (Bennett & Falk, forthcoming).

Parents and the Community: Schools normally have two major sources of external pressure upon them—the community in which they are physically embedded and the school system under which they are chartered. In the case of the community, this pressure comes from several sources: from parents, school boards, and from citizens' groups and other ad hoc sources. Let us discuss each of these briefly.

Parents are, in fact, secondary clients of the school's efforts. Although it is the pupils who will learn or not learn (and be happy or unhappy) in school, pupils are but minors and their interests will be reflected in the attitudes and beliefs of their parents. Thus, parents are important reference persons for the school, although normally they are not physically present in the school except on special occasions. Parental interaction with the school is handled in a number of ways. In some countries (for example, in the United States and New Zealand) parental involvement with the school is maximized, parents are encouraged to discuss their children's problems with school staff, and parents are brought to the school regularly for meetings with teachers and social events. In other countries (such as Britain) schools have traditionally taken the position of keeping parental involvement at a minimum, believing that education is properly the province of trained professionals. In still other countries (such as Australia) parents are allowed only to participate in non-curricular matters.

Within the wider community, parental interests in the school are merged with the interests of all adult citizens, and usually the school has some sort of formal procedure whereby it contacts the community as a whole. In some countries (again, in the United States and New Zealand) it is traditional to have an appointed or elected school (or education) board which represents the interests of the community. Although procedures vary, normally there is but a single board for each school district (which incorporates a number of schools), and under most state constitutions the school board is, in fact, the legal body which sets up the school. In the United States school boards have a wide range of powers, including the setting of standards and salaries, with state involvement in education usually limited to the provision of per capita revenue to the board for minimal pupil education. More than 20,000 separate boards presently exist in the United States with vast disparities among them as to standards of education. In New Zealand, two types of school boards exist—provincial educational boards, and boards of governors for certain secondary schools or boards of managers for technical colleges. However, none of these bodies has the wide range of decision-making powers of boards in America, and educational procedures are more homogeneous throughout the state.

Finally, schools must also deal with ad hoc pressure groups and citizens' committees as representatives of segments of their community. Since school boards are normally constituted of higher-status persons, representatives of ethnic minorities or special-interest groups sometimes feel that their interests are not adequately represented in the operation of the school. Organized pressure groups may make their impact directly on the school (by persuasion or coercion of school personnel), on the school board, or on the legislature ultimately responsible for education.

The School System: Most schools are not autonomous organizations but, rather, are incorporated into a school system or district. In some countries all publicly-supported schools are, in fact, organized into a single embracing system with various sub-units, levels of hierarchy, and an entrenched bureaucracy. In other countries, states, provinces or districts may be given the task of organizing education. In the United States, schools are organized through local school systems whose boundaries are usually roughly coterminus with the sphere of influence of the community. (However, it is also true that American school systems are loosely tied together through regional and state-wide affiliations and influence.)

In general, visible staff positions within the school system represent hierarchical levels standing above those of the school. Thus, the active teacher who has worked himself into a position of responsibility in the school, or perhaps to a headmastership, can look forward to the possibility of additional promotions to a system-wide post. Methods of organizing the school system vary widely, however. Most American systems are headed by a school superintendent who is the chosen administrator of the school board. Under the superintendent serve a variety of administrative assistants, curriculum specialists, architects, fiscal experts and others concerned with the truly big business of education. In countries where education is organized on a state-wide basis there is usually an education director who serves at the behest of the state legislature. He is also seconded by assistants, curriculum specialists, architects, fiscal experts and the like. Most larger systems also exhibit regionalism, with a certain amount of diffusion of power to regional offices. Finally, state school systems following the British model tend also to have a corps of inspectors—representatives of the central authority whose responsibility it is to visit, advise and rate individual teachers on their classroom performances. (In American schools the rating of teachers is generally the responsibility of the principal.)

An excellent study has been completed on the role of the American superintendent of schools (Gross, Mason & McEachern, 1958), but, again, the writer is unfamiliar with similar studies done in other countries. It is interesting to note, however, that schools everywhere have tended to find themselves more and more involved in bureaucracy. As is true for other types of organization, the consolidation of small units (schools) into larger units (school systems) has tended to have a number of effects that are both supportive and interruptive of the accomplishment of school tasks. For one thing, it is usually more economical to operate a group of schools than but a single school—cheaper rates may be obtained through bulk purchases, and certain services (such as an educational television station) need be provided but once for a school system containing hundreds of schools. For another, basic values of Western democracies stress both the necessity of equalizing educational opportunity and the desirability of physical mobility. It is difficult to achieve these values without some degree of effort centralization in education.

And yet, bureaucracies also tend towards rigidity and to be bound by rules that stifle individual initiative. Thus, teachers in a large school system may find that they are constrained by standardized texts, curricula and procedures that are inappropriate for a particular pupil population, or that they are bound by rules that were created for administrative convenience rather than for educational benefit, or that their promotion is determined by tenure or marital status rather than by the excellence of this instruction. The most questionable school bureaucracies are those that are 'closed'— which systematically restrict contact between themselves and outside sources of pressure such as parents, community representatives or the universities. The classic examples of such 'closed' systems often operate their own teacher-training colleges and restrict entry into the system to teachers who they, themselves, have trained. Some 'closed' systems may become self-perpetuating, archaic and even bigoted, oligarchies. It is possible, however, to open up school systems to local interests—by decentralization of authority over some issues, by appropriate use of citizens' groups, by the use of teacher aids chosen from the local community, by cooperating with the universities and being open to innovations and research.

School Characteristics and Pupil Learning

Given the complex nature of the school, it is reasonable to presume that many organizational characteristics of schools may be conceptualized and studied for their effects on pupil learning. Schools differ from one another in terms of their identity, the social positions of which they are composed and the incumbents of those positions, the rules by which they operate, the forms of interaction they exhibit, their tasks, authority structures, and needs of both staff members and their clients. They also may be differentiated in terms of their relationships with the community and school system in which they are embedded. To list all of these many characteristics would involve the reader in a morass of literally hundreds of distinctions, many of which would turn out to be interrelated. Instead, I shall list only a few of the more salient organizational characteristics of schools that have actually been studied. This listing will be organized into five topics: size, bureaucratization, structure, composition and context.

Size and its Concomitants

Size: Size is an obvious facet along which schools may be differentiated from one another, and, at several points in the chapter, I have used school size to illustrate points in the discussion. Within Western democracies schools range in size from the isolated, single-teacher school involving a mere handful of pupils to urban schools of more than 20,000 pupils and many hundreds of teachers. Although easy to measure, size is merely a 'marker' variable and not in and of itself important. However, size correlates positively with other organizational properties that affect the lives of both pupils and staff members. Corwin (1966), for example, studied twenty-eight schools located in and around Ohio, and found correlations among school size and hierarchicalization, standardization, complexity, and staff turnover. Let us, therefore, turn to some of the organizational characteristics that are most closely related to school size.

Hierarchicalization: Hierarchicalization is the number of 'levels' within the authority structure of the school. The smallest schools have but one level (teachers), larger schools add a second level (the principal), still larger schools add a third level (department chairmen), while the largest schools may have four or more levels. Increasing the numbers of levels of hierarchy has two effects—first, teachers and pupils are more isolated from the efforts of others and may specialize or concentrate more on the task at hand, while second, they are also forced to accommodate the 'red tape' engendered by a multi-level hierarchy. With low levels of hierarchicalization, then, interaction is more diffuse, personal, disorganized. Pupils of multi-level schools should learn more specialized knowledge (including how to operate 'the system'); however, their relationships with staff should be less personal and more 'official'.

Specialization: Closely related to hierarchicalization is specialization—the degree to which specific, rather than general, subjects are taught within the school. Scales measuring specialization may be found in Corwin (1966), and Fraser (1967). From the viewpoint of the teacher, specialization is the degree to which the individual teacher can concentrate on a specific subject matter. In the small school, teachers must often cover two or three fields or grade levels; however, in the larger school, a teacher may not only teach merely mathematics but may concentrate on 'remedial mathematics' or 'first-year algebra'. From the pupil's viewpoint, specialization involves the degree to which concentrated tuition is available in subjects of his interest. In the small high school, for example, only one course in chemistry may be offered, while in the large high school the talented pupil may find a half dozen specialized courses in the same subject. Again, specialization allows for higher levels of instruction, but in specialized schools the pupil is often allowed to neglect other fields in which he has no immediate interest. This problem is most acute in high schools offering *only* a specialized curriculum, such as the Music and Art High School in New York City where pupils can find the finest secondary instruction in orchestral music offered perhaps anywhere in the world, but where pupils can receive but mediocre instruction in the sciences.

Complexity: Hierarchicalization and specialization are but two facets of a more general notion commonly referred to as organizational complexity. Other aspects of complexity involve the division of labour, the number of curricular offerings, the detailedness of rules, and even the physical construction of the school building. Scales for the measurement of complexity appear in Corwin (1966) and Fraser (1967), although the latter author confines his attention primarily to hierarchicalization and specialization components. A complex school should provide the pupil with a wider range of curricular and extracurricular offerings but may also confuse or overwhelm him.

Standardization: Standardization concerns the degree to which procedures within the school are fixed by rule. In all schools the subjects to be taught are set for the school, but in some schools the texts, visual aids, techniques, timing and even manner of presentation may also be standardized. Scales measuring standardization are available in Anderson (1964) and Corwin (1966). As suggested earlier, standardization seems to be a concomitant of size in the sense that economic and administrative forces will conspire to promote standardized practices, even when staff members are determined to resist them. Pupils in schools high on standardization are likely to suffer less variability in instruction or grading but also to be treated less personally or to experience education that is tailored to their individual needs. One cannot help but feel ambivalent about standardization. Whereas the majority or 'average' pupil undoubtedly does well in a highly-standardized setting, few of us are, in fact, 'average'. Since schools are people-processing organizations, and human beings are variable, some standardization must, in fact, be detrimental to the accomplishment of educational tasks.

Anomie: It is reasonable to presume that some students in larger schools suffer through lack of personal contact with others, impersonality of the school bureaucracy, and the predominance of positionally-based rather than personally-based interaction with others. This phenomenon was first identified by Durkheim (1897) as a concomitant of urban life. The anomic process probably reaches some sort of a zenith (or nadir) in the large, American, state university where undergraduate students are often processed endlessly through classes involving hundreds or thousands of students, standardized examinations, television instruction and little or no personal contact with either instructional or counselling staff. However, secondary pupils, too, are prone to anomie, particularly in the urban setting or ethnic ghetto where neither the curriculum nor staff appear to have meaning or sympathy for the needs of pupils.

Activity/Person Ratio: Most of us have a rather firm idea of what constitutes a primary or secondary school, and there tends to be only minor differentiation of either the curriculum or the extracurricular activity structure with increasing size of the school. In the typical high school, for example, there is a minimal mathematics curriculum, and though the large high school offers some additional courses, the rate of differentiation of the curriculum does not match the rate of increase of pupils in the school. Or, to take another example, most American high schools have but a single football team. As the school gets larger its team gets more excellent, but since only a set number can participate, the proportion of boys playing football within the school population declines. In general, then, as size increases there is also an increase in the absolute number of activities within the school but a *decrease* in the number of activities per pupil. This phenomenon has been noted by Barker and Gump (1964) who present data showing that in smaller-sized high schools, where the activity/person ratio is high, activities are generally 'under-manned', and pupils are drawn into a wide variety of experiences. On the other hand, in larger high schools whose activities are more 'expert', the average pupil does not participate in as many of them. This phenomenon can be defeated, of course, by increasing the number of activities proportionate with the number of pupils. In Australian and New Zealand schools, for example, there are often football teams at several levels of competence, and pupils willing to play are drawn into a team representing their own skill level. Similarly, a number of American universities are experimenting with the use of small dormitory units as centres of activities including both competitive athletics and small group study experiences, the latter somewhat similar to the Oxbridge tutorial system. Many high schools are kept from experimenting with activities, however, not only by the rigidities of their bureaucracies but also because of the diffuseness of their goals. A football team, for example, is operated at least as much for public entertainment and community identification as it is for educative experiences, and any attempt to institute multiple football games would interfere with accomplishment of these latter tasks.

In summary, then, with increasing size there tend also to be increases in the levels of hierarchy of the school, in its specialization, in its complexity and standardization, in the anomie suffered by its pupils, and a decrease in its activity/person ratio. Although none of these effects is inevitable, most are likely. This suggests that pupils of larger schools are likely to have a wider choice of curricular alternatives that are taught more expertly, although they will, at the same time, suffer the problems of anomic isolation with fewer informal contacts and fewer pressures to enter both curricular and extracurricular activities. The direct influences of these effects upon pupil learning have not yet been studied, but it is reasonable to presume that pupils attending larger schools will do better on academic achievement tests but may be less broadly educated and less sure of themselves as integrated persons.

Bureaucratization and its Concomitants

Bureaucratization is the tendency for organizations to become managerially dominated. It is composed of a variety of separate facets that tend to be associated with one another, several of which are set forth here. Whereas there is, presumably, some tendency for larger schools (and school systems) to become more bureaucratized, Corwin (1966) advances evidence suggesting the relative independence of bureaucratization and size effects. Such components of bureaucratization as routines, rules, closeness of supervision and employee autonomy were found to be closely interrelated but more or less independent of size effects.* This finding fits well with the common observation that school systems in various countries or states differ sharply in terms of bureaucratization. Those standards, procedures or curricula one school system finds it absolutely necessary to control may be left to the autonomy of individual schools or teachers in another system. Thus, schools of various sizes within a given system are likely to be somewhat similar in their bureaucratization.

Rigidity of Rules: One of the stronger indices of bureaucratization is the extent and ossification of rules (Corwin, 1966). The more areas of school activity covered by rules, the more detailed the rules, the more rigid the rule-setting procedures, the more the bureaucratization. This is nowhere better illustrated than in *Up the Down Staircase* (Kaufman, 1964) where rules are pyramided on rules, often in complete contradiction of one another or in violation of major educational tasks.

Closeness of Supervision: Another method of bureaucratic control is that of close supervision of lower-level staff members (teachers) by their superiors. Although it is hypothesized by Anderson (1966) that the appearance of rules will vary inversely with amount of supervision, Corwin (1966) found that the two went together and seemed to be but variants of the general trait of bureaucratization.

Routine Decision Making: Another way of reflecting the impact of bureaucratization is to ask teachers whether they are free to make routine decisions (Corwin, 1966). In a school that is over-managed such decisions must be referred to someone else—the individual teacher is not judged competent to make them.

Autonomy: Perhaps the most general formulation of the problems of bureaucratization in schools has been given by Katz (1964) using the concept of autonomy. Although it is usually assumed that bureaucratization and autonomy are antithetical, Katz points out that the programming of limited autonomy is, in fact, necessary in even the most oppressive bureaucracies. Autonomy can occur within or outside of task roles and may be enacted within the organization or may be tolerated outside of it. However, in operationalizing autonomy, Corwin (1966) merely counted the frequency with which teachers consulted administrators about decisions concerning their classroom work.

In summary, bureaucratization is the tendency towards proliferation of management in organizations. It is likely to appear within both school systems and individual schools, and Corwin's data indicate that it is only partially correlated with size effects. Bureaucratization has the effects of reducing the autonomy of the individual teacher and of frittering away

---

*The relative independence of size-related and bureaucratic factors in schools is clear in Corwin's data, although passed over by the author (Corwin, 1966, Chapter V).

staff effort into activities not related to tasks. Bureaucratization, presumably, reflects a number of forces—desires for standardization, mistrust of individual teachers, drives for economy and misplaced zeal concerning the importance of administrative roles. Pupils in heavily-bureaucratized schools are likely to waste some of their efforts merely coping with the demands of the system, are less likely to learn verities that are applicable to their own conditions and may well become confused about the morality of 'bucking the system'. Oligarchies tend to generate a black-ar white morality—either one accepts or rebels against the system, anu other alternatives are not considered. In addition, 'closed' bureaucracies may also be archaic in their practices, and bureaucratic schools less open to the excitement of innovation and experiment. Thus, pupils in over-bureaucratized schools and systems are less likely to be independent or creative.

Structural Characteristics

Size and bureaucratic-associated differences among schools are almost inadvertent. Explicit decisions concerning school size are often made by random criteria while bureaucracies, like Topsy, often 'just grow'. However, some school characteristics are deliberately structured. Let us consider structural differences in both rules and tasks.

Rules: Schools differ widely in the ways in which they organize their curricula, and some rule-based distinctions have been used for typologizing schools. Primary and secondary schools differ in their rule structures, as do schools adopting 'streaming' versus those offering a standardized curriculum. In traditional schools a lock-step grade structure is de rigueur, while in newer schools a more open grading system is sometimes adopted. In some university laboratory schools in America and British infant schools, for example, pupils are taught on a self-demand schedule. Schools may vary also in the use of prefects—older pupils who are called upon for academic leadership, tutorial consultation or disciplinary control. American ghetto schools are also experimenting with the use of teacher aids, relatively untrained adults who assist the teacher in the classroom and help to bridge the gap between school and community. Such rule distinctions involve many issues, and the effects of most rule-based innovations are only now being investigated.

Tasks: Task differences among schools are also structured. Primary and secondary schools also attempt distinct tasks, as do privately and publicly-supported schools, and high schools adopting limited curricular objectives such as the grammar, technical or commercial school. However, schools may also be characterized in terms of the breadth of tasks accepted within the culture or school system in which they are embedded. As has already been suggested, American high schools commonly accept a broader definition of their tasks than high schools in most other Western countries. In general, the broader the tasks attempted by the school the more diffuse will be its effort. High schools attempting public entertainment and adult education will have fewer funds to spend per head of pupil on academically-related instruction. The primary school that offers a curriculum rich in music, art, dramatics and sports will build well-rounded pupils who are not, perhaps, quite so able to achieve high scores on competitive examinations in traditional subjects. It would seem that a reasonably broad choice of instructional tasks probably helps to produce wide interests and flexibility in pupils, but that the acceptance of non-academic tasks may well interfere with academic objectives. Task clarity is another dimension along which schools may be rated. As has been suggested by Biddle (1964), unclear tasks in the school have a variety of effects, of which confusion and the setting of arbitrary standards are but two.

Compositional Properties

Schools also differ in their compositions—in the complements of pupils and teachers who make them up. Let us consider some of these characteristics.

Pupil Characteristics: Primary and secondary schools differ, of course, in the age composition of their pupils, and in different countries schooling may begin as early as age five and as late as age eight. Pupils also differ in terms of sex composition, race, social class, ethnic affiliation, recency of migration to the community and other compositional properties. Some of these factors are relatively unimportant to pupil learning. But others— such as race—are of such transcendent importance as to have generated both armed conflict and public policy. Let us consider two examples of pupil compositional factors affecting the school, sex and race.

Schools may readily be classified as serving a pupil clientele that is all boys, all girls, or coeducational. Traditional, privately-supported schools have tended to serve pupils of but a single sex, while the majority of publicly-supported schools have tended to be coeducational—however, exceptions to this generalization may easily be found. Arguments have been advanced favouring both kinds of systems. Single-sex schools are said to involve a simpler curriculum, fewer disciplinary problems and a greater concentration on academia rather than frivolity. (In all fairness, some of the heat generated in favour of single-sex schools seems to reflect fears of sexual contact rather than educational tasks.) Coeducational schools are presumed to offer a wider range of experiences and to introduce boys and girls to one another under controlled conditions prior to actual courtship. It is reasonable to presume that both arguments have merit. As with the breadth of task dimension, single-sex schools presumably produce greater subject matter achievement but less well-rounded citizens. In fact, most Western countries are drifting towards equal opportunities for men and women to enter all occupations and professions. If this trend becomes a fact, the excuse for maintaining separate-but-equal schools by sex will have become less puissant.

Race composition, however, is another matter. As a general rule, it is reasonable to presume that school standards are likely to reflect the values of the ethnic or racial majority of pupils in the school (Herriott & St

John, 1966). For example, it is by now well known that non-white children do better academically when they are embedded in a predominantly-white school than if they attend a predominantly non-white school (for example, Coleman, *et al.*, 1966). This effect is so striking that within urban ghettoes in America non-whites are apt to lag behind their white neighbours (and their non-white neighbours attending white schools) by as many as two or three years in achievement by the time they are to enter high school. No remedy has yet been suggested for this phenomenon except to break up those schools that are predominantly non-white—and as a result a number of American school systems are now spending vast amounts of money to bus children to distant schools so as to change racial balances.

Teacher Characteristics: Teachers, too, will differ in terms of demographic characteristics within the school, and schools may be differentiated according to the age, sex, social class, education and tenure of their teachers. Both Corwin (1966) and Fraser (1967) studied the teacher composition of schools, and the latter discovered greater satisfaction among schools where teachers were relatively homogeneous. Teacher composition, however, is likely to have a variety of effects on pupils. For example, in American primary schools it is almost impossible to find a male teacher in the early grades. This is, presumably, not terribly important to the middle-class boy who comes from an intact home. But for the Negro boy from the ghetto this may be a genuine tragedy. A large proportion of Negro families are, in fact, broken, with male figures being absent entirely or merely transients. Those that are not broken are often faced with such financial problems that both parents carry a full-time job. Thus, the Negro boy may, in fact, have no successful male figure with whom to identify, and to find that his school, too, is run exclusively by women places on him a difficult burden. In general, pupils are likely to do better, academically, as well as in building egos and adult values, when adult figures are present in the school with whom they can identify. This suggests that student bodies that are ethnically, sexually, or racially heterogeneous need a heterogeneous group of teachers (Herriott & St John, 1966).

Contextual Characteristics

Finally, schools also vary in the way in which they are related to their environments. Again, some of these contextual relationships are structural. Schools are either supported by public funds, or by private sources, or by some combination of the two. The school has a defined legal status within its school system, and its relationships with the community are usually specified either by law or by well-established custom. However, within the constraints of law and custom, differences among schools may be recognized in terms of their contextual relationships. Fraser (1967) suggests two such properties. Vertical independence is the extent to which the school is controlled by an external authority, while horizontal intrusion is the degree to which the community (parents) intrude into the activities and the running of the school. As has previously been suggested, lack of vertical independence implies bureaucratization of the relationship between the school and system with predicted results that have previously been discussed. However, horizontal intrusion of the community into the school is another matter. Most educators have a horror of public involvement, feeling that their professional expertise is a far more reliable guide for planning education than parental prejudices. And yet, as Smith and Geoffrey (1968) have suggested, the process of schooling is not isolated from parental influences, and lucky is the school whose parents are, in fact, involved in and supportive of its educational efforts. Provided that it does not involve public controversy, it is reasonable to presume that pupils will do better in schools high in horizontal intrusion.

The Need for Research

This chapter closes where it began. Although schools are manifest examples of organizations, and although school characteristics may be studied and presumably have an effect on pupil learning, few if any studies of these effects have yet been made. Thus, the school planner, the educational administrator, the school board member or interested citizen must perforce make judgements about how to organize education on ad hoc grounds rather than from secure knowledge about the effects of his decisions on the tasks of education.

Examples of ad hoc planning are easy to locate. Conant (1959), for example, recommends standardization upon a relatively large high school, primarily on economic grounds. 'Neighbourhood' schools are planned with but little regard for the problems of ethnic composition of their student bodies. Bureaucratic decisions are made within the school system with but little regard for their educative consequences in schools.

And yet, not only is it possible to study school characteristics, but these may fruitfully be related to both task accomplishment and personal satisfaction. Corwin (1966) has demonstrated relationships between organizational characteristics in schools and the professionalism of its teacher staff, Fraser (1967) showed that school characteristics predicted teacher happiness and commitment, while Barker and Gump (1964) demonstrated relationships between school size and pupil participation. What is needed now is to extend such research into the central task areas of education.

In planning schools, then, as in so many areas of life—someday we shall have to get organized!

References

Anderson, J. G., 1964: An empirical study of bureaucratic rules in the junior high school. Unpublished PhD dissertation, John Hopkins University.

Anderson, J. G., 1966: Bureaucratic rules: Bearers of organizational authority. *Education Administration Quarterly*, II, Winter, 7-34.

Bakke, E. W., 1959: Concept of the social organization. In Mason Haire (Ed.), *Modern Organization Theory*. John Wiley & Sons, Inc., New York.

Barker, R. G. and Barker, Louise S., 1963: Social actions in the behavior stream of American and English school children. In R. G. Barker (Ed.), *The Stream of Behavior*. Appleton-Century-Crofts, New York.

Barker, R. G. and Gump, P. V., 1964: *Big School, Small School*. Stanford University Press, Stanford, Calif.

Barker, R. G., Wright, H. F., Barker, Louise S. and Schoggen, Maxine, 1961: *Specimen Records of American and English Children*. University of Kansas Press, Lawrence.

Barnard, C. I., 1938: *The Functions of the Executive*. Harvard University Press, Cambridge, Mass.

Becker, H. S., 1962: The career of the schoolteacher. In S. Nosow and W. H. Form (Eds), *Man, Work, and Society*. Basic Books, New York.

Bennett, W. S., Jr. and Falk, R. F. (forthcoming). *Teacher Aids: New Roles in the Instructional Process*. Holt, Rinehart and Winston, Inc., New York.

Biddle, B. J., 1964: Roles, goals, and value structures in organizations. In W. W. Cooper, M. W. Leavitt, M. W. Shelly, II (Eds), *New Perspectives in Organizational Research*. John Wiley & Sons, Inc., New York.

Biddle, B. J., 1967: Methods and concepts in classroom research. *Review of Educational Research*, 37, 337-357.

Biddle, B. J., 1969: The role of the teacher. *Encyclopaedia of Educational Research* (4th edn) AERA.

Biddle, B. J. et al., 1968: *Teacher role in four English-speaking countries*. Papers presented at 40th Congress of the Australian and New Zealand Association for the Advancement of Science. Christchurch, New Zealand.

Clark, B. R., 1962: *Educating the Expert Society*. Chandler Publishing Company, San Francisco.

Coleman, J. S., 1961: *The Adolescent Society*. The Free Press, Glencoe, Ill.

Coleman, J. S., et al., 1966: *Equality of Educational Opportunity*. Office of Education, U.S. Department of Health, Education and Welfare, U.S. Government Printing Office, Washington, D.C.

Conant, J. B., 1959: *The American High School Today*. Signet, New York.

Corwin, R. G., 1966: Staff conflicts in public schools. Cooperative Research Project No. 2637, Office of Education, U.S. Department of Health, Education and Welfare.

Cyert, R. M. and March, J. G., 1959: A behavioral theory of organizational objectives. In Mason Haire (Ed.), *Modern Organizational Theory*. John Wiley & Sons, Inc., New York.

Donovan, F. R., 1938: *The Schoolma'am*. Frederick A. Stokes, New York.

Durkheim, E., 1897: *Le Suicide* (Suicide). F. Alcan, Paris.

Erickson, D. A., 1969: *Freedom and Religion in Education*. University of Chicago Press, Chicago, Ill.

Etzioni, A., 1961: *A Comparative Analysis of Complex Organization*. The Free Press, New York.

Flanders, N. A., 1964: Some relationships among teacher influence, pupils attitudes, and achievement. In B. J. Biddle and W. J. Ellena (Eds), *Contemporary Research on Teacher Effectiveness*. Holt, Rinehart and Winston, Inc., New York.

Fraser, G. S., 1967: Organizational properties and teacher reactions. Unpublished PhD dissertation, University of Missouri.

Gordon, C. W., 1957: *The Social System of the High School*. The Free Press, Glencoe, Ill.

Goslin, D. A., 1965: *The School in Contemporary Society*. Scott, Foresman and Company, Glenview, Ill.

Gross, N, 1956: Sociology of education, 1945-55. In H. L. Zetterberg (Ed.), *Sociology in the United States of America: A Trend Report*. UNESCO, Paris.

Gross, N. and Herriott, R. E., 1965: *Staff Leadership in Public Schools: A Sociological Enquiry*. John Wiley & Sons, Inc., New York.

Gross, N., Mason, W. S. and McEachern, A. W., 1958: *Explorations in Role Analysis: Studies of the School Superintendency Role*. John Wiley & Sons, Inc., New York.

Herriott, R. E. and St John, Nancy H., 1966: *Social Class and the Urban School*. John Wiley & Sons, Inc., New York.

Hopkins, T. K., 1961: Bureaucratic authority: The convergence of Weber and Barnard. In A. Etzioni (Ed.), *Complex Organizations*. Holt, Rinehart and Winston, Inc., New York.

Katz, F. E., 1964: Autonomy structures in the school. *Harvard Educational Review*, 34, 428-455.

Kaufman, Bel, 1964: *Up the Down Staircase*. Prentice-Hall, Inc., Englewood Cliffs, N.J.

March, J. and Simon, H., 1958: *Organizations*. John Wiley & Sons, Inc., New York.

Musgrove, S., 1961: Parents' expectations of the junior school. *Sociology Review*, 9, 167-180.

Nuthall, G. A. and Lawrence, P. J., 1965: *Thinking in the Classroom: The Development of a Method of Analysis*. NZCER, Wellington, New Zealand.

Parsons, T., 1951: *The Social System*. The Free Press, Glencoe, Ill.

Peterson, W. A., 1964: Age, teacher's role, and the institutional setting. In B. J. Biddle and W. J. Ellena (Eds), *Contemporary Research on Teacher Effectiveness*. Holt, Rinehart and Winston, Inc., New York.

Rhea, B. B., 1964: Organizational analysis and education: An exercise in sociological theory. Unpublished PhD dissertation, University of Missouri.

Runkel, P. J., 1962: *The Effectiveness of Guidance in Today's High Schools: A Survey in Illinois*. Office of Educational Testing, University of Illinois, Urbana, Ill. (Draft)

Smith, L. M. and Geoffrey, W., 1968: *The Complexities of an Urban Classroom*. Holt, Rinehart and Winston, Inc., New York.

Stiles, L. J., 1957: *The Teacher's Role in American Society*. Fourteenth Yearbook of the John Dewey Society. Harper & Bros, New York.

Taylor, P. H., 1962: Children's evaluations of the characteristics of a good teacher. *British Journal of Educational Psychology*, 32, 258-266.

Waller, W., 1932: *The Sociology of Teaching*. John Wiley & Sons, Inc., New York.

Weber, M., 1922: *Wirtschaft und Gesellschaft*. Mohr, Tubingen. Partially translated by A. M. Henderson and T. Parsons as *The Theory of Social and Economic Organization*. Oxford University Press, New York.

Wilson, H. C. (forthcoming). On the evolution of education. In B. J. Biddle (Ed.), *Essays on the Social Systems of Education*. Holt, Rinehart and Winston, Inc., New York.

10

*Some Effects of Size and Organization of Secondary Schools on the Experiences of Pupils in Extracurricular Behaviour Settings**

W. J. Campbell

AMONG several concomitants of urbanization that could have significance for education is the growth of schools into very large institutions. Thus, although Brisbane, with a population of 683,500 persons, is not a giant metropolis, the average size of its state secondary schools in 1966 was 1,040 pupils, and its biggest school had an enrolment above 2,000 (*Queensland State Department of Education Bulletin*, 1965).

The influence of school size upon pupils has given rise to considerable controversy, but few scientific attempts have been made to test the validity of the conflicting viewpoints. One approach that gives promise of transferring the issue from the realm of personal opinion to that of disciplined examination is behaviour-setting analysis, and it is this which is employed in this study.

Behaviour settings may be defined as units of the environment which have the following structural characteristics:

1. a space-time locus (e.g., *English lesson* in room 16 between 9.30 and 10.10 a.m.);
2. a variety of entities and events (e.g., teacher, students, blackboard, writing in books);
3. a distinctive pattern of activities (no one confuses Miss Smith's *English lesson* setting with the *ladies' tuckshop*);
4. an orderly arrangement of entities and events (e.g., all the students and the desks face the front of the room; the furniture is in keeping with the activities);
5. nesting structures (e.g., the *English lesson* has parts, and is, itself, contained within more comprehensive units); and
6. independent existence.

A moment's reflection suggests that much of our daily round-of-life

*First published in *Australian Journal of Education*, 12, 2, 177-189.

is spent within ordered units of this kind: lectures, meal times, watching television, the community meeting, and so on, although a few minutes per day are usually spent on unstructured activities, and 'just doing nothing'.

In addition to its structural properties, each setting contains a system of controls designed to maintain the setting intact and functioning at a stable or near-stable level. This notion of a homeostatic system may appear, on first encounter, to be something like a genie, but there is really nothing mysterious about it. Some of the controls reside in the physical fixtures and paraphernalia—for example, it is easy to present an English lesson in Miss Smith's room, but difficult to set up a tuckshop there, or even give a chemistry lesson; the arrangement of the furniture in the 'TV' room facilitates viewing but makes study well nigh impossible. Some reside in the combination of opportunities and obligations which settings offer their inhabitants. A behaviour setting is a place which contains opportunities for the satisfaction of various personal motives, and it is this which attracts individuals to it. The desire for satisfaction imposes an obligation upon the inhabitants to ensure that the setting functions at the most satisfying level. Thus, when too many cooks begin to spoil the broth, the least efficient may be discouraged from further participation, but on the cook's day off the five-year old, and even father, may be pressed into peeling onions; when the English teacher digresses from the syllabus, those students who are anxious to pass the examination may introduce various tactics aimed at countering the digression, and, if these fail, they may undertake more independent study; the members of a soccer team may play harder and display greater versatility if the left full-back is absent or inefficient. Vetoing, increased pressure from others, deviation-countering tactics and variations in personal effort are among the main controls used by the inhabitants of settings to ensure stable and satisfying functioning.

If this theoretical analysis is sound, one would expect that when persons are in short supply there would be an increase in the strength and range of control forces acting upon those who remain within the setting. Some of the behavioural consequences of these increases are likely to be: *partici-pation in a wider variety of activities, participation in more difficult and more important tasks, greater functional importance within the setting, less sensitivity to, and less evaluation of, persons, greater effort, lower levels of maximal performance, more responsibility, greater functional self-identity, greater insecurity and more frequent occurrences of success and failure.* Conversely, when many persons are available, the strength and range of control forces impinging upon each individual will decrease, many are likely to have their participation vetoed or reduced to a minimum, and less effort will be required from each person.

In order to relate this commonsense 'theorizing' to the issue of school size, at least three sets of facts are required: (a) number of pupils; (b) number of behaviour settings; and (c) the availability of settings to pupils.

The study reported here involved three metropolitan state secondary schools: Town, 1,034 pupils; Hill, 1,177 pupils; and Plain, 1,534 pupils. These schools were situated in similar residential areas, they were all relatively new and modern, and they possessed very similar facilities. By many standards, all three schools would be considered large, but, in Brisbane today, the first two are average among those with a complete grade enrolment (i.e., grades 8 to 12) and the third is the second largest within the metropolitan area.

The study began with a detailed survey of all the extracurricular behaviour settings that had occurred in each of the schools during the period 1 February 1965—30 June 1965. This survey showed that the number of settings for each school was: Town, 147; Hill, 176; and Plain, 132. Thus, the simple 'density' figures (i.e., number of students per setting) were:

Town: 7.03
Hill: 6.69
Plain: 11.62

It is usual in studies of this kind to consider only number of enrolments, or, perhaps, density figures as listed above. However, it would seem desirable to give, in addition, some weighting to the availability of the settings to the pupils, and here organization of extracurricular activities becomes important. In many respects the organization in each of the three schools was similar: all schools were divided into houses for sports; all were dependent to some extent upon community facilities outside of the school boundaries; participation in some activities (e.g., hobby clubs for eighth grade pupils) was compulsory; all schools competed in zone competitions; excursions associated with academic studies (such as geography, science and zoology) were common features; school captains, prefects and form captains were elected/appointed similarly in the three schools. The only clear difference that emerged in organization was that Hill and Plain had three 'sport halves' (eighth grade pupils had sports on one afternoon, ninth grade pupils on another, and tenth, eleventh and twelfth grade pupils on still another), whereas Town had only one. This might appear to be a minor matter, but it affected the availability of about one quarter of the facilities to an appreciable extent, and when allowance was made for this, the density figures became:

Town: 7.03 (i.e., no change)
Hill: 5.58
Plain: 9.68

Assuming that these are the best indices, are the extracurricular behaviour settings in these schools likely to be undermanned, overmanned, or, like baby bear's porridge, 'just right'? It is impossible to answer this question with certainty, but, on the best comparative evidence available, all three schools would appear to have enrolments which have outstripped their use of facilities. This conclusion is obviously more true of Plain and Town than it is of Hill.

On the basis of the data presented above, it was predicted that:

(a) pupils in all three schools would report few forces aimed at increasing their participation in extracurricular activities, but, to the extent that any differences would emerge, they would be in the direction of Hill pupils reporting the greatest number of forces;

(b) pupils from Hill would report more, and higher level, participations than would those from Town and Plain;

(c) pupils from Hill would report the largest number of satisfactions associated with active participation (challenge, enjoyment and the like) and the smallest number associated with onlooker participation (vicarious enjoyment of various kinds); and

(d) the order of schools throughout would be: Hill, Town, and Plain.

There is nothing mysterious about these predictions. All but (c) are simple matters of arithmetic, and (c) is a commonsense deduction from (b).

Scope and Sample

All pupils in grades 8 (1st year), 9 (2nd year) and 11 (4th year) were given a questionnaire designed to provide information on forces to participate, extent of participation, levels of participation, and satisfactions obtained from participation in the extracurricular behaviour settings of their schools during the period under study. The list of behaviour settings, of course, varied from school to school, but the items chosen to measure forces were ones that featured in all three lists, and the questionnaire on satisfactions was identical throughout. Some idea of the nature of the questionnaire can be gathered from the following extracts, taken from the script of an eighth grade boy.

Forces (16 in complete list)

	Common-wealth Youth Day March	Library	Interhouse Swimming Carnival	School Dance	School working bee
1. I thought I might learn something there		✓		✓	
3. It gave me a chance to be with the others	✓		✓		✓
6. I like to be active and do things				✓	✓
9. Others wanted me to go	✓		✓	✓	
13. I was told to go	✓				✓
16. I knew that this activity needed to have certain things done					✓

Participations

Setting	Were You There?		What Did You Do?
1. Athletics Practice	No	Yes	Practised
3. School Boy Cross-Country	No	Yes	Ran in it
11. Cricket Practice	No	Yes	—
30. Lunch Hour Gymnastics	No	Yes	Watched

55. Red Cross Cadets Regular Meeting	(No)	Yes	—
70. Inter-School Debates	No	(Yes)	Listened
133. Election of Form Captain	No	(Yes)	Voted
144. School Fête	No	(Yes)	Sold Drinks
176. 'Air Your Grievance Day'	(No)	Yes	—

Satisfactions

Names of Activities	Explanation
(Activities which were especially good, satisfying and worthwhile.)	(What I did or what went on that made the activities good; what I enjoyed or got out of the activity.)
1. Football Practice	It's good because it's rough and tough. I like pitting my strength against others.
2. Library	I like to read about science and learn new things.
3. School Dance	It was lots of fun. I enjoyed mixing with the other boys and girls, and learning new social and physical skills.

From the total number of scripts, a matched sample of 255 pupils from each school was drawn. The matching was based upon the variables of sex, grade, age and particular academic course being taken, and the distribution by the first two of these is shown in Table 10.1.

TABLE 10.1

Matched Samples According to Sex and Grade*

	Girls	Boys	Totals
Eighth grade	54	58	112
Ninth grade	37	65	102
Eleventh grade	20	21	41
Totals	111	144	255

*The number in each cell represents that frequency of matched threes.

Forces to Participate

The questionnaire used in this section of the study was originally compiled by Willems (1963), and it has featured in several studies of this kind (Willems, 1964; Campbell, 1964). Pupils are presented with a number of school behaviour settings and are asked to indicate for each what were for them real forces or attractions towards participation. The settings used in this study (p. 178) were chosen because of their occurrence in each of the schools during the five-month period being surveyed.

In the analysis of the data no attempt was made to retain the identity of each setting; rather, responses were summed across the settings in order to find the frequency with which each pupil reported the existence of each force.

Students from Hill and Plain reported the existence of a similar number of forces associated with entry into the settings and those from Town reported fewer. Mean numbers were: Town 13.55; Hill, 14.76; and Plain,

14.51. In previous studies of this kind, forces have been classified according to *own* (arising from within the personality of the respondent: 'I thought I might learn something') and *foreign* (originating from without the respondent: 'I was expected to go'). As a first step, a similar breakdown was made here. This analysis revealed no intergroup differences in the number of own forces, but pupils from Hill and Plain reported a greater number of foreign forces than did those from Town. (Significance levels .01 and .05 respectively.)

As a final form of analysis, the forces were clustered as follows:

1. Items suggesting intellectual attraction: 'I thought I might learn something there', and 'It was a chance for me to do or see something new and different'.
2. Items suggesting external pressures: 'Others wanted me to go', 'I was expected to go', 'I was told to go', and 'This activity is required for students like me'.
3. Items suggesting anticipated enjoyment: 'I like that specific activity', 'I like to be active and do things', 'In general, I like this activity; by going I could help to see to it that it would be there for me to enjoy again', and 'In general, I like this activity; by doing something there, I could see to it that it would be there for me to enjoy again'.
4. Items suggesting social attractions: 'It gave me a chance to be with the others', 'Everybody else was going, so I wanted to go too', and 'I saw that everyone else was going, and it's not fun to be left out'.
5. Items suggesting personal responsibility: 'I knew this activity needed people', and 'I knew this activity needed to have certain things done'.
6. Items suggesting opportunity to acquire primary status: 'It gave me a chance to be someone special'.

As Table 10.2 shows, significant intergroup differences were found with respect to *external pressure* and *personal responsibility*.

TABLE 10.2

Number of Forces by Study Groups and Clusters of Forces

Clusters	Town (1)	Hill (2)	Plain (3)	Significance (Chi^2)
1. Intellectual	603	615	598	ns
2. External pressure	821	979	939	Gps 2:1 < .01 Gps 3:1 < .05
3. Anticipated enjoyment	953	938	927	ns
4. Social	641	660	668	ns
5. Personal responsibility	320	438	438	Gps 2:1 < .01 Gps 3:1 < .01
6. Primary status	117	134	129	ns
Totals	3,455	3,764	3,699	Gps 2:1 < .01 Gps 3:1 < .01

However one looks at the findings, only mixed success was achieved with the predictions concerning forces. As expected, pupils from Hill, in comparison with those from Town, reported more forces, and, in particular, more forces associated with external pressures and a sense of personal responsibility. So far, so good. Pupils from Plain, however, did not differ, in these respects, from Hill ones, whereas it was predicted that they would report even fewer forces than pupils from Town. There is no explanation for this failure in prediction. If pupils from all schools had responded similarly, one could have said that this reflected high densities throughout, but this did not happen, so here is a case of half right being almost worse than completely wrong!

Extent and Levels of Participation

As the extract given earlier (p. 178) will suggest, the questionnaire used to obtain data on participations required the pupils to indicate whether or not they attended each setting, and, if so, what they did there. The statements given in the latter part were then used to determine levels of participation. Thus:

> Level 1: 'watched', 'listened'.
> Level 2: 'practised football', 'practised my part in the play'.
> Level 3: 'was a prompter at the play', 'sold tickets for the match', 'worked with all the class on the stall'.
> Level 4: 'played in the match', 'sang a solo', 'had a part in the play', 'kept minutes of the meeting'.

In general terms, these levels range from just being present at the setting, through more active participation, to taking a responsible part in the proceedings.

When total participations, irrespective of levels, were considered, mean scores were:

> Town: 33.43 ⎫
> ⎬ $t < .01$
> Hill: 38.53 ⎭ ⎫
>   ⎬ $t < .01$
> Plain: 33.32 ⎭

As predicted, pupils from Hill scored significantly better than did those from Town and Plain.

When participations were classified according to levels, the superiority of the Hill pupils was evident in all but level 2.

TABLE 10.3

Levels of Participations and Mean Scores

	Level 1	Level 2	Level 3	Level 4
Town	22.12	7.29	.69	3.33
Hill	26.96	5.37	1.73	4.47
Plain	23.34	6.73	1.26	1.99

*t scores significant at the .01 level.

It is customary in studies of participation to distinguish between *entries* (levels 1 and 2) and *performances* (levels 3 and 4). When this was done in this study the findings were the same: Hill pupils scored consistently higher than did those from either of the other schools. However, the superiority tended to lie in performances rather than entries.

Town pupils recorded significantly more level 4 participations than did those from Plain, but the position was reversed at level 3, and, taken as a whole, pupils from these schools rated similarly.

	Entries	*Performances*
Town	29.41	4.02
Hill	32.33	6.20
Plain	30.07	3.25

A somewhat depressing feature of Table 10.3 is the low percentage of level 4 participations in *all* schools. Even at Hill, this percentage is only 11.6, and at Plain it is slightly less than 6. Certainly, in the extracurricular activities of these schools, onlooker participations appear to be the rule. This general picture supports the early suspicion that, with respect to the provision of non-academic settings, all three schools were somewhat over-populated.

Satisfactions from Participations

In this 'satisfactions' section, pupils were asked to select from the list of behaviour settings those few settings which they had found particularly satisfying and worthwhile. Then they were asked to recall what it was about the settings that made them so worthwhile. The satisfaction report protocols yielded a selection of one to eight 'worthwhile settings', with an average of 2.5 per respondent. There were no statistically significant differences among the schools with respect to numbers mentioned.

The explanations 'why it was good' were, as a first step, classified into forty-five categories, similar to those used by Gump and Friesen (1964). Subsequently, seven super-categories were formed as follows:

1 Competence; increase in or maintenance of physical fitness or skill; improved self-confidence or reduction of emotional blocks; increase in getting along with others; in handling oneself in different situations; becoming able to do new tasks, or to do old tasks better.

2 Learn about; opportunity to learn about formal and informal social relationships; to know more of human nature; learning about various skills but with no direct statement of capacity increase; learning about knowledge areas, as opposed to social and skill areas; learning about inferred from general statements that the setting was 'educational', 'interesting', etc., but with no particulars given; learning things that may help with educational or occupational planning.

3 Action and test; satisfaction in hard work, self-test, attempts to progress; zest in the same struggle or test situations as in challenge, but the opposing forces are from people; positive outcome of individual or group endeavours;

a good job, a successful job; significant help to social cause or group; doing a lot, or doing something important.

4 *Novelty*; enjoyment of novel events, places, activities; meeting, or knowing for first time, people one has not known before; escape from usual routines; enjoyment in 'doing something'.

5 *Vicarious enjoyment*; observing struggle and competition; pleasure in being stirred up, usually through watching others; liking for the 'show' put on by others.

6 *Action valence*; liking for the activity engaged in; just plain enjoyment.

7 *Social rewards*; giving minor or token help or support; support from key adults in the school; support from peers and from non-school groups; being in the focus of attention, a status person, receiving an honour or prize; companionship, fun with others, conversation; being part of an organized action group, satisfaction in functioning together; attachment to, or the immersion in, large groups, feeling of a bond with the school awakened.

The findings from this super-category comparison are shown in Table 10.4.

TABLE 10.4

Comparison of Satisfactions

Super-Categories	Town (1)	Hill (2)	Plain (3)	Significance (Chi²)
1. Competence	129	104	103	ns
2. Learn about	99	101	84	ns
3. Action and test	105	126	87	Gps 2 & 3 $<$ .01
4. Novelty	41	82	65	Gps 1 & 2 $<$ .01 Gps 1 & 3 $<$ .05
5. Vicarious enjoyment	60	38	88	Gps 1 & 2 $<$ .05 Gps 1 & 3 $<$ .05 Gps 2 & 3 $<$ .01
6. Action valence	224	296	211	Gps 1 & 2 $<$ .01 Gps 2 & 3 $<$ .01
7. Social rewards	113	116	136	ns

Pupils from Hill, as predicted, provided the fewest number of satisfactions associated with *vicarious enjoyment* ('I did enjoy watching it'; 'It's fun to see the school team in action'), and the largest number associated with *action valence* ('It is fun taking part in school plays'), *action and test* ('This gave me a chance to show that I could really act'; 'I knew that we were doing well'), and *novelty* ('This was something new for me'). In each of these four clusters, except *novelty*, pupils from Plain were at the other extreme from Hill pupils, so, again, a high degree of success was achieved with the predictions. The only surprising feature of Table 10.4 is the low novelty score attained by pupils from Town.

Discussion and Implications

This behaviour-setting analysis has enabled us to move from a consideration of an ecological fact (density of population within the settings), through the behaviours of individuals, to some of what Brunswik (1955) would call personal 'proximal achievements'. In retrospect, and conceding that any manipulations involved concerned a simple variable (density), this empirical study confirms the optimism of a number of current researchers who believe that psychologists are on the threshold of attaining considerably greater control over the personal and environmental manipulations in which they engage (Barker & Barker, 1964). One feature of the behaviour-setting approach is its apparent simplicity; there must have been few readers of this study who did not keep repeating to themselves, 'But this is only commonsense', and certainly most would have been surprised if the predictions had not been confirmed.

Probably the most important implications of this study are related to methodology and theory, but there are, also, implications for child development and school administration, and it is to a consideration of these that we now turn.

Implications for Child Development: Although there has long been evidence from industrial psychology that the larger and more bureaucratically efficient the organization the greater the degradation of the individual, this knowledge has had little influence upon schools, and the widespread concern for the organization man has not been accompanied by a similar concern for the organization child. On the contrary, the enlargement of schools has often been accepted not as an unfortunate necessity but as a welcome educational improvement.

If an entry participation were as stimulating as a performance one, size and organization of schools would be relatively insignificant factors. However, without underestimating the value of watching or listening to high-quality productions, research on child development overwhelmingly endorses the view that the more active the participation the more stimulating it is. In general, it is better to play than watch, and to contribute actively rather than to sit passively. This difference in stimulation is reflected clearly in the comparison of satisfactions reported by pupils from Hill and Plain. The former mention the thrills of challenge, novelty and personal achievements, whereas the latter obviously seek these same satisfactions but frequently have to settle for vicarious achievement of them.

It might be argued that the important outcomes are 'distal achievements' (Brunswik, 1955), such as long-term changes in attitudes, skills and knowledges, and not 'proximal' ones, like the satisfactions mentioned above. Certainly, long-term changes are extremely important, but they do not develop out of thin air. Rather, they emerge from the interaction of short-term outcomes with new stimulating experiences. To the extent that long-term outcomes cannot be divorced from short-term ones, the latter, too, have importance. Moreover, even if the proximal achievements never blossom into distal ones, their occurrence is likely to add strength to the personalities of the individuals. It is better to have loved and lost than never to have loved at all!

Implications for School Administration: Big schools are here to stay, so the most practical issues to discuss are: (a) the provision of a large number of stimulating and varied settings; and (b) ensuring that the facilities are available to all pupils under optimal conditions.

The three schools involved in this study were relatively modern, and reasonably well endowed with facilities. Their settings ranged over nine super-varieties: *sports, hobby clubs, cultural, social, excursions, religious groups, journalism, school government* and *service corps*. In these respects they were probably not markedly inferior to good schools anywhere, and it could be said that they all possessed the basic framework for rich extracurricular programmes. Moreover, in all cases, use was made of facilities, such as tennis courts and large recreational areas, which belonged to the communities which surrounded the schools. However, the final lists of settings were disappointingly short. This is evident when a comparison is made with similar studies (Barker & Barker, 1964) from Kansas, U.S.A. (see Table 10.5).

TABLE 10.5

Comparison of Brisbane and Kansas Schools in Terms of Population/Differentiation Ratios

	Population	Settings (Differentiation)	P/D Ratio
Brisbane (5 months)			
Town	1,034	147	7.03
Hill	1,177	176	6.69
Plain	1,534	132	11.62
Kansas (10 months)			
University City	945	312	3.03
Shereton	1,923	487	3.95
Capital City	2,287	499	4.58

Although the three Brisbane schools would introduce *some* new settings in the second half of the year, it is most unlikely that they would approach the richness of the Kansas schools. One conclusion is that these schools, while possessing the basic structure for rich extracurricular programmes, need to be further differentiated at the setting level. This differentiation is likely to be most effective when pupils and teachers are encouraged to establish new settings. This is already done to some extent at Hill, where teachers and pupils tend to fashion a new programme annually, rather than fit into an existing programme, and it is surely no coincidence that this school has the largest number of settings.

Probably the main hope for substantial improvement lies in more effective use of the settings. Hill and Plain are already divided into grade levels for purposes of sports, and the effect of this is reflected in the overall similarity of participation scores obtained by pupils from Plain and Town, for, otherwise Town pupils could be expected to have scored higher. It seems clear that Town could effect an improvement by following the lead of Hill and Plain in this matter.

One of the striking features of the setting lists is the large number of settings that are reserved for particular grade levels (the vetoing phenomenon referred to earlier). As a result, the effective number of settings for any individual is much lower than even the total lists would suggest. The challenge that faces all three schools is one of ensuring that the facilities that exist are available to all pupils under optimum conditions for participation. No radical departures from traditional organization are currently being experimented with, but there is a need for intelligent experimentation. This study would suggest that a significant improvement in the values that pupils in a large school gain from the extracurricular programme is likely to be dependent upon the establishment of autonomous 'little' school units within the larger one (Plath, 1965). This would certainly be a radical departure from current organization, but, assuming that schools exist for the benefit of pupils, any departure that would increase these benefits is worthy of careful consideration.

References

Barker, R. G., 1960: Ecology and motivation. In M. R. Jones (Ed.), *Nebraska Symposium on Motivation.* University of Nebraska Press, Lincoln.

Barker, R. G. and Barker, L. S., 1964: Structural characteristics. In R. G. Barker and P. V. Gump (Eds), *Big School, Small School.* Stanford University Press, Stanford, Calif.

Brunswik, E., 1955: The conceptual framework of psychology. In *International Encyclopedia of Unified Science.* Vol. 1, Pt 2, 656-750. University of Chicago Press, Chicago, Ill.

Campbell, W. J., 1964: Some effects of high school consolidation. In R. G. Barker and P. V. Gump (Eds), *Big School, Small School.* Stanford University Press, Stanford, Calif.

Gump, P. V. and Friesen, W. V., 1964: Satisfactions derived from nonclass settings. In R. G. Barker and P. V. Gump (Eds), *Big School, Small School.* Stanford University Press, Stanford, Calif.

Plath, K. R., 1965: *Schools Within Schools: A Study of High School Organization.* Bureau of Publications, Teachers College, Columbia University, New York.

Queensland State Department of Education, 1965: *Predicted Enrolments: Metropolitan High Schools, 1966-68.*

Willems, E. P., 1963: Forces toward participation in behavior settings of large and small institutions: A field experiment. Unpublished MA thesis, University of Kansas.

Willems, E. P., 1964: Forces toward participation in behavior settings. In R. G. Barker and P. V. Gump (Eds), *Big School, Small School.* Stanford University Press, Stanford, Calif.

11

Grade Organization of Schools

D. J. Drinkwater

IN THE early 'sixties the educational systems of New South Wales and Queensland differed in several, possibly significant, aspects of organization. Clearly the most striking of these was the age of transfer from primary to secondary education, and the circumstances surrounding that transfer. These included the retention of an external examination and the option of leaving at the conclusion of primary schooling in one state, against no such barrier and compulsory attendance at a secondary school at a younger age in the other. In effect, if one interprets the changes that have taken place in the age and grade level of primary-secondary articulation over the last fifty years as representing progress, when they involve the modification of structure from Eight-Four (and option to leave after eight grades) to Six-Six and secondary education for all after six grades, then it is possible to see the two organizations investigated here as representing two stages in a historical process. Yet they existed independently, side by side, in otherwise similar environments, and were thus able to be compared. The average thirteen-year old child in Queensland was still in what was called, and organized as, the primary school. In New South Wales he was into the second year of his secondary school.

Acceptable data on the problem remain to this day as indefinite as Reavis left it nearly forty years ago (Reavis, 1931). It is quite likely that such forces as cultural homogeneity and teacher personality are more important in development than technicalities of organization. Basic intelligence, for instance, and individual sociocultural background are more important variables in learning achievement than whether a subject is studied in a so-called primary or secondary environment. In those aspects of development interpreted as character or personality traits it is extremely likely that the overall effects of a homogeneous society are likely to be more influential than the idiosyncrasies of individual schools.

Nevertheless, one still finds in the literature a range of opinions, usually with no offer of substantiation from empirical research, which favour various types of organization. These still vary from such apparently arbitrary claims as: 'The junior high school has accomplished the special purposes which prompted its organisation and determined its practices.' (Reavis, 1931), through such related but cautious statements as: 'Much evidence indicates that the pattern of high school organisation is more often based on space requirements than it is on educational needs.' (Keller, 1958), to the safest summing-up of all, 'Perhaps an able teacher, given freedom to work creatively, is more important by far than any mechanical scheme [of organization], however ingenious.' (Shane & Polychrones, 1957.)

For practical reasons, the investigator had to select a limited range of characteristics for assessment. Included, however, was a range of traits associated with the more difficult to gauge, but very important, aims concerning personality development, in addition to measures of scholastic attainment in the more important subjects. These were justified by parallel statements from the published aims of education for each state.

The selection of traits will be clearly in evidence during the statement of results. Once the selection of traits had been made, it was necessary to choose or construct tests that were likely to be valid in relation to some aspects of the traits they purported to measure and, at the same time, valid in terms of the communities in which the measurement was to take place. Most attainment tests were constructed especially for the purpose of the investigation.

A pilot investigation was carried out in both states, reliability indices were assessed for all tests, and those that did not meet predetermined standards of excellence were rejected. Administration was standardized and a sample was selected.

For reasons of practical organization, and because such a plan contributed to strengthening the claim of homogeneity of the social group covered, it was decided to restrict sampling to the northern part of New South Wales (north of Sydney and east of Moree) and the southern part of Queensland (south to Bundaberg and east of Goondiwindi). Subgroups were set up and representative random samples were selected across both states. It could be demonstrated on any of the subsamples finally used that there was great closeness of final matching, and the representational spread of each subsample on each variable approximated to what one would expect in the total community. The essential variables on which these things were checked were age grouping, intelligence, and sociocultural status.

Results

Results in the attainment tests are presented in Table 11.1; the remaining quantitative results are in Table 11.2.

In both tables a double asterisk denotes statistical significance of difference at the one per cent level, a single asterisk at the five per cent level.

It seems fairly apparent that the organization of basic skills into the syllabus, and, up to a certain point, the degree to which a subject is emphasized within that syllabus, constitute strong determinants of success in terms of large group performance.

TABLE 11.1

State Superiorities in Attainment Tests

Test	'r'	City		Rural		Private		Overall Both Sexes
		Boys	Girls	Boys	Girls	Boys	Girls	
Reading	0.93	NSW	NSW*	QLD	QLD*	QLD	NSW	NSW*
Vocabulary	0.89	NSW**	NSW**	QLD	QLD*	QLD	NSW	NSW*
Social Studies	0.71	QLD**	QLD	QLD*	QLD**	QLD	QLD	QLD**
Science	0.74	NSW	NSW**	NSW	NSW	NSW	NSW	NSW
Art/Music/ Literature	0.54	NSW	NSW**	NSW	NSW	NSW**	NSW**	NSW**
General Knowledge	0.87	QLD	NSW**	NSW	QLD	NSW**	NSW**	NSW**
Mathematics	0.83	QLD**	QLD**	QLD**	QLD**	QLD**	QLD**	QLD**
Composition: Impression	—	QLD	NSW*	NSW	NSW	NSW**	NSW	NSW**
Composition: Length	—	NSW	NSW**	NSW**	NSW**	NSW**	NSW**	NSW**
Composition: Accuracy	—	QLD	QLD	QLD**	QLD**	QLD*	QLD	QLD**
Study Sources	0.81	NSW	NSW**	NSW	QLD	NSW	NSW**	NSW**

For those who think this is merely stating the obvious, the needless empiricizing of commonsense, the author should point out that class ranges obtained indicate, very forcefully, that the inclusion of a subject, or the emphasizing of it in the timetable, could not be taken as a pointer to anything concerning the performance of any given *individual*. Even at the class level, other factors such as intelligence, sociocultural level and teacher quality can distort results to the extent that no class in any one system will necessarily surpass any one in another system just because the emphasis officially given might be quite different. It is only when a cross-section of classes is taken that the overall pattern of dominance can confidently be expected to show.

Perhaps the mathematics results provide the clearest example of emphasis and the key to the whole pattern of attainment over the states. One is reminded of the earlier ACER findings (Cunningham & Price, 1934) that, beyond a certain limit, excessive time spent on repetitive treatment of a subject can be time wasted. Nevertheless, the consistent Queensland superiority in the field of mathematics is almost certainly the result of continued and excessive emphasis on arithmetical practices. Some Queensland children may have done more than was necessary; but they have certainly done enough. One must not forget, of course, that most New South Wales children tested spent over three hundred minutes per week in mathematics instruction time, and they more than shared the expressed faith in the subject as a means of developing the 'faculty' of logic revealed in another part of the study. But their groundwork has not been as thorough, and their programme has already been broadened to a greater extent than in Queensland. So the discrepancy in attainment can be attributed to the Queensland organizational additions of timetable emphasis and classroom traditions, excessive homework and external examination pressure—all of which are interrelated.

Thus, Queensland attains superiority in all three scholarship subjects, mathematics, social studies and English usage (technical skill is stressed —apparently to the detriment of other facets). It has been suggested before (ACER, 1951) that the heavy emphasis on mathematics instruction might well be contributing directly to Queensland's inferior position in other, more important, skills. Assessing Queensland's achievement against the total statement of aims it appears that a great deal of school time may be spent in practices in which the gains are not commensurate with the time expended.

TABLE 11.2

State Superiorities in Other Personality Measures

		City		Rural		Private		Overall
Trait	'r'	Boys	Girls	Boys	Girls	Boys	Girls	†
Reading maturity	—	QLD	QLD	NSW	NSW	NSW	QLD	—
Reading activity	—	QLD*	QLD*	NSW	NSW*	NSW	NSW	—
Leisure activity	—	QLD	NSW	QLD	NSW	NSW	QLD	—
Attitude to education	0.71	NSW	QLD	QLD	QLD**	QLD**	QLD	QLD**
Attitude to good workmanship	0.68	QLD**	QLD	QLD	QLD	Equal	QLD	QLD**
Attitude to authority‡	—	NSW	QLD	NSW	NSW	QLD	QLD	—
Moral judgement	—	QLD	QLD	QLD	QLD	QLD	Equal	QLD
Moral contrasts —ought	0.60	NSW	QLD	QLD*	QLD	QLD	NSW	—
Moral contrasts —might	0.76	QLD	QLD	NSW	QLD	QLD	QLD	—
Social superstitions§	0.61	QLD	NSW	NSW*	NSW	QLD	NSW	—

†Omitted when meaningless
‡State listed is the 'more authoritarian'
§State listed is the 'least superstitious'

A generalization on the attainment section of the test battery could be that New South Wales organization results in slightly better all-round development. Other results indicate that this is achieved with a more extensive subject range, in an environment in which children play more sport, go on more school visits, attend to radio, television and films more often, lose more time in travelling, and do less homework.

But the results also demonstrate that the New South Wales children are not achieving those levels in essential skills that their Queensland counterparts show *can* be reached. Indeed, both states have much to be concerned about in these attainment results.* Certainly the tests were constructed to yield means around the fifty per cent mark; but this was all too easily done with a pool of items, all of which were assessed as necessary knowledge for the good citizen.

The full test battery included a questionnaire designed to reveal three main groups of information: an analysis of reading activities, an indication of leisure-time pursuits, and further background information on the school situation and attitudes towards it. The implications of many of these answers come out in the later discussion of results. In addition to this, two quantitative indexes were worked out to cover reading activity and leisure activity. Comparisons were made in the usual way on these and the results appear together with other personality measures in Table 11.2.

Other Questionnaire Results

An attempt was made to measure sociability, group health, and social expansiveness by means of a series of sociometric questions. The results and analysis and a full discussion of implications are contained in Drinkwater (1962). Although there are some suggestions of differences that may have been related to coeducation, the overall tenor of results favours the 'homogeneous population' theory.

Great differences of group health were found but these varied within states rather than meaningfully across states.

Indeed, much of the questionnaire response seemed to reinforce the theory of comparable social groups on the Australian east coast.

Throughout, the answers given pertaining to numbers of books read and in other aspects of reading activities beyond the school situation, there were no significant differences between the states although, again, there were considerable differences between groups within states.

As the social picture expanded, one state mirrored the other. Much the same proportion of public school children in each state read their parents' books—about sixty per cent of each subgroup—and these divided similarly into those who read them 'often' and 'sometimes'. Actually, a prime reason for the inclusion of this question was to discover the incidence of those who claimed that their parents had no books. The number was small (five per cent), and evenly distributed across the states.

There were slight exceptions shown in the deficiencies of New South Wales city and Queensland private girls in their public library membership, and New South Wales private boys seemed not quite to equal the advantages of their Queensland counterparts in within-school membership. Apart from this, however, in twenty-one comparisons across the states, the pattern of library membership is practically duplicated.

*It is encouraging to note two related aspects of the secondary reforms instituted in both states since the study. In Queensland, they embrace a broadening of curriculum, with removal of scholarship, the pressure of an external examination at so young an age; in New South Wales there is increased attention to the reinforcing of basic skills, particularly for duller groups, in the early years of the 'new' secondary schools.

Neither state has solved the 'problem' of persuading children to want to read poetry or plays, to any extent, in their own time. Those that do indulge in these practices represent a small, equitably distributed percentage of all subgroups. Just where these forms of literature (compulsory in all schools) fit into the hierarchy of early adolescent literary taste can be seen by reference to Table 11.3.

Tastes

Statements of favourites (even to the number not making a choice) in terms of types of books preferred, radio and television programmes liked, and type of entertainment desired (from a select list including opera, ballet, symphony, musical comedy and the like)—showed consistent patterning across the states. There were sex and type of school differences, but no between-state differences of any acceptable proportions.

Tastes in reading are clearly revealed in Table 11.3, compiled from an original three choices allotted each child.

TABLE 11.3

Composite Table of Favourite Books (Allowing Three Choices per Child)
(Categories are arranged in rank order and expressed in percentages)

Category	Adventure	Detective	Animal	Love	Historical	Short Story	Science
NSW	24.6	17	7	7	7	8	6
QLD	24.0	18	8	7	7	6	6

Category	School	Travel	Biography	Plays	Poetry	Blank	n
NSW	4	4	2	2	0.4	11	1398
QLD	5	5	2	1	1.0	10	1398

The most striking characteristic was, as claimed, the homogeneity of choice across the states. Not only were the rank orders in both states very similar but the actual numbers of adherents to any particular kind of book were remarkably alike.

Definite sex differences showed up on the categories, 'love' and 'school' favoured by girls, and on 'science' and 'historical' favoured by boys. These differences occurred in both states and in all areas and types of school.

Clearly the most popular radio programmes for Australian east coast thirteen-year olds were those which featured hit tunes. Apart from this solid leader in all positive choices the only category extensively filled out was that of 'no particular favourite', which was also fairly evenly distributed between the states. Even the conscientious children who claimed 'the news' as their favourite radio programme, were equally provided—thirty-three in each state—and quite well matched in the various subgroups.

A table showing both the rank order and the total state choices for each category is included by way of emphasis. The orders were identical. (*See* Table 11.4.)

Perhaps this manifestation of the interaction of the potency of a mass medium of information—albeit a little dated—and the recognition of stages of development, interests, etc., may contain a lesson for the educationist who wonders what we might do to make school a more effective agency in shaping the lives of our future citizens.

When not relaying 'big' shows over an interstate 'hook-up', the commercial stations are playing the same pop, or sentimental records, and interspersing them with advertisements which vary slightly in the addresses of local retailers but which are usually peddling goods produced by interstate monopolies, in terms produced by interstate-monopoly advertising companies. It is little wonder that radio tastes do not differ from state to state; the schools are having no noticeable effect yet on this aspect of Australian community living.

TABLE 11.4

Favourite Radio Programmes

Category (ranked)	Hits	Plays	News	Comedy	Sport	Classical	Children's	Other	Religious	No Choice
NSW	171	34	33	23	19	10	7	2	1	166
QLD	144	46	33	30	10	10	9	6	2	176

A table of television viewing categories with favourites recorded is included for the edification of the reader. (*See* Table 11.5.) The propensity shown in book choices, for children of this age to take delight in adventure and detective stories, was startlingly reinforced here. Of note, if not of concern, was the utter consistency of choice irrespective of state, sex or type of school.

TABLE 11.5

Favourite Television Programmes
(Categories are in rank order and expressed in percentages)

Category	Crime	Western	Other adventure	Comic	Family	Musical	Sport	Other	Blank
NSW	43	21	8	5	4	5	3	5	6
QLD	41	20	6	5	4	3	2	8	10

On the list of selected entertainments the only consistently scoring category was the 'no favourite' column which won twenty-five to fifty per cent of the various subgroups and significantly featured more boys than girls. Other sex differences showed up: girls liked 'ballet', boys liked 'variety'. Both sexes liked musical comedy more than other things. In quite a varied pattern of results there was no suggestion of serious disbalance between the states, and in this case the sameness persisted between matched adolescents in spite of the differences in school-guided experiences of visits to these same types of entertainment that are revealed later.

Other Leisure Pursuits showing Sameness

New South Wales groups had proved to be superior in their theoretical knowledge of art/music/literature background. Few significant differences showed, however, when the children were asked about their actual performance in music. Sex and area differences showed in terms of the incidence of non-learners. Between states, there not only were no significant differences in this incidence but often the actual patterning over various instruments was duplicated. School obviously played a negligible role as an activator. The reason why two-thirds of all learners had started was simple enough—they 'liked the instrument'. These were fairly evenly balanced across the states, as were the numbers who started because their 'parents wanted it', the only other substantial reason.

One further interesting fact emerged from the inquiry as to the number of years learners had been playing their instruments. Answers indicated that much the same numbers of Queensland children—in most groups similar to New South Wales—had either continued learning or started to learn their instruments during the seventh or eighth grade years. The non-local reader might wonder at the highlighting of this fact, but to Queenslanders, surely, it is a revelation: here, in the years of heavy 'scholarship' pressure, in preparation for what was the first of the 'big' external examinations, much the same numbers of individuals were turning to the practice of music as relaxation and personality expansion as in New South Wales where the children had already passed effortlessly on to secondary school.

Another aspect of worthy leisure time that it was considered might possibly be affected by the pressures of 'scholarship' was participation by the Queensland children in club activities. There was not a shred of evidence to support this supposition. On the contrary, the consistent and remarkably even patterning of results showed as one of the strongest supports for the 'homogeneous society' theory. When a related question, too, was considered—that which revealed those who held positions of responsibility in their clubs—the similarity between states was further emphasized.

The parallels continued. With the exception of city boys there were similar distributions in both states according to hobbies. With the same exception, among those with hobbies, much the same time was spent in pursuit of this branch of worthy activities.

Regular paid jobs in the family were an equally rare phenomenon in both states; about twenty per cent of each subgroup acknowledged this characteristic. Jobs outside the family were even more rare; they fluctuated according to sex, but not significantly according to state.

Much the same proportions of all area groups have had experience on the stage as entertainers. In all areas, girls have had slightly more experience than boys. Again, the differences were within states, not between them.

Inasmuch as these and other results give support to the author's basic assumption of the one homogeneous society throughout the states, they tend, of course, to negate the possible influences of the differences that existed in school organization. By all means, both school systems might have contributed considerably to the children measured having achieved certain standards, but whatever the determinants of these activities might be, they cannot, on this evidence, be related to earlier transfer to secondary education, nor to overt differences in teacher training, nor to the existence of one-sex or coeducational schools.

These social samenesses in early adolescents were so striking that, so far, they have dominated discussion. Yet there were differences, too, that showed up in analysis of the questionnaire results.

Individual Questions showing Differences

New South Wales children spent more time listening to the radio; in the country they went to the pictures more often, and in the city they watched more television. In all of these groups they spent less time on homework.

The dominant pattern of the questions relating to the playing of sport emphasized a direct effect of school organization. New South Wales children played more regular sport, on the whole. This coincides with the organizational factor that all New South Wales secondary schools had one half-day of the school week set aside for organized sport; in this time most interschool, interhouse and even regular interclass competitions were run. In the Queensland situation there was some allowance made on the time-table for regular sport but the period was not always used to advantage; there was less interschool competition, and much of what did go on was of an irregular nature—such as the supervision of a game between impromptu sides by the non-expert general teacher. This lack of expert attention was likely to be more pronounced for girls. It is no strain on the imagination to suspect a causal relationship in these results.

One further point of interest regarding the questions on sporting activities was brought to light by a third set of answers, those relating to the regular watching of sport. Here the effects of differential school organization, and the resultant participation, have quickly diminished; one is again confronted by the homogeneous society. There was a consistent sex difference revealed; boys watched sport more than girls; but there was no difference of any note between the related state subsamples.

Another combination of results which both reveals an organizational difference and yet strengthens the homogeneous society theory was seen in the analysis of answers to those questions pertaining to visits and trips made, in the first instance, with the school, and, second, independently of school. There was no doubt about the fact that school-organized, extra-mural activities involving visits to concerts, trips to factories and the like were more widespread in New South Wales, in all areas and types of schools and for both sexes. Here was a significant procedural difference between the states.

The results on visits outside school showed that there was no carry-over of proportion of activity from the within-school situation. In all subgroups Queensland made relative advances and in seven of twelve comparisons the Queensland children actually reversed the pattern of frequency of visits; in all other cases they cut the differences to insignificant, mostly negligible, proportions. This constituted a strong suggestion that the carry-over into life of worthy school activities might not always be what the fond theorist surmises.

The other state differences that unequivocally existed between the thirteen-year olds surveyed were those directly influenced by timetable inclusions or equally immediate aspects of school organization. One dramatic difference showed between proportions in various categories on the basis of why children dislike the subject they most dislike. Similar numbers (in some cases, identical numbers) were 'bored', 'can't do it', 'don't do well in it', and so on, but ten per cent to twenty per cent in New South Wales, against none in Queensland, disliked a subject because of the 'teacher' ('The teacher is a nong'—as one child so charmingly put it). Queensland primary teachers were spared this particular piece of projection because they were responsible for all subjects (all three; Queensland children disliked either English, maths, or social studies). The Queensland teacher may have been the reason that a child disliked school altogether, but he did not become identified with a single subject.

Another difference between the daily activities of public-school children in the two states which was directly related to a school organizational point was that concerning travel time. In both city and rural areas the New South Wales children spent longer each day travelling to and from their schools. This was particularly so in the cities where the selective organization of the Sydney schools resulted in much more travelling than any sort of area system, whether of primary or secondary schools, would require. This finding was reinforced by that which showed that New South Wales children travelled by train, tram or bus, in much greater numbers than Queenslanders.

School Subjects

All Queensland children, in all areas and types of school, did more homework than the boys and girls of New South Wales. This extra homework time was spent mainly on mathematics and social studies; English ran a very poor third among the three subjects pursued by Queenslanders. No meaningful interstate comparisons can be made on these bases as the fundamental difference that existed is that of the wider dispersion of energies by the New South Wales children among the greater range of subjects that they studied. This also affected the results on favourite subject, most disliked subject, and subject desired.

It was of interest that the definite patterns-according-to-sex of likes and dislikes in English (favoured by girls) and mathematics (favoured by boys) within Queensland was not repeated in New South Wales when a greater spread of subjects was being considered.

When asked about their most disliked subject a significantly greater number of Queenslanders claimed that they had none. This implication, that Queenslanders were more contented with what their schools had to offer, turned out to be consistent with other findings of the survey. When asked how long they would like to stay on at school, fewer Queenslanders claimed that they would 'leave as soon as possible' and a greater number than New South Wales could provide declared that they would 'stay on as long as possible'. Much the same numbers in both states indicated that their parents would make them stay or that they would 'have to leave'. The differences found could not be shown to be significant but the consistency of direction on those questions which provided background on attitude to school is worthy of note. This consistency of direction carried over to the results on the Attitude to Education scale.

Attitude to Education

New South Wales city boys revealed a slight but negligible margin (0.05) over their Queensland counterparts; but in all other subgroups the children from the northern state displayed a more desirable attitude.

Actually, the attitudes revealed by the New South Wales groups were quite acceptable—from the private boys, who scored lowest of all, to the city boys who scored higher than four of the Queensland subsamples. They fell slightly below the English grammar school figures produced by Glassey (1945) and Campbell (1952) but they were considerably above even the best of the secondary modern results assessed by Hill (1956). Hill's scores ranged from 6.28 for his rural sample to 7.15 for his suburban groups. The overall Queensland score of 8.0 closely approached Glassey's mean for grammar school pupils (8.1) and the New South Wales figure was considerably closer to the British grammar school than to the secondary modern. Both Australian groups come into that category designated by Campbell as 'moderately favourable'; but the Queenslanders definitely have the better general attitude.

Attitude to Good Workmanship

The impression of greater 'piety' among the Queensland children was built up further by the results on this scale. Although only one subgroup, the city boys, and the overall figure, could be accepted with confidence as being superior, the consistency of direction intensified the suggestion of a better attitude in Queensland.

The consistently better performance of girls against the relevant boys' subgroups was also worthy of note. Such a finding, were it more definite, would be quite compatible with one's general impression of the roles played by the sexes in Australian society. It was also in the spirit of other findings of this study, pre-eminently those pertaining to 'moral' behaviour.

The regularity with which New South Wales groups covered a greater spread of scores than the Queenslanders, although most differences between S.D.'s were negligible, was suggestive of a possibly variant pattern within the New South Wales system. This could be heavily dependent on the emphasizing and stereotyping of individual differences at a fairly early stage of development by the organizational procedure, fairly common from the early years, of grading classes on overall ability. By this system the brighter and more promising children might be stretched a little, but those who came to regard themselves as 'D' class material could well tend to develop a 'D' class outlook on most things in life—including the 'if-it-works-it's good enough' attitude shown up by this particular test.

In the remainder of the tests assessing personality traits there appeared either no difference between states or differences which favoured Queensland.

On the moral judgements test, girls were more pious than boys—considerably so in terms of these raw scores. There did not appear to be area or type of school differences that could have meaning, but it was of interest that the private boys' samples of both states, all of whom were affiliated with some religious denomination or other, were not outstanding for their superior 'morality'.

Further analyses strengthened the suggestion that New South Wales children might really be inclined to view the activities mentioned with less disapproval than the Queenslanders. It is of interest that item 2,* the one which could be most easily associated with early adolescent development in a society where the 'independent' teenager is commercially inspired, indicated the greatest aberration from the 'straight and narrow'. More than half the children from both states, and in most individual subsamples, condoned lying to a parent in order to protect a member of the peer group from censure for a typically adolescent activity.

In the results for item 6† there was a significant difference between the states that could be related, if not directly attributed, to a school organizational difference. New South Wales children were less likely to be honest in the buses. One remembers from earlier results that New South Wales children utilized public transport (including buses) to a greater extent than Queenslanders. Here is a further dilemma. More New South Wales children have actually faced the problem presented in item 6. Their responses were less desirable, but would undoubtedly have been more 'real'. Was the moral superiority of the Queenslanders a valid one, or was it the result of a theoretical piety superimposed onto an insufficient experiential background? In other words, if more Queenslanders used public transport, might they not have 'morally collapsed' to the same extent?

One further clue was given. In only one group, the private boys, did Queenslanders use bus and tram transport to the same extent as New South Wales boys. In item 6 it was the Queensland private boys who achieved an 'immorality' score equivalent to that of New South Wales.

It seems a logical conclusion that there was a relationship here between the development of the 'immorality' indicated and a facet of school organization which required excessive travelling, and, thus, created the situation of temptation.

*The child indicated degree to which behaviour was wrong in the statement, 'Mary told her mother that Bill was at the pictures because she knew he would get into trouble if it was known he was with the gang in the park.'

†'Shirley had her money ready to pay the bus conductor but, as he didn't get as far as her before the bus arrived at her stop, she got off and put the money back into her pocket.'

Moral Contrasts

The sex differentiation, which had shown up as a characteristic of results on the previous test covering aspects of social conformity, was absolutely maintained in both sections of the test that asked children, not only what they '*should*' do in a given situation, but also what they would be likely to do—what they '*might*' do. The coincidence with what one would expect according to the sexes, in all cases considered, led to a strengthening of one's confidence in other patterns indicated in the results.

Of interest in those results which showed the degree to which the various groups had a knowledge of desirable social behaviour, was the fact that a number of the within-states differences were found to be statistically acceptable. But the only between-states difference of note was found between groups of rural boys and is acceptable at only the five per cent level. More Queensland groups than New South Wales were superior but these results could represent chance fluctuations. These results, therefore, tended to give less support, than those just considered, to state differences. They suggested quite strongly that, in this respect, differences within states were more assertive than those between.

More interesting were the results which indicated the degree to which the groups admitted they might deviate from modes of behaviour they knew to be more 'proper'. Even with the most 'righteous' group, Queensland city girls, there was an admission of twenty per cent deviation from what these children 'knew' to be acceptable behaviour in society. In the most extreme cases, those of Queensland rural boys and New South Wales private boys, the groups would have to improve their likely behaviour by as much as sixty per cent in order to have achieved the levels indicated as what ought to be done. With the exception of the rural boys, all Queensland groups had higher means and S.D.'s but, though some of the differences approached significance, none was acceptable at the five per cent level or better. The pattern, however, was remarkably close to previous ones in which Queensland groups were more 'moral' than New South Wales equivalents, boys were less socially conformist than girls (a number of these differences were significant) and denominational schools were not outstanding for their avowed piety.

Attitude to Authority

Attitude to authority was seen as an important background variable, and worthy of perusal.

The investigation was set up, not to demonstrate, on some subjective assumption, that there were, or were not, 'moral' differences between the states, but to indicate the degree to which various groups within the states identified themselves in a variety of more or less authoritarian situations. The classic studies of Lewin, Lippitt and White (1939) have left educational and psychological circles firmly—and sometimes naïvely—convinced of such 'facts' as the presence in authoritarian organized and dominated groups of more signs of authoritarian behaviour and attitudes between the members of the group. The present writer was aware of the prevalence, among critics from outside (including some from New South Wales), of severe condemnation of what appeared to be 'outdated', excessively authoritarian, methods and attitudes in both classroom procedures and interpersonal relationships in Queensland schools. It was in order to assess factually such criticisms that the attempt was made to set up an 'authoritarian' scale.

The results were clear: there were no groups which were highly authoritarian on all traits; nor were there any which were consistently liberal. But where one state, or group, was liberal, so was the other; where one was apparently harsh it showed as part of what is probably an Australian pattern—not a manifestation of anything provided by one state only. The attitudes revealed might well be engendered by state agencies including education—but such agencies are obviously provided by both states and could not be attributable to the organizational differences being considered.

And how did this section of society feel about the phenomena cited? On only one item—'That delinquent boys should be caned' did they surpass the fifty per cent mark for the authoritarian approach. Flogging for crimes of violence was only moderately opposed and more than a third of each state thought the 'prefects should be obeyed even when they were being unfair and bullying'. Against the extreme penalties, however, the thirteen-year old critic hardened appreciably; over eighty-five per cent of children would not have soldiers shot for disobeying their officers, and more than three-quarters of all asked agreed that the death penalty did not stop people from committing murder. It was not surprising, perhaps, that not much more than one-quarter of the children thought there should be more 'rod' and less 'spoiling' of children thereby. The relevant point of all these patterns is that they applied similarly across both states, and, to a great extent, across all subgroups.

Social Superstitions

The creators of the California F scale (Adorno, *et al.*, 1950) offer a reasoned statement of the likely relationship between attitudes of an authoritarian or antidemocratic kind and tendencies to superstition and stereotypy. Indeed, they included in the revised form of the scale such items as 'Some day it will probably be shown that astrology can explain a lot of things'. The argument is developed that superstition and stereotypy embrace, beyond mere lack of intelligence, certain dispositions in thinking which are closely akin to prejudice.

If this is an indictment of certain groups in 'democratic' society, then it is no small order that the schools of both states have set themselves to train the children 'in the exercise of discrimination and in a healthy habit of scrutinizing new facts and judgments' (N.S.W. aims); 'to develop the power of competent judgment' (Queensland aims).

A true-false test involving twenty popular fallacies resulted in a figure that suggested, overall, that New South Wales children were slightly more sophisticated than those from Queensland. But this was only a suggestion; to claim a definite state difference would be to strain the import of the results and to ignore the inconsistency of direction revealed in closer analysis of the results. Of far more concern was the revelation of social superstitions to a greater extent than, even in the thirteen-year olds, might be condoned with comfort.

Sociometric Study

The boundaries of sociometry are not yet agreed upon by competent people in the field. The author is inclined, however, from personal experience and previous studies, to accept some of the broader implications of earlier work which emphasized relationships between certain group characteristics and the degree of adjustment of the members of that group. In terms of the present study the investigator had desired some measures of the degree to which the two state systems encouraged, allowed, or, at least, resulted in, 'sociability'—that 'living with and for their fellows' referred to in the aims.

The total sociometric findings revealed the complexity of the within-state situations. But they did suggest, too, that there might be some differences pertaining to sociability between the states that could be attributed to aspects of organization.

That the results were not more definite is not surprising if one is at all convinced by the author's allegations of homogeneity throughout the communities represented and full cognizance is taken of the importance of home and local environment on individual development. To a great extent the school in both states stands outside the community. It is an externally imposed institution, basically authoritarian in comparison to most home atmospheres, and, in this respect, therefore, a similar factor in individual development in most cases, whatever the subtleties of its organization that professional educationists might come to feel so strongly about. Although the aims are common, neither state does much directly towards 'sociability' beyond class grouping, lip-service to 'mateship' concepts, team sport procedures (which, it was seen, did not directly affect all—and are of doubtful value anyhow*) and an official liaison with the basic Christian ethic.

Beyond this, and in practice, both systems militate strongly against dependence on one's fellows—and, hence, one's mixing with them for 'work' purposes—by an excessive emphasis on individual rivalry. Not only does this happen through examination-dominated procedures in the classrooms of both states, still, but it is also built into the administrational and, particularly, promotional structure of teacher development. Representatives of one particular state might see 'big' differences in the activities of another

---

*Drinkwater (1956) contains a full discussion of the possible value of team sports in character development.

but, compared with those between active stressing of individual competition and any real education for cooperation and 'working-togetherness', such differences as an extra external examination in Queensland, or a longer and slightly more liberal teacher education in New South Wales, become so relatively slight as to make no overall impression. And what the socio-metric study might have revealed as desirable aspects of coeducational groups were negated, or became clouded by a complex of other pertinent factors.

General Discussion of the Personality Findings

A consensus of indications from the individual personality assessments would more strongly favour a generalization of sameness across the states rather than differences between them. But the above-mentioned specific and significant differences *did* show up, and where they showed, they favoured Queensland. So some attempt at elucidation should be offered.

So limited was the coverage of traits, as against a total personality picture, and so complex the variables that could not be controlled in this assessment, that the following attempt at explanation can only be offered as suggestive. It is an explanation, however, that fits all the facts that have come to light.

A clue given in the sociometric results sets the basis for this theory. There appeared to be signs of greater social expansiveness, among some Queensland classes, which could be explained as one of the effects of the more long-term stability of the groups concerned. This stability is the key. On the whole, the educational environment of the Queensland thirteen-year old had not been seriously disturbed for eight years. The school building, the majority of the peer group and the main social forces working within and upon the school, had varied little; where they had changed, and where teaching personnel had come and gone, these experiences had been shared by a cohesive and relatively permanent coterie, so that any emotional or disturbing effects were accepted as externally imposed events which did not upset the essential nature of things. The schools were, to a greater extent than those checked in New South Wales, more local in their intake and other aspects or organization; it was more likely that to some extent their social outlook is more parochial than in New South Wales. The children had the problem of adjusting to a number of adult person-alities but, on the whole, at the rate of only one per year, and their adjustment had had a greater chance of completeness when they had shared the procedures of all 'school' work, together with such experiences as games, visits, special functions and any other event that happened along, with a single guide and mentor.

The New South Wales children, on the other hand, had undergone a considerable organizational upset eighteen months prior to the adminis-tration of these tests. Following six years of a background such as that just described for Queenslanders, they had suffered a change of school environment, they had to adjust to their knowledge coming in discrete 'packages' each with its own subject label, and, possibly most impressive of all, they had faced an adaptation to regular but frequent changes of adult guidance (and example) during any one school day or week. The common secondary device of appointing one of the subject teachers as a 'form' master is an attempt at compensation, but in many respects is an inadequate substitute for the single-teacher organization of the primary school.

The New South Wales children had also made the personal adjustment from being the biggest, and therefore the most important, people in their 'little' school to relatively insignificant roles in their new 'big' school. In the case of city children in New South Wales this modification had been further complicated by the fact that a percentage of the children would have been feeling relatively successful in having achieved placement in a better (selective high) school while others would have been aware of the fact that they had been relegated to a second-grade school—in spite of the terminology, junior technical or domestic science.

What were the apparent effects of these organizational differences? The New South Wales children appeared to be more 'sophisticated' than those of Queensland. This judgement was based on their slight ascendency in attainments, both measured and assessed, the tendency to be less socially 'superstitious' on some items than the Queenslanders, and the superiority of their standard in independent study skills. The sociometric results showed that the children had quite quickly welded into fairly healthy social groups. But, as observation and such phenomena as the projection of subject weaknesses against individual teachers revealed, they had achieved an existence which was more independent of any particular adult guide, and, therefore, more independent of adults, than they previously had. The social unit was more essentially the class, rather than the class-and-the-class-teacher as was the case in primary school.

This increased independence had apparently not been without cost. In making their more responsible adjustment to the increased pressures of living represented by a more complex school organization the New South Wales children had suffered some emotional and moral disturbance. In their moral judgements they were inclined to be more tolerant of aberrations from the strict demands of society; they tended to be a little less definite in their awareness of those actions considered more ethical in society and were likely to perform at a relatively 'worse' level; their attitude to the doing of a good job for its own sake was significantly less desirable; the only indication of differences in attitude to authority showed that New South Wales thirteen-year olds generally were more highly authoritarian in their attitude to the treatment of criminals, a possible reaction to increased social pressure; and, in spite of the apparently more relaxed and recreative time they were allowed to have, both in and out of school, their attitude to education did not equal that of their harder worked, more stable neighbours.

Support for this theory came when we could directly trace one case of 'moral breakdown' to the fact that the New South Wales children had been forced to come to grips with their total social environment to a greater extent—and this, by school organization. The groups who showed that they most had to use public transport also showed that they were least opposed to dishonesty in that environment. The further possible differences in 'moral lassitude', although not demonstrably significant, were 'damning' in the preponderance of their direction; these could have been a function of the alleged 'sophistication', which, in its turn, was a result of an earlier forced dependence—the result of school organization.

Thus, the phenomena can be explained in a logic which takes account of all those aspects of education and children with which this study purports to be concerned. The author has deliberately refrained from evaluating all this—and apologizes for what might seem, therefore, the excessive use of inverted commas in describing 'moral' terms. The point is, of course, that only the society concerned can evaluate the worth or, if it is discovered that dilemmas exist, the relative merits of effects revealed. Postponement of temptations may not be really desirable. It is possible that Queenslanders might yet have to go through this stage, as an unavoidable aspect of maturation and preparation for responsible social living. On the other hand, what appear to be unwelcome concomitants of certain aspects of education might be modifiable by greater educational effort—including further refinements in organization.

School Organization and the Homogeneous Society

Having discussed where organization might have had some influence on the traits of pupils, it is of interest to consider, in toto, where—and why, if possible—it did *not* have an expected effect.

The alleged broadening of horizons, and what has been called sophistication, in the New South Wales groups, have had no apparent effect on tastes that seem to be characteristic of age and sex.

The reorganization of children into secondary schools obviously had no effect, in itself, in determining the aspects of reading considered in this study.

If selection of favourites in other fields, too, in radio, television and various forms of organized entertainment, is alleged to be a manifestation of some aspect of maturity, then in these respects there are no maturity differences between the states.

Whatever constitutes maturity in terms of class social structures, and this would vary somewhat according to subjectively established criteria, there is no basis in the sociometric results for a firm decision on whether the children of one state or the other definitely make more mature social adjustments. Revelations of greater social expansiveness in rural groups in Queensland—which have been attributed to the longevity of the class structure—are balanced by suggestions of beneficial effects in New South Wales which seem to be complicated by whether organization is coeducational or not. And the point has been made that New South Wales groups have achieved their position of fairly widespread equivalence in a shorter time together. But to decide arbitrarily which of these patterns is more mature would only distort the main contribution of the sociometric study, that the characteristics of groups in both states are very similar and are conditioned by larger social and personal environmental factors more than by school organization.

The major social determinants of behaviour also diminish the effects of school in most activities relating to the use of leisure time, the worthy conditioning of which is an avowed aim of both school systems. Not only the assessed Leisure Activity Index but most of the questions pertaining to special aspects of leisure pursuits indicated remarkable similarities between the representatives of the subgroups as well as across states. It is fairly obvious from this that the schools are doing jobs of equal 'efficiency' in respect to this aim.

It would be much more difficult and hazardous to conjecture on the efficiency of the job that *both* systems are doing. One would have suspected, from a theoretical consideration of efforts made, that New South Wales with its increased sport, greater and freer inclusion of art/music/handwork, more school visits, and at the time of the study, greater expenditure per head on education, would have produced a potential citizen who was more worthily active in his leisure moments. The fact that this had not happened indicates fairly conclusively that the determinants of such characteristics are more in the nature of sex, age, sociocultural background and overall social emphases on recreational patterns than they are in primary or secondary school organization, exact geographic location, or even, in this case, in modifications of curriculum and timetable.

None of this is to say, of course, that schools *could not* have a powerful effect in conditioning such facets of character, but it is extremely likely that to do so the formal educational institutions would have to be working along with other agencies of education in the total society, such as the mass media and legislation affecting the overall structure of social living.

References

ACER, 1951: English and Arithmetic for the Australian Educational Research.

Adorno, T. W., Frenkel-Brunswik, E., *et al.*, 1950: *The Authoritarian Personality*. Harper & Bros, New York.

American Educational Research Association (AERA), 1931: *Review of Educational Research*, 1, 3. School Organization, National Education Association, Washington, D.C.

Campbell, W. J., 1952: The influence of home environment on the educational progress of selective secondary school children. *British Journal of Educational Psychology*, 22, Pt II, 89-100.

Cunningham, K. S. and Price, W. T., 1934: *The Standardization of an Australian Arithmetic Test*. Melbourne University Press, Melbourne.

Drinkwater, D. J., 1956: An assessment of the value of physical education in character training for boys. Unpublished MA thesis, University of London.

Drinkwater, D. J., 1962: A comparative study of the effects of different types of school organisation on the traits of pupils. Unpublished PhD thesis, University of London.

Glassey, W., 1945: The attitude of grammar school pupils and their parents to education, religion and sport. Unpublished MA thesis, Manchester University.

Harris, C. W. (Ed.), 1960: *Encyclopedia of Educational Research* (3rd edn). Macmillian & Co., New York.

Hill, C. G. N., 1956: An evaluation of some aspects of the development of pupils in secondary modern schools. Unpublished PhD thesis, University of London. Summarized in *British Journal of Educational Psychology*, 28 (1958), Pt II, 177-180.

Keller, R. J., 1958: Secondary education—organization and administration. In C. W. Harris (Ed.), *Encyclopedia of Educational Research* (3rd edn). Macmillian & Co., New York.

Lewin, K., Lippitt, R. and White, R. K., 1939: Patterns of aggressive behaviour in experimentally created 'social climates'. *Journal of Social Psychology*, 10, 271-299.

New South Wales, 1957: *Report of Committee on Secondary Education.* N.S.W. Government Printer, Sydney.

Queensland Department of Public Instruction, 1952: The syllabus of course of instruction in primary and intermediate schools, Books 1-4. Government Printer, Brisbane.

Reavis, W. C., 1931: Evaluation of the various units of the public school system. *Review of Educational Research*, 1, 3, 173-193.

Shane, H. G. and Polychrones, J. Z., 1957: Elementary education—organization and administration. In C. W. Harris (Ed.), *Encyclopedia of Educational Research* (3rd edn). Macmillian & Co., New York.

12

Chemistry Scholars in School and University Contexts: A Study of Transition from School to University

J. M. Genn

Introduction

As STERN (1961) has said, 'Our knowledge of transition from high school to college has been limited in the past to attempts to predict college grades from high school performance.' He has further remarked that it is only recently that 'a body of literature dealing with high school and college as social processes has begun to emerge'. Goodstein (1960) has spoken of 'the crucial importance of understanding students as complicated human beings in equally complex social-psychological environments', and this view is increasingly widely held. If, then, an effective study of transition from school to university is to be made, it seems that what is required is a model which can cope with the complexity of the interaction of unique personalities with school and university environments that are uniquely perceived.

The study reported here draws heavily on Murray's need-press theory which first appeared in his *Explorations in Personality* (1938). Only a bare outline treatment of this theory is possible here, and the reader should consult some of the following for further details: Pace and Stern (1958), Stern (1962a, 1963a, 1963b, 1964, 1967), Stern, Stein and Bloom (1956), Murray (1938), and Murray and Kluckhohn (1953).

The Lewinian equation, $B = f(P,E)$, (behaviour is a function of the person and the environment), is well known and it has been given a wider psychological relevance by the new topologists who have taken it out of the original context of Lewin's theorizing concerning the instantaneous total situation or life space. Lewin's novel idea of conceptualizing behaviour as a molar event involving an actor and a broad contextual setting is now foundational in much educational and psychological research. But until Murray presented his need-press theory, and until more adequate measures of E (environment) were available, the Lewinian equation was more admired than used. Almost all measurement before this time was of P (person).

In Murray's writings, 'the concept of need represents the significant determinants of behavior within the person, and the concept of press represents the significant determinants of behavior in the environment'. (Pace, 1963). The model for studying behaviour then becomes 'the inter-action between personal needs and environmental press' (Pace, 1964).

'Just as needs are inferred from the characteristic modes of response of an individual, so press are reflected in the characteristic pressures, stresses, rewards, conformity-demanding influences of the college culture.' (Pace & Stern, 1958.) Press, for Stern (1967), is a 'taxonomic classification of characteristic behaviors manifested by aggregates of individuals in their mutual interpersonal transactions'. He says press 'may be inferred from events reported in the objective perceptual field of the participant' (1967), and he points out that there may be 'genuine disparity between the per-ceived situation and the veridical one' but 'no disparity for the perceiver under ordinary circumstances'.

It is important at this point to raise the issue of idiosyncratic perception versus consensual perception. Stern (1962a) has written:

> In the ultimate sense of the term, press refers to the phenomenological world of the individual, the unique and inevitably private view which each person has of the events in which he takes part . . . [but] . . . there is a point at which this private world merges with that of others. . . . Both the private and the mutually shared press are of interest in their own right, but, in the final analysis, the inferences we make as observers about the events in which others participate are the ultimate source of a taxonomy of situational variables. (p. 29.)

Congruence is an important concept as we consider individuals inter-acting with environments. 'The congruence-dissonance dimension is based on a hypothetical psychological symmetry between person and environ-ment.' (Stern, 1967.) An individual has, perhaps, a high need for affilia-tion. He may find himself in an environment where the press towards affi-liation is very low. Stern (1967) says that, 'For the individual case, a con-gruent relationship would be one producing a sense of satisfaction or fulfillment. Discomfort and distress are concomitants of dissonance.' When we match students with environments we want to know about the relation-ship between individuals' needs and the environmental press. But which press? Stern (1967) says 'It might be concluded inasmuch as phenomenal reality is idiosyncratic, the entire problem can only be resolved by working with each subject as an individual unit, matching his needs with *his* press.' He admits that greater precision in prediction would follow use of idio-syncratic rather than consensual press.

The two fundamental measuring instruments used in the advancement of need-press theory have been the Activities Index (AI) measuring needs, and the College Characteristics Index (CCI) measuring environmental press. In each case the instruments consist of 300 questions, 30 groups of 10, each group relating to a particular psychological dimension. The same 30 dimensions used for describing needs are used in the description of press. The actual 30 dimensions used are indicated below, and brief descriptions of each are provided. This listing and the descriptions are taken from Stern (1963*b*).

Need-Press Scale Definitions

1 ABA *Abasement*—ass *Assurance*: self-depreciation versus self-confidence.
2 ACH *Achievement*: striving for success through personal effort.
3 ADA *Adaptability*—dfs *Defensiveness*: acceptance of criticism versus resistance to suggestion.
4 AFF *Affiliation*—rej *Rejection*: friendliness versus unfriendliness.
5 AGG *Aggression*—bla *Blame Avoidance*: hostility versus its inhibition.
6 CHA *Change*—sam *Sameness*: flexibility versus routine.
7 CNJ *Conjunctivity*—dsj *Disjunctivity*: planfulness versus disorganization.
8 CTR *Counteraction*—inf *Inferiority Avoidance*: restriving after failure versus withdrawal.
9 DFR *Deference*—rst *Restiveness*: respect for authority versus rebelliousness.
10 DOM *Dominance*—tol *Tolerance*: ascendancy versus forbearance.
11 E/A *Ego Achievement*: striving for power through social action.
12 EMO *Emotionality*—plc *Placidity*: expressiveness versus restraint.
13 ENY *Energy*—pas *Passivity*: effort versus inertia.
14 EXH *Exhibitionism*—inf *Inferiority Avoidance*: attention-seeking versus shyness.
15 F/A *Fantasied Achievement*: daydreams of extraordinary public recognition.
16 HAR *Harm Avoidance*—rsk *Risktaking*: fearfulness versus thrill-seeking.
17 HUM *Humanities, Social Science*: interests in the humanities and the social sciences.
18 IMP *Impulsiveness*—del *Deliberation*: impetuousness versus reflection.
19 NAR *Narcissism*: vanity.
20 NUR *Nurturance*—rej *Rejection*: helping others versus indifference.
21 OBJ *Objectivity*—pro *Projectivity*: detachment versus superstition (AI) or suspicion (CCI).
22 ORD *Order*—dso *Disorder*: compulsive organization of details versus carelessness.
23 PLY *Play*—wrk *Work*: pleasure-seeking versus purposefulness.
24 PRA *Practicalness*—ipr *Impracticalness*: interest in practical activities versus indifference.
25 REF *Reflectiveness*: introspective contemplation.
26 SCI *Science*: interests in the natural sciences.

27 SEN   *Sensuality*—pur *Puritanism*: ιnterest in sensory and aesthetic experiences.

28 SEX   *Sexuality*—pru *Prudishness*: heterosexual interests versus their inhibition.

29 SUP   *Supplication*—aut *Autonomy*: dependency versus self-reliance.

30 UND   *Understanding*: intellectuality.

To measure, for example, a student's need for achievement, the student is asked to indicate whether he likes or dislikes such tasks as the following: setting difficult goals for himself, working for someone who will accept nothing less than the best that is in him, competing with others for a prize or goal, taking examinations, choosing difficult tasks in preference to easy ones, sacrificing everything else in order to achieve something outstanding.

To measure, for example, the press of the environment towards achievement, the students in the environment are asked to answer whether such descriptions of their college, as follow, are true or false: the competition for grades is intense; it is fairly easy to pass most courses without working very hard; most courses require intensive study and preparation out of class; personality, pull and bluff get students through many courses; students who work hard for high grades are likely to be regarded as odd; students set high standards of achievement for themselves.

While there is a nomological parallelism between the AI and the CCI, it has been found that the factorial dimensions of need and press are by no means as parallel as the input constructs (Stern, 1967). This, of course, raises problems when it comes to the measurement of congruence. Stern (1967) says that the 'common space in which need and press dimensions interact still remains to be isolated'. However, Webb and Crowder (1965) present a useful rationale for the comparison of need and press and seem to have somewhat qualitatively solved Stern's quantitative problem. They say:

> One possible resolution of the difficulty might involve considering strength for initiating action as a basic common characteristic of need and press. The needs might be regarded as inner motives or directional forces. The press might be considered as external (environmental) forces to which motivating properties have been attached or projected from the several individuals of the environment through the process of cathexis. Then it might be possible to scale need and press in terms of their motivating strength. (p. 431.)

Pace and Stern (1958) have supplied basic hypotheses to keep researchers busy for some time. For example, they say, *inter alia*, 'It is possible that the total pattern of congruence between personality needs and environmental press will be more predictive of achievement, growth and change than any single aspect of either the person or the environment', and in particular they suggest a close look at 'the significance of congruence between needs and press in determining successful performance and/or satisfaction in the college environment'. Stern (1962*b*) asks: 'Is dissonance or stress a motivating factor in student growth?' He further asks: 'What is an optimal environment—one that satisfies, or one that stimulates?' and somewhat light-heartedly points out that while pearls come from 'aggravated oysters' you can only get milk from 'contented cows'.

Clearly there are enormous potentialities for institutional self-study and analysis in the need-press theory. Any academic institution can now get both a broad and a detailed view of what students bring to the institution, and what the institution does to them. Also, the institution can learn much from syndromes of student achievement and satisfaction. In the study which follows, the attempt is made to realize some of these theoretical potentialities when the institution is a university department.

Aims of this Research Study : Basic Hypotheses

The general aim was to focus on chemistry education and to isolate and consider some educational and psychological issues relevant to transition of students from school to university.

In particular the aims were:

(a) to study the nature of chemistry education environments in school and university and the nature of the differences between the school and the university environments; and

(b) to see if information about students' personality needs and their perceptions of the press of their school and their university chemistry education environments contributes

(i) to our understanding of the nature of success and satisfaction in first-year university chemistry studies, and

(ii) to the prediction of success and satisfaction.

Basic hypotheses relating to these aims were generated. However, certain measuring instruments and statistical procedures were required before these hypotheses could be tested. These instruments and procedures are described in the next section on the methodology of this research, and the hypotheses, with the results of their testing, are set out subsequently.

Methodology

Only an outline treatment is possible here. For details concerning methodology see the full report of this study (Genn, 1969).

Measuring instruments

The Activities Index (AI) was used to measure needs.

To measure the environmental press of the chemistry education environment a special instrument called the CEEI (Chemistry Education Environment Index) was constructed.

It is necessary to discuss briefly the concept of a chemistry education environment. Astin (1965) and Pace (1964) have shown the reality of subenvironments in colleges and universities. Often, naturally, these environments are centred on academic subjects. Falk (1967) has noted that 'The environment of a department will embody the attitudes conventional in that field', and she asks: 'Do knowledge, skills and attitudes to be acquired in a particular field differ in ways which will make generalisations about "good teaching" .... misleading guides when applied to a particular subject?'

In secondary schools, of course, the 'chemistry department' is not as visible or separate as it is in university. However, in terms of the specialist teachers, the distinctive group of students, the specialist laboratories, lecture rooms and libraries, the other peculiar behaviour settings and the general ethos characterizing chemistry learning and teaching at school, it seems a sufficiently realistically-based idea to speak of a school 'chemistry department'. In any case it is reasonable to ask students, whether they are at school or at university, about their perceptions of the environmental press which they experience in their chemistry classes.

It was decided to measure separately faculty press (the influences ascribable to teacher behaviour) and student press (the influences ascribable to student behaviour), each along the 30 usual dimensions. Some items in existing press scales of Murray (1938), Pace and Stern (1958), Stern (1963b) and Thistlethwaite (1962) were adapted for the chemistry education environment. Many other new items had to be generated. It is important to note that the same scales and items were used for measuring school environmental press and university environmental press.

A scale called SATTCH, (Satisfaction with Teaching), was developed on the basis of the Satisfaction with Faculty scale in the College Student Questionnaires (Peterson, 1965).

The results of students in the end-of-first-year university chemistry examination were available. So, too, were the results of the end-of-school Senior Public Chemistry Examination (matriculation).

The sample and test administration

One hundred and thirty-five medical students (95 men, 40 women), in the Chemistry I class, 1967, at the University of Queensland, Brisbane, constituted the main sample. There was also a sample of science students at the University of Queensland, Brisbane ($n = 86$ or 85), and a sample of students at the Townsville University College ($n = 69$ or 68 or 54), and some data from these samples are used for comparative purposes in this study.

In March 1967 the students completed the AI. At this time, also, they completed the CEEI and SATTCH in terms of their 1966 secondary school experience. In July 1967, after two terms at university, they completed the CEEI and SATTCH again, this time in terms of their university experience.

Instrument properties and checks

Parsimony, Factors, Factor Scores: Having administered 150 scales, each of 10 items (30 scales for needs and 30 scales for each of faculty press at university, student press at university, faculty press at school, student press at school), it was desirable in the interests of parsimony to reduce the dimensionality of the need and press measurement. Using principal components analysis, retaining those factors for which the latent roots were greater than unity, and then using Varimax rotations, the following factors were extracted and named—

From the 30 needs scales : 8 factors
- V1   Conforming, humble
- V2   Emotional, expressive
- V3   Achievement-striving
- V4   Reflective, academic
- V5   Unsociable, shy
- V6   Projective
- V7   Passive, cautious
- V8   Orderly, organized

From the 30 faculty press scales when measuring *faculty press : university* (FPU) : 4 factors
- V9   Academically unencouraging
- V10 Dominating, suspicious
- V11 Unexpressive, restrictive
- V12 Humane, friendly

From the 30 student press scales when measuring *student press : university* (SPU) : 7 factors
- V13 Deferential, restrained
- V14 Industrious, studious
- V15 Confident, objective
- V16 Unreflective, insensitive
- V17 Dependent, friendly
- V18 Unconcerned with self and sexuality
- V19 Ambitious, imaginative

From the 30 faculty press scales when measuring *faculty press : school* (FPS) : 4 factors
- V20 Academically unencouraging
- V21 Aggressive, dominating
- V22 Social involvement
- V23 Unrestrictive, relaxed control

From the 30 student press scales when measuring *student press : school* (SPS) : 7 factors
- V24 Not academic, not studious
- V25 Insensitive, unexpressive
- V26 Introverted, not practical
- V27 Objective, confident
- V28 Independent, unhelpful
- V29 Unconcerned with self and sexuality
- V30 Aggressive, disrespectful

Factors are hypothetical variables. It is possible to calculate for a person his score on a factor, knowing his score on each of the 30 variables involved in the domain and knowing the loadings of each of these variables on the factor. The factor scores were obtained as standard scores, with a mean of zero and a standard deviation of unity, and factors in a domain were uncorrelated. Having factor scores both as standard scores and as virtually normalized (central limit theorem), permitted ready comparisons within and across domains. (*See* Difference scores, below.)

Parallelism: It was of considerable interest to see if the factorial dimensions of need and FPU (faculty press : university) were comparable, because one was interested in matters of need-press congruence in the university context. The reader can see that essentially comparable parallel dimensions exist if need and press are compared as follows:

Need		Faculty Press : University
V2	and	−V11
V3	and	−V9
−V5	and	V12
V7	and	V10

Difference scores

Four 'difference variables', to be called faculty press difference variables, 'FAPR-DF', were established.

As the reader can see, the factors for FPS and FPU are essentially identical in nature and this and the psychometric properties already mentioned meant that it was possible to find for each student his difference score when his FPU score for a certain factor was subtracted from his FPS score for the corresponding factor. For each student four such scores were available, viz.

B1 (change of academically unencouraging press)   V20–(V9)
B2 (change of aggressive, dominating, suspicious press)   V21–(V10)
B3 (change of social involvement, humane, friendly press)   V22–(V12)
B4 (change of unrestrictive, relaxed, expressive press)   V23–(−V11)

Four difference variables, to be called need-press difference variables or 'ND-PR-DF' variables, were also established.

As has already been noted, it is possible to select needs factors which are parallel to particular FPU factors, and for reasons given earlier it is valid to find for each student his difference score when his FPU score for a certain factor is subtracted from his need score for the corresponding need factor. For each student four such scores were available, viz.

A1 (need for achievement-striving minus corresponding press) V3–(−V9)
A2 (need for passivity, caution minus corresponding press)   V7–(V10)
A3 (need for sociability and outgoing minus corresponding press)
                                                         −V5–(V12)
A4 (need for emotional expressiveness minus corresponding press)
                                                         V2–(−V11)

Definitions of achievement and satisfaction levels

Those students who, in the first-year university chemistry examination, failed outright (N) or were given supplementary examinations, (NZ, NS), constituted the lowest level of achievement (27 students); those who gained the award of pass (P), pass-minus (P−), or pass conceded (PC), constituted the next or medium level of achievement (72 students); those who gained awards of credit (C), distinction (D), or high distinction (HD) constituted the third or highest level (36 students).

Those students scoring below 33 out of a possible 60 in SATTCH (Satisfaction with Teaching) at university constituted the 'not satisfied' category (36 students); those scoring 34 to 41 constituted the 'satisfied' category (66 students); those scoring 42 or higher constituted the 'very satisfied' category (33 students).

Concepts of 'over' and 'under' achievement and 'over' and 'under' satisfaction

Scores on the matriculation chemistry examination and on the first-year university chemistry examination were normalized and the difference (university minus school) between normalized scores on the examinations found for each student. When this difference was sufficiently great and positive a student was labelled as an 'overachiever'; when the difference was sufficiently great and negative a student was labelled as an 'underachiever'. All other students were described as 'achieving as expected'.

Similarly, by working with scores on SATTCH (Satisfaction with Teaching) at school and university, it was possible to arrive at groups that could be labelled, respectively, 'undersatisfied', 'satisfied as expected' and 'oversatisfied'.

Experimental design and major statistical analysis, with an explanatory note on discriminant analysis

Essentially, the study was concerned with comparisions of the kind where a group called 'school' was compared with a group called 'university', or where, say, a group called 'high achievers' was compared with groups called 'medium achievers' and 'low achievers'. Also, the comparisons were to be holistic, i.e., they were to be made taking full account of a number of variables (*m*), all operating together in each of the groups being compared.

Multivariate techniques appear to be highly relevant in a study of the nature of learning environments or of the interaction of unique persons with uniquely perceived environments. Such techniques, with the exception of factor analysis, have not as yet been much used in educational and psychological research. Because the reader may be unfamiliar with the particular multivariate techniques to be used in the testing of the research hypotheses in this study, an explanatory note on these techniques follows. Cooley and Lohnes (1962) and Tiedeman (1951) are useful references.

Using multivariate analysis of variance it is possible, taking cognizance of the m variables simultaneously operating, to decide whether groups are, in fact, different, or whether differences are not sufficiently great to warrant rejection of the null hypothesis, Ho. This hypothesis would be to the effect that the groups being compared on the m variables have arisen from the same population. If Ho is rejected one can proceed to make a separate univariate analysis, in which one sees what differences, if any, exist among the groups on each variable.

If Ho is rejected, one can also proceed to a discriminant analysis which essentially gives to each of the variables a discriminant weight indicating the contribution that the variable makes to the separation of the groups. It is possible to discover which of the variables are most important in causing the differences among the groups. A discriminant function is obtained, and an individual's score on this function is calculable, knowing his score on each of the m variables and knowing the discriminant weight for each of the variables. The discriminant scores for each of the groups cluster around the respective group centroids. A centroid is the average discriminant score for a group on the discriminant function. The purpose of the discriminant analysis is, as it were, to pull the centroids as far apart as possible and to make the discriminant scores in particular groups cluster as closely as possible around the respective centroids. This discriminant function is a new hypothetical variable which can usually be named and given psychological meaning, and, as we shall presently see, this is a very useful way of arriving at a condensed and empirically-based statement about what constitutes the essential difference between or among groups. The naming or interpretation of the discriminant function is accomplished by noting the variables which are most heavily weighted on the function or which are most highly correlated with the function. (*Note*: where more than two groups are being compared it is possible to arrive at more than one discriminant function. The maximum number obtainable is $g - 1$ or m, whichever is smaller, where g is the number of groups and m is the number of variables. Where there are two discriminant functions the centroids and clusters of discriminant scores are in a two-dimensional space; if there are three functions then a three-dimensional space is involved, and so on.)

Supposing one has just the one discriminant function, and one knows where the centroids for particular groups are, as well as the variability of discriminant scores for members of particular groups around the respective centroids. Suppose, then, that one is presented with the m scores for some person not involved in any of the experimental work up to this point. The question is: which group does this new individual most resemble, on the basis of his m scores? This question can be readily answered by calculating his discriminant score. Sometimes, knowing this score, one can, at a glance, answer this question. More accurately, and in general, one uses probability theory, working out which group the individual is most like, this theory taking account of the position of the population centroids and the dispersion of population scores around each. The population characteristics are inferred from the sample data. The procedure just outlined indicates the extreme usefulness of discriminant analysis and allied classification procedures.

Sometimes, to indicate just how good a discriminant function will prove in prediction, one can proceed as follows. Suppose there were, in the analysis, 27 people in group A, 72 in group B and 36 in group C, 135 in all. One knows, of course, which group a particular person is in. Suppose for each of the 135 people the discriminant score is calculated. One can take each of the 135 scores in turn and see what population it most resembles. Naturally, if the discriminant function has power, most people will be 'assigned' as it were, by the computer, to their 'right' population or group, i.e., the one to which they actually belong. A correct placement is called a 'hit'. One might finally get a table as shown below:

		Group Entered			
		A	B	C	
	A	17	33	1	51
Group Predicted	B	7	24	6	37
	C	3	15	29	47
		27	72	36	135

Proportion of 'hits' $\dfrac{17}{27}$ $\dfrac{24}{72}$ $\dfrac{29}{36}$ $\dfrac{70}{135}$ Total

Testing Hypotheses

In this section the hypotheses are presented in a form amenable to statistical analysis and the results of the analysis are provided.

HYPOTHESIS 1

That, taking all thirty faculty press variables together, there is no difference between the perceived faculty press in the chemistry education environments at school and at university.

Analysis

One hundred and thirty-five students answered the faculty press scales twice, first in terms of their school experience, then in terms of their university experience.

$$F = 17.22 : df = 30, 105 : P = .0000$$

Only one discriminant function was obtained.
Discriminant weights $> |.2|$ were found for ABA (.28), ACH (.36), AFF (.22), AGG (.30), CTR (.26), NUR (.35), SUP (.36) and CHA (−.22).

School centroid = 10.67
University centroid = 5.49

Variables for which correlation with the discriminant function was greater than .5 were: ACH (.67), ADA (.67), AFF (.73), CTR (.70), E/A

(.58), F/A (.64), HUM (.51), NUR (.75), ORD (.51), REF (.54), SUP (.68).

On the basis of the high correlations just listed, it appears that the discriminant variable could be described as the extent to which faculty press is friendly, humane, helpful, encouraging of striving, critical, and encouraging of dependency. The higher the discriminant score, the more school-like is the faculty press.

In univariate F tests (degrees of freedom = 1, 134 : P = .05), school faculty press was found to be significantly less than university faculty press on DFR and DOM. School faculty press was significantly greater than university faculty press on all other scales except ABA, CHA, OBJ, PLY and SEX.

Summary

Ho is rejected. There *is* a difference between the perceived faculty press in the chemistry education environments at school and at university. The discriminant variable is virtually identical with 'hovering concern' (Alpern, 1966), by which he meant that school teachers are, in general, more friendly, concerned and supervisory than the university lecturers.

HYPOTHESIS 2

That, taking all thirty student press variables together, there is no difference between the perceived student press in the chemistry education environments at school and at university.

Analysis

One hundred and thirty-five students answered the student press scales twice, first in terms of their school experience, then in terms of their university experience.

$$F = 10.68 : df = 30, 105 : P = .0000$$

Only one discriminant function was obtained.
Discriminant weights $> |.2|$ were found for AFF (.56), CTR (.24), DOM (.27), NUR (.20), PLY (.24), PRA (.21), ABA (−.35) and DFR (−.21).

School centroid = 2.61
University centroid = −0.74

Correlations of variables with the discriminant function, where $r > |.3|$, were for AFF (.54), AGG (.39), CTR (.31), DOM (.49), IMP (.36), PLY (.37), PRA (.54), ABA (−.40), DFR (−.53).

The discriminant variable could be described as the extent to which the student press is friendly, playful, counteractive, dominating, aggressive, not abasive, not deferential, and practical. The higher the discriminant score, the more school-like is the student press.

In univariate F tests (df = 1, 134 : P = .05), school student press was significantly less than university student press on ABA, CNJ, DFR, ENY, HAR, REF and SEN. School student press was significantly greater than university student press on ADA, AFF, AGG, CTR, DOM, EMO, EXH, IMP, PLY, PRA and SUP.

Summary

Ho is rejected. There *is* a difference between the perceived student press in the chemistry education environments at school and at university. The discriminant variable is meaningful. It is in line with differences between school and university students one would expect on the basis of the selection factors one knows are at work.

HYPOTHESIS 3

That a small university, as far as the press of its chemistry education environment is concerned, is somewhere between a typical school and a large university.

Analysis

The groups involved were, for faculty press, 68 'school' students, i.e., students reporting on their school experience before they enrolled at Townsville University College, 54 students of a small university (Townsville University College), and 85 students of a large university (Brisbane). The numbers involved, for student press, were 69, 54 and 86 respectively. A table was constructed in which, for each of the 30 dimensions of faculty press, the actual mean scores for school, the small university and the large university were inserted.

As far as faculty press is concerned, in 23 out of 30 three-way comparisons the small university was intermediate in position, i.e., between school and large university.

A similar table was constructed for student press, and, in this case, in 16 out of 30 three-way comparisons, the small university occupied the intermediate position.

In both tables, and particularly in the first, it appeared that there were good grounds for upholding the hypothesis. What is more, when satisfaction with teaching (SATTCH) was looked at, in the three environments, the small university was again intermediate, and comparison indicated that satisfaction decreased from school, through small university to large university.

These results are interesting and significant. A small university is something like school and something like a big university. Students in a small university must have a different 'transition experience' from those in a large university.

HYPOTHESIS 4A

That there are no differences among three 'achievement' groups on the basis of scores of members of each group on the thirty need and press factor variables. (V1—V30, i.e., eight needs, four FPU variables, seven SPU variables, four FPS variables, seven SPS variables).

Analysis

Low achievers $n = 27$
Medium achievers $n = 72$

High achievers $n = 36$
$$F = 1.405 : df = 60, 206 : P = .04$$

Only one discriminant function was significant (73.91% of variance). Discriminant weights $> |.2|$ were as follows:

Positive: V3 (.26), V7 (.23), V12 (.20), V22 (.23), V24 (.33), V26 (.23), V28 (.21).

Negative: V9 (−.39), V11 (−.30), V14 (−.20), V20 (−.21), V21 (−.27).

Centroids:
Low achievers   = −0.41
Medium achievers = −0.25
High achievers   = 0.79

Correlations of variables with the discriminant function, where $r > |.17|$, $(P = .05)$, were:

Positive: V3 (.26), V5 (.30), V7 (.41), V8 (.22), V22 (.19), V26 (.24).

Negative: V9 (−.34), V11 (−.23), V18 (−.31), V27 (−.17), V29 (−.27).

Note that the high achievers get a high positive score on the discriminant function. The essence of the matter here is that the discriminant variable is related to:

(a) need for achievement-striving, unsociable, shy need, and passive, cautious need;
(b) faculty press at university perceived as academically encouraging, expressive and unrestrictive;
(c) student press at university perceived as concerned with self and sexuality;
(d) faculty press at school perceived as towards social involvement; and
(e) student press at school perceived as introverted, not practical, not objective or confident, and concerned with self and sexuality.

In univariate F tests $(df = 2, 132 : P = .05)$, there were only three variables on which significant differences occurred, viz.; V7 (need for passivity, caution), V9 (FPU as academically unencouraging) and V18 (SPU as unconcerned with self and sexuality). These differences were consistent with the nature of the discriminant function.

Summary

Ho is rejected. There *are* differences among the three 'achievement' groups on the basis of their needs and press scores. The main finding is the emergence, in the discriminant function, of a clear and meaningful achievement syndrome.

HYPOTHESIS 4B
That there are no differences among the three 'satisfaction' groups on the basis of scores of members of each group on the thirty need and press factor variables (V1—V30).

Analysis

'Not satisfied' $n = 36$
'Satisfied' $n = 66$
'Very satisfied' $n = 33$
$F = 1.959 : df = 60, 206 : P = .0004$

Only one discriminant function was significant (72.92% of variance). Discriminant weights $> |.2|$ were as follows:

Positive: V9 (.42), V10 (.31), V11 (.46), V20 (.33).
Negative: V14 (−.23), V24 (−.21), V27 (−.21).

Centroids:
'Not satisfied' $= 0.75$
'Satisfied' $= 0.18$
'Very satisfied' $= -1.18$

Correlations of variables with the discriminant function, where $r > |.17|$, $(P = .05)$, were as follows:

Positive: V9 (.52), V10 (.46), V11 (.48), V16 (.22), V20 (.33), V21 (.18), V23 (.18), V24 (.31).
Negative: V4 (−.18), V5 (−.21), V8 (−.27), V14 (−.55), V15 (−.25), V17 (−.27).

The discriminant variable is such that the extent to which a score resembles that of the 'very satisfied' is related to:

(a) the unsociable, shy need, to the orderly, organized need;
(b) faculty press at university perceived as academically encouraging, not dominating or suspicious, and as expressive and unrestrictive;
(c) student press at university perceived as industrious and studious, confident and objective, reflective and sensitive, dependent and friendly;
(d) faculty press at school perceived as academically encouraging; and
(e) student press at school perceived as academic and studious.

In univariate F tests $(df = 2, 132 : P = .05)$, there were six variables on which significant differences occurred, viz.: V9 (FPU as academically unencouraging), V10 (FPU as dominating and suspicious), V11 (FPU as unexpressive, restrictive), V14 (SPU as industrious, studious), V20 (FPS as academically unencouraging), and V24 (SPS as not academic, not studious). The differences found among the three groups on each of these six variables were consistent with the nature of the discriminant function.

Summary

Ho is rejected. There *are* differences among the three 'satisfaction' groups on the basis of their needs and press scores. The strong relationship between perception of faculty press at university and satisfaction is salient.

HYPOTHESIS 5A
That there are no differences among the three 'change of achievement'

groups on the basis of scores of members of each group on the four 'FAPR-DF' (faculty press difference, i.e., school faculty press minus university faculty press) variables.

Analysis

$$\text{'Achieving as expected' group } n = 86$$
$$\text{'Overachievers'} \quad n = 23$$
$$\text{'Underachievers'} \quad n = 26$$
$$F = 1.010 : df = 8, 258 : P = .43$$

F was not significant
No further analysis was meaningful.

Summary

Ho is accepted. 'Change of achievement' is not related to the 'FAPR-DF' variables. This result is somewhat unexpected in that it might have been thought reasonable that changed perception of faculty would be connected with change of achievement.

HYPOTHESIS 5B

That there are no differences among the three 'change of satisfaction' groups on the basis of scores of members of each group on the four 'FAPR-DF' variables.

Analysis

$$\text{'Satisfied as expected'} \quad n = 76$$
$$\text{'Oversatisfied'} \quad n = 30$$
$$\text{'Undersatisfied'} \quad n = 29$$
$$F = 8.019 : df = 8, 258 : P = .0000$$

Only one discriminant function was significant (92.64% of variance).
Discriminant weights:

B1 (change of academically unencouraging faculty press from
school to university) .34
B2 (change of aggressive, dominating, suspicious faculty press
from school to university) .89
B3 (change of social involvement, humane, friendly faculty press
from school to university) −.14
B4 (change of unrestrictive, relaxed, expressive faculty press
from school to university) −.25

Centroids:
'Satisfied as expected' = −0.04
'Oversatisfied' = 1.09
'Undersatisfied' = −1.03

Correlations of variables with the discriminant function:
B1 (.40), B2 (.87), B3 (−.22), B4 (−.34)

The essence of the matter is that the discriminant score increases in the direction of the 'oversatisfied' when change from school to university means

(a) increase in perceived academically encouraging faculty press;

(b) decrease in perceived aggressive, dominating, suspicious faculty press;

(c) increase in perceived social involvement, humane, friendly faculty press; and

(d) increase in perceived unrestrictive, relaxed, expressive faculty press.

In univariate F tests $(df = 2, 132 : P = .05)$, significant differences among the groups were found on three of the four 'FAPR-DF' variables, viz.: B1 (change of academically unencouraging press), B2 (change of aggressive, dominating, suspicious press), and B4 (change of unrestrictive, relaxed, expressive press). The nature of these differences was generally consistent with the nature of the discriminant function.

Summary

Ho is rejected. There *are* differences among the three 'change of satisfaction' groups on the basis of their 'FAPR-DF' scores. Satisfaction increases when perceived anabolic press increases. 'Anabolic press are represented in those stimuli which are potentially conducive to self-enhancing growth.' (Stern, 1967, p. 13.) Anabolic press is sometimes linked with developmental press, catabolic press with controlling press (Stern, 1967, p. 430). Stern says catabolic press are 'those which are antithetical to personal development or which are likely to produce countervailing responses'. (Stern, 1967, p. 13.)

HYPOTHESIS 6A

That there are no differences among the three 'achievement' groups on the basis of scores of members of each group on the four 'ND-PR-DF' (need-press difference, i.e., need minus faculty press at university) variables.

Analysis

Low achievers $n = 27$
Medium achievers $n = 72$
High achievers $n = 36$
$F = 2.432 : df = 8, 258 : P = .0150$

Only one discriminant function was significant (70.49% of variance).
Discriminant weights:

A1 (need for achievement-striving minus corresponding university faculty press) .10

A2 (need for passivity, caution minus corresponding university faculty press) −.29

A3 (need for sociability and outgoing minus corresponding university faculty press) .92

A4 (need for emotional expression minus corresponding university faculty press) .25

Centroids:
Low achievers = −0.03
Medium achievers = 0.34
High achievers = −0.65

Note that these centroids are not sequential. This points to some lack of linearity in regression of the criterion (achievement), on the four measures. See, for example, Tiedeman (1951, p. 79).

Correlations with the discriminant function:

A1 (.19), A2 (−.32), A3 (.90), A4 (.25)

Interpretation of this discriminant analysis is complicated by the lack of sequence in centroids. However, taking low and medium achievers at one pole and high achievers at the other, we see that the higher the 'friendly', 'expressive' and 'achievement-striving' discrepancy scores the more a person is like the low and medium achievers, and the higher the 'passivity' discrepancy the more a person is like the high achievers. When it comes to separating low achievers from medium achievers we note that the higher the 'achievement-striving', 'friendly' and 'expressive' discrepancy scores the more a person is like medium achievers, while the higher the 'passivity' discrepancy score the more a person is like low achievers.

In univariate F tests ($df = 2, 132 : P = .05$), significant differences among the groups were found on two of the four 'ND-PR-DF' variables, viz.: A2 ('passivity' discrepancy) and A3 ('friendly' discrepancy).

On A2, high achievers have a fairly high positive discrepancy score, low achievers have a substantial negative score, with medium achievers in a neutral position. On A3, high achievers are substantially negative, low achievers are somewhat negative while medium achievers have a fairly high positive discrepancy score. This variable is the main source of the lack of linearity of regression mentioned earlier.

Summary

Ho is rejected. Pace and Stern's fundamental hypothesis has been confirmed to the extent that need-press congruence has been related to achievement. However, clear-cut conclusions are prevented by the lack of sequence in the centroids which means that low achievers are more like the high achievers than they are like the medium achievers. One can say that high achievers have negative 'ND-PR-DF' scores (i.e., press greater than need), for 'friendly', 'expressive' and 'achievement-striving' discrepancies and a positive score for the 'passivity' discrepancy. Therefore, the high achievers are those for whom what might be called anabolic or developmentally desirable needs are more than satisfied by 'good' anabolic press, and for whom the catabolic press towards 'passivity' is not large relative to the need for 'passivity'. This result might have been predicted on the basis of Maslow's theory of the hierarchy and prepotency of motives.

HYPOTHESIS 6B

That there are no differences among the three 'satisfaction' groups on the basis of scores of members of each group on the four 'ND-PR-DF' variables.

Analysis

'Not satisfied' $n = 36$

'Satisfied' $n = 66$

'Very satisfied' $n = 33$

$$F = 4.570 : df = 8, 258 : P = .0001$$

Only one discriminant function was significant (91.03% of variance). Discriminant weights:

A1 (need for achievement-striving minus corresponding faculty press) .47

A2 (need for passivity, caution minus corresponding faculty press) −.52

A3 (need for sociability and outgoing minus corresponding faculty press) .36

A4 (need for emotional expression minus corresponding faculty press) .62

Centroids:

'Not satisfied' = 0.64

'Satisfied' = 0.23

'Very satisfied' = −1.16

Correlations with the discriminant function:

A1 (.54), A2 (−.52), A3 (.32), A4 (.67)

The lower the 'achievement-striving', 'friendly' and 'expressive' discrepancies, and the higher the 'passivity' discrepancy, the greater is the resemblance to the 'very satisfied'.

In univariate F tests ($df = 2, 132 : P = .05$), significant differences among the groups were found on three of the four 'ND-PR-DF' variables, viz., A1 ('achievement-striving' discrepancy), A2 ('passivity' discrepancy) and A4 ('expressive' discrepancy). The nature of these differences was largely consistent with the nature of the discriminant function.

Summary

Ho is rejected. Pace and Stern's fundamental congruence hypothesis is again confirmed to the extent that need-press congruence has been related to satisfaction. High satisfaction with teaching at university is linked with negative anabolic need-press discrepancies, i.e., with anabolic press greater than anabolic needs, and with positive catabolic need-press discrepancy. This result could have been predicted on the basis of Maslow's theory.

HYPOTHESIS 7

That the power of the need-press theory in the prediction of achievement of students in the first-year university chemistry examination is at least equal to the power of the end-of-school matriculation (Senior) chemistry examination score.

To put this into testable form one might say that the proportion of 'hits', i.e., correct predictions, attained by the use of classification computer programs following discriminant analyses relating to the 'achievement' groups, and involving need and press variables, is equal to the proportion of 'hits' when the matriculation score is used.

Analysis

If, out of 135 students who have already passed the matriculation (end-of-school) chemistry examination, 36 are to be predicted as high-level achievers, 72 as medium-level achievers and 27 as low-level achievers in the first-year university chemistry examination, then the obvious way to predict membership of various groups would be to use the matriculation order of merit.

If this is done we get the following matrix (Matrix 1).

MATRIX 1

'Achievement' Group Entered

		L	M	H	
'Achievement' Group Predicted	Low L	12	14	1	27
	Medium M	15	42	15	72
	High H	0	16	20	36
		27	72	36	135

Proportion of 'hits': $\dfrac{12}{27}$ $\dfrac{42}{72}$ $\dfrac{20}{36}$ $\dfrac{74}{135}$ Total

Concerning the 'hits', one notes that 12 students predicted to be in the lowest level did score at that level, that 42 predicted to be in the medium level did score at that level and that 20 predicted to be in the highest level did score at that level. This is quite an accurate prediction and consistent with a correlation of .58 between school chemistry achievement and university chemistry achievement.

The discriminant analysis relating to hypothesis 4A used 3 'achievement' groups and 30 need and press factor variables. Using this analysis in conjunction with a classification programme Matrix 2 was obtained.

MATRIX 2

'Achievement' Group Entered

		L	M	H	
'Achievement' Group Predicted	L	17	33	1	51
	M	7	24	6	37
	H	3	15	29	47
		27	72	36	135

Proportion of 'hits': $\dfrac{17}{27}$ $\dfrac{24}{72}$ $\dfrac{29}{36}$ $\dfrac{70}{135}$ Total

The discriminant analysis relating to hypothesis 6A used the same 3 'achievement' groups and 4 'ND-PR-DF' (need minus university faculty press) variables. Depending on the type of classification procedure used (Cooley & Lohnes, 1962, Chapter 7), these matrices below were obtained:

MATRIX 3

'Achievement' Group
Entered

		L	M	H	
'Achievement'	L	6	31	4	41
Group	M	9	22	9	40
Predicted	H	12	19	23	54
		27	72	36	135

Proportion of 'hits': $\dfrac{6}{27}$ $\dfrac{22}{72}$ $\dfrac{23}{36}$ $\dfrac{51}{135}$ Total

MATRIX 4

'Achievement' Group
Entered

		L	M	H	
'Achievement'	L	0	0	0	0
Group	M	22	67	26	115
Predicted	H	5	5	10	20
		27	72	36	135

Proportion of 'hits': $\dfrac{0}{27}$ $\dfrac{67}{72}$ $\dfrac{10}{36}$ $\dfrac{77}{135}$ Total

The 'hits' achieved by the use of matriculation chemistry score are real predictions, while the computer programme 'hits' indicate only the degree of minimum overlap among the three groups. (Cooley & Lohnes, 1962, p. 143). Nevertheless, it is clear that, even if the computer were asked to cope with real prediction work, it could do quite well, and perhaps even better than matriculation score, particularly in predictions at some levels.

It would obviously be a matter of interest to see how well the computer could do, in what amounted to a cross-validation study of the predictive power of the discriminant function. In this present research, cross-validation of a kind could be achieved with the present sample if, say, only half the group were used to arrive at the discriminant function and then the function was tried out on the other half to see how well it could classify members of the other half. The problem here is that when a sample is halved the quality of the discriminant function would suffer because of its being based on the small sample. (*See*, for example, Horst, 1966, p. 139.)

It might not be irrelevant here to add that, while reasonable success is attainable by the computer as a predictor of achievement, considerably greater success is attained in the prediction of satisfaction, using the need and press variables and various discriminant analyses involving 'satisfaction' groups.

Summary

To conclude this report, a summary appraisal of work that has been done in this research is now supplied.

1. Work has been done in determining the nature of school and of university chemistry education environments. This work is useful in that:

   (a) Some empirical grounds are now available for discussion of differences between school and university, and less reliance on polemics is now required (Stern, 1965); and

   (b) The university, in the consensual press data, is now better informed on what it is doing to students. When it looks at school-university differences it may ask if the differences are in what it deems to be the 'right' direction, i.e., in line with its objectives. Objectives, according to Pace and Stern (1958), indicate 'directions in which a college means to influence the behavior of students'. Also, Pace and Stern say 'Institutional press should have some clear relationship to institutional purpose.' They speak of implicit press, which is what students say exists. There is also an explicit press, which the institution or the faculty says it is providing. Pace and Stern (1958) note that 'A serious lack of congruence between implicit press and explicit objectives would suggest to faculty members and administrators that certain aspects of the environment ought to be changed in order to make the total impact of the institution more consistent or more effective.'

2. Need-press theory has been used to improve understanding of the behaviour of unique personalities in the uniquely perceived environments of their chemistry education. In this regard note that:

   (a) Understanding of what is involved in achievement and satisfaction in chemistry education environments has been furthered. It has been shown that, associated with the achievement in the university environment, there is a distinct pattern of personality needs and perceptions of school and university environmental press. There is also a distinct pattern of needs and press perceptions associated with satisfaction. The patterns or syndromes are valuable information, but are they what the university would prescribe as ideal?

   (b) Understanding of transition dynamics has been furthered by the findings concerning the relationship between how students' faculty press perceptions change and how satisfaction changes. In fact, a relationship has been established between change of anabolic press perception and change of satisfaction. The result is of considerable theoretical interest.

(c) Understanding of interaction dynamics in the university environment has been furthered by findings concerning the relationship between need-press congruence and satisfaction and success. Relationships have been established between anabolic need-press discrepancy and both satisfaction and success. As mentioned earlier there is here some vindication of Maslow's theory.

3. A fair degree of success in prediction has been achieved by need-press theory in this research. Without the aid of information concerning previous achievement, reasonable success has been achieved in predicting academic success at university. The success in predicting satisfaction is more striking. Also, prediction of change of satisfaction has proved to be successful.

4. As a general and inclusive statement it could be said that multivariate statistical techniques in conjunction with need-press theory have coped with the complexities of research into the nature of environments and particularly their influence on their inhabitants. Campbell, in the Preface to this book, (p. vi), describes behaviour as a response to a *pattern* of interacting variables. Multivariate analysis in this research has coped with interacting variables and has provided information concerning just what *pattern* is involved. This pattern emerges in the discriminant weights for variables. In these weights some considerable progress has been made towards discovering more about the elusive 'f' in the Lewinian equation, $B = f (P,E)$. Campbell rightly says 'techniques of multivariate analysis are not well advanced'. However, they are already sufficiently advanced to be profitably employed in the inherently multivariate situations where scholars are studied in context.

5. This research has demonstrated only a fraction of the potential power of need-press theory to extend educational psychological theory and to throw light on practical educational problems. A more comprehensive study of transition will take cognizance of more environmental variables, will employ a wider range of behavioural variables and will be concerned with discovering whether scholastic aptitude can profitably combine with need and press variables, and their combinations, to increase understanding of academic behaviour and efficiency in its prediction.

References

Alpern, D. K., 1966: In place of recitations: An experiment in teaching. *Teachers College Record*, 67, 589-594.

Astin, A. W., 1965: Classroom environment in different fields of study. *Journal of Educational Psychology*, 56, 5, 275-282.

Cooley, W. W. and Lohnes, P. R., 1962: *Multivariate Procedures for the Behavioral Sciences*. John Wiley & Sons, Inc., New York.

Falk, B., 1967: The use of student evaluation. *The Australian University*, 5, 2, 109-121.

Genn, J. M., 1969: Chemistry scholars in school and university contexts—A study of transition from school to university. Unpublished PhD thesis, University of Queensland.

Goodstein, L., 1960: A summing up. In H. T. Sprague (Ed.), *Research on*

College Students. Interstate Commission for Higher Education, Boulder, Colorado.

Horst, P., 1966: An overview of the essentials of multivariate analysis methods. In R. B. Cattell (Ed.), *Handbook of Multivariate Experimental Psychology*. Rand McNally & Co., Chicago, Ill.

Murray, H. A. (Ed.), 1938: *Explorations in Personality: A Clinical and Experimental Study of 50 Men of College Age by the Workers at the Harvard Psychological Clinic*, New York.

Murray, H. A. and Kluckhohn, C. K., 1953: Outline of a conception of personality. In C. K. Kluckhohn, H. A. Murray and D. M. Schneider, *Personality in Nature, Society and Culture*. Alfred A. Knopf, New York.

Pace, C. R., 1963: *CUES: College and University Environment Scales: Preliminary Technical Manual*. Educational Testing Service, Princeton, N.J.

Pace, C. R., 1964: *The Influence of Academic and Student Subcultures in College and University Environments*. Co-operative Research Project, No. 1083, University of California, Los Angeles, California.

Pace, C. R. and Stern, G. G., 1958: An approach to the measurement of psychological characteristics of college environments. *Journal of Educational Psychology*, 49, 5, 269-277.

Peterson, R. E., 1965: *Technical Manual: College Student Questionnaires*. Educational Testing Service, Princeton, N.J.

Stern, G. G., 1961: Continuity and contrast in the transition from high school to college. In N. C. Brown (Ed.), *Orientation to College Learning—A Reappraisal*. American Council on Education, Washington, D.C.

Stern, G. G., 1962a: The measurement of psychological characteristics of students and learning environments. In S. J. Messick and J. Ross (Eds), *Measurement in Personality and Cognition*. John Wiley & Sons, Inc., New York.

Stern, G. G., 1962b: Environments for learning. In R. N. Sandford (Ed.), *The American College: A Psychological and Social Interpretation of the Higher Learning*. John Wiley & Sons, Inc., New York.

Stern, G. G., 1963a: Characteristics of the intellectual climate in college environments. *Harvard Educational Review*, 33, 5-41.

Stern, G. G., 1963b: *Scoring instructions and college norms. Activities Index: College Characteristics Index*. Psychological Research Center, Syracuse, New York.

Stern, G. G., 1964: B = f (P,E). *Journal of Projective Techniques*, 28, 161-168.

Stern, G. G., 1965: Student ecology and the college environment. *Journal of Medical Education*, 40, 132-154.

Stern, G. G., 1967: *People in Context: The Measurement of Environmental Interaction in School and Society*. Syracuse University, New York.

Stern, G. G., Stein, M. and Bloom, B. S., 1956: *Methods in Personality Assessment*. The Free Press, Glencoe, Ill.

Thistlethwaite, D. L., 1962: Fields of study and development of motivation to seek advanced training. *Journal of Educational Psychology*, 53, 2, 53-64.

Tiedeman, D. V., 1951: The utility of the discriminant function in psychological and guidance investigations. In 'The Multiple Discriminant Function —A Symposium', *Harvard Educational Review*, 21, 2, 71-80.

Webb, S. C. and Crowder, D. G., 1965: Analyzing the psychological climate of a single college. *Teachers College Record*, 66, 425-433.

13

Some Effects of Australian University Education on Asian Students

Daphne M. Keats

THE RESEARCH reported here differs from other studies related to foreign students in several ways. First, it attempts to combine a social psychological orientation with a concern for educational outcomes. Second, it is a longitudinal study, and, as such, is concerned with changes over a relatively extended period of time which allows for the effects of acculturation processes to occur. Third, it uses a control group of local students, a circumstance which makes necessary the development of techniques and the adoption of a theoretical orientation which satisfy the exacting demands of being equally valid for members of all the cultures involved.

It is only in the last two decades that substantial numbers of foreign students have come to Australian educational institutions, and little research has been carried out in this field. Two aspects have been emphasized in the past. On the one hand are those studies involving levels of academic success generally (Tylee, 1964; Sanders, 1954), and those relating special abilities such as English to academic success (Keats, D. M., 1962). On the other hand are a number of studies of the 'adjustment' kind, for example, by Hodgkin (1966) on Asian students in Western Australia, by Noesjirwan (1966) on Indonesian students in New South Wales and Benn (1961) on Thai students, also in New South Wales. These studies have drawn heavily on the work done in the United States of America by research workers such as Brewster Smith (1956a and b), Lesser and Peter (1957) and Beals and Humphrey (1957) whose pioneering work has provided basic models of stages of adjustment. Valuable though this early work has been, the failure of most research both here and elsewhere to compare the adjustment of foreign students with the degree of adjustment of local students severely limits the extent to which generalizations can be made from the results obtained. Although these models do attempt to account for the foreign study period as an intervening one, they do not fully consider it as a stage in general intellectual and social development. Those who apparently adjust best to the foreign environment may be those who do not adjust satisfactorily to their home environment, a possibility supported by the work of Bennett, *et al.* (1962) on Japanese students in the United States. It would seem preferable, therefore, to substitute for the concept of adjustment the concept of the development of cognitive structures, which can be studied not only in terms of how well a foreign student likes or fits in with the host culture, but also cross-culturally, by comparing the development of foreign students with that of their fellow students in the host country.

The problems of such a cross-cultural approach are many. In the case of foreign students in Australia, who are principally of Asian origin, there are unique problems arising from essential differences between Asian and Australian (or European) cultural orientations, particularly in modes of communication and social interaction. One of the greatest problems is to devise methods which will overcome the considerable language difficulties from which foreign students generally suffer, especially if they have not attended English medium schools in their home country, as is the case with students from Thailand and Indonesia.

The difficulties of selecting and matching samples of foreign and local students, and of achieving equivalence in the research tools used, are a considerable deterrent to using control groups of local students. Cultural equivalence is required if tests or measures are applied to subjects of different cultures. To be culturally equivalent the items must be equally valid for both the groups and the source data used to make up the items must have similar meanings in both cultures. For example, if a standardized attitude scale such as the F scale is used, there is need for considerable caution in directing questions which involve ethnic groups like Jews or Negroes to people of Asian cultures, for whom the presence of such people does not have the same social implications as it has in the United States of America.

There must also be cultural equivalence in the task required of the testee. For the tasks themselves to be meaningful they must ideally be without cultural bias. There has been a great deal of work done (e.g., by the Educational Testing Service) to develop' so-called culture-free or culture-fair tests of ability (Coffmann, 1963; Campbell, 1964), but there are many problems yet to be solved.

There must also be cultural equivalence in motivation, and for this to obtain, the purpose of the tasks set or the questions asked must appear to be the same for representatives of both cultures. Boesch's work in Thailand illustrates the difficulty of motivating Thai children in the same way as European children in group tests in which the instructions exhort them to strive to excel others, a type of behaviour socially unacceptable in that culture (Boesch, 1958).

Finally, a necessary type of equivalence is that of the research worker's style of data collection. The difficulties of obtaining equivalence are not always resolved by mere translations. We must come to terms with a quality strongly developed in Asian cultures, the necessity for preserving face. If face is to be preserved, there often cannot be exact verbal equivalence in the phrasing and stating of questions and one must look for a functional equivalent which expresses the intention of the question rather than sustaining the same wording for every subject. This need cuts across some of the important requirements of consistent and precise measurement of attitudes.

The problems of obtaining functional equivalence in methods and research tools are also related to the choice of an appropriate theoretical orientation. The conceptual framework adopted ought to be one which can include members of the host group as well as members of the foreign student group, and ought to be able to account for the fact that the period of university study is, for the foreign student, an intervening one, preceded and followed by behaviour and experiences in the home cultures which will, in the long run, be of greater importance to the student than his temporary experiences while in a foreign country.

Because the environment which the foreign student enters is not itself a static one, an appropriate conceptual framework will be one which can account for dynamically changing interpersonal relationships between foreign students and members of the host country. These relationships will change considerably over a fairly lengthy period of time. As university courses generally last from three to six years, one could expect that a short period of study such as one year would be insufficient to demonstrate the changes which occur.

Finally, since the main activity in which both foreign and local students are jointly involved is, or should be, the pursuit of their academic studies, the conceptual framework adopted must be one which is, or can include, a theory of learning.

To meet the third condition referred to above an appropriate conceptual framework must also be one which can include social learning of many kinds as well as the acquisition of knowledge or specific skill required for university studies. This last need encompasses those aspects of adjustment on which many previous studies of foreign students have concentrated. But theories of learning from which the most precise methodologies can be derived do not lend themselves to considering social variables. In a cross-cultural setting, the complex of variables cannot be broken down by isolating the learning variables in the laboratory, since the parts of the whole may be dynamically related to each other in a different way in all of the cultures being compared. Theories of cognitive development based on phases of biological development, of which the principal proponents are Piaget and Bruner, have been shown to have promise of cross-cultural validity (Greenfield & Bruner, 1966) but they have not been refined at the stages of cognitive development with which we are concerned at the university level, and they have generally been less concerned with social variables than a cross-cultural study must be.

These conditions are all met by Lewinian cognitive field theory. In essence, this theory is relativistic. Instead of aiming to eliminate the variables of cultural environment in order to obtain experimental precision,

Lewin's approach attempts to bring behaviour and environment into one integrated construct. The relativistic treatment of perception and reality is particularly useful for considering the differences between meanings of an apparently similar experience to culturally dissimilar groups. For both groups, this experience represents a part of their total psychological fields, a part in which the life spaces of the members of the two groups temporarily overlap and impinge upon each other. In so far as cultural antecedents and aspirations for the future are perceived at the time as traces or goals, the cognitive field approach accounts for the different cultural backgrounds and the different purposes in the two groups, and, as learning is regarded as a restructuring of the life space, it may be either problem-solving behaviour, or learning of the academic kind or the development of new relationships of a social-interpersonal kind.

It was hypothesized that patterns of differentiation in the life space would be found which would distinguish the Asian students from the Australian students. At the beginning of their Australian sojourn these patterns would be considerably different, but after some years in Australia the Asian students could be expected to show some change away from these Asian differentiation patterns in the direction of adopting more typically Australian behaviours and attitudes.

This study tried to locate some of these differences and to trace the extent to which changes did occur. The construct of the force field was used to show the relative valences of various behaviours and goals of the Asians compared with the Australian students. The period during which changes were investigated was three years of university study. An attempt was made to produce a series of cognitive maps delineating relevant regional patterns of differentiation of the life space on particular occasions of contact. With Lewin's approach to the notion of contemporaneity, such cognitive maps could include not only present conditions, behaviour and attitudes, but also traces of former behaviour and plans for the future. The extent and detail of the regional differentiation of these cognitive maps would depend on the degree of complexity required. As Lewin (1951) points out in his discussion of k, the size of the units (wholes, W) is relative to the need for detail in the analysis, but the same principles apply no matter what size units are chosen.

In terms of methodology this means that not all regional phenomena would need to be included to construct such maps, but that an array of data should be obtained of sufficient width and detail to bring out the differences and changes with which one is concerned, and the regions to be tapped for these data should be those thought likely to be relevant to university study experience. At the outset, it was not known in which regions differences would be found between the Asians and Australians, and the initial collection of data necessarily had to be exploratory. However, if the array of data obtained was wide enough and tapped relevant regions or sub-regions, typical patterns of locomotion and regional differentiation would be revealed.

One of the methodological problems of this approach is that, to some extent, the nature of the regional patterns could be generated by the kinds of instruments used. Tools were therefore selected or designed so that the maximum spontaneity of responses could be obtained—for example, instruments which used open-ended rather than forced choice questions.

Sampling

Because of difficulties in obtaining subjects, the initial sample was built up gradually over a period of two months to a total of 67 students, approximately 75 per cent of the total Asian first-year enrolments. The interviewing programme began before the complete sample was gathered, and it soon became clear that it would be difficult to retain some Asian subjects for the whole of the interview and the test battery. Although it would have been a neater research design had all subjects done all tasks, it was decided not to exclude the incomplete cases. If some Asian subjects failed to keep their interview appointments, the cause could have been merely an Asian unconcern about time, but, on the other hand, the cause could also have been in their anxiety, which overrode a genuine intention to be helpful. If this were so, it was an important facet of the whole situation, just as omitted items in some projective tests may be significant responses.

To obtain a comparable Australian sample required a somewhat different technique in that only about 50 students taking courses similar to those taken by the Asians had to be selected out of a probable total of about 1,000 full-time first-year enrolments. Because of the difficulty of building up the Asian sample, no early prediction could be made as to what would be its likely composition by courses. The Australian sample wanted was a characteristic sub-sample of the Australian first-year population rather than a sample matched individually with Asians.

The method used to obtain the sample was to administer a questionnaire paralleling in written form the questions put orally to the Asians in the interviews. Approximately 800 questionnaires were distributed to groups of students in first-year courses taken by the largest numbers of students from all faculties, and from these 499 replies were received. From this number a small group of 50 was selected at random within the faculty groups required. The cooperation of 46 of these students was obtained to take part as subjects for the remainder of the research. The data obtained from this survey were also used to provide background information about the general first-year population and to check the extent to which the selected Australian sample was, in fact, representative of the total first-year group.

The composition of both the Asian and Australian samples in the second and third years of the study was contingent on the academic progress of the students in addition to their continued cooperation. A considerable decrease occurred in the number of Asian students, a drop from 67 to 37, but there was a smaller loss among the Australians, whose numbers dropped from 46 to 39. This loss of subjects was partly accounted for by failures, partly by the high mobility of the Asian students, and partly by anxiety on the part of those who wanted to avoid being questioned on the difficulties they were experiencing. A few cases also occurred in which a student had to leave because of illness or parental pressure.

The Research Tools

The research tools and tests used were selected or constructed to meet the criteria of being valid in a cross-cultural context and of contributing to the delineation of patterns of cognitive structure in Lewinian terms. The principal research tool used was a tape-recorded interview. This was supported by a non-verbal test of general ability, a reading comprehension test, a vocational interests inventory and an attitude scale. The ability tests used were Raven's Progressive Matrices, 1947, and the Co-operative Reading Test B2.

In addition to whatever questions on vocational goals were to be included in the interviews a more objective measure was required by which the choice of university courses could be related to more basic patterns of vocational interests. Here, the criterion of cultural equivalence was particularly difficult to meet. Inventories standardized in the United States, which are commonly used in Australia, had to be rejected because of cultural biases which would have introduced situations and occupations unfamiliar to Asians. No scale or inventory designed specifically for Asian conditions was available, and even if there were, the Australian sample could not have used it appropriately. The only alternative possible, therefore, was to use an inventory which was standardized in Australia for Australian conditions and to try to cope with the cultural discrepancies in relation to the Asian subjects as they occurred.

The Rothwell Miller Vocational Interest Blank was chosen because it used material which was relevant to both Australian and Asian occupational conditions, and it used as its examples a wide range of occupations rather than only those for which university training is preparatory. Moreover, it required minimum verbal instructions and allowed for explanations of meanings required by the Asian subjects. Finally, it was relatively simple to complete and had built-in checks on whether the instructions had been fully understood.

A projective test of attitudes was required. The Rohde Sentence Completion Test was selected because it was easy to administer to those without high language skills, it did not obviously present potentially threatening statements to which only face-saving replies would be a culturally acceptable response, it did not present alternatives which might be culturally inappropriate from which to make a forced choice, but, by the use of open-ended items, allowed each subject to reply in terms of his own cultural background. The indirectness of the projective approach was likely to be acceptable to the Asians, whereas a direct probing of motivations and anxieties would definitely be unacceptable.

The interview was given on three principal contact occasions but the actual schedules used were modified slightly in the later years to suit the changed conditions, and questions which had not proved effective in the first administration were omitted. All interviews were tape-recorded and transcribed verbatim for analysis. The time taken for each interview varied from half an hour for the most fluent to nearly three hours, spread over two or more sessions, for those with severe communication problems.

The great variability in the duration of each interview demonstrated the advantage which a flexible interview technique had over more rigid forms of questioning. Many of the subjects who took this protracted time would not have replied to an instrument of all written questions, for the task of coping with the difficulties involved in expressing their attitudes correctly would have been too burdensome. An apparent failure in communication could also mean that the question as phrased was face threatening and should be re-worded or left temporarily to be returned to later by a different, less threatening route, a safeguard which would not have been available in pencil and paper tests.

In addition to the oral questions a number of written items were incorporated into the interviews. These instruments, designed to supplement the data obtained orally, included questions asking for background data, items concerned with vocational interests and reasons for choosing university courses, attitude items concerned with Asian and Australian students' reactions to each other, acculturation items derived from Taft's scale of 'Australianism' (Taft, 1962) and items concerned with participation in student activities and informal discussions. The method of analysis varied according to the questions and the data obtained.

Groups of questions were arranged around a theme with the aim of eliciting a general pattern of attitudes or behaviour. These basic themes represented likely main regions of the life space. They could be hypothesized to exist for all subjects but they could be shown to vary individually in centrality and differentiation and to be subject to different locomotive forces. These main themes (or main regions) were: the university, accommodation, school, vocation, financial and economic activity, social and peer-group activities, the family, the sociological background, socio-political identification, religious beliefs and attitudes, and physical and mental health. The theme of principal concern in the study was the university region.

Analysis of the Results

The first task in the analysis of the results was to classify the academic performance of the students in the samples. Relatively few Asians proceeded straight through their course; three quarters suffered some failure, compared with approximately a third of the Australians. Among the Australians, the most frequent alternative behaviour after a failure was to repeat the year or to give up the university completely. This was not the case with the Asians. Whereas some repeated the same course, an equally frequent strategy after failure was to change to another course.

The General Ability and Reading Tests: In both 1962 and 1964 the Australian students performed significantly better on Raven's Progressive Matrices Test than did the Asians. The Asian means were 26.63 in 1962 and 30.14 in 1964, compared with Australian means of 33.41 in 1962 and 35.68 in 1964. The mean differences between the samples in both 1962 and 1964 were significant at the .01 level of confidence.

The Reading Comprehension Test was also analysed by comparing differences in means. The scores were expressed as raw scores adjusted for error but not scaled. As was expected, the performance of the Australian students was significantly better than that of the Asians in both 1962 and 1964 (mean difference 1962, 17.08, $t = 9.13$, significant at .01 level of confidence; 1964, 15.57, $t = 5.50$, significant at .01 level of confidence).

The Rothwell-Miller Vocational Interest Inventory: The method of analysis used for the Rothwell-Miller Interest Inventory was based on the Lewinian theory of development as an increase in differentiation of the life space. The making of a vocational choice involved making a commitment to incorporate into the life space a complete system of interrelated persons and activities which, in Lewinian terms, together made up a distinctly bounded region. Such a commitment required a reorganization of the life space as new sub-regions became differentiated and boundaries between regions were re-defined.

It was hypothesized that, for a student who expressed a strong preference for one particular vocational goal and strong dislikes of others, the regions of the life space would be highly differentiated, and selected and rejected vocational goals would be separated by strong boundaries, whereas, for a student who felt no strong attraction to any one goal and who had not identified his personal goals with a particular vocational field, the boundaries between regions would be weaker, the regions amorphous, and the life space less differentiated. If a subject expressed a strong commitment to a particular goal, but had neither a liking for nor dislike of other occupations, that region would be clearly differentiated and surrounded by strong boundaries, but at the same time the life space would be undifferentiated in regard to other regions of vocational choice.

In the Rothwell-Miller Interest Blank the subject is required to rank examples of twelve categories or occupations in order of attractiveness to him. Each set of twelve occupations is presented nine times but in a slightly varying order and with a different example for each category so that it is not readily apparent to the subject that he is not ranking 108 unrelated unclassified occupations. The hypotheses were tested by examining the internal consistency of each set of nine rankings using Kendall's coefficient of concordance (W). If W was found to be significant, the distribution of choices, from high positive valence through to strong negative valence, would not be attributable to a chance effect, but if W was not significant, the implication would be that the array of occupations to be ranked would not have strong positive and negative valences for that subject. High differentiation would occur only if W were significant. Furthermore, as the total rank order was obtained from the summation of each set of rankings on the basis of certain classifications of occupations in an Australian setting, the significance or otherwise of W would test, in a sense, the cross-cultural validity of those classifications for the Asian subjects.

It was predicted that the successful students would be more likely than unsuccessful students to differentiate strongly between vocational regions and would be more likely to show preference patterns which were in harmony with the interests and activity of their chosen course. It was also predicted that Asian students who were culturally most divergent from Australian students would be likely to have vocational interest patterns which were dissimilar to those of Australian students in the same course.

The hypotheses were tested by comparing the incidence of non-significant W's in the successful versus the less successful students. Rank order correlations (*rho*) were carried out on the results of each Asian student, relating his individual rank orders of preference to the rank order of the Australian group in the same type of academic course. The *rho* coefficients were then compared with indices of social similarity obtained from the analysis of the sociological background.

The results showed a high degree of internal consistency: W was found to be significant in over 90 per cent of cases $(165/176)$. In both 1962 and 1964, all Australian students, all Asian women students, and all but one of the successful Asian men, made internally consistent choices. All the insignificant W's were found in the group of Asian students who had experienced failure. The successful Asian students showed preference patterns similar to Australian students in the same courses. There was no significant relationship between similarity of preferences and socio-economic background.

These findings indicate that for most subjects the inventory did present meaningful contrasts in types of occupation which had positive and negative valences for them. Differentiation had occurred in the vocational region. The fact that many Asian as well as Australian students showed this high degree of differentiation may be taken to indicate a degree of cross-cultural validity in the test.

The Rohde Sentence Completion Test: In the analysis of the Rohde Sentence Completion Test, the responses were first classified into the themes which appeared most often, representing possible regions of the life space. The principal themes obtained were: the university, school, theoretical, vocational, economic-financial, parents, affiliation, sex, political-social, leisure, sport, health, food, personal environment, accommodation, exploration and travel, religion, aesthetic-literary activities and personal appearance. Each protocol was then scored on the basis of an overall rating of resultant forces operating in each of the nineteen regions. The total conflict, negative and neutral and unclassifiable responses were obtained and the differences were compared (by chi^2).

Regions which showed the greatest degree of concern could be distinguished from areas of low concern, and these were found to differ for the Asian and Australian groups. In 1962, central regions for Asians were health, food, religion, financial-economic activities and university, and for the Australians health, economic-financial activities, religion, affiliation, sex and food. In 1964, central regions for Asians were affiliation, religion, parents, economic-financial activities, good health, and for Australians health, university, sex, religion, personal appearance, economic-financial activities, parents and affiliation.

Regions of low concern for the Asians in 1962 were school, personal environment, leisure, sport, aesthetic-literary activities and, to a lesser degree, the theoretical, exploratory, and political-social regions, while for the Australians the exploratory, political-social, aesthetic-literary and theoretical regions were of little interest. In 1964, the Asians again showed little concern for the aesthetic-literary, sport and exploration regions and the Australians again were little concerned with exploration and aesthetic-literary activities. These patterns of centrality-peripherality showed little change for the two groups from one occasion to the next.

The Interviews

The analysis of the interviews was divided into two parts, the sociological background and the analysis of regions and changes in cognitive structure. Only some of the more interesting results can be presented here.

First, factual data were extracted to give a picture of the sociological background. Differences between Asians and Australians were compared (by chi^2) in cases where the same categorization was appropriate to both groups, and an index of social similarity was constructed on the basis of these results. The aspects of the sociological background from which this index was derived included: political identification, race or ethnic grouping, medium of at-home and at-school communication, father's occupation, family structure (i.e., whether the family was of the primary or extended kind), age of the student, social-sexual behaviour, whether the type of geographical background was urban, small town or rural, the religion formally adhered to by the family, and the extent of previous cross-cultural experiences.

There was cultural dissimilarity between the two groups in family size and organization, in the predominantly rural background of Asians compared with an urban background of the Australians, and in the language spoken in the home. Successful Asian students were not more like the Australians than were the less successful. The Chinese students were found to be more similar to the Australians than any other ethnic group, followed by Indians and Indonesians.

Four major clusters of sub-regions obtained in the analysis of the university region were: techniques of acquiring knowledge, interactions between staff and students, interpersonal relationships between students, and concepts of the university as an institution. Differences between the

Asians and Australians in 1962 and 1964 were examined and the nature of changes was explored.

In 1962, the Asians were less ready to express critical opinions, had more difficulty in taking notes, did not participate in class discussions and did not believe that students should 'sow their wild oats'. Asian students took very little part in student societies apart from joining their own national associations, and when they did join societies they often chose activities not favoured by Australians of the same sex. Asian students entered into fewer discussion topics and favoured topics not popular with Australians of the same sex. They were also more likely to prefer school to university than were the Australians, who generally appeared to be well pleased with the change over from school to university.

Of particular interest in this group of findings were the results concerned with problems of taking notes. Differences between the Asians and Australians in this regard were considerable on both occasions (Asian v. Australian 1962: chi^2 22.38, .01 df 2, Asian v. Australian 1964: chi^2 19.45, .01 df 2). There was very little change in the Asian students between 1962 and 1964 (chi^2 ns) and only a slight change in the Australian students—the differences between them remaining extreme. This result must surely be disturbing to those who would hope that in a three-year period at university students would learn these skills, and that by their third year at university Asian students would no longer have difficulties in taking notes.

Many university teachers would claim that one of the most important aspects of university teaching is to encourage critical thinking. A higher incidence of the expression of critical thinking could be expected to occur in the later years of university study when classes are smaller and seminar methods are in more common use than in first year. There is, of course, a difference between developing the ability to think critically and expressing these critical thoughts in a group setting, and it may well be that the correlation between critical thinking and the willingness to express oneself is slight. Only the willingness to express oneself could be noted in these interviews.

Very striking differences were brought out on this variable. In 1962, the Australians were not only more ready to speak up than were the Asians but also a much larger proportion of the Asians accepted things non-critically, whereas the Australians were critical, if reticent (Asian v. Australian 1962: chi^2 11.60, .01 df 2). In 1964, most of the Australian students were still confident of expressing their criticisms. Among the Asians there was a slight change from non-critical acceptance to being more critical but remaining reticent. At the same time the differences between the Asians and the Australians had become, if anything, even more pronounced (Asian v. Australian 1964: chi^2 34.69, .01 df 2). In other words, the Asian students had not learned to express their ideas freely in the seminar or classroom. This reticence on the part of Asian students has been noted by many who have been involved in teaching them and it would seem that here is a cultural barrier which a three-year period and the efforts of lecturers and tutors have been unsuccessful in breaking down.

The other regions analysed were: attitudes to school and the continuing influences of school, communication media, vocational interests, economic and financial activities, family and parental relationships, affiliation with peer groups, sex behaviour, political and social interests, sport, aesthetic activities, health, food, the domestic environment and religious performance and beliefs. In a relatively small number of cases, other regions which had emerged in the sentence completions did appear in the interviews but in an insufficient number of cases to allow for a group analysis (for example, travel and exploration, and attitudes to self in regard to appearance and dress).

Differences between the Asians and Australians occurred in nearly all these regions. The Asians were less clear about their future vocations, were less likely to have made the choice themselves, and less likely to attribute their choice to idealized social motivations than were the Australians. The Asians had not received vocational guidance, and, unlike a large number of the Australian group, had not had the experience of part-time or vacation employment. They were less likely to have conflicts with their parents, but, at the same time, their parents had less control or influence in their choice of friends. The Asians claimed friendships with Australians more often than the Australian students did with Asians. Australian students had more casual friendships with members of the opposite sex and were generally more attracted to these activities than were the Asians. The Australian students were much more likely to participate in sport than were the Asians.

The Australian students enjoyed better health and expressed fewer anxieties in terms of suffering from poor health or being hindered in their studies by headaches and other illnesses. Australian students enjoyed their food, Asians had difficulty with it. The Asians were less satisfied with their accommodation and changed it more often. Whereas Australian students who lived away from home were most likely to live in colleges and boarding houses, the Asian students were most likely to share flats or houses. During the three years both the Asian and Australian patterns changed somewhat, the Asians perhaps more than the Australians, but most of the differences obtained in 1962 remained in 1964.

Participation in student affairs was investigated by a question which asked the students whether they belonged to or worked for any university societies such as faculty or subject societies, drama groups, political groups, student magazine, newspaper, religious clubs, commemoration festivities, choirs, the free thought society or the international club. There was a sizeable interest in faculty and subject societies (42 per cent), in sporting clubs (21 per cent), and religious groups (24 per cent), but only limited support for commemoration organization (5 per cent).

Of the 58 Asians, 47 (81 per cent) did not join in any student activities. Not only was this a greater proportion than in the case of Australian students, but there were differences, also, in the kinds of activities which were preferred. Sporting activities were most popular and accounted for 38 per cent of all memberships, followed by the international club (29 per cent); faculty societies attracted only 14 per cent while other categories were of negligible size. When the rank orders of the Asians were correlated with those of the Australian group the correlation of .43 (*rho* ns) was obtained, demonstrating the lack of agreement between the two sets of rankings. By 1964, the extent of participation had changed somewhat for the Asian students but only slightly for the Australian group.

In another question, the students were asked whether they became involved in discussions on 'serious subjects other than their own work'. Eight examples were given and others invited if they did not appear among the eight. Those given were politics, religion, world affairs, the state of the world generally, sport, the opposite sex, social topics, and philosophical ideas.

The Asians discussed fewer topics than did the Australians in both 1962 and 1964. A high proportion of Asians said that they did not enter into discussions at all. As expected, there was also a difference in preferences in 1962; whereas the Asians talked most about religion, followed by world affairs and social topics (tied), sport and politics (tied), the opposite sex, and lastly philosophical ideas, the Australian group talked about sport, the opposite sex, politics, world affairs and religion, followed by social topics, and lastly philosophical ideas. The only correspondence in the Asian and Australian students' preferences appeared to be in their lack of interest in philosophical ideas, an attitude common to nearly all the men students. Discussions of philosophical ideas were more favoured by the women students, both Asians and Australians. In 1964, however, a positive correlation (.80, *tau*) was obtained between the Asian and Australian rankings. This appears to represent mainly a change in the Australian interest, although there was a slight change within the Asian group.

Another written item explored motivations for the choice of courses. This item was presented to the subjects as a set of eleven possible sources of motivation for choosing their career goal which the subjects were asked to rank in order of importance. From the initial rankings of all eleven stimuli, the five most frequently ranked reasons were selected and analysed by the multi-dimensional unfolding method. The first five rankings were given to: interest in the content of the course, parents' wishes, the wish to help one's fellow man, a desire to gain a good financial position, and response to vocational guidance.

The location of the Asian subjects relative to the location of the Australians suggested that, in general, the Asians did not give similar reasons to Australians for choosing similar courses. There seemed to be an emphasis amongst the Asians on an other-directed choice rather than an internalized interest. No substantial change between the 1962 and 1964 results occurred in the case of Australians, but for the Asians there were some changes. Not only could fewer be placed in 1964, but the locations of those who could be placed were more likely to fall within the Australian pattern.

The multi-dimensional unfolding method was also used to explore the relative valences of contrasting sources of reference for making decisions in difficult situations. The reference sources used for this item were parental influence, opinions of members of the peer group, moral or ethical tenets and religious beliefs, advice from older people, and reliance on the self alone.

The Australians, as a whole, did not use older people as reference sources, but the Asians did. The Australian women referred to older people more than did the Australian men, but not frequently even so. These results suggested a greater reliance by the Asians than the Australians on external rather than internalized reference sources. A tendency to deference in their preference for the advice of parents or other older persons contrasts with the Australian students use of peer-group reference sources.

In another item exploring attitudes to four popular stereotypes—saints, scholars, heroes, artists—the multi-dimensional unfolding technique was again used. Some strong faculty differences appeared in the results of the survey group. The Asian students, even in engineering and science, appeared to choose patterns favoured by Australian arts and medical students rather than by the engineers and commerce students. The high favour given to scholars by the Asian students was similar to a pattern found by J. A. Keats using this item on Malaysian data. (Keats, J. A., 1962.)

A group of ten items from Taft's Australianism scale was included under the title of Social Opinions. Asian-Australian differences were significant on three items in 1962. Very few changes occurred from 1962 to 1964. The Asians differed in 1964 from their attitudes in 1962 on only one item, that concerned with respect accorded to a family on the basis of its high social standing. The Australians, too, however, had changed on this item.

Individual Differences in Acculturation

In the final stage of the analysis an acculturation scale was constructed by collecting all the items on which significant differences between Asian and Australian students had been found. Each Asian student's responses on these items, 54 in all, were scored as being either like or unlike the behaviour or attitude found most frequently in the Australian students. The number of responses like those of the Australians was then totalled to produce the acculturation score.

The items making up the acculturation scale are set out below.

The Acculturation Scale

I Item from the Performance Tests—The Asian student's response is scored as positive, i.e., more like the responses of Australian students than like those of Asian students, if:

    1. His Reading Comprehension score is not less than 1 standard deviation below the mean of the Australian students.

II Items from the Rothwell-Miller Vocational Interest Inventory—The Asian student's response is scored positive if:

2. He differentiates between the vocational interest categories.
3. He favours vocational interest patterns which correlate significantly with those of Australian students in similar courses.

III Items from the Sentence Completion Test—The Asian student's response is scored positive if:

4. He expresses optimistic attitudes and positive locomotions towards the university.
5. He expresses optimistic attitudes and positive locomotions towards his financial prospects and present financial position.
6. He expresses conflicting attitudes towards his parents.
7. He expresses positive locomotions towards sex.
8. He expresses positive locomotions towards sport.
9. He expresses favourable attitudes towards his physical well-being.
10. He expresses positive enjoyment of food.
11. He does not express interest in travel.
12. He expresses anxieties about his personal appearance.

IV Items from the Socio-Economic Background—The Asian student's response is scored positive if:

13. He comes from a family which is not active politically.
14. He has previously had an English-medium education.
15. He speaks English in the home.
16. His father is a business executive, professional man or higher-grade public servant.
17. His family structure is of the nuclear rather than the extended type.
18. He comes from an urban rather than rural background.
19. His family are formally adherents of the Christian religion.
20. His age is not more than 1 standard deviation above the mean age of the Australian students.
21. There are no more than three other children in his family.
22. He has had previous contact with Europeans before coming to Australia.

V Items from oral questions in the interviews—The Asian student's response is scored positive if:

23. He has no difficulty in taking lecture notes.
24. He expresses critical opinions in class rather than remaining reticent or uncritical.
25. He participates actively in seminars, laboratory work and tutorials.
26. He participates in informal discussions with other students.
27. He participates actively in student clubs and societies other than foreign national students' societies.
28. In discussions and informal conversations with students he prefers to talk about sport and the opposite sex rather than politics, world affairs and philosophical ideas.

29. He approves of students 'sowing their wild oats'.
30. He prefers university to school.
31. He is clear rather than vague about his vocational future.
32. He has made the vocational choice himself rather than carrying out the wishes of others.
33. He has had professional vocational guidance.
34. He has chosen his vocation with altruistic motivation.
35. He has had part-time or vacation employment experience while a student.
36. He is sometimes in conflict with his parents.
37. He makes friends amongst Australian students rather than with Asians.
38. He is influenced by his parents in making peer-group friendships.
39. He has informal friendships with members of the opposite sex but is neither married nor subject to promises of marriage or marriage arrangements made by his family.
40. He has a generally positive attitude towards sex.
41. He plays sport actively.
42. He enjoys good health.
43. He enjoys the food provided for him by others.
44. He lives in college or boards privately.
45. He is satisfied with his accommodation and the personal relationships he makes with others there.
46. He does not make frequent changes in his accommodation.

VI Items from the non-standardized written questions in the interviews—The Asian student is scored positive if:
47. His motivations for choosing the course he enters are strongly based on interest in the course and not related to parental influence.
48. His preferred reference sources for making decisions are himself and his peer group rather than parents and other authority figures.
49. He admires scholars and heroes rather than saints and artists.

VII Items from the Taft Australianism Scale—The Asian student is scored positive if:
50. He disagrees with the statement that the clergy should keep completely out of politics.
51. He disagrees with the statement that parents have a right to expect their children to support them when they are old.
52. He disagrees with the statement that a person whose family has had a high social standing for many generations is entitled to some respect.
53. He agrees with the statement that it is all right for a girl to have dates with as many boys as she pleases.
54. He disagrees with the statement that a country is far more enjoyable to live in when the people come from a wide range of racial and national backgrounds.

The scores of 32 Asian students who had completed these items on both occasions were used to examine changes from 1962 to 1964, using tests of differences between means. The relationship between success and acculturation was also examined. Each of the 32 students was given a success rating using an eleven-point ranking scale. The difference between their 1962 and 1964 acculturation scores was found and these differences were correlated with the success scores.

The mean acculturation score for 1962 was 22.09, and for 1964, 22.13. The difference between the means, .04, was not significant. The relationship between change in acculturation and success was found to be positive ($rho = .45$, $t = 2.76$, df 30, significant at .01 level of confidence).

Summary and Conclusions

The purpose of this research was twofold: first, to develop techniques for exploring and identifying differences between Asian and local students in an Australian university, and, second, to examine the changes which occurred over a three-year period.

The methods have been successful as exploratory tools. The use of the Lewinian theoretical orientation has made it possible to demonstrate what is central and what is more peripheral in the Asian students *vis à vis* the Australians. At the outset of this research only hunches could be expressed as to where the difference between Asian and Australian students would lie, and these hunches could, at best, be informed guesses based on a knowledge of the differences between the cultures as reported by anthropologists and sociologists. There would seem to be sufficient evidence from these results to support the contention that Asian students can be considered to be a group, in that they are different from Australian students, no matter how extensive the differences between them and between their cultures might be. By emphasizing functional equivalence, rather than verbal consistency, the methods used have overcome the considerable communication difficulties as well as possible and have provided a way of making successful cross-cultural comparisons.

A relationship has been established between change in acculturation and level of success, showing that the greatest degree of change towards Australian behaviour patterns occurred in the most successful Asian students. The amount of change in the Asian students, however, was small. These results are depressing for those who hope that a sojourn in Australia will produce substantial changes in the Asian students' attitudes. Differences between Asians and Australian students tended to remain. It is possible of course that the effects of these changes are of the delayed action kind, but that is an issue which is to be explored in a later study.

References

Beals, R. and Humphrey, N. D., 1957: *No Frontier to Learning. The Mexican Student in the United States.* University of Minnesota Press, Minn.

Benn, R. W., 1961: The adjustment problems of a group of Asian students at an Australian university. Unpublished MEd thesis, University of Sydney.

Bennett, J. W., *et al.*, 1962: *In Search of Identity. The Japanese Overseas Scholar in America and Japan.* University of Minnesota Press, Minn.

Boesch, E. E., 1958: *Problems and Methods in Cross-Cultural Research.* UNESCO Expert Meeting on Cross-Cultural Research on Child Psychology, Bangkok.

Brewster Smith, M., 1955: Some features of foreign student adjustment. *Journal of Higher Education,* 26, 4, 231-241.

Brewster Smith, M., 1956a: Cross-cultural education as a research area. *Journal of Social Issues,* 12, 1, 3-8.

Brewster Smith, M., 1956b: A perspective for further research on cross-cultural education. *Journal of Social Issues,* 12, 1, 56-68.

Campbell, J., 1964: Testing of culturally different groups. College Entrance Board Research and Development Reports. RDR 63-4, No. 14, E.T.S.

Coffman, W. E., 1963: Evidence of cultural factors in responses of African students to items in an American test of scholastic aptitude. E.T.S. Research Memorandum, No. RM 63-6.

Greenfield, P. M. and Bruner, J. S., 1966: Culture and cognitive growth. *International Journal of Psychology,* 1, 2, 89-108.

Hodgkin, M. C., 1966: *Australian Training and Asian Living.* University of Western Australia Press, Perth, W.A.

Keats, D. M., 1962: English ability and success of Asian students. *Australian Journal of Education,* 6-7, 37-46.

Keats, J. A., 1962: Attitudes to idealised stereotypes in Australia and Malaya. *Journal Social Psychology,* 57, 353-362.

Lesser, S. O. and Peter, H. W., 1957: Training foreign nationals in the U.S. in some applications of behavioural research. UNESCO.

Lewin, K., 1951: *Field Theory in the Social Sciences.* Harper & Bros., New York.

Morris, R. T. and Davidsen, O. M., 1960: *The Two-Way Mirror. National Status in Foreign Students' Adjustment.* University of Minnesota Press, Minn.

Noesjirwan, J., 1966: A study of the adjustment of some Indonesian students studying in Australia. Unpublished MA thesis, Victoria University, Wellington.

Sanders, C., 1954: Examination results of students from S.E. Asia, enrolled in Australian universities during 1953. University of Western Australia, Report No. 2.

Taft, R., 1962: Opinion convergence in the assimilation of immigrants: A problem in social psychology. *Australian Journal of Psychology,* 14, 41-54.

Tylee, A. F., 1964: *Foreign Students in Technical Schools and in Industry in Australia.* Swinburne Technical College, Melbourne.

Part VI
The Classroom Context

14

The Classroom Context

Raymond S. Adams

ONLY a few short years ago the field of classroom research remained relatively virginal. Researchers, in general, seemed convinced that the study of classrooms, unglamorous as they were, offered neither excitement nor reward. The reasons for their disdain are not hard to trace. In the first place, there was abroad a common delusion that, because everyone had been to school, everyone knew all about education. Second, no one seemed inclined to consider that the real world of classroom practice might be any different from the way that the precepts and strictures of educational philosophy said it ought to be. Third, classrooms, schools, and indeed most educational enterprises, were regarded with poorly veiled suspicion—the cost of investing in them was apparent, the returns from the investment, doubtful. Consequently, to consider incrementing the cost by engaging in educational research was to add insult to injury.

In this general atmosphere of disinterestedness few researchers felt inclined to waste intellectual energy on educational fieldwork. However, the situation is vastly different now. Research into the 'real world' of the classroom is burgeoning—blatant and unashamed. Already, books are appearing that almost proudly proclaim their interest in the classroom phenomenon.*

Again, papers are burgeoning too. At the 1968 convention of the American Educational Research Association there were more than forty papers concerned with the act of teaching, teacher-pupil interaction, or discourse analysis. Finally, in the U.S.A., Flanders' (1960) interaction analysis—a packaged method for discerning aspects of the teacher-pupil interaction—is currently enjoying an unprecedented and unexpected vogue.

One wonders what accounts for this sudden popularity of the Cinderella-like classroom. What has brought about her emancipation? There are three main reasons that seem to have face validity. First, there has been a

*TEPS, 1966: *The Real World of the Beginning Teacher*; ASCD, 1966: *The Way Teaching Is*; Ira J. Gordon, 1966: *Studying the Child in the School*; G. W. Moore, 1967: *Realities of the Urban Classroom*; P. W. Jackson, 1968: *Life in Classrooms*; R. S. Adams and B. J. Biddle, 1969: *Realities of Teaching*.

general re-evaluation of education's significance to society. America, affronted by Sputnik 1, began, in 1958, to regard education as a means of social investment with the return measurable in terms of human capital gain. Second, within the ranks of educators themselves there had been growing frustration over their own continuing inability to demonstrate professional expertise. Educationists, it seemed, knew little more about the facts of educational life than did anyone else. Furthermore, their conventional props—educational philosophy and educational psychology—were proving unequal to the task of single-handedly shoring up education's growing edifice. Something, it seemed, was needed both to convert into action the fine intentions of normative philosophy, and to link the esoteric world of experimental psychology with the mundane world of teaching. Third, as technology began to encroach on educational practice, doubts and uncertainties were raised in the minds of educators over the consequences of an impending brave, new, machine-bound, educational world.

These and other factors conspired to focus attention on the place where school learning ostensibly occurs—the classroom. Questions began to proliferate. How can we improve what the teacher does? How can we facilitate the learning process? Will smaller classes help? Will a more congenial environment produce greater learning? How can subject matter be systematized better? How can subject matter be reduced to manageable proportions? What organizational procedures will facilitate learning best? Are some things learned better in small groups, others in large groups and others in isolation? Why should this new book be used? Why should this new method be introduced? Why not use a number of teachers working as a team? Why not use a machine instead of the teacher? Increasingly, however, the main thrust of the questions became more and more pragmatic. In effect the questions asked, 'What will happen if this, that or the other change is introduced?' Slowly it became apparent that this question could not be answered authoritatively. Inevitably, attempted answers were couched in terms that were as nebulous as they were optimistic. Phrases like, 'we believe', 'we hope', 'we expect', 'we intend', featured prominently. Inevitably, when the practical (and legitimate) rejoinder, 'How do you know?' was made, no direct, factually-based reply could be given.

Educationists were faced with a dilemma. They recognized that teaching and learning ought to be improved. They assumed that improvement was possible. They also recognized that the 'good ideas' being advocated wholesale had a considerable amount of apparent validity. Plausible arguments could be invoked to defend them and an abundance of enthusiastic advocates were available to proselytize them. But there seemed to exist genuine reasons for doubting if the freely-advocated changes would, in fact, accomplish the purposes desired. Furthermore, it was not at all clear that even if the changes were successful they would not, at the same time, vitiate other legitimate goals of education.

Given this dilemma, what are the conditions that need to be met in order to resolve the problem? So that we may attempt an answer to this question here, we must, first of all, digress temporarily from the main line of discussion. Consider, for a minute, the issues involved in determining whether *any* educational innovation could work. In simplest terms the problem can be seen as involving: (a) a pre-condition (before the change is introduced); (b) a treatment condition (when the change is implemented); and (c) a post-condition (when the effects of the change are to be discerned). Determining whether change has occurred and how it occurs, seems to depend on discovering differences between the pre-condition and the post-condition. Now, most attempts at evaluation of innovations have assumed that this is *all* that needs to be known. Consequently, most often the pre-condition of learners is measured (say, their arithmetical knowledge). Then the new programme is introduced. Then learning gain is measured after the programme has been implemented. However, as a variety of reviewers have testified (Barr, 1940, 1943, 1946, 1948, 1949; Domas & Tiedeman, 1950; AERA, 1952, 1953; Gage, 1960; Mitzel, 1960; Ryans, 1960; Biddle & Ellena, 1964), the single, most impressive piece of information resulting from such evaluation is that what really determines the success or failure of a programme is still unknown. We are left wondering then, what other conditions need to be fulfilled if the effects of innovation are to be discerned systematically and comprehensively.

It seems apparent that whether a particular innovation succeeeds in accomplishing what it sets out to do will depend in large degree on what happens to it *when it is put into action*. For example, a teacher who is unaware of the conceptual bases, assumptions and procedures appropriate for the use of Cuisenaire rods can do little better than employ them as mere adjuncts to his old formalistic methods. By contrast, the teacher sophisticated in their use may change his whole teaching style to accommodate to them. It is conceivable, for instance, that the introduction of the new system of arithmetic may have a variety of side effects that would not be revealed by any simple, single-minded evaluation of arithmetic attainment alone. For example, children exposed to the new method may learn to like (or dislike) arithmetic intensely. They may also find that the 'new' arithmetic suddenly becomes a significant, dominant feature of their classroom lives. New groupings emerge in the classroom, new timetables are observed, repeated allusions are made to arithmetic during other lessons. Arithmetic becomes glamorous, other subjects pale. New leaders emerge, the social structure is altered. New definitions of 'good' and 'bad' behaviour are promulgated and accepted.

All this suggests that if any definitive knowledge about the effects of the innovation are to be gained, we ought to know what was happening in the classroom *before* its implementation, what happened *during* its implementation and what happened *after* it had been implemented. We ought to be able to state exactly how the innovation was introduced, explained, practised, augmented and supported. As well, we also ought to be able to discern changes in the social system of the classroom, changes in classroom organization, changes in interaction and in the character of teacher-pupil discourse *as well as* any learning increment that might have occurred.

There is here, then, one practical reason for the rapidly-increasing interest shown in the classroom as a learning context—knowing about it may lead to a better understanding of how the learning process is promoted, and hence how it may be controlled. There are two other reasons that also deserve mention—even if only briefly. First, classrooms are a pervasive social phenomenon. There are more classrooms than there are factories. There are more classrooms than there are hospitals. There are more classrooms than there are prisons. There are more classrooms than there are election days. There are more people in classrooms than there are people who smoke, than there are people involved in automobile accidents, than there are investors on the stock exchange. In other words, classrooms merit study in their own right, simply because they represent a significant region of human behaviour. Second, classrooms also merit study because in them the young are presumably being inducted into society. In them, the citizens of tomorrow, the industrialists, the doctors, the soldiers, the policemen, the housewives, the motorists, the politicians, the electors, are all being moulded and shaped. Society might do well to know and note how this moulding process proceeds.

Predictably, attempts already made at studying the classroom have shown considerable variety. Some have been simple studies confined to identifying single phenomena, for example: Urban (1943) investigated sneezes; and Harrington (1955) focused on smiles. Others more ambitious have sought to tap the behavioural complexity of the classroom. For instance, the extensively used Medley and Mitzel's (1958) 'OScAR' lists seventy different kinds of observable behaviours, while Cornell, Lindvall and Saupe's (1953) check list exceeds that number by thirty-two. The techniques used have also varied considerably. Sometimes hand-written verbatim records provide basic data, e.g., Barker and Wright (1951, 1954, 1961). Sometimes audio records serve instead, e.g., Withall (1949), Smith, et al. (1964), Solomon and Miller (1961). Sometimes films are used, e.g., Kounin (1968), Garfunkel (1968). Sometimes video tapes provide the data, e.g., Adams (1965).

Again, researchers have been trying to accomplish different purposes. Urban (1943) was concerned with influencing the health habits of children, Flanders (1961) with improving teaching, Kounin (1968) with eliminating deviant behaviour, Withall (1956) with assessing social climate, Soar (1962) with perfecting statistical procedures, Ryans (1963) with providing a basis for conceptualization, etc.

Predictably, investigations have been concerned with children of different ages and different grade levels. Anderson (1939), Anderson and Brewer (1945, 1946) and Fisher (1967) undertook work at the kindergarten level. Primary classrooms have been investigated more frequently, notably by: Hughes, et al. (1959), Taba, Levine and Elzey (1964), Jackson (1965), Gump (1967). Work done at secondary level reflects a greater concern for (a) subject matter; e.g., Bellack, et al. (1966), Wright and

Proctor (1961), and (b) intellectual processes; e.g., Smith, *et al.* (1964, 1967) and Nuthall and Lawrence (1965).

Although there are now quite a number of behavioural studies that have been undertaken in classroom settings, few general research reviews have used the classroom concept as a basis for delineating the field. Thelen (1950), in *Human Dynamics in the Classroom*, overviewed some empirical work, but showed greater concern with substantiating some 'educational principles' thought to derive from studies of human interaction. Jensen and Parsons (1959) presented a model for 'conceptualizing' or, to be more precise, categorizing, group phenomena in the classroom. One section in the *Encyclopedia of Educational Research* (1960), entitled 'Classroom organization', focused exclusively on teaching methods, while another, dealing with 'group processes' gave brief attention to the educative setting and asserted enthusiastically, but without supporting evidence, that: 'the school grade or class is a special case. . . . However many of the facts and principles of group structure and dynamics are definitely applicable.'

Again, in the 1960 *Review of Educational Research*, Withall gave a polished but encapsulated overview of the field by way of introduction to an equally cryptic descriptive account of some recent studies. He noted, it seems, with surprise, 'some research reported gives distinct signs of having been guided by implicit theories or models'. A more detailed treatment is to be found in Medley and Mitzel's chapter in Gage (1963) where observational methodology is examined and where experiments, both early and recent, are described. The most recent of the reviews has been undertaken by Biddle (1967). He dealt with classroom studies under the broad headings of: coverage, methods of data collection, unit of analysis, conceptual posture and concepts used. Biddle's review is essentially a systematic analysis of the current state of research methodology and conceptualization in the area. As such, it followed a more expansive treatment of general observational research by Boyd and deVault (1966) in an earlier issue of the same journal. It thus continued a tradition established by the *Review of Educational Research* no earlier than 1953, when Wann's rather free-ranging chapter entitled 'Action research in schools' gave brief, tacit recognition to the existence of the classroom as a behavioural setting.

It might be anticipated that, with research activity increasing, there would be an abundance of new insights and information available. This is only partly true. For instance, with the exception of Smith's (1959) small brochure, no extensive list of 'findings' derived from this kind of research is available for general consumption. In fact, findings have seemed to play a rather incidental part up to the moment. Most researchers have been interested in the problem of devising research tools that will enable them to go into the classroom and identify and measure supposedly significant aspects of human behaviour. Sometimes these instruments have been ad hoc, consisting of lists of items that have been selected either arbitrarily or without an explicit rationalization of the bases for their selection. Sometimes they have been accompanied by an assertion claiming that, 'This is the way the classroom world is'. However, rarely has any instrument been supported by an integrated theory of human behaviour with its postulates and hypotheses clearly stated.

This state of affairs, though regrettable, is not surprising. The situation confronting the classroom researcher is not too different from the one which confronts today's incipient lunar biologist or geologist. Lunar biology and lunar geology are, at the moment, very inexact sciences. Presumably, the first task of their researchers will be to accumulate samples of relevant phenomena. Of necessity, this will have to be done indiscriminately with selection determined by the locality of the collector (man or machine) and his (its) range of mobility. Whether any sample found may be collected or not will depend on its size, weight, and whether appropriate tools are available for detaching it. Discerning the compositional character of samples will, at first, be determined by the number and kind of earth-originated tests that the researchers think are appropriate. Later, no doubt, other moon explorers will select samples more discriminately and will come to develop research tools not limited by earth-bound perceptions and conceptions, nor restricted to a perhaps irrelevant earth-bound view of the nature of the biological and geological universes.

In a similar way, the pioneers of classroom research have been forced to start with the ideas, perceptions and concepts currently available. Consequently, we find researchers talking about classroom behaviour in conventional pedagogical terms, e.g., 'deviancy' (Kounin, 1968), 'questions' (Perkins, 1964), 'milk money time' (Gump, 1967), 'repeats—summarizes' (Oliver & Shaver, 1963), 'responding' (Bellack, et al., 1966), 'defining' (Smith & Meux, 1963), and so on. Others have invoked psychological concepts, e.g., 'learner supportive' (Withall, 1949), 'positive affectivity' (Hughes, et al., 1959), 'accepts feelings' (Flanders, 1960), 'warmth' (Ryans, 1960). Some others, again, have used the language and concepts of anthropology and sociology, e.g., Adams (1965), Moore (1967), Smith and Geoffrey (1968). However, new concepts are also beginning to appear. For example, Smith, et al. (1964, 1967) developed the term *venture* to account for segments of discourse that could be classified in terms of nine underlying objectives, viz., conceptual, causal, evaluative, reason, rule, procedural, interpretative, particular and informatory. Bellack, et al. (1966) defined *teaching cycles* and talked about the rules of the *games that teachers play*. Kounin (1966), who has a flair for the picturesque, coined the phrases, *'teacher withitness'* and *'ripple effect'*.

New terms such as these carry a certain appeal, possibly because novelty tends to intrigue anyway, but more likely because the orientations suggested also generate additional new insights.

However, new insights, if they are really new, also generate their own problems. First of all they require a new nomenclature which is both precise and clearly discriminable from other naming systems so that confusion can be avoided. In this respect, research faces a major difficulty.

Most of the descriptive terms used so far were used previously to refer to individual behaviour. There are, it seems, surprisingly few words in the English language that are exclusively group terms. Cohesiveness (Festinger, et al., 1950) is one and syntality (Cattell, 1948) is another, but by and large today's language lacks a group-orientated vocabulary. Researchers are, consequently, left with two unattractive alternatives: either to use words more appropriate for describing individual behaviour, thus creating confusion, or to coin new words, thus inviting hostility.

The generation of new insights also gives rise to an even more important problem—the problem of explanation and prediction. The human appetite for knowing why, is, it seems, insatiable. The relevance of this point needs illustration. Adams (1965) discovered that nearly seventy per cent of all verbal exchanges in the classroom occurred in a narrow band that extended from the centre front of the room directly towards the centre back. He also discovered that, within this band, the closer the pupil is to the front of the room the greater the likelihood that he will be involved *directly* in the verbal action of the classroom. The existence of this phenomenon is not of interest by itself. It becomes interesting only because of the questions it provokes. For example, is pupil achievement a function of location in the classroom? Again, if direct involvement in the interaction process is desirable, why is interaction circumscribed in this particular way? Again, what are the consequences of selective interaction—perhaps in terms of teacher satisfaction, pupil attitude, and the like. Raising questions of this kind carries an important implication. Virtually, they require not only that the relationship between the two phenomena (say, location and achievement) be discovered, but also, that its existence be explained. However, providing explanations depends on the existence of conditions that make explanation possible. It is at this point of the discussion that we are forced to confront one serious, basic deficiency of educational research, viz., that we have not yet created the necessary conditions. We are, consequently, not equipped to provide authoritative explanation yet. We are obliged to ask, however, what conditions would have to obtain if adequate explanatory and predictive power is to be achieved.

Basically, any explanation of any phenomenon is a statement of a special kind of relationship—an 'if A then B' relationship. How good any given explanation is depends on whether the relationship stated is a necessary and sufficient one—whether or not the relationship can be stated as: 'only if A, *and* if A only, then B'. In this case we know that B will occur only if A occurs, and that nothing else other than A is needed. Regrettably, however, relationships as neat as this are seldom to be found in the behavioural sciences (even though much behavioural research assumes they are). Inevitably, we find that the relationship between A and B needs to be qualified. The first qualification that has to be made is to recognize the nature of the conditions that obtain in the context in which the relationship occurs, and to acknowledge these 'givens'. To take an example from the physical sciences: calculating the trajectory of missiles differs according to the context in which the missile has to perform. One set of calculations is appropriate for earth, another for the moon, and yet another for outer space. In a similar way there are 'givens' that have to be recognized when human behaviour is the subject under examination. For instance, it is obvious that the relationship between the actual speed of driving and the probability of an accident varies according to whether the context is a super highway or a road in the outbacks. It is also obvious that other 'givens' might be equally relevant to the same illustration; for instance: the surface of the road; the camber of the turns; obstructions to vision; the size of the vehicle; the mechanical state of the vehicle and so on. But this is not all. There are, as well, other 'givens' that also pertain to the context but which derive from the human beings involved; for instance: the age of the driver; his skill level; his reaction time; his powers of concentration; his perceptiveness; his physical condition in general; his state of sobriety in particular, etc. When 'givens' like these are taken into account, then, in contrast with the austere simplicity of the 'if A then B' statement, the relationship equation comes to look somewhat baroque. Now we have something after this fashion: if $A + C + D + E + F + \text{not } G + \text{not } H$, *then* B— or more likely B^1 (as distinct from B^2, B^3, B^4, etc.).

The second qualification that has to be made about the A—B relationship concerns the delineation of A and B themselves. Sometimes social scientists are guilty of assuming that all things entitled A are the same—as they should be—when in fact they are not. Perhaps the best way to illustrate this is to make use of a familiar example. The measurement of intelligence has been a popular educational pastime for some years now. As a consequence, the term IQ has achieved considerable status, and a variety of tests have been devised to measure it. Some tests, however, are more restrained than others. Klausmeier (1961) states, 'The WISC (Wechsler Intelligence Scale for Children) yields considerably lower IQ's especially at 115 and above than did older forms of the Stanford Binet.' Consequently, IQ has differing connotations according to the test used. More insidious than this is the assumption that is taken to lie behind the IQ concept; namely, that there is a certain quantum of mental power each person has and that an IQ provides an accurate index of it. Consequently, a Stanford Binet IQ score, which is, in reality, no more than a particular way of rating answers given to certain specific questions, is presumed to give a measure of how much innate capacity an individual has. However, intelligence tests must be regarded really as achievement tests—tests, if you like, of the range and variety of experiences to which a child has been exposed previously. The fallibility of the earlier idea of innate intelligence with its attendant implication of predetermined intellectual potential has been exposed by recent experiments in which brain damaged children at the *age of three* have been taught to read what their superior 'normal' brethren customarily undertake at five or six. The point of all this is that intelligence, rather than being the nice, precise concept everyone would like it to be, is really rather nebulous. Furthermore, IQ— the name given to measures of intelligence—is no more precise than the concept itself. In fact, when a particular score is under consideration, unless the actual test from which it was derived is specified, it is even less precise.

Given a situation as fraught with potential ambiguity as this, what would have to be taken into account if a reasonably full and sufficient explanation of human behaviour were to be provided? In a particularly intimidating piece of work, Sells (1963) estimated that more than one hundred and eighty different variables would have to be accommodated if a full and sufficient explanation of human behaviour were to be achieved. Irrespective of the correctness of Sells' number, it seems obvious that the behavioural scientists will have to be satisfied with either partial explanation or conditional explanation as an interim alternative to perfection. Probability theory and social science are predestined to go hand in hand for some considerable time yet. Consequently, the law of parsimony becomes exceedingly important. In any situation the behavioural scientists' quest increasingly becomes a matter of delineating the *key variables*—the variables that will give greatest predictive and explanatory power with a minimum of effort. This is no less a necessity for the classroom researcher than for any other student of behaviour.

It is precisely at this point that education runs up against its own history and becomes ensnared in its own good intentions. The reason is simple, the 'key variables' bequeathed us by years of educational scholarship have not been operationalized. They are either incapable of operationalization, or the necessary steps to give the concepts operational status have not been taken. What are education's 'key concepts'? A relatively representative selection would include; aims, goals, democracy, personality, needs, motivation, the whole child, equality of opportunity, IQ, curriculum, discipline, performance, conformity, cooperation, attitudes, readiness, evaluation, subject matter and development. One is immediately impressed with the range and scope of these concepts and with the complex nature of the universe from which they have been extracted. But, at the same time, one notes that many of the concepts are nebulous—they defy definitional precision—that they are value laden, and that they appear united only in their common educational orientation. In other words, such concepts are likely to be extremely hard to treat in a scientific manner and even harder to organize in respect to one another. This is merely another way of saying that education lacks undergirding integrative theory that provides: (a) defined operational concepts; and (b) a statement of the relationships thought to exist between them. Education is empirically and theoretically bereft. It not only lacks the means for subjecting its own elements to test, but it also has neglected to describe these elements in an unambiguous and exclusive fashion. It is small wonder then, that when attempts are made to rationalize educational policies and procedures, the arguments seem confused and unscientific.

It would be pointless merely to inveigh against this regrettable state of affairs without attempting at least one small step in the direction of amelioration. Later in this chapter a tentative framework for an empirically-testable model which conceptualizes one segment of the educational domain —the classroom—will be offered. However, before this can be done, it is necessary to take note in fuller detail of some of the complexities of the classroom phenomena that have to be taken into account during the process.

In the field of classroom behaviour, the researcher is faced with an *'embarras de richesse'*. Consider, for a minute, the number of pupil-based variables that have already been thought worthy of attention: viz., intelligence in various forms, many facets of personality, attitudes, educational achievement, adjustment, health. These have all, at one time or another, featured prominently. Teacher variables also considered have included: intelligence, personality, training, attitudes, social class, religion and age. In fact, there are relatively few human attributes that have failed at one time or another to be given serious consideration as likely to be influential in the teaching-learning interaction. There is, as well, another class of variables that has to be taken into account, but this one has been relatively neglected. It comprises the various physical properties of the situation— the variety of things that Sorokin (1947) has called 'vehicles'. These include, for example: books, pencils, pens, pencil sharpeners, film strips, desks, tables, pictures, teaching machines—in fact, any material phenomenon that, because of the part it plays in the educational transaction, helps to render that transaction meaningful. There are, of course, other physical properties of the situation that are not directly involved in the educational transaction but which nonetheless appear to exert an influence over it: for example, the size of the room, its acoustic properties, its light intensity, its temperature, its aesthetic appeal, etc. To date, research in this area has mostly been concerned with the health, comfort and the physical safety of the inhabitants.

The classroom, then, is a multi-stimulus environment. In considering it as such, we are, in effect, recognizing it as a context which has 'meaning' for those who inhabit it. We are literally saying, here is a plethora of sensations that can impinge on pupils and teachers and which may affect their behaviour. However, as an earlier statement implied, just as there is a certain futility in trying to see an individual apart from his environment, there is equal futility in trying to see the environment apart from the individual. Consequently, we must also recognize some of the characteristics of the individual that serve to censor the environment for him. We must recognize that individuals perceive the same environment differently, and that some of these different perceptions can be explained in terms of the individual himself. For instance, it is obvious that a small six-year old refugee from Hitler's Europe finding himself in an American first-grade classroom would see the situation very differently from the way it was seen by other children. To use a less obvious illustration of the same point, Loflin (1968) reports discovering in Negro nonstandard English a unique grammatical structure which allows users to distinguish between a temporary state of affairs and a permanent state of affairs. For example, the phrase, 'he sick' states a temporary condition, whereas, 'he be sick' states a (relatively) permanent one. Consequently, for a white middle-class teacher to ask; 'when will he be better?' in reply to a statement that 'Johnny be sick', is for the teacher to behave in a fashion incomprehensible to the pupil.

However, there is no real reason for stopping here—for confining our attention only to what is observable within the four walls of our classroom. A classroom is *not* a closed system. Apart from the fact that the inhabitants carry with them powerful residual influences from their own 'outside' experiences, there are other forces from the world beyond the classroom that impinge directly on it. For example, the school as an organization makes demands on the classroom. Its insistent bells have to be heeded, its administrative demands met. The rest of the school not only surrounds the classroom, it infiltrates its defences too. What classroom is immune from the football team's defeat of the school's arch rivals? What classroom remains unaffected by the imminence of the school dance, and so on?

Again, the informal social system of the school exerts its influence on the classroom. Waller (1932), Gordon (1957) and Coleman (1961) have all documented the subtle ways in which peer groups create value systems for children. They have also pointed out that these values are often antithetical to school objectives. Classroom behaviour is coerced and constrained by these values. Consequently, in the classroom the teacher is often left fondly imagining that he is accomplishing his own educational objectives, while in reality a hidden, pupil determined, agendum is repeatedly subverting him.

We are confronted, then, with a situation of great complexity and, if we are honest about it, much confusion. Some resolution of this confusion can be achieved by using the stratagem of differentiating between the classroom *qua* classroom and the inhabitant *qua* inhabitant. Although the distinction is an artificial one, there is nonetheless a certain advantage in employing it at the moment. Let us deal with the inhabitants first.

As Biddle and Adams (1967) have argued, each inhabitant in the classroom, whether he is a teacher or a pupil, brings with him certain characteristics or properties. These properties include not only physical characteristics (whether the owners are short or tall, blond or red headed, etc.) but cognitive, affective and psycho-motor properties as well. Furthermore, each inhabitant's behaviour is coerced by experiences previously undergone in a variety of different social contexts. Consequently, in any given situation it is probable that an individual's behaviour is affected by both his own properties and these background experiences. Assuming that human beings tend to maximize their own gratifications and minimize their own discomforts, the apparent choice facing each classroom inhabitant is how to behave so that violence is done to neither the values that have been engendered by his background experiences, nor to his present psychological predisposition. However, this does not represent the entire choice. There are factors in the current situation that also have to be taken into account. Consequently, we need to direct attention now towards the classroom itself.

The classroom as a behavioural setting has its own rituals, its own rules and its own persisting patterns of behaviour. There is such a thing as a discernible classroom culture. Furthermore, this culture is relatively invariant. Consequently, although the inhabitants change from year to year, the pattern of behaviour stays very much the same so that an individual socialized in one classroom usually has little difficulty in accommodating to another. It is convenient to borrow the sociological term, 'norm', to describe the invariant nature of classroom behaviour. Many classroom norms are readily discernible. For example, there are organizational norms that are reflected in the way books are collected, in the way papers are ruled up, in the way children leave the room, and so on. There are also less readily discernible, or at least less readily admitted, norms that prevail in classrooms. As Adams (1965) and Jackson (1968) have pointed out, one classroom norm is a 'waiting' norm. Children wait a great deal—mostly while other individual children are receiving exclusive attention from the teacher. Again, the public character of classroom interaction can be regarded as norm based. What occurs in classrooms mostly occurs in full view of everyone else—with, of course, the prospect of public commendation or condemnation. In large part these norms of classroom behaviour are initiated or engendered by the teacher—or by the long succession of teachers who have gone before. These norms are buttressed by an intricate reward system that ensures that those who conform receive appropriate recognition. Jackson (1968) makes the telling point that despite assertions to the contrary, schools and teachers reward intellectual enterprise only when it occurs in conformity with established norms and procedures. Being 'bright', it seems, is not enough—being 'bright' and 'good' is.

To some extent the inhabitants of a classroom know and accede to the established norms, sometimes they do not, and sometimes again, they 'know' them but do not accede to them. When the norms are not known or when the expectations are different, there is the prospect of overt conflict. As might well be expected, then, a considerable amount of care and attention goes into ensuring that the norms are known and acceded to. Adams (1965) recorded that more than ten per cent of all classroom time was spent on organizational matters. He also reported that rationalization of organizational procedures seldom occurs at grade 1, features prominently at grade 6 but is no longer of any moment by grade 11. It is also a well-known fact that problems of discipline and control loom large in the eyes of administrators, teachers and parents alike.

At this point we can return to the main topic of discussion—the multistimulus character of classrooms. We have, in essence, been advocating a model in which the inhabitants of the classroom are subjected to potentially competing influences deriving alternatively from their own background experiences, their own personality characteristics and the immediate classroom environment as it is constituted as a set of norms and expectations. In any given situation, behaviour is a result of the reconciliation of these competing influences. This reconciliation, however, may now favour one influence, now another. In Figure 14.1 below, the interaction of these influences as they bear on an individual has been represented paradigmatically. In the figure, the three influences, personal properties, background

FIGURE 14.1

Influences on Behaviour

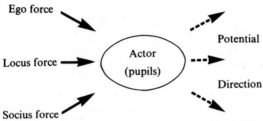

experiences and what might be called environmental press have been renamed respectively as ego force, locus force and socius force. Each force is seen to apply its influence differently on the individual (the actor in Figure 14.1), thus 'encouraging' behaviour to be directed along a line that represents an extension of one of the forces.

The paradigm bears discussion because it postulates what is essentially a conflict situation. In the diagram it is assumed that the forces must operate in opposition to each other. This is, of course, not necessarily so. It is theoretically possible for background experiences, personal properties and environmental press—or any two of them—to be in complete harmony with each other. However, whether they are or not, or the extent to which they are or not, is an empirical question. In fact, one of the major thrusts of research into the education of underprivileged children is concerned with this very question. Repeatedly it is asked, to what extent are pupil expectations and background experiences at odds with the objectives of the teacher.

The model in Figure 14.1 can also provide a basis for looking at the classroom from a broader perspective. If we see in the classroom a number of actors each of whom is being influenced to act by the nature of the forces impinging on him, we have the potential for determining which force tends to predominate. For instance, is a given classroom essentially pupil-properties oriented, is it background-experience oriented, is it environmental-press oriented? Do we have here a 'child-centred', 'permissive' setting or a society-bound 'conservative' one or an organization-bound 'institutional' one. Examples of the three different types are not hard to find. For instance, Summerhill, perhaps, represents the nearest to a 'pure' example of a school (classroom) in which pupil properties, interests, wishes, preferences, etc., determine what will be done at any given time. Again, in many American classrooms, a great deal of reverence is given to the local society. Curricula are organized around local points of geographical, social and industrial interest. In addition, pupils are deliberately taken into this society to see and experience social 'reality'. By contrast, schools in Australia maintain themselves inviolate. They are relatively immune from outside intrusions. The educational mystique is a product of the educators themselves. They made the system and they and their successors preserve it.

Necessarily, any attempt at interpreting a classroom (or a school system) in terms of the extent to which the three forces are manifested in pupils requires an aggregatory, averaging approach. To this extent the classroom becomes no more than the sum of its parts. Such a state of affairs is essentially dissatisfying. As any observer of classrooms will assert, classrooms have character of their own. Some seem happy, some busy, some depressing, some hostile, some apathetic and so on.* How, then, can an attempt be made to tap some of the uniqueness of classrooms *qua* classrooms? The answer seems to lie in recognizing the things that make classrooms unique as classrooms—their educational function.

Such a task is easier in the stating than in the executing. For years, educationists have been engaged in debating 'what is education'. The interpretations have ranged freely. For the purposes of the immediate discussion, the word education is taken as connoting the transactional process that occurs between teachers and pupils. In this process, the teacher-in-action becomes an agent who himself stands for a discernible cognitive, affective or psycho-motor position. In other words, the teacher's behaviour can be interpreted as exhibiting cognitive or affective or psycho-motor meanings.

It is a first premise of the argument that follows that the 'meaning' of the teacher's behaviour is available for imitation by the pupil—that one of the consequences of the pupil's exposure to the teacher's behaviour is that the pupil may or may not 'learn it'. However, the meaning of the teacher's behaviour may be open to different interpretations. For instance, the teacher himself can see his behaviour as having one particular meaning (e.g., encouraging intellectual enterprise), the pupil may see it differently (e.g., as deliberate goading), while an independent observer may see it differently again (e.g., as authoritarian intimidation). The question arises, 'what advantage lies in taking these different perspectives into account'? Let us accept, at the outset, that our chief objective is to better understand how classrooms function. Will it follow, then, that knowledge of the pupil's perception will help us? The answer to this question can be 'yes' only under certain limited—and rather peculiar—conditions, namely, when all pupils uniformly misperceive the situation in the same way. Usually, however, pupil misconceptions are idiosyncratic. Consequently, knowledge of pupil perceptions (misperceptions) is of most use when particular insights into the specific pupil's behaviour is needed. Will knowledge of the teacher's perception help predict what will happen in the classroom? Again, it will do so only under exceptional circumstances, namely, when (a) the teacher's perceptions are accurate, and (b) when

*We are forced here to recognize once again the limited vocabulary available to describe group phenomena. All the terms used are terms more commonly applicable to individuals.

her adaptation of her perceptions to her educational intention is perfect and (c) when her subsequent action is completely consistent with her intention. However, as before, knowing the teacher's perception may help us to understand *the teacher herself*—to know why she did or did not do some particular thing.

Is there any utility, then, in knowing the observer's interpretation of the situation? If the observer is an amateur—a purveyor of a casual opinion, the most likely answer is 'no', because this observer is subject to the personal biases, prejudices and misperceptions that any human being is. On the other hand a 'trained observer', a systematic observer, can help in this process of understanding classroom behaviour. Obviously, his helpfulness will depend on his system of observation and the extent to which it succeeds in mapping the 'reality' of the classroom. In other words, his potential power depends on the extent to which his system can identify the key variables. The reason why an independent observer may do this better than the local inhabitants can, is principally because he is not involved in the classroom process itself. He is not part of the classroom interaction (even though he may be in the room). Consequently, he is freer to ask what is this process doing; rather than asking what is this process doing to me. Because of his objective stance he is in a better position to state what the process 'means'. He is also in a better position to know what the process means because, as a systematic observer, he has predetermined the parameters of behaviour according to a (presumably integrated) theoretical framework. The proof of the effectiveness of the independent observer is yielded when he can show that his system for categorizing and relating behaviours does allow him to (a) explain why some behaviours occurred and (b) to predict that others will. Now, if the occurrence of behaviour is determined in large measure by how the actors perceive the situation, it follows that the independent observer must attempt to interpret the actor's interpretation of the situation. In other words, his own observations serve as a substitute for information that is impossible to gain, namely, a continuous consensus. More than this, however, the independent observer's system can have the potential for mapping hidden agenda—for describing goings-on that are not always fully appreciated by the participants themselves.

While the independent observer has the potential for comprehending the classroom behaviour setting better than the separate actors can, tapping the perceptions of the separate actors will give additional power. In particular, it will enable judgements to be made about the reasons for the effectiveness or failure of the educational task. Presumably, if the pupil perceives the teacher's requirements differently from the way the teacher perceived them herself, learning is inhibited. Presumably, if the observer (as consensus substitute) perceives the teacher's behaviour differently from the way the teacher perceives it herself, his understanding can be used to help the teacher. Presumably, if the observer (as a hidden agenda discerner) perceives the situation differently from the ways that both teacher and pupil do, his interpretation may generate new insights for both. There is some usefulness, then, in contemplating the possible disjunctions between teacher, pupil and observer perception. The following logical alternatives result:

Subsequent pupil behaviour is *compatible with*;
(a) The pupil's perception of the teacher's behaviour
(b) The teacher's perception of her own behaviour
(c) An observer's perception of the teacher's behaviour
(d) a + b
(e) a + c
(f) c + b
(g) a + b + c

The full pedagogical implications of these contingencies need not be discussed but there is one that needs to be recognized. Given the purposive character of education, it seems reasonable to assume that teachers are trying to induce certain kinds of behaviour in children. However, the behaviour they are trying to induce need not be consistent with the behaviour they themselves engage in, for example: the teacher who uses sarcasm when inveighing against the use of sarcasm; the authoritarian teacher who gives lip service to democratic ideals; the teacher who publically ingratiates herself with other teachers but who punishes pupils for telling tales.

We are led by the alternative contingencies to recognize that whether a given behaviour can be induced in pupils depends on a number of conditions being met. They are:

(a) That there is compatibility between the teacher's intention and the way in which she presents the behaviour she is trying to induce in the pupils.
(b) If there is not compatibility between the teacher's own behaviour and the behaviour she is trying to induce in the pupils, then the pupils must be able to make appropriate discriminatory judgements.
(c) That there is compatibility between the behaviour the teacher is trying to induce in the pupils and the pupil's perception of that behaviour.

It should be noted that these conditions have nothing to say about whether or not the behaviour that the teacher is trying to induce is worth inducing. For example, the teacher may meet all three conditions with superlative thoroughness and finish up teaching his pupils that $2 \times 0 = 2$. This implies that if any educational act is ever to be judged successful, there are at least two dimensions that have to be recognized. The first is concerned with whether the teacher teaches what he sets out to teach. The second is concerned with the veridicality of what was taught. These two dimensions might be called, respectively, teacher reliability, and teacher validity. These two dimensions yield a latin square where one cell represents something valid taught reliably, another square represents something valid taught unreliably, another, something invalid taught reliably, and the last, something invalid taught unreliably. Figure 14.2 illustrates the issues.

FIGURE 14.2

Teacher Success

Teacher

	Reliability	Unreliability
Validity	1.1	1.2
Invalidity	2.1	2.2

Teacher

The four cells in Figure 14.2 yield one kind of teaching that can clearly be designated as 'good'—cell 1.1. The figure also yields two kinds of teaching that are clearly 'bad' (cells 1.2 and 2.1). Ironically, the last cell (cell 2.2) can yield teacher behaviour that can turn out to be quite 'good' by accident—when the teacher teaches something wrong badly.

In brief review of the discussion so far: two sets of conditions have been postulated. One is related to factors or forces that influence the way in which the inhabitants react to a given situation in the classroom. The other is related to the possible consequences of that reaction—the effect of imposing a pedagogical purpose on the interaction.

When these two sets of conditions are combined, the resulting model can serve a double purpose. It can be used to provide a framework to account for the single education incident. It can also be used as an aid in describing classrooms in general. This model is presented in Figure 14.3.

The figure reads from left to right. The teacher begins the transactional process with some idea of the behaviour she wishes to induce in the pupils. She then mediates her 'intention' through her own behaviour which has the effect of activating one, some, or all the forces that affect the pupil's predisposition to react. The pupil's behaviour reaction will tend to be in the direction of the strongest force. His behaviour once emitted can then be evaluated against: (a) the teacher's original intention, (b) the pupil's perception of the meaning of the teacher's inducing behaviour, and (c) an independent observer's interpretation of the meaning of that behaviour. Thereafter, it is possible to talk about each educational incident or transaction in terms of (i) the compatibility or incompatibility of the resulting pupil behaviour with any of the three criteria advanced, and (ii) the forces influencing the direction of the response. In a similar way it is also possible to talk about the extent to which a given classroom manifests compatibility or incompatibility with all pupils and over a number of

FIGURE 14.3

Educational Transactions

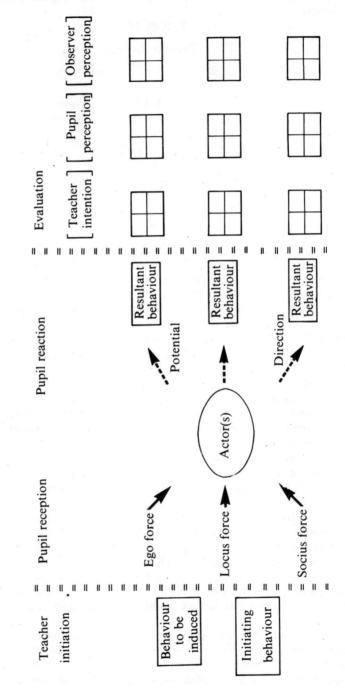

incidents. Success in this latter case, then, is averaged success. Each classroom could also be judged on the basis of its tendency to be influenced by any or all of the forces. Subsequently it would be possible to discuss the relationship between achieved compatibilities and the predomination of ego, locus or socius forces.

The model as it stands can be used to provide a broad basis for classifying most of the research that has been undertaken in classroom settings. Two comments need to be made about it, however. Although the model is appropriate for empirical studies only, it can accommodate the vast number of teacher-evaluation studies that have occurred merely by the addition of a further set of 'boxes' at the right-hand end. These boxes would carry the heading 'normative criterion' to refer to the external (ideal) standard that is invariably invoked when teacher competency measurement is attempted. Second, the various categories of the model represent broad general classes. For example, teacher intentions can themselves be classified in an intricate variety of ways. So can teacher behaviours. Again, the specification of the kinds of ego, locus and socius forces would result in considerable elaboration. Similarly, pupil behaviours can be viewed in various ways and classified in many more. No doubt future research will continue to be preoccupied with both enunciating relevant categories and establishing their salience. However, the model, gross though it may be, does provide a basis for mapping the field of classroom research. Accordingly the chapters that follow can be fitted into its roomy categories.

Summary

Initially this chapter discussed some of the reasons for the growing interest manifested in classroom field research. It then confronted some of the conceptual difficulties involved in attempting to explain the nature of the relationships existing among different kinds of classroom phenomena. The argument which was developed rested on two raw assumptions, viz., that the relationships exist because (a) that is the way people are, or (b) because that is the way educational settings are. In other words, individuals coerce the relationship or the environment does. Consequently, the relationship could be explained in terms of human behaviour theory or social interaction theory.

Obviously, this is a gross oversimplification of the issue, and one that does great injustice to the way that environments and individuals complement and supplement each other. It did, however, serve the purpose of drawing attention to two matters of some importance. First, any full understanding of the nature of behaviour in the classroom depends on the development of a theory that provides an accurate and systematic specification of (a) the various concepts involved, (b) the nature of the relationships to be found between them and (c) the rules that underly the ways in which the relationships are formed. Second, that any full and complete theory will have to take into account not only the properties and characteristics of individuals in the setting, not only in the fact that the properties and characteristics of individuals impinge on the setting and help determine the character of the setting itself, but also that the setting itself coerces, constrains and affects the individuals.

The benefits likely to result from taking this sort of eclectic view are of two kinds. First, once theory has been constructed, once empirical verification has been sought, it will become possible to talk about the *effects* of classroom conditions on the pupils. Second, it will also be possible to talk of differences between one classroom and another and, more importantly, to do so in terms of the effects different settings have on different pupils. It follows that if we accept 'the profit that accrues to students' as the ultimate criterion for judging any educational enterprise, then the route research must take is clear. Educational theory that defines, describes and relates will have to be generated. Such a theory, if it is to be comprehensive enough to provide explanations that are fuller and more satisfactory than those currently available, will have to recognize the individual in context as well as the interaction between context and individual. Thereafter, the theory will have to be subjected to empirical test and experimental manipulation until validity is accomplished.

Meeting such a need implies no small task, especially since no theories of teaching or instruction exist at the moment.* Theories of learning are seldom classroom derived, and conventional educational theory is essentially hortative and normative rather than empirical.

Whatever its eventual nature, however, a 'practical' theory of education will have to be many-faceted. Essentially, it will have to take into account the fact that the classroom is a multi-stimulus environment and that many of the stimuli to be found therein will have to be reckoned with.

*Bruner (1967) comes closest, but his book is appropriately entitled, *Towards a Theory of Instruction*.

References

Adams, R. S., 1965: The classroom setting: A behavioural analysis. Unpublished PhD dissertation, University of Otago, Dunedin.

Adams, R. S. and Biddle, B. J., 1969: *Realities of Teaching*. Holt, Rinehart and Winston, Inc., New York. (forthcoming)

American Educational Research Association (AERA), Committee on the Criteria of Teacher Effectiveness, 1952: Report of the *Review of Educational Research*, 22, 238-263.

American Educational Research Association (AERA), Committee on the Criteria of Teacher Effectiveness, 1953: Second Report of the *Journal of Educational Research*.

Anderson, H. H., 1939: The measurement of domination and of socially integrative behavior in teachers' contacts with children. *Child Development*, 10, 73-89.

Anderson, H. H. and Brewer, Helen M., 1945: Studies of teachers' classroom personalities. I: Dominative and socially integrative behavior of kindergarten teachers. *Applied Psychological Monographs*, 6.

Anderson, H. H. and Brewer, J. E., 1946: Studies of teachers' dominative and integrated contacts on children's classroom behavior. *Applied Psychological Monographs*, 8.

Association for Supervision of Curriculum Development (ASCD), 1966: *The Way Teaching Is*. A report of the Seminar on Teaching. Association for Supervision and Curriculum Development and the Center for the Study of Instruction of the National Education Association, Washington, D.C.

Barker, R. G. and Wright, H. F., 1951: *One Boy's Day*. Harper & Row, New York.

Barker, R. G. and Wright, H. F., 1954: *Midwest and its Children,* Row, Petersen and Co., New York.

Barker, R. G., and Wright, H. F., 1961: *Specimen Records of American and English Children*. Social Science Studies, University of Kansas, Lawrence.

Barr, A. S., 1940, 1943, 1946, 1949: The measurement of prediction of teaching efficiency. *Review of Educational Research*, 10 (1940), 182-184; 13 (1943), 218-223; 16 (1946), 203-208; 19 (1949), 185-190.

Barr, A. S., 1948: The measurement and prediction of teacher efficiency: A summary of investigations. *Journal of Experimental Education*, 16, 203-283.

Bellack, A. A., *et al.*, 1966: *The Language of the Classroom*. Teachers College Press, Columbia University, New York.

Biddle, B. J., 1967: Methods and concepts in classroom research. *Review of Educational Research*, 37, 337-357.

Biddle, B. J. and Adams, R. S., 1967: Teacher behavior in the classroom context. In L. Siegel (Ed.), *Instruction: Some Contemporary Viewpoints*. Chandler Publishing Company, San Francisco.

Biddle, B. J. and Ellena, W. J., 1964: *Contemporary Research on Teacher Effectiveness*. Holt, Rinehart and Winston, Inc., New York.

Boyd, Robert D. and Vere de Vault, M., 1966: The observation and recording of behavior. *Review of Educational Research*, 36, 529-551.

Bruner, J. S., 1967: *Toward a Theory of Instruction*. The Belknap Press of Harvard University, Cambridge, Mass.

Cattell, R. B., 1948: Concepts and methods in the measurement of group syntality. *Psychological Review*, 55, 48-63.

Coleman, J. S., 1961: *The Adolescent Society*. The Free Press, New York.

Cornell, G. F., Lindvall, C. N. and Saupe, J. L., 1953: *An Exploratory Measurement of Individualities of Schools and Classrooms*. College of Education, Illinois Bureau of Educational Research, University of Illinois, Urbana, Ill.

Domas, S. J. and Tiedeman, D., 1950: Teacher competence: An annotated bibliography. *Journal of Experimental Education*, 19, 101-218.

Festinger, L., *et al.*, 1950: *Social Pressure in Informal Groups*. Harper Bros, New York.

Fisher, Virginia, 1967: Role conception of head start teachers. Unpublished dissertation, University of Missouri.

Flanders, N. A., 1960: *Teacher Influence, Pupil Attitudes and Achievements: Studies in Interaction Analysis*. Final Report, Cooperative Research Project No. 397, University of Minnesota, Minn.

Flanders, N. A., 1961: Interaction analysis: A technique for quantifying teacher influence. Paper presented to the American Educational Research Association, February 23, 1961. A department of the National Education Association, Washington, D.C.

Gage, N. L., 1960: Address appearing in Proceedings, *Research Resume*. California Teachers Association, Burlingame, Calif.

Gage, N. L. (Ed.), 1963: *Handbook of Research on Teaching*. Rand McNally and Co., Chicago, Ill.

Garfunkel, F., 1968: Unpublished study. Boston University.

Gordon, C. W., 1957: *The Social System of the High School*. The Free Press, Glencoe, Ill.

Gordon, Ira J., 1966: *Studying the Child in School*. John Wiley & Sons, Inc., New York.

Gump, P. V., 1967: *The Classroom Behavior Setting: Its Nature and Relation to Student Behavior*. Final Report, Project No. 2453, Bureau No. 5-0334, Contract No. OE-4-10-107. United States Department of Health, Education and Welfare, Washington, D.C.

Harrington, G. M., 1955: Smiling as a measure of teacher effectiveness. *Journal of Educational Research*, 48, 715-717.

Hughes, Marie M., *et al.*, 1959: *Development of the Means for the Assessment of the Quality of Teaching in Elementary Schools*. United States Office of Education Report, Washington, D.C.

Jackson, P. W., 1965: Teacher-pupil communication in the elementary classroom: An observational study. Paper presented at the American Educational Research Association, University of Chicago, Ill.

Jackson, P. W., 1968: *Life in Classrooms*. Doubleday & Co., New York.

Jensen, Gale and Parsons, T., 1959: The structure and dynamics of classroom groups and educational systems. *Review of Educational Research*, 29, 344-352.

Klausmeier, H. J., 1961: *Learning and Human Abilities: Educational Psychology*. Harper & Row, New York.

Kounin, J. W., 1966: Managing emotionally-disturbed children in regular classrooms. *Journal of Educational Psychology*, 57, 1-13.

Kounin, J. W., 1968: Unpublished study. Wayne State University.

Loflin, M. D., 1968: Unpublished study, University of Missouri.

Medley, D. M. and Mitzel, H. E., 1958: A technique for measuring classroom behavior. *Journal of Educational Psychology*, 49, 86-92.

Medley, D. M. and Mitzel, H. E., 1963: Measuring classroom behavior by systematic observation. In N. L. Gage (Ed.), *Handbook of Research on Teaching*. Rand McNally and Co., Chicago, Ill.

Mitzel, H. E., 1960: Teacher effectiveness. In C. W. Harris (Ed.), *Encyclopedia of Educational Research* (3rd edn). Macmillan & Co., New York.

Moore, G. A., 1967: *Realities of the Urban Classroom*. Doubleday & Co., New York.

Nuthall, G. A. and Lawrence, P. J., 1965: *Thinking in the Classroom*. New Zealand Council for Educational Research, Wellington.

Oliver, D. W. and Shaver, J. P., 1963: *The Development of a Multi-Dimensional Observational System for the Analysis of Pupil-Teacher Interaction*. AERA (Based on a section of a larger report by the United States Office of Education, *The Analysis of Public Controversy: A Study in Citizenship Education*).

Perkins, H. V., 1964: A procedure for assessing the classroom behavior of students and teachers. *American Educational Research Journal*, 1, 249-262.

Ryans, D. G., 1960: *Characteristics of Teachers: A Research Study*. American Council of Education, Washington, D.C.

Ryans, D. G., 1963: *An Information-System Approach to Theory of Instruction With Special Reference to the Teacher*. System Development Corporation, Santa Monica.

Sells, S. B., 1963: *Approaches to the Taxonomy of Social Situations*. Technical Report No. 4, ONR.

Smith, B. O., et al., 1964: *A Tentative Report on the Strategies of Teaching*. Cooperative Research Project No. 1640, Bureau of Educational Research, University of Illinois, Urbana, Ill.

Smith, B. O., et al., 1967: *A Study of the Strategies of Teaching*. Bureau of Educational Research, College of Education, Urbana, Ill.

Smith, B. O., and Meux, M. O., 1963: *A Study of Logic in Teaching*. University of Illinois, Urbana, Ill.

Smith, L. M., 1959: *Group Procedures in Elementary and Secondary Schools*. AERA, Washington, D.C.

Smith, L. M., and Geoffrey, W., 1968: *The Complexities of an Urban Classroom*. Holt, Rinehart and Winston, Inc., New York.

Soar, R. S., 1962: *Multivariate Statistical Procedures in Predicting Teacher-Pupil Classroom Behavior*. Cooperative Research Project No. 1170, University of South Carolina, Columbia, Sth Carolina.

Solomon, D. and Miller, H. L., 1961: *Explorations in Teaching Styles: Report of Preliminary Investigations and Development of Categories*. Center for the Study of Liberal Education for Adults.

Sorokin, P. A., 1947: *Society, Culture and Personality: Their Structure and Dynamics*, Harper & Bros, New York.

TEPS (National Commission on Teacher Education and Professional Standards), 1966. *The Real World of the Beginning Teacher*. A report of the Nineteenth National TEPS Conference.

Taba, Hilda, Levine, S. and Elzey, F. F., 1964: *Thinking in Elementary School Children*. Office of Education, Cooperative Research Project No. 1574, United States Department of Health, Education and Welfare, San Francisco State College, San Francisco.

Thelen, H. A., 1950: *Human Dynamics*. Chicago University Press, Chicago, Ill.

Urban, J., 1943: *Behavioral Changes Resulting from a Study of Communicable Diseases*. Bureau of Publications, Teachers College, Columbia University, New York.

Waller, W., 1932: *The Sociology of Teaching*. John Wiley & Sons, Inc., New York.

Withall, J., 1949: The development of a technique for the measurement of social-emotional climate in classrooms. *Journal of Experimental Education*, 17, 347-361.

Withall, J., 1956: An objective measurement of a teacher's classroom interactions. *Journal of Educational Psychology*, 47, 203-212.

Wright, F., Muriel, J. and Proctor, Virginia H., 1961: *Systematic Observation of Verbal Interaction as a Method of Comparing Mathematics Lessons*. USOE Cooperative Research Project No. 816, Washington University, St. Louis, Mo.

15

Interaction in Classrooms

Raymond S. Adams

THERE is more to a chair than meets the eye. By its very presence, a chair is both suggestive and seductive. It invites us to sit in it, and we often do. Moreover, because of its shape and location, it dictates to us how we shall sit, where we shall sit, and, to some extent, with whom we can interact. Just as a chair exerts its influence over behaviour, so do other aspects of the physical environment. In general, we are only marginally conscious of such constraints. Yet the pattern is repeated all about us— in the buildings we work in, the trafficways we use, the sports fields we play on and the gardens in which we potter about. All of them in their own undemonstratively insistent ways coerce, control, and condition our behaviour.

There is no reason to believe that classrooms provide an exception to this general rule, but the nature and effects of their environmental influences have seldom been investigated. Some slight attention has been given to such things as sound proofing, lighting and ease of exit in the event of fire, but classroom design and classroom construction are seldom evaluated against any *educational* criterion. The principal determinants of the size, shape and material form of classrooms appear to be economic ones.

The varied paraphernalia to be found within classrooms have been similarly neglected. For example, the colour, shape and size of exercise books, pads and paper used in the classroom usually represent a nice compromise between manufacturers' enterprise and administrators' intuition. Textbooks also (with some notable exceptions) are seldom pretested or evaluated. It seems as if only mechanical devices (teaching machines, movies and TV, etc.) qualify for this kind of evaluative scrutiny.

The central concern of this paper is with the relationship between such physical characteristics of the classroom and teacher and student roles. The issue is not merely an academic one. Take, for example, a phenomenon only too characteristic of the mid-twentieth century—noise. Teachers are certainly well aware of the disturbing effects that the building project next door has on their own frames of mind. Again, in wooden-floored classrooms, the noise of a scraping chair or dropped ruler often leads the teacher to enact preventative and sometimes punitive roles. One can only conjecture about the effects on the learning process that might follow from the use of carpeted classrooms where this kind of problem is minimized.* Again, it is often assumed that students participate in lessons equally, so that differences in achievement that emerge after, say, the use of a new teaching method, are attributable solely to individual differences among the students. But are they? Do environmental factors permit the teacher's behaviour to be mediated to different children equally? Does every child in the classroom setting have equality of educational opportunity? We are repeatedly deluded by our own 'good' intentions and our idealistic hopes. We intend all children to participate equally, but do they?

It was in order to put such questions to the test that a research programme which involved the video-taping of classroom behaviour was inaugurated in 1962.

The study that is reported here is a segment of that larger investigation. It was concerned with the location of various actors in the setting, and with the effect that this location has upon communication.

The task, as it was first conceived, demanded the development of a theoretical model that would be appropriate for the observational study of classroom behaviour within a sociological frame of reference. The behaviour of individual teachers or of individual pupils was not an initial concern—the behaviour of the classroom collectivity was. Subsequently, a theoretical model based on a conceptualization of the classroom as a communication system which possessed certain structural and functional characteristics was devised. (The conceptual model used is reported in Adams (1965).) Within this classroom communication system, the existence of a number of greater or lesser communication sub-systems was envisaged. Each of these was identified by the presence or absence of three kinds of communication agents: *emitters*, who send the communication, *targets*, to whom the communication is directed, and *audience*, which comprises those others who 'observe' the process. These three terms need to be defined more precisely, but their definition is contingent on a further concept, the episode. The episode was used to provide a basis for a systematic analysis of classroom behaviour. Unlike Flanders (1960) who delimits an episode chronologically as a three second period, and Barker and Wright (1954) who see it as a logical sequence of goal-orientated behaviour, the episode here was defined as a period of classroom time wherein no functional or structural change occurred. Episodes can be of any length of time but their defining characteristic is that for the entire duration of each episode, a static state exists.

*The author had occasion to make a video-tape recording of an eleventh grade carpeted classroom. Not only were the working conditions pleasant, but the quality of interaction was delightfully civilized and the intellectual quality of the discussion extremely high.

Emitter, target and audience can now be defined formally.

(a) *An emitter is the transmitter of communication signals at the onset of a given episode.* Emitters may be single emitters (a teacher or a pupil), multiple emitters (a choir), or non-human emitters (a movie projector).

(b) *A target is the subject to whom a communication is directed.* Targets also may be single targets, multiple targets or even (rarely) non-human targets.

(c) *An audience is any inhabitant of the setting, or any group of inhabitants, whose manifested behaviour may be observationally interpreted as 'attendant' on a given emitter.*

In arriving at the *functional* characteristics of the classroom system, the communications of the actors were subjected to analysis on two dimensions: (i) the content, or subject matter of the communication, and (ii) the mode, or educational character of the communication. The *structural* properties of the classroom were defined by the relationships existing between the actors and the functional properties of the communication, and, as well, among the various actors themselves. An elaboration of this interpretation is to be found in Adams (1966) and Biddle and Adams (1966).

The operationalization of the rather complex, multivariate model devised, was made possible through the use of a method of data collection unique to classroom research—video-tape recording. Two remotely controlled cameras were placed inconspicuously in classrooms. One, with a wide-angle lens, covered most of the classroom, and the other, with a zoom lens, focused on, and followed, the teacher. Four microphones were suspended from the ceiling at strategic places round the room and the teacher also wore a cordless microphone. Two audio channels enabled the teacher's communications and the students' communications to be recorded separately. The monitored visual image from the cameras, together with the audio records, were all preserved on magnetic tape.

The advantages of the method of data collection were principally threefold. First, an extremely comprehensive record of classroom behaviour could be preserved for subsequent and repeated examination. Second, the fidelity of the system was extremely good; the television cameras found no difficulty in dealing with the conventional classroom setting, the teacher's microphone missed virtually nothing that the teacher said, and the classroom microphones also recorded the greater proportion of all public utterances. Third, the playback control mechanism on the tape recorder permitted extremely fast stopping and rewinding. As a consequence, during data coding, sequences of behaviour could be viewed and re-viewed at will. Many viewings of each tape were required in order to identify behaviour, measure it in terms of elapsed time, and record it onto category sheets from which IBM cards could be punched. The coding procedure used (which required approximately twenty hours of coding for every one hour of recorded time) converted the visual data into quantified terms of two kinds: (a) *incident* counts which registered each occasion on which every variable occurred,* and (b) *duration* counts which recorded the length of duration of each incident. Subsequently, computer analysis provided data on number of incidents and total time spent for each variable. It also permitted the calculation of significances of differences when the data were grouped on the basis of four selected independent variables: (a) grade level of class, (b) subject taught, (c) age of teacher, and (d) sex of teacher.

Such, in brief compass, are some of the more general features of the larger study. This current report, however, is concerned with only one aspect of the structural analysis—location.

All emitters, targets and audiences as active agents in the classroom communication process occupy identifiable geographical locations. Two questions immediately come to mind. First: in what way are different classroom locations occupied by the different inhabitants of the setting? Second: what relationships between the occupancy of given locations and other classroom behaviour variables may be hypothesized? Answering either question is conditional on the development of a system for identifying agent location. Location within actual classrooms was conceptualized in such a way that a grid design permitting a uniform apportioning of floorspace from setting to setting could be used. The grid subdivides the classroom into numbered segments which can be then used to indicate the location of any or all of the agents. The grid is reproduced in Figure 15.1 below.

FIGURE 15.1

Location Grid

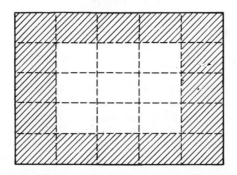

The grid quite arbitrarily cuts the classroom into twenty-five equal-sized segments so that a relatively detailed description of the use of classroom space results. The number of classifications, which facilitate systematic and consistent coding procedures, was based on a vertical and horizontal

*An incident is the basic unit of measurement for all structural and functional categories (variables). It could never be shorter than an episode but could be (and often was) longer.

division of classroom floorspace. The first digit in each number indicates vertical location, the second the horizontal location. The complete code appears below:

Vertical Dimension	Horizontal Dimension
1 = Diffuse (General)	1 = Diffuse (General)
2 = Front	2 = Left
3 = Forward	3 = Left centre
4 = Middle	4 = Centre
5 = Rearward	5 = Right centre
6 = Rear	6 = Right

All emitters, targets and audiences were coded on both dimensions and were given a location number on the coding sheet. Thus, a 66 entry in the target column located the target at the rear right of the classroom. The number 1 was used to denote the special case when interaction was not confined to single locations. Thus, 21 indicates that the communication/ interaction occurred across the front of the classroom, while 11 indicates general diffuseness throughout the whole setting.

Because classrooms are not necessarily of the same size and shape as one another, a set of rules was devised to deal with classrooms of different dimensions. A convention was observed which required, in general terms, the following procedure. The outer boundaries of the setting (front, sides and back, the shaded area in Figure 15.1) were set first, and the middle area was then expanded or shrunk depending on the total number of desks and rows in the room.

The data reported in the study were derived from sixteen pairs of lessons in sixteen classrooms. The sample was selected so that half the lessons were social studies lessons and half were arithmetic or mathematics lessons. Half of the teachers were women and half were men. Half of the teachers were over forty years of age and half were under thirty. Half the lessons came from primary classes and half came from secondary classes. Three grade levels were used—grades 1, 6 and 11. In order to obtain a measure of regularity throughout the whole sample, the following ancillary conditions also had to be met: (a) any participating teacher must have had more than two years' teaching experience; (b) only regular class groups were to be used—team teaching situations were excluded; (c) no 'special' classes were acceptable; (d) teacher trainees should not be participating in the teaching programme; (e) the students should not be representative of a single minority social group; and (f) the students should not come from a single social-class background. These conditions ensured that teachers who participated would be teaching uninterrupted class groups with which they were thoroughly familiar and that student groups did not display features that distinguished them markedly from other groups.

Most of the hypotheses initially formulated were concerned with antici- pated relationships between the independent variables (grade level, sex of teacher, age of teacher, and subject matter) and the locations of emitters, targets and audience. However, because there seemed no a priori reason why any particular location should be regarded as significant in its own right, attention was directed towards the extent to which the three actor roles would be differentially located or not differentially located.

The first hint of an unexpected result came when the general distribution of emitter scores was subjected to examination. It was immediately apparent that certain specific locations attracted a disproportionate number of communications. In Figure 15.2, below, is shown the distribution of proportions of emitter incidents for each of the twenty-five locations over the whole sample. Diffuse locations are recorded in the separate box at the base of the grid. Figure 15.3 deals similarly with the distribution of proportions of emitter time over the various locations.

FIGURE 15.2

Emitter Location
% Incidents

	2	3	4	5	6
6	–	–	–	–	–
5	–	2	6	2	–
4	1	4	9	3	1
3	1	4	12	2	3
2	–	2	34	5	–

Front

Diffuse $\boxed{8}$

FIGURE 15.3

Emitter Location
% Duration

	2	3	4	5	6
6	–	–	–	–	–
5	1	2	5	2	–
4	–	3	6	2	1
3	1	2	9	2	2
2	–	1	55	3	–

Front

Diffuse $\boxed{3}$

The overall pattern shown in Figures 15.2 and 15.3 is quite distinct in both cases. Clearly, location 24 (front centre) is the dominant one and the line of central locations 34, 44 and 54 feature prominently. Equally clear is the fact that insufficient emissions emanated from the locations at the back of the room for any one of them to register one per cent of the total. It is also apparent that side-of-the-room locations do not feature to any extent either.

The principal points of difference between the durational data of Figure 15.3 and the incident data of Figure 15.2 are that duration scores for location 24 are substantially larger than incident scores and that the diffuse category occupies a place of lesser importance in Figure 15.3.* Not unexpectedly, diffuse emissions, though quite numerous in quantity, tend to be relatively short lived. In the current sample only three per cent

*Discrepancies between incident data and duration data were not uncommon throughout the whole study. This suggests that behavioural observation that relies on check listing the incidence of a particular kind of behaviour (e.g., Withall, 1949, Social-Emotional Climate Index, and Medley and Mitzel, 1958, OSCAR) does not necessarily permit the interpretation of the behaviour in terms of salience for participants.

of the total time was taken up with diffuse emissions. There is little overall dissimilarity between Figures 15.2 and 15.3 on the relative importance of locations other than 24.

Interestingly enough, the target location data replicates the pattern set by the emitter location data. Figures 15.4 and 15.5 contain the relevant information.

FIGURE 15.4

Target Location
% Incidents

	2	3	4	5	6
6	–	–	–	–	–
5	–	2	5	1	–
4	1	3	9	4	1
3	2	3	11	4	1
2	–	3	43	2	–

Front

Diffuse 2

FIGURE 15.5

Target Location
% Duration

	2	3	4	5	6
6	–	–	–	–	–
5	1	3	4	1	–
4	1	4	8	3	1
3	1	3	11	3	1
2	–	1	50	2	1

Front

Diffuse 1

The centre line locations which dominated in the preceding two figures also dominate in Figures 15.4 and 15.5. As in the earlier figures, again the difference between incident data and duration data was one of degree, not kind. The most noteworthy fact is that throughout all four figures the pattern of distribution of the scores is remarkably similar.

Sufficient evidence has been presented to corroborate the assertion that, at least for this sample, communication among members of the classroom setting is customarily confined to those who occupy certain specified centre-of-the-room locations. However, the data so far have only been concerned with emitter and target locations and have neglected audience location.

In comparison with the other results, the audience location data are distressingly uniform. The reasons for this are that the data for audience location merely confirm the obvious. Given the usual case of a teacher emitter to a majority audience, the audience location must (except in quite unusual circumstances) be diffuse-diffuse (11). Again, given both the coding system's bias towards identifying the teacher's role and the teacher's tendency to occupy the front of the room, the use of location 24 also seems obvious. These two locations 11 and 24, account for ninety-eight per cent of all instances of audience location occupation and for ninety-nine per cent of the total time. The inference that can be made from these data is that independent group work and small group discussions were extremely rare in the classrooms of the sample.

The uniformity of the audience result makes it unnecessary to pay more detailed attention to audience information in this study. However, the three role concepts, emitter, target and audience, do make it possible to conceptualize the classroom communication system as having two different kinds of communicatory interaction. Emitters and targets can be regarded as being involved directly in the communication system while audience members are indirectly involved. The extent to which given locations play a part in the direct communication system can be deduced by considering the emitter and target location data together. As a result of doing so it is possible to enunciate a location-communication principle, viz.

The greater the distance a location is from the centre line of the room, and the greater the distance it is from the centre front of the room, the less the likelihood that inhabitants of the location will be involved in the direct communication-interaction system.

The mechanistic nature of the system used for plotting locations precludes an interpretation of the data in 'task' terms. For instance, although locations 23, 24 and 25 represent the 'front-centre' part of the room, it does not necessarily follow that the teacher's table, or, for that matter, a blackboard was located there. Similarly, it does not follow that a teacher who characteristically occupied a non-front location therefore had his (her) table placed at the location occupied most. However, certain general points can be made. The teachers were more often in front of the class than elsewhere (thirty-nine per cent of incidents). Nonetheless, they were in other locations frequently (thirty-seven per cent of incidents) and did engage in walking about the room to some extent (twenty-four per cent of incidents).

The duration figures heighten the impression that the teacher's spiritual home was at the front of the room. Locations 22, 23, 24, 25 and 26 were occupied for sixty-eight per cent of the total time while the proportion of the time spent walking about the room accounted for fifteen per cent of the total time.

It would seem as if there is another location occupation principle operating in the classroom. It might be expressed thus:

The further a location is from the middle front of the room, the less likely it is to be visited by the teacher.

The extent to which one can generalize from these findings depends essentially on three factors: (a) the extent to which the sample was a representative one; (b) the extent to which the test situation was a replica of the 'real' situation; and (c) the accuracy with which the behaviour was recorded.

Representativeness of Sample: The education districts within which the participating schools fell would be rated among the better ones in the State of Missouri. Each district was relatively well-endowed, enjoyed effective public support, paid good salaries and seemed to be characterized by a progressive, positive approach towards education. The schools selected were ones that would be attractive to teachers. Child deviancy was minimal, conditions of employment were good, and plant and equipment were more than adequate. In general, the educational environment appeared congenial, if not luxurious. An attempt was made to discourage the authorities from putting their best teachers 'on show'. However, even if they resisted the temptation to do so, the very nature of the enterprise itself would probably commend itself more to teachers who were confident in their own ability than to those who were not.

All this suggests that when characteristics of teachers and classroom settings are taken into account, the sample was above average in certain respects that relate to quality of personnel, administration, plant and equipment. In terms of the actual way the classes and lessons were organized and the work was carried out, however, there is no way of telling whether the sample was unduly atypical. Unsystematic observation of other schools and other systems would suggest that it was not.

The Reality of the Test Situation: Whether or not the introduction of TV cameras into the room affected normal classroom procedures will probably never be known adequately. 'The problem of comparing observed and unobserved behaviour is akin to that of the small boy who turned out the bedroom light and could never quite make it to his bed before the room got dark.' (Medley & Mitzel, 1963.) Conclusions about the intrusion of the equipment can consequently only be made indirectly from observation and from reports. The equipment did not *appear* to be unduly distracting. Because the cameras were remotely controlled there was no operator in the room during the actual lesson. The cameras drew little attention to themselves. They operated without noise and the black shroud covering the camera and the black interior of the glass fronted boxes which contained them made it very difficult for camera movement to be discerned. The classes, too, were 'acculturated' to the impending observation. Dummy boxes, initially placed in the classrooms prior to the study, excited a certain amount of interest among the students. They peered into the boxes and asked questions about them, of both the teacher and research workers. The children's questions were answered truthfully. The explanation was given that the cameras were part of a university research project and that their class would be televised sometime during the next two days. They were also told that they might ask further questions if they wished. As a final injunction they were encouraged to 'forget' that the cameras were there. During the televising of the lessons proper, very little interest was shown in the cameras. Occasionally children looked at the boxes speculatively but no action was ever directed towards the cameras by groups, and even individual action was extremely rare. Once or twice, prior to leaving the room or upon entry, some children re-examined the boxes and occasionally 'performed'. Once class work got underway however, the cameras were disregarded almost completely.

Whether the cameras influenced teacher behaviour or not is also an issue that is unlikely to be resolved. As part of the research programme however, each teacher was given an 'open-ended' interview. Among the questions asked were: (1) Did your class behave as it normally does?

(2) Were you conscious of the cameras while you were teaching? In all cases the answers to question (1) were an unequivocal 'yes'. The answer to question (2) was not quite so definite. All teachers claimed that they were not unduly influenced by the cameras and stated that once the lesson was underway they became virtually unaware of them. However, two teachers admitted to one occasion each when they modified their behaviour because of the cameras. One decided against putting his feet on the table, the other resisted an initial temptation to castigate a pupil who interrupted the class. Another teacher also considered that he was 'subliminally' conscious of the cameras. He thought that they seldom obtruded but that they exercised a mild restraint on his conduct throughout. However, when it is remembered that literally thousands of teacher acts were recorded by the cameras these few instances constitute an infinitesimal proportion of the total behaviour sampled.

It is always distressing to concede uncertainty. And yet this particular study has given rise to a number of questions for which reasonable answers do not seem readily available. Why, for instance, are the centre line locations so consistently prominent in the classroom communication exchange? Is it because the more vocal students migrate to, or are put in, these locations? Do teachers (presumably operating from the front of the room) have a peculiar myopia that prevents their giving other than marginal attention to the fringe dwellers in their classrooms? Does the physical plant somehow coerce behaviour—do non-swivel chairs and fixed lecterns somehow determine a teacher's forward looking stance? Is distance a factor? In a classroom where quietness is valued, does a far off student fear to raise his voice? Does a soft-voiced teacher, conserving strength and energy, eschew the strain of shouting? Why do teachers apparently feel 'at home' at the front of the classroom? Are they seeking attention or do they dread insurrection?

Such questions could be proliferated further, but without more data presently available there is little advantage in doing so. Attempting to find equally hypothetical answers would, as well, be but another exercise in plausibility. However, some merit might be found in thinking briefly of potential theoretical frameworks within which answers might be sought. For instance, does the customary location of the teacher at the front of the room, and does the customary placement of desks facing him, indicate that people have an inclination to attend best to what is in their direct line of vision?

Again, have (unrecognized) norms of classroom procedure developed to coerce teacher and pupil communication patterns subtly into this particular mould? Do we have a classic example of the domination of what Getzels has called, the nomothetic dimension?

At a more mechanistic level, can physiological factors be invoked to explain the state of affairs? For example, the use of peripheral vision is a skill that has to be developed, as any basketball player or jungle soldier knows.

Finally, it is possible that, consistent with the earlier discussion of the coercive effects of physical properties of the environment, more satisfactory solutions than any of these may be found within the boundaries of human ecological study.

Whatever the ultimate solution to the issue there remains the important question: what are the educational implications of the findings of the study?

The initial temptation is to question the 'justice' of the unequal distribution of communication participation in the classroom and to suggest procedures that might prevent the development of such a state of affairs. To this end, regular relocating of all pupils might be employed, teachers might be advised to deliberately take up new stations in the classroom or to make a point of encouraging fringe members to communicate.

However, there are two matters of greater significance implied by the data. First, does participation in the direct communication system of the classroom help or hinder learning—if so, under what conditions? There are arguments that suggest that children profit from receiving the teacher's direct attention. But if the teacher is a 'poor' teacher or if the attention is essentially negative, does profit then accrue? Second, if many students spend much of their time as peripheral members of the group, learning, as it were, vicariously through the experiences of others, what sort of vicarious experiences are likely to be best for them? If the naughty, restless, short-sighted or hard-of-hearing youngster is specially placed within the classroom's 'zone of influence' does he, ipso facto, provide the ideal model for the marginal members.

Problems like these lead to the prospect of redesigning classrooms. For instance, if greater participation is thought desirable, perhaps a circular classroom would achieve it. Alternatively, if selective communication is thought to be inevitable, perhaps classrooms deliberately designed to provide defined stage and audience areas might prove to be educationally more appropriate.

Irrespective of the kind of plausible argument that might be used to support these or other suggestions, one point is abundantly clear—we are remarkably ignorant about the nature of the classroom's socio-educational environment. Clearly, a great deal of research is necessary in order to establish a sound basis for decisions that would lead to the restructuring of classroom settings. Such research would need to be concerned not only with the structural features of the classroom but, more importantly, with functional characteristics and, more importantly again, with the inter-relations between the two. Ultimately, it may be possible to arrive at an educationally defensible rationalization not only of teachers' behaviour in the classroom but of the other physical properties of the situation as well.

References

Adams, R. S., 1965: The classroom setting and behavioural analysis. Unpublished PhD thesis, University of Otago, Dunedin.

Adams, R. S., 1966: The classroom as a communication setting. In B. J. Biddle and R. S. Adams, *et al.*, *Essays on the Social Systems of Education*. University of Missouri, Columbia, Mo.

Barker, R. G. and Wright, H. F., 1954: *Midwest and its Children*. Row, Peterson and Co., New York.

Biddle, B. J. and Adams, R. S., 1966: Teacher behaviour in the classroom context. In L. Siegel (Ed.), *Contemporary Theories of Instruction*. Chandler Publishing Company, San Francisco.

Flanders, N. A., 1960: *Interaction Analysis in the Classroom*. University of Minnesota Press, Minn.

Medley, D. M. and Mitzel, H. E., 1958: A technique for measuring classroom behavior. *Journal of Educational Psychology*, 49, 86-92.

Medley, D. M. and Mitzel, H. E., 1963: Measuring classroom behavior by systematic observation. In N. L. Gage (Ed.), *Handbook of Research on Teaching*. Rand McNally and Co., Chicago, Ill.

Withall, J., 1949: The development of a technique for the measurement of climate in classrooms. *Journal of Experimental Education*, 17, 347-361.

16

A Study of Kindergarten Interactions

Anne Silcock

THIS STUDY, which is focused on the interactions of children and their environments, attempts to provide answers to a number of questions. To what extent is the behaviour of the young child determined by his environment? How often is his ongoing behaviour interrupted by adults and by other children making demands upon him in relation to goals they set for him? How does the child view these demands of others? Does he change the direction of his behaviour in order to move towards these environmentally-determined goals? Is he coerced into compliance? How free is the child to choose his own goals? How successful is he in inducing the social agents to assist him? Does conflict result from the attempts of other people to direct the child's behaviour, or from the child's efforts to elicit their support in relation to his own goals? Does more conflict arise from interactions with adults or with children? What are the specific sources of conflict between the child and his environment? These are the kinds of questions for which answers were sought.

The investigation was carried out within the theoretical framework of psychological ecology as developed by Barker (1957, 1960, 1963a, 1963b, 1964, 1965), from concepts formulated by Lewin. One of Barker's co-workers, Willems (1965), suggests that the eco-behavioural approach is characterized by the following interests.

1. Discovery of the distribution of the phenomena of psychology in nature.
2. Emphasis upon the discovery of naturally-occurring phenomena as opposed to the observation of arranged and contrived phenomena.
3. Continuity—the continuous, interdependent flow of the stream of behaviour and the stream of environmental events.
4. Description and taxonomy of the environment with which organisms can and do interact, in which they behave, and to which they adapt.
5. Formulation of a conceptual representation of the environmental complex.
6. Developing ways to conceptualize the relations among phenomena which obey different laws.

The ecological psychologist is concerned primarily with behaviour in its environmental context, the behaving individual and the milieu forming one interdependent unit. Gump and Kounin (1960) define the milieu stream as 'the flow of environmental conditions within which the individual behaves —his social associates and their behavior, his activity props and arenas— and the changes of these over time. The milieu stream may be visualized as supporting, provoking, or restricting the behavior stream.' Behaviour and the environment are mutually causally-related systems.

Behaviour is viewed as an ongoing stream which is characterized by temporal continuity. It has sequential as well as simultaneous complexity. Within this stream naturally-occurring units of molar behaviour exist, occurring singly, concurrently and in overlapping formations. The boundaries of these inherent, self-generated behaviour units can be perceived in the easily observed breaks that occur in the flow of the behaviour stream. The units can be identified and classified according to their structural-dynamic characteristics or by their material-content properties.

The study of behaviour from an ecological viewpoint necessitates specialized methods of investigation that are consonant with the eco-behavioural approach. In order to examine behavioural phenomena, the ecological psychologist acts as a receiver and discoverer of events as they exist in nature, uncontrived and uncontaminated by the purposes and the methods of the investigator. Barker (1965) refers to the ecological research worker as a transducer, and to the methods of investigation that he employs, as T methods. Ecological methods have input only: there is one way communication between them and the phenomena to which they are applied. The techniques used are gentle, non-interfering, and non-destructive of the ordering and patterning that exist under natural conditions. Barker and his colleagues have developed two highly-specialized research methods which meet the requirements of T type data-generating systems. One of these is based on the identification of behaviour settings, a procedure which permits the investigation of the ecological environment inhabited by the individual. The other utilizes specimen description, a technique which enables the research worker to examine the behavioural phenomena that are present in the ongoing stream of behaviour.

Behaviour settings are patterned and ordered events that exist in the eco-logical environment, independently of the particular individuals who inhabit the milieu. They have time and space loci, they have objects and inhabitants and standard patterns of performance that are synomorphic with or appropriate to the setting. These latter relate to characteristic and predictable patterns of behaviour of people en masse. Behaviour settings have a system of controls that ensure the participation of the optimal number of persons, and the performance of the standard patterns of behaviour that are apposite to the setting. These controls are sometimes highly coercive. Within each setting there is an hierarchy of positions relative to the responsibility for ensuring that the settings function effectively—the positions of greatest responsibility being accompanied by greatest power and authority. Within the classroom the position of teacher has more influence and responsibility over the behaviour patterns of the settings than has the position of pupil.

The behaviour-setting technique has been used in a variety of research projects. For example, it has been applied to descriptive studies of Americans in their milieus, such as that of Barker and Wright (1954) at Midwest, and to comparative studies of American and English people and the settings they inhabit. By surveying the array of behaviour settings available in these two milieus, Barker and Barker (1961) were able to compare the characteristic behaviour patterns of American and English children and adults. The technique has been used, also, to study the effects of different properties of the ecological environment, such as the size of schools, on the behaviour of the inhabitants. A number of investigations in this area have been reported (Barker & Gump, 1964).

Wright (1956) used the behaviour-setting technique in his study of preschool children and community behaviour settings in Midwest, and in his city-town project (1961), in which he examined the after-school visits of children to activity settings in the community. Shure (1963) investigated various characteristics of the behaviour of children in five different behaviour settings within the kindergarten environment. Gump and Kounin (1960) studied the behaviour of boys in three camp behaviour settings: swimming, cook-out and dining hall. Gump and Sutton-Smith (1955) examined social interactions in four camp activity settings: cook-outs, boating, swims and crafts.

The second method, that of specimen description, allows the investigation of the individual's stream of behaviour. The technique of compiling a specimen record involves the continuous observation and narrative recording of behaviour as it occurs under natural conditions. A prolonged segment of the ongoing behaviour of the child is observed and recorded, together with the situation in which the behaviour occurs, in atheoretical, descriptive prose. This results in a deliberately unselective specimen record of behaviour. Wright (1960) points out that time sampling and similar methods of recording behaviour do not respect naturally-occurring units within the behaviour continuum, and he and Barker (1954) recommend observation of prolonged sequences of behaviour such as a complete day in the life of a child (Barker & Wright, 1951). To examine behavioural phenomena within the behaviour stream the ecological psychologist allows the data to dictate the unit of measurement, instead of imposing a preconceived, alien form of classification upon the data. Naturally-occurring units such as behaviour episodes, are identified and analysed.

Specimen records have been used to describe the behaviour of young people in a number of different milieus. They have been employed in the study of children in their homes (Schoggen, 1963; Fawl, 1963; Dyck, 1963; Simpson, 1963; Hall, 1965), in nursery schools (Hartley, Frank & Goldenson, 1952), in schools (Schoggen, Barker & Barker, 1963), in a research hospital (Jordan, 1963), in a summer camp (Gump, Schoggen & Redl, 1957), and in the community at large (Barker & Wright, 1954). The milieu of the present study was a Brisbane kindergarten.

The Ss used in the investigation were twenty-four children aged between 3.1 and 5.4 years, in regular attendance at the kindergarten. They formed three groups of eight children, with mean ages of 3.3, 4.1 and 5.1 years. Nine trained kindergarten teachers, about fifteen student teachers, and several other members of the staff, interacted with the Ss during the periods of observation. Detailed observations of each child's ongoing behaviour for three consecutive hours on each of two successive mornings at kindergarten were set down in specimen record form, as devised by Barker and Wright (1954). Approximately 2,200 pages of primary data were gathered in this way. The Ss were tested for level of intelligence, extent of vocabulary and relationships with members of their families. The staff at the kindergarten and the parents of the Ss completed schedules concerned with behaviour and personality characteristics of the Ss and their parents, as well as with parental attitudes.

The analysis of the forty-eight specimen records was based on a goal-directed unit of behaviour, the Environmental Force Unit (EFU). This unit, an outgrowth of Barker and Wright's behaviour episode, was developed by Schoggen (1963). He defines an EFU as 'an action by an environmental agent which: (1) occurs *vis-a-vis* the child, and (2) is directed by the agent towards a recognizable end-state with respect to the child, and (3) is recognised as such by the child'. The environmental agents operating within the kindergarten are the teachers, the student teachers, and boys and girls in the same age groups as the Ss. When the action stems from the S, instead of an environmental agent, the unit is termed an Organismic Force Unit (OFU).

The following excerpt from the first specimen record of Alison Sutherland, aged 3 years 4 months, provides an example of an EFU. Alison had been playing in the block corner during the indoor play period. She had reluctantly helped the teacher (T) and the other children to tidy away a few of the blocks, stacking them in the cupboard. When the other children left the block corner to go to the piano Alison walked over to another block cupboard.

10.13 She took out two of the large, hollow blocks.
She began to push them across the floor.

$$20, 3, A◊S*$$

T called to Alison, telling her that it was time to go to the piano for music.
Alison continued to push the blocks across the floor.
T walked over to Alison and told her again that it was time for music.

---

*The bracket denotes the interaction from initiation to termination. The first numeral (20) indicates the sequential order of the unit in the specimen record. The second numeral (3) indicates the duration of the interaction in minutes. The symbols A◊S indicate that the unit was initiated by an adult and that the subject was the target. The title of the unit, which identifies the action, is shown on the vertical line.

Alison picked up the blocks and stood up, holding them. She carried them across to the cupboard and put them away again.

10.14   T walked across the nursery to the piano, leaving Alison to follow.

Alison left the block corner and walked across the room. She stopped beside the table on which the puzzles had been set out earlier in the morning.

The puzzles had now been tidied away.

She climbed on top of the table and lay down on her tummy.

T left the piano and walked across to Alison.

She said to her 'Come and sit next to me'.

10.15   Alison sat up and climbed off the table.

T tucked her blouse and jumper into her long pants.

Together they walked across to the piano.

Alison sat down on the mat near T.

She looked up at T and smiled at her.

T says to go to the piano

Then she swung round to look at the student teacher who was seated at the piano.

The following extract from the first specimen record of Keith Mulholland, aged 4 years 11 months, illustrates an OFU. Keith was standing beside a small table playing with the pieces of a construction set, during the indoor play period.

10.54   He stood beside the table and lifted up the bowl that contained pieces of the set.

He tipped them out on to the table.

He put the bowl down on the table again.

He sorted through the brightly coloured pieces of wood.

Keith began to separate out the circular pieces.

He placed them on a felt board that was lying on the table.

He started to build with them.

He arranged some of the circles inside each other, making concentric circles.

He seemed to be interested in this formation.

10.55   He continued until he had made a number of concentric circles.

Then he left the rest of the pieces on the table and moved away.

39, 2, S◊A

He hurried across the nursery to T.

He said to her 'Come and see what I did'.

T followed him over to the small table.

He showed her the patterns that he had made. T talked about them with him.

She pointed to some solid semicircles in the bowl.

She suggested that he might like to use some of these.

Shows T his patterns

10.56   Warren walked over to the table as T and Keith talked
         together.
         He leaned on the table and watched.
         T walked away.

         Keith pulled out a chair and sat down.
         Picking up some pieces of the set he began to make more
         patterns.

The 6,172 goal-directed interactions identified in 144 hours of recorded observations were classified according to such criteria as the goal of the initiator, the method used in the transaction, success in goal achievement, and congruence between the goal of the initiator and that of the target. The statistical techniques used in the analysis of the results were chi², Spearman rank correlation and, on occasions, the Sign Test.
Some of the findings related to the various hypotheses tested in the investigation are presented.

A. *Investigation of the attempts of the social agents in the environment to modify the behaviour of the Ss.*

Initiation of Interactions: The Ss initiated a significantly larger proportion of the interactions than did the environmental agents ($p < .01$). Accordingly, the Ss were able to move actively towards the attainment of their own goals more often than they were called upon to modify their behaviour, by changing it in the direction indicated by the social agents in their environments. The Ss were not merely targets of environmental action.

Within each 60 minutes an average of 43 interactions was recorded between each S and one or more of the social agents, indicating a high degree of interdependence between the Ss and their environments. Of the total interactions 77.4 per cent lasted for a period of one minute or less, and 92.7 per cent for 4 minutes or less. Only 0.77 per cent persisted for 20 minutes or longer. The interactions of four-year old Ss and environmental agents persisted significantly longer than did those of the three-year olds and the five-year olds, due, perhaps, to greater adult emphasis on participation in programme activities by this group of Ss. These activities necessarily occupied longer periods of time than goal-directed behaviours such as seeking approval or comfort.

Tables 16.1, 16.2 and 16.3 show the sources and targets of the interactions between environmental agents and Ss at each age level.

Within the three ages represented in this sample the four-year olds were the most outgoing in initiating contacts with the social agents (4 and 3, $p < .05$). Whereas the actual number of interactions recorded at the two younger ages were almost identical, an increase of about one-third was registered at five years. Thus, the volume of activity between environmental agents and Ss was significantly greater at the five-year level. These Ss demonstrated their ability to do more things in the same space of time, and to carry out comparable tasks at a greatly accelerated speed of performance, than the younger Ss.

TABLE 16.1

Interactions between Environmental Agents and Subjects

Source	3 years n	Per cent	4 years n	Per cent	5 years n	Per cent
A	431	23.17	464	25.00	458	18.67
SP	230	12.37	175	9.43	419	17.08
OP	161	8.66	108	5.82	150	6.11
P	18	0.96	8	0.27	26	1.07
S	1020	54.84	1104	59.48	1400	57.07
Totals	1860		1859		2453	

TABLE 16.2

Sources of EFU Initiated by Environmental Agents

Source	3 years n	Per cent	4 years n	Per cent	5 years n	Per cent
A	431	51.30	464	61.46	458	43.49
SP	230	27.38	175	23.18	419	39.79
OP	161	19.17	108	14.30	150	14.25
P	18	2.15	8	1.06	26	2.47
Totals	840		755		1053	

TABLE 16.3

Environmental Targets of OFU Initiated by Ss

Target	3 years n	Per cent	4 years n	Per cent	5 years n	Per cent
A	507	49.70	393	35.59	498	35.71
SP	255	25.00	382	34.60	587	41.79
OP	187	18.33	249	22.55	175	12.50
P	71	6.96	80	7.26	140	10.00
Totals	1020		1104		1400	

Legend: A = adults   P = groups of peers
         SP = same sex peers S = subjects
         OP = opposite sex peers

Source of Environmentally-Determined Interactions: Of the total EFU originating from the social agents in the kindergarten environment 51.1 per cent were initiated by the adults and 48.9 per cent by the child agents. Adults initiated significantly more of the environmentally-determined contacts at four years than at three and five years ($p < .001$), and peers were responsible for making significantly more of the contacts at five years than at the younger ages ($p < .001$). These findings support Schoggen's statement (1963) that 'With increasing age, adults play a less prominent role while peers play an increasingly important role in the socialization process'.

Overall, and at each age, significantly more contacts were made with Ss of the same sex, than with those of the opposite sex, the proportion increasing from 59 per cent at three years to 72 per cent at five years. Approximately two-thirds of the peer contacts were with children of the same sex ($p < .01$). At each age EFU emanating from groups of peers were very infrequent, accounting, overall, for less than 2 per cent of the contacts initiated by environmental agents. At the preschool level, children do not appear to act spontaneously in groups of more than two or three. Through 144 hours of recorded behaviour there was almost no evidence of what could be termed group goals, or behaviour regulated in accordance with these.

Goals of Environmental Agents: Within the interactions initiated by adult agents, programme-centred behaviour occurred significantly more often than child-centred and adult-centred actions ($p < .01$). At each age level of Ss the three most frequently occurring adult imposed goals were programme-centred: attempts to persuade Ss to participate in specific sections of the programme, in ritual-associated activities (such as going to the toilet, or eating lunch), or in some common group activity such as tidying away play things, predominated in the behaviour of adults in their contacts with Ss of all ages. The six child-centred goals (such as assists or gives help, or gives attention or approval) accounted for 32 per cent, and the one adult-centred goal (asking the child to do something for the adult) for 2.7 per cent of the adult-initiated interactions.

Spearman rank correlations between the rank order of the adults' goals for Ss at 3 and 4, 4 and 5, and 3 and 5 years were .91, .98 and .91 respectively, all significant at well beyond the .001 level. Accordingly, much the same goal classes provided the impetus for EFU directed by adults to Ss of all ages. Behaviour related to certain classes of adult-imposed goals occurred with greater frequency at some ages than at others.

Although the adults showed that they were aware of the immediate needs of individual children by meeting a large proportion of these, they tended to deal with the requirements of individual children by planning a programme of activities which they believed would meet the needs and appeal to the interests of all the young children in their care, and by attempting to persuade all the children to participate in this programme of events in the approved manner. Thus, programme-centred considerations tended to take precedence over child-centred behaviour, and ensuring that the various sections of the programme were put into effect smoothly appeared to be the primary concern of the adults while the children were in their care. Perhaps this is inevitable when one adult is responsible for the physical and psychological well-being of 15 to 20 preschool children.

As only 38.4 per cent of the EFU initiated by child agents were concerned with child-centred or ego-centred goals, the interactions initiated by peers were more often instigated by social than by personal interests. Four of the fourteen goal classes accounted for more than two-thirds of all the EFU originating from child agents. These goal classes were:

1. Makes or engages in social contact (peer-centred).
2. Follows own play interests or preferences (child-centred).
3. Directs or changes child's play or behaviour (peer-centred).
4. Joins in play or child's ongoing activity (peer-centred).

These appear to represent the predominating interests of the child agents. Certain types of goal-directed behaviour were characteristic of the actions of children at the different ages. The majority of the goals of three-year old child agents were child-centred, while peer-centred behaviour was more prevalent amongst the older children.

Method Transactions: Adults used very mild methods in 50.7 per cent and temperate methods in 46.2 per cent of all adult-initiated EFU. Methods classed as coercive or strong (gives vigorous instruction or order and uses physical proximity to support instruction given) were used in only 44 out of 1,408 interactions, or 3.1 per cent of all method transactions. Five behavioural techniques, one temperate (uses statement, instruction or direction) and four very mild (requests, encourages or reassures or gives help, makes matter-of-fact suggestion, and speaks to or engages in conversation), were employed in 85 per cent of adults' contacts with Ss. Apparently the adults very seldom felt any necessity to use coercive methods in their attempts to modify the behaviour of the children in their care.

The three methods most frequently used by child agents in their contacts with Ss were speaks to or engages in conversation, interferes with child's play material or ongoing activity, and joins in the child's ongoing activity. They employed antisocial techniques in one third of their attempts to achieve their goals. The greatest amount of antisocial behaviour, 42.2 per cent of all methods used, was found amongst the youngest children, the percentage falling progressively with increasing age of the peers to 32.8 per cent at four years and 22.9 per cent at five years.

In general, three-year old peers used non-verbal techniques, together with physical aggression against the child's play things. Murphy (1943) also found that three-year olds showed a higher incidence of snatching another child's toy or molesting or aggressively attacking his play material than attacking the person of the child. Four-year old child agents tended to use a combination of verbal and non-verbal methods, and they used physical aggression against the child's person. Five-year old peers employed verbal methods of communication and they expressed their hostility verbally.

Goal Achievement: Adults (87 per cent) were significantly more successful than child agents (71 per cent) in modifying the behaviour of Ss ($p < .001$). The four-year old Ss were somewhat readier to comply with the wishes of the adults than were the three and five-year olds, but the differences between the groups were slight. Child agents were most successful in achieving their goals when they interacted with five-year olds, and least successful with four-year olds but, again, the differences were slight. Examination of the percentage of goals attained by each subgroup of child agents showed that five-year old same-sex peers were considerably more successful than same-sex peers at the two younger ages, whereas three and four-year old opposite-sex peers were considerably more successful than the oldest opposite-sex peers. Overall, the environmental agents were highly successful in modifying the behaviour of Ss so that it conformed to their own expectations and demands.

Harmony in Interactions: The goals of adults were congruent with the goals of Ss significantly more often than occurred with the goals of child agents and Ss ($p < .001$). Significantly more congruent than non-congruent acts were found in adult-initiated EFU ($p < .01$), Ss viewing two-thirds of the adults' goals as acceptable to them. The difference between congruent and non-congruent interactions originating from child agents was not significant. Thus, the Ss demonstrated greater willingness to move towards the goals set by adults, than to help their peers achieve goals of their own choosing, in which the Ss were implicated. With increasing age Ss showed more inclination to change their behaviour in the direction indicated by the adults, the percentage of adults' goals that were congruent with the goals of Ss rising from 62.9 per cent at three years to 67.3 per cent at five years. Overall, there was a discrepancy of more than 20 per cent between the behavioural changes of Ss in order to meet the goals that the adults set for them, and their preferred behaviour in these situations. To this extent they were coerced into meeting the demands of the adult agents.

In contacts initiated by child agents, a significantly greater amount of congruence existed at the five-year level than amongst the younger children. The discrepancy between the actions of three and four-year old Ss in response to the demands of peers and what they wanted to do in these circumstances was more than 25 per cent, whereas the difference fell to 10 per cent at the five-year level. These figures indicate the extent to which the Ss were coerced into modifying their behaviour by the child agents in their environments.

At the three-year level, contacts originating from opposite-sex peers were somewhat more harmonious than those emanating from peers of the same sex. At four years, approximately the same amount of harmony (45 per cent) was found in interactions with each group of peers. At the five-year level there was a small increase in compatibility between opposite-sex peers and Ss, and a significantly large increase in the harmonious interactions with peers of the same sex (65 per cent). Throughout the study a high degree of cooperation and mutual good will was found in the social relationships of five-year old Ss and peers of the same sex.

B. *Investigation of the active attempts of the Ss to attain their own goals through the social agents in their ecological environments.*

Agents as Targets of Interactions: The total group of Ss directed significantly more OFU to child agents than to adult agents ($p < .001$), but this phenomenon did not occur at the three-year level where half of the interactions were directed to each group of social agents. A significant change in the proportion of contacts with adults and with peers occurred at four years and persisted thereafter, with both four and five-year olds directing 65 per cent of their actions to child agents and 35 per cent to adult agents. Two-thirds of all the interactions with peers were directed to children of the same sex. The percentage of contacts with same-sex peers rose significantly from 58 per cent and 60 per cent at three and four years respectively, to 77 per cent at five years. Therefore, a slight preference for playmates of the same sex shown by three-year olds increased with age until by five years nearly 8 out of every 10 contacts were with same-sex peers.

Goals of Ss: There were differences between the types of goals of Ss in relation to behaviour directed to adult agents and to child agents. Zero order correlations were found between the rank order of the goal-directed behaviour of three and four-year old Ss relative to adults and to child agents as targets. A nonsignificant relationship was found at the five-year level. Thus all Ss were highly selective in the targets of their goal-directed behaviour, the five-year olds displaying the greatest flexibility in choice of targets. Behaviour concerned with joining in the various sections of the programme, as well as actions related to personal goals such as seeking attention, approval, assistance, reassurance or information, were customarily addressed to adults, whereas making social contacts and aggressive acts were more usually directed to peers.

Although some differences were apparent, in general, Ss tended to direct OFU related to the same goal classes to peers of either sex. In the minority of instances where behaviour related to programme and personal goals was not directed to adults, acts concerned with personal goals were more commonly directed to peers of the same sex, while the sex of child agents appeared to be irrelevant in relation to programme-centred goals. Ss tended to make no distinction between taking the hand of a boy or a girl to join in a game or to go to lunch. Antisocial behaviour was more often directed to opposite-sex than to same-sex peers.

Despite stability in the order of goal classes throughout the three to five-year age span, some changes in the pre-eminence of particular goal classes were found with increasing age of Ss. Three-year olds were more concerned with following their own play interests than were the four-year olds ($p < .05$), and with joining in play, than were five-year olds ($p < .01$). The desire for attention or approval instigated a significantly larger amount of the behaviour of four-year old Ss than that of the threes and the fives (4 and 3, $p < .05$; 4 and 5, $p < .01$). Making or engaging in social contacts took place least often at four years (4 and 3, $p < .01$; 4 and 5, $p < .05$). Attempts to direct or change the play or behaviour of other children, and also to gain information, were most common at five years ($p < .001$). Ss in this age group made significantly fewer spontaneous attempts to join in the programme (5 and 4, $p < .01$; 5 and 3, $p < .001$). These variations in the frequency with which certain goals were sought reveal changing patterns in the personal and social needs of preschool children, with increments in age.

Method Transactions: Nonsignificant correlations of .25 and .22 were found at three and four years between the rank order of the methods used by Ss in interactions with adults and with peers, showing that different techniques were employed by these younger Ss in their contacts with each group of social agents. At the five-year level, a significant relationship of .67 ($p < .01$) indicated that the oldest Ss used similar methods in their interactions with both groups of targets. Within the cultural setting of the kindergarten environment certain techniques were appropriate to interactions with adults, and others to contacts with peers. The Ss appear to have learned the patterns of communication appropriate to each group. The significant relationship found at five years was due to the preponderance of verbal methods of communication, equally suitable for interacting with each group of targets. One particular verbal method, that of speaking to or engaging in conversation, was used in one-third of all their interactions.

Significant differences in the frequency of usage of some techniques at the various ages were found. These are illustrated in Figure 16.1.

FIGURE 16.1

Variations with Age of Subjects in Frequency of Occurrence of Method Transactions

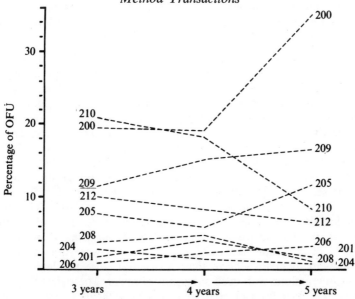

Legend:
200 Speaks to or engages in conversation
201 Plays roughly or wildly in fun
204 Smiles or laughs
205 Requests or asks a question
206 Uses verbal aggression
208 Manhandles, hits with object

209 Calls out or makes noise to attract attention
210 Approaches without speaking, looks at
212 Shows or holds up play material

Two nonverbal methods, shows or holds up ($p < .01$), and smiles or laughs ($p < .001$) were used significantly more often at three than at five years. Playing roughly or wildly in fun was most characteristic of the four-year olds (4 and 3, $p < .01$; 4 and 5, $p < .001$). The nonverbal methods of approaches without speaking, looks at, or points to (3 and 5, 4 and 5, $p < .001$) and the antisocial methods of manhandles, pushes, shoves or hits with object (3 and 5, 4 and 5, $p < .001$) were employed significantly more often by the two younger groups of Ss. The verbal methods of speaks to or engages in conversation (5 and 4, 5 and 3, $p < .001$), verbal aggression (5 and 3, $p < .001$), requests (5 and 4, 5 and 3, $p < .001$), and calls out or makes a noise to attract attention (5 and 3, $p < .001$; 4 and 3, $p < .05$) were more typical of the older than of the youngest Ss.

Although some differences were apparent, Ss usually employed similar methods of achieving their goals in interactions with same-sex peers and with opposite-sex peers. The methods of plays roughly in fun, shows play material, and approaches without speaking, were commonly used with peers of the same sex. The four antisocial methods, as well as the use of light physical contact (such as taking the child's hand), and calling out or making a noise to attract attention, were more often employed in interactions with peers of the opposite sex. The more frequent use of antisocial techniques with opposite-sex peers, especially at the youngest age level, was the major difference between the methods used in the interactions of Ss with same-sex and with opposite-sex child agents.

Goal Achievement: Overall, and at each age, Ss attained significantly more of their go   in interactions with adult agents than with child agents ($p < .001$). Adults assisted Ss of each age to achieve their goals in 9 out of every 10 occasions. In interactions with peers, three, four and five-year old Ss were successful in 81.9 per cent, 70.9 per cent and 84.4 per cent respectively, of their goal-directed behaviour. Thus four-year old Ss were significantly less successful than the other two groups of Ss ($p < .001$), while the five-year olds recorded the highest level of goal achievement. The five-year old Ss were the most successful group in contacts with same-sex peers (5 and 4, $p < .001$; 5 and 3, $p < .05$), and the youngest Ss with opposite-sex peers (3 and 4, $p < .01$). The findings suggest that the three-year olds were highly successful in goal attainment irrespective of the particular target of the OFU, being least successful with peers of the same sex. The four-year olds were able to persuade adults to help them to achieve their goals, but were the least successful group in interactions with each subgroup of peers. The oldest Ss generally experienced a high level of goal achievement with all targets, being least successful with peers of the opposite sex.

The percentage of goals attained within the different goal categories varied with the age of the Ss. These are illustrated in Figure 16.2. The three-year old Ss were the most successful group in attaining goals related to their own play interests (3 and 4, $p < .05$; 3 and 5, $p < .01$). With increasing age of Ss, this child-centred goal was achieved less often. The four-year old Ss were significantly less successful than the three and the five-year olds in gaining attention and approval ($p < .001$), which they sought more often. They were not permitted to join in play ($p < .01$), or to make social contacts (4 and 5, $p < .001$), as often as were the younger and older children. The oldest Ss experienced fewer setbacks in their attempts to join in the programme (5 and 3, $p < .05$) and were less successful in guarding or reclaiming play materials than were the younger Ss. These age differences highlight the three-year olds' concern for their own play interests, and the difficulties experienced by the four-year olds in making social contacts and in gaining the attention and

FIGURE 16.2

Success in Goal Achievement within Classes
by Subjects at Different Age Levels

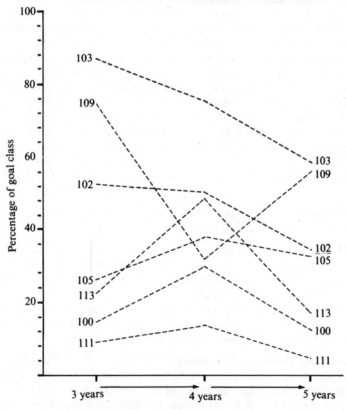

Legend: 100   Seeks attention or approval
          105   Follows own play interests or preferences
          107   Joins in section of programme
          109   Guards or reclaims play material
          111   Engages in social contact
          113   Joins in play or ongoing activity

approval they sought so frequently. The five-year olds demonstrated that they were able to attain their own goals through the social agents in their environments more consistently than were the younger Ss.

Harmony in Interactions: Of the OFU directed by Ss of each age to adult agents and to child agents, a significantly higher proportion of the adult-oriented goals were congruent with those of the adult agents than were the child-oriented goals with those of the child agents ($p < .001$). As the adults showed their willingness to assist Ss of each age to achieve their goals on almost 9 out of every 10 occasions, the social relationships between Ss and adults were very harmonious. Apparently the Ss were skilful at keeping their requests of adults within approved limits. Perhaps the consistent application throughout the kindergarten of clearly defined rules, procedures and discipline enabled even the youngest child to learn, and to accept, the fundamentals of adult-child relationships and to function effectively within these set limits.

The goals of peers and those of Ss of three, four and five years were compatible in 70 per cent, 60 per cent and 80 per cent of instances respectively, although peers assisted Ss to attain their goals more frequently. Apparently the Ss were able to apply sufficient pressure to achieve some of their goals despite resistance from the child agents. At the five-year level the size of the discrepancy between preferred and actual behaviour dropped to half ($p < .001$) due, perhaps, to greater skill in handling social relationships. Thus a much higher degree of harmony prevailed between Ss and peers at the five-year level than at the younger ages, especially in interactions with peers of the same sex. The lowest amount of congruence registered by Ss of each age occurred in contacts with opposite-sex peers, four-year old Ss experiencing the greatest difficulty here.

C. *Conflict between Ss and environmental agents, its source, and the types of interactions which result in conflict.*

Source of Conflict: Significantly more conflict, overall, and at each age, stemmed from the acts of environmental agents than from those of Ss ($p < .001$). The Ss were more successful in persuading the environmental agents to help them to achieve their goals, than were the environmental agents in persuading the Ss to change their behaviour in the direction indicated. The Ss registered more resistance to attempts to modify their behaviour than did the environmental agents.

Environmentally-Determined Conflict: Overall, and at the three and four-year levels, conflict was engendered significantly more often by the actions of child agents than by those of the adults ($p < .001$). In interactions with five-year old Ss no significant difference was found between the discord generated by each group of environmental agents. More than one-third of all the adult-subject interactions were discordant. Conflict resulting from adult-initiated EFU decreased from 39.2 per cent at three years to 34.1 per cent at five years, but the differences between the groups were not significant. When the interactions originated from the child agents, almost 6 out of every 10 contacts at the two younger ages were discordant. By five years the proportion of conflictful interactions dropped to less than 4 out of 10, indicating that these Ss experienced a greater degree of compatibility with their peers ($p < .001$). No significant difference was found between the amount of conflict with Ss recorded at the two younger ages in contacts initiated by peers of the same sex and by those of the opposite sex. However, the five-year old opposite-sex peers registered a much greater amount of conflict than did peers of the same sex as the Ss ($p < .001$).

Certain types of goal-directed behaviour resulted in more conflict at some ages than at others. Joining in play, a socially oriented action, led to more discord at the younger age levels (3 and 5, $p < .001$). Attempts to direct or change the play or behaviour of other children also caused most conflict at three years and declined with increasing age of children (3 and 4, 3 and 5, $p < .05$). Perhaps the older children had developed a measure of tolerance and had learned to deal with interference and temporary frustration without an overt display of emotion, or without recourse to retribution. Attention-seeking behaviour resulted in more discord at four years than at three and at five years ($p < .05$). The goal of follows own play interests led to significantly less conflict amongst the oldest children (5 and 4, $p < .05$) due, perhaps, to increased social maturity and sophistication.

Subject-Determined Conflict: Significantly more subject-determined conflict had its source in OFU directed to child agents than to adult agents ($p < .001$). About 10 per cent of the interactions with adults were discordant, whereas conflict between three, four and five-year old Ss and their peers resulted from 30 per cent, 40 per cent and 20 per cent, respectively, of their contacts. The amount of conflict with adults was equally small within all groups of Ss. In interactions with peers, the five-year old Ss experienced significantly less conflict, and four-year olds significantly more discord (5 and 3, 5 and 4, $p < .001$; 4 and 3, $p < .01$). The four-year olds registered more conflict with each subgroup of child agents than did the younger or the older children, and were noticeably 'out of step' with their environments. They initiated a significantly greater proportion of the contacts, directing the majority of these to peers, and experienced significantly more difficulty than the three and the five-year olds in their dealings with other people. Between four and five years of age the Ss acquired an insight into social roles and relationships, and developed the social skills that are prerequisites for the harmonious relationships that characterized the five-year olds' interactions with the social agents in their environments.

More than one-third of the Ss' contacts with opposite-sex peers were discordant. Although associations between children of the opposite sex were a little more harmonious at the oldest age level than at three and four years, at each age there was less congruence between the goals of

Ss and of peers of the opposite sex than between Ss and any other group of environmental agents. From three years upwards relationships with peers of the opposite sex were much less congenial than those existing between Ss and peers of the same sex as themselves. While the amount of conflict with opposite-sex peers fell slightly, the amount of discord with same-sex peers fell rapidly with increasing age until, at the oldest age level, the relationships between Ss and peers of the same sex as themselves were exceedingly harmonious. These findings support those of Helen Koch who says (1957): 'It appears, then, that even by five years greater congeniality exists between the members of a given sex than between those not similar in sex'.

Areas of Environmentally-Determined Conflict: Overall, and at each age, significantly more conflict was associated with the attempts of the adults to attain programme-centred goals than child-centred goals ($p < .001$). At three, four and five years the five programme-centred goals accounted for 79.9 per cent, 83.7 per cent and 78.2 per cent of all the adult-initiated conflict. The six child-centred and one adult-centred goals were responsible for less than 20 per cent of the discordant interactions. Attempting to persuade Ss to join in sections of the programme was the largest single cause of conflict. Only slightly less conflictful were the adults' efforts to persuade Ss to join in common activities (such as tidying the nursery), and in ritual-associated activities (such as going to the toilet and drinking milk at mid-morning). In the latter situations, the physiological needs of the children could be expected to exert pressure towards compliance with the adults' demands. Within particular goal categories the greatest amount of conflict (86.5 per cent) resulted from the adults' attempts to protect other children from the Ss. Attempts to persuade Ss to abide by the rules and regulations and to use kindergarten play material in the approved manner led to conflict on more than 70 per cent of occasions.

In contacts originating from child agents, significantly more discord was associated at each age level with ego-centred (child-centred) than with peer-centred goals. Much more conflict resulted from the attempts of peers to attain their own personal goals, such as following their own play interests or preferences (which accounted for 31.5 per cent of all the discordant EFU), than from their efforts to play with, or to influence the behaviour of, the Ss. Actions associated with the two goal categories of directs or changes child's play or behaviour and shows aggression, which ranked second and third in size of contribution to the discord between peers and Ss, together were responsible for less conflict than the child agents' attempts to follow their own play interests. Child-centred behaviour became increasingly important as a source of conflict at the four and five-year levels ($p < .05$).

The proportion of discord associated with antisocial techniques of attaining goals was significantly greater than that concomitant with socially-approved methods ($p < .01$). The four antisocial methods which were used in 31 per cent of all contacts were associated with 55 per cent of the conflict that stemmed from the acts of child agents. Each of these methods was accompanied by conflict on more than 84 per cent of the occasions it was employed. The most commonly used antisocial technique, interference with a child's play material or ongoing activity, accounted for nearly 30 per cent of all discordant EFU, the greatest amount being recorded for the youngest children. Same-sex peers resorted to these methods most frequently at three years, and opposite-sex peers, at four years.

Areas of Subject-Determined Conflict: As only one contact in every 10 with adults resulted in discord, relationships between Ss and adult agents were generally very harmonious. However, on the occasions that conflict did ensue, it was almost invariably associated with attempts to achieve one of three particular goals: attention or approval (most noticeable at four years), assistance or support, and follows own play interests or preferences (which caused more discord at five years than at the younger ages).

Significantly more conflict was recorded in interactions of Ss with child agents than with adult agents ($p < .001$). Examination of the discordant OFU revealed that two of the fourteen goals, seeks attention or approval and follows own play interests or preferences, both child-centred goals, accounted for 40 per cent of all the conflict. Four peer-centred goals, two of them with antisocial overtones, (a) directs or changes child's play or behaviour, (b) shows aggression, (c) makes or engages in social contact, and (d) joins in play, accounted for more than 40 per cent of the discordant OFU. Behaviour related to these six goal classes, then, comprised most of the demands that Ss made of the social agents in their environments.

Several types of goal-directed behaviour resulted in more discord at some ages than at others. These are illustrated in Figure 16.3.

Showing aggression led to more conflict at three years than at five years ($p < .01$) where the children had developed some degree of tolerance. Guarding or reclaiming play material resulted in more discord at three than at four years, though the difference fell short of significance at the .05 level. Consonant with other findings, peer-centred goals resulted in significantly more conflict at four years than at three years ($p < .05$). The four-year old Ss experienced more discord in relation to joining in play (4 and 3, $p < .01$; 4 and 5, $p < .001$), and in seeking approval and attention ($p < .001$). They found the greatest amount of difficulty in making harmonious social contacts (4 and 5, $p < .001$). Following their own play interests also led to more conflict at four than at three years. Less discord resulted from attempts of five-year old Ss to direct or change the play or behaviour of others, but the differences between the groups fell just short of significance at the .05 level. Again this reflects the improved social relationships existing amongst the oldest children.

The Role of the Teacher: Lastly, the role of the teacher, as seen in this study of kindergarten interactions, should be mentioned. While attention has generally been focused on the limitations and opportunities imposed

FIGURE 16.3

*Variations in the Conflict Associated with some
Goal Classes at the Different Age Levels*

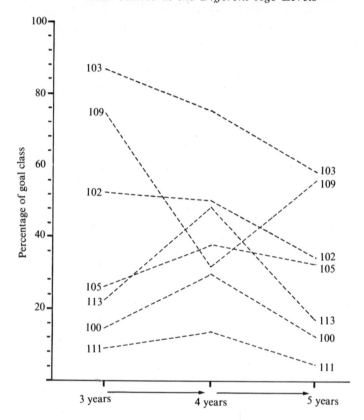

Legend: 100 Seeks attention or approval
102 Directs or changes child's play
103 Shows aggression
105 Follows own play interests
109 Guards or reclaims play material
111 Engages in social contact
113 Joins in play or ongoing activity

by behaviour settings on the behaviour of the children, it is apparent that, in the same way, the behaviour of the teacher is influenced by the structure of a given activity and that the teacher's role varies from one setting to another. If a behaviour setting is to function at a level which ensures satisfaction for the individual participants, the teacher must engage in a pattern of behaviour which is consonant with the requirements, the opportunities and the limitations that are inherent in the setting.

Gump (1964) suggests that research into teacher effectiveness should be directed towards the teacher's manipulation of the environment, or his 'behaviour-setting management'. 'The teacher', he says, 'can arrange time, space, objects, pupils, and himself into various constellations of learning environments.' Having done so his behaviour is, in part, 'a reflection of the possibilities and necessities imposed by the arrangement itself'. As well, his behaviour is influenced by the responses of the children as they deal with the particular supports and coercions of the activity settings entered.

In the present study, the teachers arranged a succession of behaviour settings and concurrent subunits of settings in order to provide the machinery, as it were, which permitted or encouraged the children to move towards the goals that the teachers set for them. Most of the settings established in the course of the morning at kindergarten were learning situations concerned with programme activities, ritual-associated activities, or responsibilities common to all members of the group. If the degree of success in modifying the behaviour of the children in the required direction can be considered a criterion of teacher effectiveness, then the present study provides decisive evidence of this phenomenon.

In summary, the amount of interacting that took place between the twenty-four Ss and the social agents in their kindergarten environments was very considerable, averaging 43 contacts per S in every 60 minutes. The great majority of these interactions were of very brief duration, nearly 8 out of every 10 persisting for a period of one minute or less. The findings of this study give an unmistakable indication of the interdependence of the behaving individual and his environment. They highlight the fallacy and the futility of attempting to understand the behaviour of the individual without, at the same time, taking cognizance of the environment with which he interacts.

References

Barker, R. G., 1957: Structure of the stream of behavior. In *Proceedings of the 15th International Congress of Psychology*, 155-156.

Barker, R. G., 1960: Ecology and motivation. In M. R. Jones (Ed.), *Nebraska Symposium on Motivation*. University of Nebraska Press, Lincoln.

Barker, R. G., 1963a: On the nature of the environment. *Journal of Social Issues*, 19, 4, 17-38.

Barker, R. G., 1963b: *The Stream of Behavior*. Appleton-Century-Crofts, New York.

Barker, R. G., 1964: Observation of behavior: Ecological approaches. *Journal Mt. Sinai Hospital*, 31, 4, 268-284.

Barker, R. G., 1965: Explorations in ecological psychology. *American Psychologist*, 20, 1, 1-14.

Barker, R. G. and Barker L. S., 1961: Behavior units for the comparative study of cultures. In B. Kaplan (Ed.), *Studying Personality Cross-Culturally*. Harper & Row, New York.

Barker, R. G. and Gump, P. V. (Eds), 1964: *Big School, Small School*. Stanford University Press, Stanford, Calif.

Barker, R. G. and Wright, H. F., 1951: *One Boy's Day*. Harper & Row, New York.

Barker, R. G. and Wright, H. F., 1954: *Midwest and its Children*. Row, Peterson and Co., Evanston, Ill.

Dyck, A. J., 1963: The social contacts of some midwest children with their parents and teachers. In R. G. Barker (Ed.), *The Stream of Behavior*. Appleton-Century-Crofts, New York.

Fawl, C. L., 1963: Disturbances experienced by children in their natural habitats. In R. G. Barker (Ed.), *The Stream of Behavior*. Appleton-Century-Crofts, New York.

Gump, P. V., 1964: Environmental guidance of the classroom behavioral system. In B. J. Biddle and W. J. Ellena (Eds), *Contemporary Research on Teacher Effectiveness*. Holt, Rinehart and Winston, Inc., New York.

Gump, P. V. and Kounin, J. S., 1960: Issues raised by ecological and classical research efforts. *Merrill-Palmer Quarterly*, 6, 145-152.

Gump, P. V., Schoggen, P. and Redl, F., 1957: The camp milieu and its immediate effects. *Journal of Social Issues*, 13, 1, 40-46.

Gump, P. V. and Sutton-Smith, B., 1955: Activity-setting and social interaction: A field study. *American Journal of Orthopsychiatry*, 25, 755-761.

Hall, E. R., 1965: An ecological study of parent-child influencing behavior. Unpublished MA thesis, University of Kansas.

Hartley, R. E., Frank, L. K. and Goldenson, R. N., 1952: *Understanding Children's Play*. Columbia University Press, New York.

Jordan, N., 1963: Some formal characteristics of the behavior of two disturbed boys. In R. G. Barker (Ed.), *The Stream of Behavior*. Appleton-Century-Crofts, New York.

Koch, H. L., 1957: The relation in young children between characteristics of their playmates and certain attributes of their siblings. *Child Development*, 28, 175-202.

Murphy, L. B., 1943: Social behavior and child personality. In R. G. Barker, J. S. Kounin and H. F. Wright (Eds), *Child Behavior and Development*. McGraw-Hill Book Co., New York.

Schoggen, P. H., 1963: Environmental forces in the everyday lives of children. In R. G. Barker (Ed.), *The Stream of Behavior*. Appleton-Century-Crofts, New York.

Schoggen, M., Barker, L. S. and Barker, R. G., 1963: Structure of the behavior of English and American children. In R. G. Barker (Ed.), *The Stream of Behavior*. Appleton-Century-Crofts, New York.

Shure, M. B., 1963: Psychological ecology of a nursery school. *Child Development*, 34, 979-992.

Simpson, J. E., 1963: A method of measuring the social weather of children. In R. G. Barker (Ed.), *The Stream of Behavior*. Appleton-Century-Crofts, New York.

Willems, E. P., 1965: An ecological orientation in psychology. *Merrill-Palmer Quarterly*, 11, 317-343.

Wright, H. F., 1956: Psychological development in midwest. *Child Development*, 27, 265-286.

Wright, H. F., 1960: Observational child study. In P. Mussen (Ed.), *Handbook of Research Methods in Child Development*. John Wiley & Sons, Inc., New York.

Wright, H. F., 1961: *The City-Town Project: A Study of Children in Communities Differing in Size*. An interim digest prepared for limited circulation, University of Kansas.

17

Some Determinants of Teacher Behaviour*

M. J. Dunkin

Introduction

WRITING in 1963, Gage makes a strong plea for the development of teaching theories alongside learning ones, and he goes on to add that we really know very little about three fundamental issues: '. . . how teachers behave, why they behave as they do, and with what effects' (Gage, 1963). The study reported here is concerned with the second of the issues, namely the determinants of teacher behaviour, and it focuses upon two specific facets, warmth and directiveness, which other studies have shown to be particularly significant in teaching (Campbell, 1967; Sears & Hilgard, 1964).

Attempts to explain the behaviour of teachers have seldom explored further than teachers' personality characteristics. In several studies, scores obtained by teachers on the Minnesota Teacher Attitude Inventory (MTAI) have been correlated with displays of warmth and directiveness by these teachers towards their pupils in the classrooms, and, in most instances, coefficients have been found to be positive, but low to moderate in size (Leeds, 1950, 1952; Callis, 1953; Chappell & Callis, 1954). Similarly, when the California F Scale, which is based upon the concept of 'authoritarian personality', has been used to obtain a measure of teachers' personalities, coefficients of correlation with classroom behaviour have been only moderate (Levin, Hilton and Leiderman, 1957; McGee, 1955). Finally, as examples, Alexander (1950), using the Adult-Child Interaction Test, and Ryans (1960), using the Teacher Characteristics Schedule, to measure teachers' personalities, report correlation coefficients with displays of both warmth and directiveness ranging from zero to around .40, with medians approximating .30. It seems clear from these studies that the personality of the teacher is one of the factors which influence his classroom behaviour, but the low order of correlation coefficients suggests that it is not a sufficient explanation.

*First published in the *Australian Journal of Education*, 11, 3, 252-266.

Although environmental influences upon the behaviour of teachers feature prominently in research paradigms (Gage, 1963), few studies of teachers' warmth and directiveness have incorporated environmental influences into their research designs. The study by Hoehn (1954) is one exception. In this an attempt was made to establish the effects of the social-class status of pupils upon the frequency and kinds of contacts initiated by the teacher. No differences in frequency were found, but teachers tended to interact with lower-class children in a dominative way, and with higher-class children in a cooperative way. Although these findings cannot be interpreted confidently in terms of social class alone (achievement may have been the crucial variable), they do offer some support to the thesis that teachers' warmth and directiveness are affected, to a degree, by environmental influences.

The psychological theory which gives greatest recognition to the personality and the environment in the determination of behaviour is 'field theory', which has been developed from the early theorizing and research work of Kurt Lewin (1935, 1936, 1952). To Lewin, behaviour is the outcome of interactions among psychological forces applying within the life space. Some of these forces have their source in the personality and may take the form of needs which seek a level of satisfaction in behaviour. In addition, some forces are induced by the environment. These 'induced' forces often have their source in social interactions and take the form of expectations perceived to be held by significant others. Thus, behaviour may be determined by the resultant of interactions among relevant needs, and pressures applying from others with whom there is interaction.

Since Lewin's earliest work, a number of focal points have been developed by writers interested in filling in the details of field theory. Of special significance to the issues being investigated here are the notions being advanced by a group of field theorists who concentrate upon analyses of social systems.

A social system is viewed by these theorists as a network of positions whose incumbents interact with one another largely on the basis of accepted rights and obligations attached to the positions which they occupy. Thus, within the family system, the incumbents of the mother, father and offspring positions interact on the basis of ideas about appropriate behaviour for persons occupying these positions, almost irrespective of the particular individuals involved. Similarly, there are attached to the positions of principal, deputy principal, teacher and pupil, within the school system, various sets of prescribed forms of behaviour. These sets of prescriptions are called roles, and, as prescriptions, they indicate what other persons think the occupants of the positions should do.

It is claimed that a teacher, as an occupant of a position in a complex social system, will experience, firstly, various 'own' forces concerned with the degrees of warmth and directiveness to be displayed in his relations with pupils. Some of these forces will be associated with the personality needs which he brings with him into the teaching situation and which will seek a level of satisfaction within his teaching behaviour. In addition to own forces, the teacher will experience 'socially-induced' forces, in the form of attributed roles, emanating from the occupants of the various other positions—inspector, headteacher, parents and pupils, among others —with whom he interacts.

Most of the hypotheses in this study are concerned with the influence upon behaviour of perceived roles, and are predicated on an assumption of frequent conflict between attributed roles and needs, and among attributed roles related to the teacher's display of warmth and directiveness. It is appropriate, therefore, at this stage to consider the contributions which previous research has made to the theories of role conformity and of role conflict resolution.

These studies have produced findings which suggest that role behaviour is dependent upon:

1. Specific own forces, such as needs, having their sources in the personality (Gross, et al., 1958);
2. The degrees of agreement between own forces and socially-induced forces, such as attributed roles (Dinitz, et al., 1962);
3. The strength and intensity of socially-induced forces as seen, for example, in the expertise ascribed to a role definer, and the rigour with which he demands conformity (Gross, et al., 1958; Videbeck & Bates, 1959);
4. The extent to which the behaviour concerned is observable by role definers (Stouffer, 1949; Sutcliffe & Haberman, 1956);
5. A general personality orientation, such as 'authoritarianism' or 'morality' which seems to act as an integrating force and which may predispose the occupant of a position towards conformity to socially-induced forces (Stouffer & Toby, 1951; Sutcliffe & Haberman, 1956; Mishler, 1953; Gross, et al., 1958).

In the light of these generalizations, and within the framework of psychological field theory, the following propositions form the basis of the hypotheses tested in this study.

Proposition I. Behaviour is partly determined by psychological forces arising from within the personality.

Proposition II. Behaviour is partly determined by psychological forces arising from the psychological environment.

Proposition III. Interactions between own and prevailing socially-induced forces are influenced by general personality orientations.

Such orientations are conceptualized as integrating forces which determine the significance attached to socially-induced forces. They have their source in central regions of the personality and, as it were, orientate towards conformity to own forces related to certain types of behaviour, or towards conformity to socially-induced forces. Internally-oriented, or 'self-oriented' individuals attach less significance to socially-induced forces in that conformity to them is relatively unattractive. Externally-oriented, or 'other-oriented' individuals attach strong significance to socially-induced forces and find conformity to them attractive. Thus, for 'self-oriented' individuals the behaviour which is valued most coincides with needs, while for 'other-oriented' individuals the behaviour which is valued most coincides with prevailing socially-induced forces.

Proposition IV. Performance is determined by interactions among specific own forces, prevailing socially-induced forces, and general personality orientations, giving rise to a system of values.

On the basis of these propositions, then, the following hypotheses were formulated and tested in this study:

HYPOTHESIS I
(a) Teachers who, on the basis of central personality needs, can be classified as 'self-oriented', will attach low measures of significance to socially-induced forces related to warmth and directiveness;
(b) Teachers who, on the basis of central personality needs, can be classified as 'other-oriented', will attach high measures of significance to socially-induced forces related to warmth and directiveness; and
(c) Teachers who, on the basis of central personality needs, cannot easily be classified as either 'self-oriented' or 'other-oriented', will attach medium measures of significance to socially-induced forces related to warmth and directiveness.

HYPOTHESIS II
Teachers, whose needs for warmth and directiveness coincide with prevailing socially-induced forces, will have professional values which coincide with both.

HYPOTHESIS III
Teachers, whose needs for warmth and directiveness do not coincide with prevailing socially-induced forces, and who, on the basis of central personality needs, can be classified as 'self-oriented', will have professional values which coincide with their needs for warmth and directiveness.

HYPOTHESIS IV
Teachers, whose needs for warmth and directiveness do not coincide with prevailing socially-induced forces, and who, on the basis of central personality needs, can be classified as 'other-oriented', will have professional values which coincide with prevailing socially-induced forces.

HYPOTHESIS V
Teachers, whose needs for warmth and directiveness do not coincide with prevailing socially-induced forces, and who, on the basis of central personality needs, cannot easily be classified as 'self-oriented' or 'other-oriented', will have professional values which coincide with their needs for warmth and directiveness as frequently as they do with prevailing socially-induced forces. However, where possible, their professional values will be a compromise between their needs and prevailing socially-induced forces.

HYPOTHESIS VI

Teachers will display approximately the same degrees of warmth and directiveness in their classroom performance as they do in their professional values.

*Method**

In broad terms the study involved (a) selecting a sample of teachers; (b) assessing the warmth and directiveness of the teachers' professional values; (c) assessing the warmth and directiveness of the roles attributed by members of the sample to significant other role definers; (d) determining the degrees and types of social power which these other role definers have over members of the sample; (e) assessing the degrees of warmth and directiveness displayed by members of the sample in the classroom; (f) assessing the significance attached by members of the sample to roles attributed to other role definers; and (g) assessing manifest personality needs of the members of the sample.

The Sample: The study involved 114 male teachers in the state primary schools of Queensland who were each employed on a full-time basis in charge of one class of pupils. Some were undertaking part-time evening courses at the University of Queensland, some were external students of the same University and were teaching outside the Brisbane metropolitan area, and others were not enrolled as students but were teaching within the city limits.

Warmth and Directiveness of Teachers' Professional Values: These were assessed on the basis of *H*-scales developed from a questionnaire which asked teachers to indicate which mode of behaviour they considered would have the most desirable effects upon their pupils in a number of classroom problem situations.

Below are examples of the situations and response alternatives. Example (i) is a 'warmth' item and Example (ii) is a 'directiveness' item:

Example (i): During the past few weeks, the pupils of your class have complained about losing pencils and erasers. Cathy is discovered to be the culprit. She comes from a middle-class family and is provided with more spending money than the average pupil.

(a) Discuss, in a friendly way, her behaviour with Cathy, pointing out its consequences. Offer to lend her any equipment she needs and to return the articles privately to the owners for her.

(b) Give Cathy an opportunity to return the articles privately without risk of being discovered.

(c) Inform the class that Cathy is the culprit and suggest that they retrieve their belongings and keep a watchful eye on her in future.

(d) Reprimand Cathy and tell her to return the articles to their owners immediately or to make alternative compensation.

---

*Details of the methodology adopted in this study are to be found in Dunkin (1966).

Example (ii): Dorothy knows the difference in the spelling of 'their' and 'there' but through carelessness often uses one when she should use the other. You have corrected her again and again but in her latest composition she has repeated the mistake.

(a) Indicate the error whenever it is made but wait for Dorothy to learn the difference as she matures.

(b) Give Dorothy daily drilling in the use of the two words and insist that she read over her composition and show that she has checked these words by underlining them.

(c) Tell Dorothy to make a card with two pictures—one illustrating the use of 'there', the other illustrating the use of 'their'—and instruct her to refer to it whenever she uses one of the words.

(d) Refer to the words incidentally during the course of teaching and indicate the error whenever it is made.

It will be seen in sections (3) and (5) below that subjects completed nine other sets of responses for the situations included in the *H*-scales of warmth and directiveness.

Warmth and Directiveness of Roles Attributed to Significant Others: These were assessed on the basis of the *H*-scales developed to measure warmth and directiveness of teachers' professional values. The teachers attributed prescriptions for their behaviour in the 'warmth' and 'directiveness' situations to eight role definers: the Department of Education, their inspectors, their headteachers, their senior assistants, their fellow assistant teachers, their pupils, the parents of their pupils and the local community served by the school.

Social Power of Significant Others over Teachers: Among the many conceptualizations of social power which appear in the literature, that of French and Raven (1959) seems particularly appropriate for this study. These two writers identify the following types of social power:

(a) *Referent*, arising from a desire by the subject to model his behaviour upon that of another person because of liking or respect.

(b) *Expert*, which applies when the subject acknowledges the superior knowledge or skill of another.

(c) *Legitimate*, based upon an acknowledgement by the subject that another person has a right to expect certain behaviour of him.

(d) *Coercive*, in which it is perceived that another person is able to apply negative sanctions for behaviour of certain kinds.

(e) *Reward*, in which it is perceived that another person is able to apply positive sanctions for behaviour of certain kinds.

French and Raven point out that the last two types of power are associated not only with ability to punish or reward, but also with the likelihood that this ability will be actualized and with whether or not the subject's behaviour is likely to be observed by those who are able to punish or reward.

The primary aim in this section of the study was to obtain an estimate of the strength of the psychological forces which particular role attributions would constitute, so, in the instrument used, the teacher respondents were asked (a) to indicate the likelihood that rewards and punishments would be used by the role definers if they knew of the teacher's behaviour; (b) to indicate the likelihood that pertinent behaviour would be observed by the role definers; (c) to indicate the likelihood that personal regard for the role definers would make conformity to their wishes preferable to nonconformity; (d) to assess the expertise possessed by each role definer in the pertinent areas of teacher-pupil relations; and (e) to assess the right of each role definer to expect conformity to his prescriptions in those areas.

The items devised to measure these variables were arranged in four-point Likert scale form to which weights ranging from one to four were assigned. On the basis of combinations of scores obtained on each variable, overall assessments of the social power of each role definer over each teacher were made. These assessments were used as indicators of the relative strength of forces in the form of attributed roles and enabled prevailing socially-induced forces to be determined.

Warmth and Directiveness of Teachers' Classroom Performance: These 'performance' data were obtained with a questionnaire in which the teachers were asked to indicate their most likely responses to the classroom problem situations included in the *H*-scales of warmth and directiveness.

Significance Attached to Attributed Roles: Included in the instrument used to measure the social power variables were two items designed to measure the positive and negative internal sanctions experienced by the teachers as a result of their conforming or not conforming to the roles attributed to significant others. Members of the sample were asked to disregard rewards and punishments but to indicate on four-point Likert scales how pleased or disappointed with themselves they would be if they conformed or did not conform to the prescriptions attributed to each of the eight role definers. On the basis of responses made to these items, teachers were assigned scores for significance of socially-induced forces.

Manifest Personality Needs: After a survey of standardized instruments purporting to measure personality needs, the Edwards Personal Preference Schedule (EPPS) (Edwards, 1953) was chosen as the most appropriate one for this study. This instrument was designed as a quick and convenient measure of fifteen of the manifest needs presented by Murray, *et al.* (1938), whose terminology was used in naming the variables.

In this study, the EPPS was used to measure manifest personality needs relevant to warmth and directiveness displayed by teachers in interaction with their pupils, and as a measure of a personality orientation to conform to pressures exerted by significant others.

The need considered to be most relevant for displays of warmth is nurturance, which is described as follows:

> nur Nurturance: To help friends when they are in trouble, to assist others less fortunate, to treat others with kindness and sympathy, to forgive others, to do small favours for others, to be generous with others, to sympathize with others who are hurt or sick, to show a great deal of affection toward others, to have others confide in one about personal problems. (Edwards, 1959, p. 11.*)

A strong need for nurturance, then, as measured by the EPPS, was taken as an indication of a strong own force to display warmth toward pupils.

A cluster of needs might seem relevant to directiveness, for example, achievement, order, dominance and endurance. However, two appear to stand out. The first is order, which is described thus:

> ord Order: To have written work neat and organized, to make plans before starting on a difficult task, to have things organized, to keep things neat and orderly, to make advance plans when taking a trip, to organize details of work, to keep letters and files according to some system, to have meals organized and a definite time for eating, to have things arranged so that they run smoothly without change. (Edwards, 1959, p. 11.)

The second is dominance:

> dom Dominance: To argue for one's point of view, to be a leader in groups to which one belongs, to be regarded by others as a leader, to be elected or appointed chairman of committees, to make group decisions, to settle arguments and disputes between others, to persuade and influence others to do what one wants, to supervise and direct the actions of others, to tell others how to do their jobs. (Edwards, 1959, p. 11.)

High scores obtained on these variables were taken as indications of strong own forces to be directive in classroom relations with pupils.

On the basis of the findings of previous studies and simple face validity deference, autonomy and succorance were accepted as needs related to a general personality orientation to conformity:

> def Deference: To get suggestions from others, to find out what others think, to follow instructions and do what is expected, to praise others, to tell others that they have done a good job, to accept the leadership of others, to read about great men, to conform to custom and avoid the unconventional, to let others make decisions.

> aut Autonomy: To be able to come and go as desired, to say what one thinks about things, to be independent of others in making decisions, to feel free to do what one wants, to do things that are unconventional, to avoid situations where one is expected to conform, to do things without regard to what others may think, to criticize those in positions of authority, to avoid responsibilities and obligations.

*These quotations are reproduced by permission from the Edwards Personal Preference Schedule Manual. Copyright 1959 by The Psychological Corporation, New York, N.Y. All rights reserved.

suc Succorance: To have others provide help when in trouble, to seek encouragement from others, to have others be kindly, to have others be sympathetic and understanding about personal problems, to receive a great deal of affection from others, to have others do favours cheerfully, to be helped by others when depressed, to have others feel sorry when one is sick, to have a fuss made over one when hurt. (Edwards, 1959, p. 11.)

High scores on deference and succorance, together with a low score on autonomy, were taken to indicate 'other-orientedness', that is, a strong general personality orientation to conform to others, while low scores on deference and succorance, together with a high score for autonomy, were taken to indicate 'self-orientedness', that is, a strong general personality orientation to conform to own needs rather than to prescriptions attributed to others.

TABLE 17.1

A Comparison of the Number of Correct Predictions Obtained on the Basis of a Theory of Professional Values with the Number Expected on the Basis of a 'Proportionate-Expectancy' Model

Behavioural Continuum	No. of Cases	No. of Correct Predictions by the 'Theory'	No. of Correct Predictions by 'Proportionate-Expectancy'	χ^2	p
Warmth	114	62	40	12.1	<.001
Directiveness	114	66	39	18.7	<.001

Results

Two criteria were invoked in testing the theories concerning professional values of teachers and the performance of teachers in the classroom. First, the number of correct predictions made on the basis of these theories had to satisfy a criterion of statistical significance. Second, the theories had to satisfy a criterion of parsimony in comparison with other theories employing fewer independent variables.

HYPOTHESIS I

The null hypothesis was tested, namely that there is no significant positive correlation between 'other-orientedness' and measures of significance attached to socially-induced forces related to warmth and directiveness. The Spearman rank correlation coefficient between the two variables was .20 ($p<.05$). While the coefficient is small, it is accepted as providing significant support for hypothesis I.

HYPOTHESES II, III, IV *and* V

These four hypotheses were derived from a theory which may itself be regarded as a single general hypothesis about the ways in which the three predictor variables—needs, prevailing socially-induced forces, and general personality orientation—are related among themselves, and how these, in turn, are related to the criterion, professional values. In this chapter, therefore, only the results obtained in testing the theory as a whole are reported.

As can be seen in Table 17.1, for 62 of the 114 cases concerning warmth, and for 66 of the 114 cases concerning directiveness, the theory led to the correct prediction. Since it was known that various degrees of warmth and directiveness of professional values did not occur with equal frequency, significance levels based on comparisons of the proportions of correct predictions with the proportions expected by simple chance appeared to be, as Gross, *et al.* (1958) put it, 'if not a capitalization on chance, at least a misrepresentation of realistic possibilities'. Instead, therefore, significance levels for the numbers of correct predictions were calculated by comparison with the 'proportionate-expectancy' which takes disparities among the known frequencies into account, and requires that a behavioural category be selected by chance with the frequency with which it is known to occur. The difference between the numbers expected in respect to both warmth and directiveness according to the 'proportionate-expectancy' model and the numbers obtained on the basis of the theory were significant at the .001 level. It is concluded, therefore, that the data provide significant support for the theory concerning both warmth and directiveness of professional values.

TABLE 17.2

A Comparison of the Numbers of Correct Predictions Obtained on the Basis of a Theory of Behaviour with the Numbers Expected on the Basis of a 'Proportionate-Expectancy' Model

Behavioural Continuum	No. of Cases	No. of Correct Predictions by the 'Theory'	No. of Correct Predictions by 'Proportionate-Expectancy'	χ^2	p
Warmth	114	64	46	7.04	<.01
Directiveness	114	73	33	48.48	<.001

HYPOTHESIS VI

Table 17.2 shows that, with respect to warmth, predictions made from professional val es to anticipated performance were correct in 64 cases of the total 114, and that, for directiveness, the number of correct predictions was 73 out of 114. The fact that both these numbers are significantly larger than the proportions expected in terms of the 'proportionate-expectancy' model provides significant support for hypothesis VI.

So far, the theory and hypotheses guiding this study have been tested in terms of the number of correct predictions made to teachers' professional

TABLE 17.3

Tests of Parsimony of Theory of Professional Values

| Behavioural Continuum | Number of Correct Predictions on the Basis of | | | |
	1 Theory	2 Needs	3 Induced Forces	4 Proportionate-Expectancy
Warmth	62	49	48	40
	$[\chi^2_{(1,2)} = 3.45, p<.10]$		$[\chi^2_{(1,3)} = 4.08, p<.05]$	
	$[\chi^2_{(2,4)} = 2.03, p>.10]$		$[\chi^2_{(3,4)} = 1.60, p>.20]$	
Directiveness	66	40	62	39
	$[\chi^2_{(1,2)} = 16.90, p<.001]$		$[\chi^2_{(1,3)} = 0.26, p>.50]$	
	$[\chi^2_{(2,4)} = 0.03, p>.80]$		$[\chi^2_{(3,4)} = 13.56, p<.001]$	

TABLE 17.4

Tests of Parsimony of Theory of Classroom Behaviour

| Behavioural Continuum | Number of Correct Predictions on the Basis of | | | |
	1 Professional Values	2 Needs	3 Induced Forces	4 Proportionate-Expectancy
Warmth	64	39	57	46
	$[\chi^2_{(1,2)} = 16.03, p<.001]$		$[\chi^2_{(1,3)} = 0.86, p>.30]$	
	$[\chi^2_{(2,4)} = 1.07, p>.30]$		$[\chi^2_{(3,4)} = 2.63, p>.10]$	
Directiveness	73	40	55	33
	$[\chi^2_{(1,2)} = 27.23, p<.001]$		$[\chi^2_{(1,3)} = 5.59, p<.02]$	
	$[\chi^2_{(2,4)} = 1.48, p>.20]$		$[\chi^2_{(3,4)} = 14.67, p<.001]$	

values and their own anticipations of their classroom performance. The question which now needs to be considered concerns the parsimony of the theory. Could professional values and anticipations have been predicted as accurately on the basis of fewer variables than were actually used?

In answering this question a number of tests needs to be made. The numbers of correct predictions to professional values and anticipations made on the basis of the theory underlying the study need to be compared with the numbers of correct predictions that could have been made on the basis of manifest personality needs alone, and prevailing socially-induced forces alone. The criterion of parsimony will be met if either of the two following conditions holds:

(a) The theory leads to a significantly larger number of correct predictions than could have been made from either needs alone or prevailing socially-induced forces alone;

(b) The theory leads to a statistically significant number of correct predictions while neither needs alone, nor prevailing socially induced forces alone, lead to a statistically significant number of correct predictions.

Table 17.3 shows that, where warmth is concerned, the theory is a superior basis for predicting professional values to either needs alone or prevailing socially-induced forces alone. However, where directiveness is concerned, it appears that while the theory is parsimonious in comparison with manifest needs, it is not parsimonious in comparison with prevailing socially-induced forces.

Table 17.4 shows that, where both warmth and directiveness are concerned, professional values are superior bases for predicting anticipated behaviour to either manifest needs alone or prevailing socially-induced forces alone.

Summary and Implications

The following conclusions may be drawn from the study:
1. There is a significant, though quite small, positive relationship between 'other-orientedness' and significance attached to socially-induced forces upon warmth and directiveness.
2. In a significant number of instances, the warmth and directiveness of teachers' professional values can be predicted on the basis of 'self-orientedness' and 'other-orientedness', manifest personality needs for warmth and directiveness, and prevailing socially-induced forces upon warmth and directiveness.
3. With some qualification, the theory of professional values is parsimonious.
4. In relation to warmth and directiveness, teachers' anticipations of their classroom performance can be predicted from their professional values in a significant number of instances.
5. In predicting to teachers' anticipations of their classroom performance, the theory of teacher classroom behaviour is parsimonious when applied to teacher warmth and directiveness.

Assuming that these conclusions have some general validity, what are the implications for those who guide our educational system?

Before any attempt is made to discuss the implications of the major findings of this study, a number of other issues needs to be raised. First, there is the question of optimal degrees of warmth and directiveness to be displayed in teachers' interactions with pupils. In general, it seems that high warmth and medium to low directiveness are desirable qualities of teachers' classroom performance (Campbell, 1967; Sears & Hilgard, 1964). For the purposes of the following discussion, therefore, it will be assumed that pressures militating against high warmth and medium to low directiveness are adverse influences upon teachers' classroom performance.

The majority of teachers involved in this study were in conflict with regard to the levels of warmth and directiveness to be displayed in the classroom. In particular, there was conflict between teachers' own inclinations and the pressures they perceived from their superordinates in the teaching profession and there was a strong tendency for teachers to see their superordinates as prescribing low warmth and high directiveness. Moreover, superordinates were assessed to have strongest social power over the teachers concerned. In other words, the teachers in this study tended to experience strong pressures from their superordinates to perform at other than optimal levels of warmth and directiveness in the classroom, and 'other-oriented' teachers, especially, were likely to be induced to conform to these adverse pressures.

If teachers' perceptions of superordinates' prescriptions are accurate, the anomalous state of affairs exists where those who are given great responsibility for ensuring that children are well taught are themselves the source of adverse influences upon teaching.

If it is true that inspectors, headteachers and others are able, by virtue of their social power, to induce conformity to expectations which are educationally unsound, a number of questions arise concerning potential remedies. Is it possible, for example, to change the expectations which a headteacher has for the classroom performance of members of his staff? Can the social power hierarchy within the teaching profession be restructured so that teachers might enjoy higher degrees of autonomy? Is it possible to select, from the ranks of teachers, superordinates who will value teaching behaviour which is optimal and who will demand such behaviour from teachers? Or is the education system such that, in spite of any potentialities they might have for valuing high warmth and medium to low directiveness, superordinates are coerced into being cold and authoritarian in their dealings with teachers?

On the other hand, if teachers' perceptions of the prescriptions of their superordinates are inaccurate and the latter really prescribe optimal levels of warmth and directiveness, the problem seems to be one of communication.

Is it possible, for example, for teachers to discuss educational questions with their superiors without feeling as though they are being evaluated? Is it a necessary consequence of bureaucratic educational administration that teachers associate authority with lack of warmth and high directiveness?

For some teachers—those who are 'self-oriented'—classroom performance appears to be determined more by their own needs than by pressures from outside. In so far as their personality needs are consistent with optimal levels of warmth and directiveness, these teachers are likely to be effective according to the warmth and directiveness criteria. However, personality needs which are inconsistent with optimal warmth and directiveness may be adverse influences upon the performance of 'self-oriented' teachers. There are implications here involving procedures by which candidates for entry to the teaching profession are selected. In particular, there may be some basis for expanding these procedures to include criteria such as assessments of personality needs. Or can it be assumed that programmes of teacher training can provide formative experiences which ensure that by the time teachers enter the profession they have personality structures essential for teaching success?

References

Alexander, T., 1950: The prediction of teacher-pupil interaction with a projective test. *Journal of Clinical Psychology,* 6, 273-276.

Callis, R., 1953: The efficiency of the Minnesota Teacher Attitude Inventory for predicting interpersonal relations in the classroom. *Journal of Applied Psychology,* 37, 82-85.

Campbell, W. J., 1967: Excellence or fear of failure: The teacher's role in the motivation of learners. *Australian Journal of Education,* 11, 1, 1-12.

Chappell, T. L. and Callis, R., 1954: *The Efficiency of the Minnesota Teacher Attitude Inventory for Predicting Interpersonal Relations in a Naval School.* Report No. 5, ONR 649 (00), University of Missouri, Columbia.

Dinitz, S., Angrist, Shirley, Lefton, M. and Pasamanick, B., 1962: Instrumental role expectations and post-hospital performance of female mental patients. *Social Forces,* 40, 248-254.

Dunkin, M. J., 1966: Some determinants of teacher warmth and directiveness. Unpublished PhD thesis, University of Queensland.

Edwards, A. L., 1953: *Edwards Personal Preference Schedule.* Psychological Corporation, 522 Fifth Avenue, New York.

Edwards, A. L., 1959: *Manual to the Edwards Personal Preference Schedule* (rev. edn). Psychological Corporation, 522 Fifth Avenue, New York.

French, J. R. P. Jr. and Raven, B., 1959: The bases of social power. In D. Cartwright (Ed.), *Studies in Social Power.* University of Michigan, Ann Arbour, Mich.

Gage, N. L., 1963: Paradigms for research on teaching. In N. L. Gage (Ed.), *Handbook of Research on Teaching.* Rand McNally and Co., Chicago, Ill.

Gross, N., Mason, W. S. and McEachern, A. W., 1958: *Explorations in Role Analysis: Studies of the School Superintendency Role.* John Wiley & Sons, Inc., New York.

Hoehn, A. J., 1954: A study of social class differentiation in the classroom behavior of nineteen third grade teachers. *Journal of Social Psychology,* 30, 269-292.

Leeds, C. H., 1950: A scale for measuring teacher-pupil attitudes and teacher-pupil rapport. *Psychological Monographs,* 64 (whole no. 312).

Leeds, C. H., 1952: A second validity study of the Minnesota Teacher Attitude Inventory. *The Elementary School Journal,* 52, 398-405.

Levin, H., Hilton, T. L. and Leiderman, Gloria F., 1957: Studies in teacher behavior. *Journal of Experimental Education,* 26, 81-91.

Lewin, K., 1935: *A Dynamic Theory of Personality.* Translated by D. K. Adams and K. E. Zener. McGraw-Hill Book Co., New York.

Lewin, K., 1936: *Principles of Topological Psychology.* Translated by F. and G. M. Heider. McGraw-Hill Book Co., New York.

Lewin, K., 1952: *Field Theory in Social Science.* Edited by D. Cartwright. Tavistock Publications, London.

McGee, H. M., 1955: The measurement of authoritarianism and its relation to teachers' classroom behavior. *Genet. Psychol. Monogr.,* 52, 89-146.

Mishler, E. G., 1953: Personality 'characteristics' and the resolution of role conflict. *Public Opinion Quarterly,* 17, 115-136.

Murray, H. A., *et al.*, 1938: *Explorations in Personality*. Oxford University Press, New York.

Ryans, D. G., 1960: *Characteristics of Teachers*. American Council of Education, Washington, D.C.

Sears, Pauline S. and Hilgard, E. R., 1964: The teacher's role in the motivations of the learner. In E. R. Hilgard (Ed.), *Theories of Learning and Instruction*. *NSSE Yearbook*, LXIII, Pt I, University of Chicago Press, Chicago, Ill.

Stouffer, S. A., 1949: An analysis of conflicting 'social' norms. *American Sociological Review*, 14, 707-717.

Stouffer, S. A. and Toby, J., 1951: Role conflict and personality. *American Journal of Sociology*, 56, 395-407.

Sutcliffe, J. P. and Haberman, M., 1956: Factors influencing choice in role conflict situations. *American Sociological Review*, 21, 695-703.

Videbeck, R. and Bates, A. P., 1959: An experimental study of conformity to role expectations. *Sociometry*, 22, 1-11.

18

Environmental Events and Inherited Traits as Determinants of Individual Differences in Classroom Performance

G. T. Evans

Introduction

CLASSROOMS are characterized by teachers attempting to arrange the environment of their pupils in such a way that certain goals will be achieved. Of course, the goals vary widely from classroom to classroom, but there is always *some* set of goals. Just as surely, one can predict that for any given classroom, pupils' responses to this special environment will all be different. Given the same school experiences, some children succeed well in terms of these goals, others fail, and most fall in between.

Some educational and administrative procedures seem to assume that nearly all students can achieve the same learning goals, provided their school experiences are suitably varied. Programmed texts and teaching machines work on this principle; any 'normal' student using a programmed text is expected to master its material eventually. Other procedures take for granted that, whatever the environment, no matter how the school or teacher caters for individual differences, there will always be a large range from low to high in the final performance. Procedures like streaming and subject-setting, and the use of grammar and secondary modern schools in Britain, are based on this second belief.

In either case the teacher must know on which continua individual differences are important determinants of goal achievement, and he must have some measure of these variables for each pupil. With the first of the above beliefs, he will try to arrange his pupils' experiences so that, while they all achieve the immediate goal, each does so in what is the most efficient way for him. With the second belief, the teacher attempts to arrange his school, or his class, in such a way that each child can 'do his best' given the kind of person that he is.

The reader may argue that, in the long run, it matters little which of these two beliefs one has. Both courses of action would presumably lead to maximum development of students if we had sufficient knowledge of individual differences. Unfortunately, the situation is more complex than this. Solutions like those of streaming, or having a tripartite school system, usually entail a prejudging of what children will be able to achieve at some time in the future, that is, *before* they have had a chance to try. The other kind of solution could be just as unfair, leading to possible frustration and failure for those not capable of some kinds of achievement.

One may, of course, decide to be like Estragon as he waited for Godot, and say 'Don't let's do anything. It's safer.'. But not doing anything usually involves ignoring individual differences, either in student traits or in the appropriateness of goals. This leads to inevitable frustration and failure for some, boredom and lack of self-realization for others, and an inadequate education for nearly everyone. Continuing studies into individual differences in learning would thus seem imperative if one is to have an adequate rationale for the several possible courses of action.

It is the purpose of what follows to discuss, in part, the results of two investigations into individual differences. These studies did not examine teaching methods or ways of catering for individual differences. Rather, each followed students through their secondary school course for three or four years, attempting to discover what were the main types of individual differences, that is, the main variables, in the students' development. The first study, which provides most of the data for the discussion, was concerned with the development of performance in mathematics; the second with general educational development. One of the major questions of each study was to ask just what part teachers, classrooms or schools play in *creating* individual differences among students. More directly we ask, 'Does a person's educational progress depend on what school he attends, and, if so, in what areas is the school's effect important?'

Development in mathematical performance illustrates progress in a school 'subject'. The tests used to measure such progress set tasks requiring rather specialized knowledge available from a formal and systematic course of work, although there are many elements of secondary school mathematics on which most schools in most countries agree.

The second study looks at a rather different kind of school achievement, that measured by the Iowa Tests of Educational Development (ITED). This battery of nine tests is intended to measure very general outcomes of education resulting from learning both in and outside the school, as contrasted with the results of specific courses in particular subject matter. The skills and knowledge measured are not only considered necessary to successful achievement in the normal secondary school courses, but they are assumed also to sample a core of knowledge necessary in a wide variety of vocational and social settings. The ITED have been accepted for over twenty years in a large number of schools throughout the United States as being good measures of such general educational outcomes.

In both studies, either the same tests, or accurately matched parallel forms of the same tests, were administered annually to the same students. This procedure gives a strict meaning to the term 'progress', which can really be accurately measured only by comparing increases in performance on the same set of tasks over a period of time.

Procedures

The mathematics study was carried out in Brisbane, Australia, using two samples, overlapping in time. The main sample consisted of 383 students from twelve secondary schools who were in grade 9 in 1961. Some 135 of these students provided a complete set of data through to grade 11. The second sample comprised 210 students from seven of the twelve schools who were in grade 11 in 1961, 83 of whom also provided complete data sets for grade 12 in 1962. Each school provided a single class of students, chosen in such a way that the final sample was as representative as possible in terms of sex, type of school attended, type of course taken and achievement in early grade 9.

A battery of twenty-three tests was administered in late July of each year of the study. Seven of the tests were achievement tests constructed with the assistance of a panel of teacher 'judges' in the process areas of routine skill and knowledge, understanding of mathematical concepts, and problem solving. The tests covered the content fields of arithmetic, algebra and geometry and were built from a very large set of items in such a way that all items had been judged by the panel of teachers to be good measures of what they thought were desirable outcomes of mathematics education. Thus, in a very real way, the tests might be thought of as reflecting the *goals* of mathematics teaching in Queensland. The final items of each test were also chosen to form a set whose difficulty and content gradually increased from that appropriate for grade 9 to that appropriate for grade 12.

The remaining tests of the battery form four groups and are described schematically in Table 18.1. Those in the first group test performance in tasks requiring what Inhelder and Piaget (1958) call 'formal operations', the thinking characteristic of the final stage in the development of logical thought. The second group contains three time honoured measures of 'g' or general intellectual ability, and the third, four tests based on a theory of mathematical processes due to Hamley (1934). The final group provides reference tests in the well-known verbal and numerical factors.

The various sets of results from the study provided the raw data for several types of factor analyses. Factor analysis is a procedure whereby a large set of test scores for a sample of subjects may be represented in terms of a few new hypothetical variables or 'common factors', together with a set of 'unique' components, one unique component specific to each test. Although factor analysis need not be used in this way, it has become accepted that these common factors may correspond to fundamental or underlying psychological variables. It is also possible to find for each student a score on each of these variables or factors. Thus, one thinks of

TABLE 18.1
Specifications of the Test Battery

Test	Group	Rationale	Materials	Time (min)	No. of Items	Re-liability*	Author
1 Combinations A	Piaget Operations	Combinatorial	N,† V, Symbols	20	30	.69	Investigator
2 Combinations B		Schema	N	8	25	.56	Investigator
3 Combinations C			N, V	30	30	.66	Investigator
4 Proportions		INRC group	N, Spatial	20	20	.62	Investigator
5 Reversibility A		Reversibility	N, Symbols	20	30	.70	Modified
6 Reversibility B		Operations	N, Symbols	30	30	.67	From Keats (1955)
7 Verbal Reas. A	g	Spearman's Educ-tion of Relations and Correlates	V, Analogies	10	19	.64	Investigator
8 Verbal Reas. B			V, Syllogisms	10	22	.64	Investigator
9 Raven's P.M.			Spatial	20	22	.67	Raven
10 Classifications A	Hamley Operations	Classification	N, Symbols	15	20	.55	Modified from Lee
11 Classifications B		Classification	Spatial	15	20	.44	Lee
12 Order		Seriation	N	15	21	.63	
13 Correspondences		Finding correspondences	N, Symbols	15	30	.65	
14 Mill Hill Vocab.	N, V† Reference	Synonyms	V	7	33	.77	
15 ACER Addn		Numerical speed and accuracy	N	5	140	.89	ACER
16 ACER Multn			N	5	160	.89	ACER
17 Algebra A	Mathematics Achievement	Concepts	N, Symbols	20	26	.72	Investigator
18 Geometry A			Spatial, N, V	20	23	.74	Investigator
19 Arithmetic A			N, V	20	19	.76	Investigator
20 Algebra B		Routine	Symbols, N	15	20	.70	Investigator
21 Arithmetic B		Processes	N	15	18	.64	Investigator
22 Algebra-Arithmetic		Problems	N, Symbols, V	30	19	.71	Investigator
23 Geometry B			Spatial, N	30	18	.68	Investigator

* Test-Retest reliability over a 12-month period

† N: Number-content; V: Verbal-content

the original test scores as coming about because each student has a 'score', or relative status, on each factor, while these factors, in turn, are of varying importance in performance on the original tests. The numbers which show just how much each factor contributes to each test are called factor loadings. For a further exposition of the analysis, see, for example, Thomson (1951).

An important preliminary result in the present study was that, irrespective of what grade the students were in or of whether they were to continue at secondary school for several years, or leave after one year, performance on the twenty-three tests could be largely accounted for by the same six factors, and the loadings on these factors were relatively constant for the different types of student. This means that one could speak generally of *the* factors of mathematical ability for this group of Queensland students, and it is on these six factors that the main arguments of the next section are based.

Complete descriptions of the nine ITED variables used in the second study are given in the test manual (1963). Shortened titles are used in Table 18.8. The complete results of annual ITED administrations throughout the state of Iowa were available for the years 1961 to 1965. A sample of forty schools, representative for size of school, but otherwise random, was chosen from all Iowa secondary schools in which the 1964 senior class had taken the test in each of the four years from their freshman year on. In each school forty seniors were picked at random, and as many of these as had complete ITED data were retained in the final sample of 999 cases. These data were cross validated with those from the 1965 seniors, with very close agreement for correlations and factor loadings.

The analytical technique used in this case differed from the mathematics study, the nine tests on four occasions being regarded as thirty-six variables. Details of the method may be found in Evans (1967a and b).

Development in Mathematical Ability

The loadings for the six factors which emerged from the mathematics study are given in Table 18.2. The factors may be described as follows.

Factor I *Numerical Facility*: Defined completely by the two speeded tests of automatic numerical facility, there is little doubt that this is the N factor found in many other studies. It is the most stable of all the factors found and appears to reflect a relatively permanent and well-developed skill, which, once minimum competence is reached, has only a small relationship with what is regarded as mathematics in secondary education. Indeed, its correlation with all but the arithmetic tests is of zero order.

Factor II *Verbal Comprehension*: This is the well-documented Verbal (V) factor of many studies, and is defined in the present study by the vocabulary and the two verbal reasoning tests. There is good evidence that it represents a skill of verbal recognition and comprehension rather than one of verbal reasoning.

Factor III *General Reasoning*: This factor correlates with all tests involving some form of reasoning, correlating highly with the 'Piaget' tests, the verbal reasoning tests, the achievement tests, and most highly with the Raven's Progressive Matrices, a test of intelligence. It is undoubtedly the same as, or similar to, Spearman's general intelligence, and the most important of all reasoning factors.

Factor IV *Mathematical Education*: This factor loaded strongly on all of the mathematics achievement tests, especially those of mechanical algebra and algebra concepts. It also loads highly on those other tests in the battery which have items phrased in mathematical terms or requiring any mathematical facility. In contrast, it has zero order loadings on such tests as the Raven's, the verbal reasoning tests, and the classification tests,

TABLE 18.2

Model 1 Factor Analysis: Sample 1, 1961-1963
Rotated Orthogonal Factor Loadings*

Tests	I (No.)	II (Verbal)	III (Reasoning)	IV (Math. Ed.)	V (Problems)	VI (Arith. Reas.)	h^2
1 Combinations A	25†	14	54†	28†	22	23	56
2 Combinations B	30†	−02	24	46†	23	33†	52
3 Combinations C	21	32†	53†	24	02	05	50
4 Proportions	−02	13	41†	31†	39†	32†	54
5 Reversibility A	13	21	41†	68†	03	13	73
6 Reversibility B	11	28†	44†	55†	16	24	65
7 Verbal Reas. A	05	57†	52†	18	08	08	64
8 Verbal Reas. B	12	38†	41†	12	19	29†	46
9 Raven's P.M.	08	05	69†	15	18	16	55
10 Classifications A	16	21	39†	17	08	26†	34
11 Classifications B	−04	10	31†	−01	21	01	15
12 Order	24	21	42†	44†	16	11	52
13 Correspondences	17	18	39†	48†	21	25†	55
14 Mill Hill Vocab.	19	55†	17	32†	16	09	50
15 ACER Addn	81†	04	19	20	09	05	75
16 ACER Multn	83†	12	06	17	04	01	73
17 Algebra Concepts	12	20	46†	67†	28†	03	81
18 Geom. Concepts	10	25†	52†	45†	37†	−01	69
19 Arith. Concepts	25†	27†	27†	54†	37†	35†	75
20 Mech. Algebra	13	17	44†	71†	08	04	78
21 Mech. Arithmetic	30†	24	20	46†	23	16	47
22 Alg. Ar. Problems	20	27†	39†	42†	48†	21	72
23 Geom. Problems	07	20	30†	53†	42†	04	60
Percentage Variance-Criteria	3.4	5.4	14.4	30.2	11.8	2.8	68.9
Percentage Variance-Total	8.5	6.8	16.8	17.4	5.4	3.5	61.9

* Decimal points omitted
† Loadings greater than or equal to .25

which appear to demand the perception of novel relationships. If the general reasoning factor represents an ability for new learning, the mathematics education factor represents an aspect of *past* learning which is independent of the former trait.

Factor V *Problem Solving*: Performance in the mathematics tests which require problem solving is only partly explained by the factors mentioned so far. In the case of the two 'problems' tests, and, to a lesser extent, in the case of the concepts tests, there is a third important factor which appears to be independent of intelligence as it is usually measured, which seems to stem rather from an ability to solve novel problems. It is as if, for really 'sticky' problems, just being 'intelligent' is not sufficient; some kind of creative or problem-solving flair is also involved.

Factor VI *Arithmetical Reasoning*: This last, rather unimportant factor, is involved in just those tests which are arithmetical or arithmetical-verbal in nature, and whose items require some reasoning for successful completion. This appears to be the kind of verbal reasoning taught in some primary schools to help students solve arithmetical problems. It 'works' for only certain kinds of problems, depends heavily on verbal cues and is likely to be used only in the kind of situation in which it was originally learnt.

When a student enters secondary school we might think of him as being subjected to two sets of forces. The first comes from the momentum of what he has been and now is, i.e., the sum total of his hereditary and environmental endowments. The other force comes from the new environment with which he is interacting. With the above description of the six factors, we here try to disentangle those effects due to the new environment, i.e., the secondary school, from those due to the personality the student brought to the secondary school with him.

This may be done in part by examining the pattern of school means in each of the three years. If the patterns of means are highly conforming, this implies that the schools are having little effect on changes in the factor. If not, the schools are themselves contributing to individual differences in rate of development.

Before doing this, we examine the correlations between the same factor on successive occasions to see if there are any factors for which there are genuine changes in the relative status of students from occasion to occasion. That is, we wish to know for what factors the relative superiority of some students definitely appears to change.

Table 18.3 shows the correlations between the *estimated* factor scores, which, because they are estimates, are somewhat unreliable. The five per cent confidence limit shown is the possible lower limit of between-occasion correlations which might be expected were the *true* factor scores perfectly correlated from occasion to occasion, taking into account the unreliability of the estimates. There is no clear evidence of instability in any factor except factor IV, the education factor. In this case, the results show quite plainly that the ordering of the students on the true factor scores suffered a definite change from year to year.

TABLE 18.3

**Correlations between Estimated Scores on the Same
Factor on Different Occasions**

Occasions Compared	I (N)	II (V)	III (GR)	IV (ME)	V (PR)	VI (AR)
			Factors			
1961-1962	.76	.59	.75	.59*	.52	.60
1961-1963	.78	.64	.66	.50*	.45	.41
1962-1963	.84	.64	.68	.66*	.60	.55
Lower 5% confidence limit	.75	.46	.59	.69	.43	.34

TABLE 18.4

**Ranks of School Means on the General Reasoning
Factor for Various Occasions***

Year	11	09	12	04	05	02	08	10
				School Number				
1961	1	2	3	4	5	6	7	8
1962	1	2	3	4	5	6	8	7
1963	1	3	2	4	6	7	5	8

$$W = .98$$

*Only eight of the schools had sufficient of the original sample remaining in 1963 for the means to be reliable.

TABLE 18.5

**Ranks of School Means on the Education
Factor for Various Occasions**

Year	02	09	10	05	12	08	04	11
				School Number				
1961	1	2	3	4	5	6	7	8
1962	2	5	4	6	1	3	7	8
1963	2	1	3	8	6	5	4	7

$$W = .60$$

It can be demonstrated further that this upsetting of the order of merit is closely associated with the school attended. In Table 18.4 are shown the ranks of the school means on the general reasoning factor for the three occasions of testing. In Table 18.5, corresponding results are shown for the mathematics education factor. It is evident that, in the former case, agreement from year to year is high, the coefficient of concordance being .96. In the latter case, the coefficient of concordance is relatively low

FIGURE 18.1

*Mean Factor Scores for Boys and Girls
at Various Dropout Levels*

Mean Factor Scores

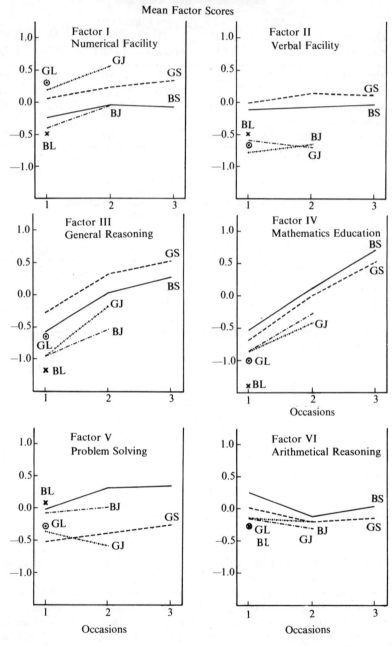

(.60), and there are fairly large alterations in the ranks of the means from occasion to occasion. With some confidence, it may be asserted that the mathematics education factor reflects those aspects of performance which teachers are both able to manipulate, and deliberately do manipulate. By contrast, teachers appear to have much less influence on relative performance in the other factors. In these, a student would probably improve about as well whatever school he attended, and by whatever teacher he was taught.

It will probably surprise few readers that schools themselves are sources of individual differences between students. However, the finding is not as at first appears. In considering the development of all students in an educational system, two types of change or growth may occur. First, there is the kind in which the students change in such a way as to preserve their previous ranks or status in the group. Some special cases of this are those in which nobody changes at all, or in which everybody's score alters by exactly the same amount, or everyone's score alters by an amount proportional to his original score, and so on.

The second kind of change occurs when some students develop in such a way as to alter their rank order in the group. Gross changes of this second type are usually *not* expected. The changes in the mathematics education factor are, however, changes of this second type.

The nature of the various kinds of individual differences in development and their relationship with gross school effects is more clearly grasped when one considers the mean development of various types of students on the six factors. The graphs of Figure 18.1 show the mean factor scores for the various 'drop-out' groups of both boys and girls. Membership of the 'drop-out' groups was determined according to when the students left secondary school, i.e., at the end of grade 9 (Group L), at the end of grade 10 (Group J), or at the end of grade 12 (Group S). A condensed summary of the information contained in the graphs may be made in the following way:

Mean Increase in Factor Scores

		Little or no increase	Large increase
Stability of Factor Scores	High	Numerical Facility Verbal Facility Problem Solving Arithmetical Reasoning	General Reasoning
	Low		Mathematical Education

In four of the six factors there is little or no change at all, either of the first or second type, although, with those students continuing on to grade 12, there is a slight increase in scores on the problem-solving factor, and between grades 9 and 10 there is some improvement in numerical facility. The education factor has both large increases and low stability, and this latter characteristic is almost certainly tied up with school differences. It is also certain that the large improvements made in the scores on this factor are due to secondary schooling. What of the increases in the ability represented by the general reasoning factor? Were the twelve secondary schools uniformly, and all in like manner, causing increases in this ability over the period studied, or were these increases inherent in the prior personalities of the students? Unfortunately, this study stops short of answering this question. It may be that the general fare of secondary education, whatever the school is like, offers a common thrust in the development of this kind of reasoning. More likely, however, it is something which emerges from the large common environment of things and ideas which goes with our type of society, together with the developmental momentum of prior experience and hereditary equipment.

When one examines the graphs, some striking differences between the means for boys and girls are apparent. In the period of the study, a much smaller percentage of girls than boys continued at secondary school into the senior years, grades 11 and 12, and more girls dropped out from school at the end of grades 8 and 9. Consequently, the girls were increasingly becoming more 'selected' than the boys. There is good evidence from this study, and other studies, that those students who drop out from school are those who, in general, have been performing relatively badly in their school work. Dropouts usually also perform less well on standardized intelligence tests. The graphs for factors III and IV tend to demonstrate this point. Because more girls dropped out than boys, one would expect the girls who remained behind to have a higher mean intelligence than the boys, merely because the girls represent the cream, and the boys do not. This fact is illustrated by the graph for factor III. The general reasoning ability of the girls is superior to that of the boys for every group. One would not ordinarily expect girls to be any more intelligent than boys on the average, so that we may attribute the sex differences of factor III to the community practices with regard to girls leaving school, or to the sampling procedures used in the study.

We note, too, that girls are clearly superior in numerical facility. This is probably a true *sex* difference, over and above the initial sampling differences. What is important is that in spite of the initial selectivity of the girls, the boys are a little superior in the mathematics education factor, and very much superior in the problem-solving factor. There appears to be a major difference between the cognitive styles of boys and girls.

It is not at all easy to explain these sex differences. One kind of explanation is in terms of biological differences, the other in terms of differences in the ways our kind of culture treats boys and girls; that is, how they are reared from infancy on, and what we expect from them. This author takes the 'cultural differences' point of view. Perhaps women and girls are expected to conform more closely to social customs than are men and boys. 'Conforming' girls would certainly tend to work harder to achieve their teachers' expectations in learning number facts and skills than 'nonconforming' boys. The same tendency to conform, to keep to the learnt routines, may well be a disadvantage in problem solving where imagination and looking for new ways seem to be required. Perhaps the changing role of girls in the 'sixties will bring about a change in the pattern.

While such explanations are attractive they are highly speculative, and the terms used will need much clearer definition and the deductions will require a rigorous experimental examination, before any such theory of sex differences is acceptable.

The other notable feature of the graphs is with reference to dropouts. While, for most of the factors, the students who leave school prematurely are inferior to those who continue, this is clearly not the case for the problem-solving factor. In this case, those who left school at the end of grade 9 were somewhat superior to the rest in terms of their mean score, although, by grade 10, the position was reversed.

Performance in the problem-solving tests and scores on the problem-solving factor were found to be excellent predictors of success in first-year university mathematics and important correlates of success in the matriculation mathematics tests. It was apparently less important in the early secondary school as judged by its correlation with success in an external examination at the end of grade 10, and, as shown here, by its lack of correlation with whether or not students finish secondary school.

We complete this section by making several important points about individual differences which have been demonstrated by the data presented.

(a) Individual differences arise from a variety of sources. At any particular stage of schooling we can think of a person as having a set of traits or characteristics, often measurable, which he possesses by virtue of his previous life history or because of genetic makeup. In the present case, the numerical facility factor, the verbal factor, the general reasoning factor and the problem-solving factor are clearly of this kind. Modification of these traits and new sources of individual differences may be, and usually are, present in the current environment. The modification may be of a kind which preserves the subject's previous rank or status on the trait, as with the general reasoning factor, or it may genuinely alter the pattern of individual differences as with the mathematical education factor.

(b) The school itself, or, more precisely, the classroom and the teacher, can be an important source of individual differences. Some human traits can be modified in the classroom. The point is made now, in the light of some evidence, to reiterate the distinction made in the second paragraph of this chapter. The teacher must teach for optimal development but he should not too readily assume that any given child's maximum is a low one. There is a danger that increasing use of psychometric prediction will lead to a kind of circularity of expectations. A student might too readily be judged by the accident of his first experiences or his first contact with a testing programme.

(c) There appear to be some very stable, difficult to change, types of individual characteristics. Differences between the sexes and differences in problem-solving ability are two examples. At this time the most help the research findings can give to the teacher is to make him aware of them. One hopes that continuing research will reveal the sources of these differences. One also hopes that continuing action research in the classroom will, in fact, find some chink in the armour of unchangeability that such traits wear.

(d) Of the vast range of individual differences only a few are relevant to what is judged as success in school. What is judged as success, however, is largely a cultural, or even community, decision. Sometimes these judgements are quite irrational. In the study outlined here, it could be shown that official and rewarded success in early secondary mathematics had little or no problem-solving component. In the senior school and at university it did. Some students who could satisfy the early goals could not satisfy the later, and in some cases the reverse applied although, because of the selection procedures, most students who could not satisfy the early goals were 'turned off' a career in mathematics.

School subjects, whether 'traditional' or 'new', tend to be considered in terms of content. What distinguishes the 'new mathematics' from the old is much more the terminology and content than the behaviours of the students. Yet the main sources of individual differences in mathematics are behavioural ones. One might ask that goals in the teaching of a school subject be arrived at by considerations of community needs and realistic goals of student development as well as the content objectives of subject areas.

With reference to the second, there is the possibility suggested by Guilford (1959), that when new types of individual differences are discovered, these be studied to see if nurturing the trait would either improve the development of a large number of students, or, alternatively, provide a pool of skills of use to the community.

General Educational Development

The data of the second study differed in several ways from that of the first. The performances tested were such as lead to conclusions on general educational development rather than on learning in a specific school study. It was accepted in the second study that adolescents do not all develop in the same fashion, while much of the first was devoted to demonstrating just this point. The focus of interest in the Iowa investigation was the different types of growth curves themselves. Again, it was necessary to use a particular mathematical model properly to analyse the data. It was supposed that for a group of tests like the ITED a number of perhaps changing traits are involved, different traits being more or less important for different tests and at different times, the subjects possessing each of these different traits or growth factors to different degrees. In mathematical terms the model is expressed as follows.

$$x_{kji} = (b_j + c_{kj}) + (a_{kj1}f_{1i} + a_{kj2}f_{2i} + \dots a_{kjm}f_{mi}) + (e_{kji})$$

The quantity x_{kji} is the score which person i makes on test j on occasion k.

The terms b_j and c_{kj} are quantities which do *not* change from person to person, but merely reflect the arbitrary nature of the zero point with regard to test scores, and, in the case of c_{kj}, the fact that for at least some tests there may be a component on which everyone's score changes by the same amount. The term e_{kji} does vary from person to person, but such terms are meant to indicate the extent to which data departs from theory, and are hopefully small.

The really important terms are those like a_{kjp}, the primary factor pattern loadings, and f_{pi}, where p is the particular factor being considered. The former indicates how important factor p is in performance on test j on occasion k; the latter, f_{pi}, is the score of person i on factor p. The value of the various a_{kjp} are given in Table 18.6. In the present case, terms like a_{kjp} can be further subdivided as follows:

$$a_{kjp} = u_{kp} v_{jp}$$

where the u_{kp} indicates how factor p changes from occasion to occasion. Thus, if as k increases, i.e., for later occasions, u_{kp} increases, this indicates that the overall importance of factor p and the extent of individual differences in it are increasing. Similarly v_{jp} shows how important factor p is to test j compared with other factors. Let us call the u_{kp} values growth factor loadings, to be found in Table 18.7, and the v_{jp} the test factor loadings, shown in Table 18.8.

TABLE 18.7

Growth Factor Loadings on Various Occasions

$Occ.^n$	1	2	3	4
Factor I	.35	.43	.46	.51
II	.40	.40	.47	.49
III	.44	.46	.44	.41
IV	.43	.44	.45	.43

The primary factors I and II of Table 18.6 are quite highly correlated, meaning that there is some overlap in nature between the trait represented on factor I and that represented on factor II. There are no other inter-factor correlations. With this in mind, an inspection of Table 18.8 shows that the first two factors define two correlated, but distinct, achievement variables. Factor I loads on tests which are all concerned with measuring knowledge of facts and principles in natural science, arithmetic, social studies, and, to some extent, reasoning in these areas. Factor II is a 'literary' variable with high loadings on tests involving correctness of

TABLE 18.6

Primary Factor Pattern Loadings: 1964 Sample, ITED Scores

Factor	I				II				III				IV			
Occ.[n]																
Test	1	2	3	4	1	2	3	4	1	2	3	4	1	2	3	4
1	.58	.71	.78	.84	.32	.29	.36	.38	.46	.52	.52	.46	.29	.37	.39	.39
2	.93	1.02	1.05	1.10	.22	.13	.15	.16	.37	.33	.29	.23	.45	.44	.41	.42
3	−.20	−.28	−.23	−.25	1.12	1.23	1.29	1.33	.36	.42	.42	.39	−.03	−.06	−.06	−.10
4	.53	.73	.82	.94	.30	.28	.30	.31	.31	.37	.36	.35	−.11	−.21	−.20	−.19
5	.39	.53	.55	.58	.21	.24	.34	.46	.79	.78	.76	.69	.22	.27	.25	.25
6	.41	.59	.59	.67	.32	.30	.46	.46	.67	.70	.65	.63	.18	.19	.17	.17
7	.11	.18	.22	.24	.62	.60	.75	.77	.68	.72	.69	.68	.36	.40	.44	.36
8	.14	.16	.15	.21	.84	.89	.95	.96	.45	.50	.46	.41	.55	.57	.58	.58
9	.29	.27	.31	.31	.71	.79	.91	.92	.37	.40	.34	.30	.18	.19	.20	.19

Correlations Among Primary Factors

Factor	I	II	III	IV
I	1.00	.70	−.06	−.07
II	.70	1.00	.13	−.08
III	−.06	.13	1.00	−.04
IV	−.07	−.08	−.04	1.00

TABLE 18.8

Test Multipliers for Growth Factors: Factor Pattern

Test	Factor			
	I	II	III	IV
1 Basic Social Concepts	*1.66*	0.77	*1.12*	0.83
2 Background in Natural Sciences	*2.34*	0.38	0.70	*0.99*
3 Correctness of Expression	−0.54	*2.85*	0.91	−0.14
4 Quantitative Thinking	*1.72*	0.68	0.80	−0.41
5 Interpretation: Social Science	*1.18*	0.71	*1.72*	0.57
6 Interpretation: Natural Science	*1.29*	0.88	*1.51*	0.41
7 Interpretation: Literature	0.43	*1.56*	*1.59*	0.89
8 General Vocabulary	0.38	*2.09*	*1.04*	*1.30*
9 Use of Sources of Information	0.67	*1.91*	0.80	0.43

expression, vocabulary, literary interpretation and the 'sources' test. Success in this last test depends on an acquaintance with, or a working knowledge of, a wide variety of source materials, such as dictionary and encyclopaedia, implying that students successful in the test are those most likely to read widely. These two factors might tentatively be named *Achievement: Scientific and Social Knowledge* and *Achievement: Literary Knowledge*. It is easy to speculate that the kinds of threads which connect them are the same kinds of educational and general reasoning factors postulated in the previous study.

Factor III loads on those tests where reading comprehension is needed and appears to be a verbal reasoning factor. Factor IV is a not very important source of individual differences and might be regarded as a general knowledge factor, loading, as it does, on tests in which knowledge might most easily be gained outside the classroom. Suitable names to describe these two factors are *Verbal Reasoning* and *General Knowledge*.

The loadings of Table 18.7, the growth factors, show how the contributions which the factors made to individual differences increased with time. Both factors III and IV showed a high degree of stability in this respect.

In factors I and II, by contrast, there is evidence of increasing variability and growth. While the data from the second study are much less detailed than that of the first, it seems that we are again observing marked developmental changes in some areas and little change in other areas. The type of analysis used in the Iowa study produces factors on which there is no change in factor scores from year to year. Instead, all changes are reflected in the factor loadings, hence the name growth factors. If a student had high 'scores' in factor II and factor III and a low 'score' in factor I, he would do fairly well in the quantitative thinking test (number 4) in its first administration, since, according to Table 18.6, the loading for factor I, test 4, occasion 1 (.53), is not much higher than the corresponding values for factors II and III (.30 and .31). By the fourth administration, however, the factor I loading has nearly doubled to .94, while the other two have remained nearly the same at .31 and .35. The contribution of factor I to the variance of test 4 is now about nine times that of either factors II or III, thus, our student in the example above would do relatively much worse on the last occasion in the quantitative thinking test than on the first occasion. The existence of growth factors with different gradients or different rates of growth implies that some students will suffer changes in relative status in some tests.

In a different way, we have here uncovered the same kind of effect as that observed with the mathematics education factor in the Brisbane study. Educational tasks call for complex performances. The tasks are not homogeneous over time, but can be conceptualized as having components which are homogeneous. Different students improve on different components at different rates. This, combined with the fact that some components become relatively more important, and some less, as time goes on, implies that we must observe what appears to be an uneven growth for some students in some tasks.

The evidence from both studies is that there are some areas for which the apparent uneven growth is more marked than others. We can speculate—the evidence is not quite detailed enough to provide a strong conclusion—that those areas of instability, that is, of changes in individual differences, are just those areas in which teachers are concentrating their major efforts of teaching, and this area seems to be mainly that of new understandings and new routine skills in mathematics and in school subjects generally. The areas teachers don't alter much at the secondary level are the well-established skills of verbal comprehension and numerical facility, nor do they appear to develop or make use of problem-solving performance, that is, the solution by students of genuine novel problems.

Environmental Factors in the Development of Cognitive Performances

Let us make an attempt at explanation of individual differences by building up a diagram which attempts to depict what a student is like, in terms of cognitive abilities, at any given time in his life. In such a diagram one must indicate not only the different broad types of individual traits, but also how they came to develop, and how they might develop in the future. Before Figure 18.2 can be understood the variable called intelligence must be very carefully defined.

Intelligence is commonly conceived as a general level of intellectual functioning (e.g., see Hebb, 1949) but we choose here a more specific definition. Over the past twenty years, the study of intellectual development has been dominated by the work of Jean Piaget and his co-workers at Geneva. According to his theory, intelligence develops by a series of adaptations. The adaptation known as *accommodation* occurs when the person's thought structures are changed by a new sensory input. That known as *assimilation* occurs when the new information itself is changed or altered by the person to fit in with his existing structure of knowledge. These ideas have their analogies in biology. The intake of food results in both a change in the food as it is assimilated and a change in the body structures as they accommodate to the food. The psychological processes of assimilation and accommodation are obviously an interaction with the environment. On the basis of his data, Piaget describes an ongoing developmental pattern in the state of the 'thought structures' themselves; a pattern which may depend partly on environment, partly on an inherited developmental capacity. Intellectual development, in Piaget's terms, is a progression through various stages. There are, of course, no abrupt changes but, rather, the stages merge into one another. For every person, the thinking characteristic of each stage is different from that of other stages. The essence of the difference is not only a difference in the amount of knowledge, but a difference in the way this knowledge is organized. Some aspects of knowledge are always more important than others; in particular, those aspects which enable the person to adapt to an environment which may be either novel or familiar. The more developed the person, the more control he will have over his environment. The key to the organization, according to Piaget, is in sets of interrelated thought structures, concepts or schemata. Some of these concepts in adults are very general and highly integrated. In young children, many of the structures do not exist, those that do are much less connected, and the kinds of concepts are different. The reader is referred to one of the many references for further explanation of this point (e.g., Flavell, 1963; Peel, 1960; Piaget, 1963).

For our present purpose, a definition of intelligence, we note that each person can be considered as having a particular set of thought structures which at any time impose a kind of structural possibility on his performance and achievement. Leaving Piaget's theory, let us now subtract from this total structural possibility any and all knowledge which is too particularized or too specialized or too esoteric; that is, any knowledge which is not part of the *general* social and physical environment in which the person lives. We are left with only those concepts which everyone has had a chance to develop. It is this remainder which seems to come closest, in a theoretical sense, to what most students of individual differences would regard as intelligence.

According to this theoretical position, intelligence is essentially *knowledge*. One may even want to go further and speak of this knowledge in terms of stimulus-response patterns, but this kind of reduction is not at present necessary. We will assume, with Piaget, that the *development* of cognitive structures is an inherited biological function. On the other hand, the *content* of the knowledge or information organized in the structures is very much environmentally determined. We also assume that the traditional intelligence tests, almost by definition, call into play some of the culture-common structures about which we have been speaking.

We now make an important distinction. *Structural possibility is not the same as performance*. A direct one-to-one correspondence should not be inferred between how a person performs on particular tests and the stage of mental development he has reached. This warning is suggested by data like that from the Brisbane study. Any test necessarily contains items with a particular content, and this content will not always be as culturally common as we have supposed. This last statement is fairly obvious, but there is, however, a possibly more important way in which people perform at a level less than their 'structural potential'.

Concepts are supposedly formed by abstractions from the environment and Piaget would call this process of representing the environment in the brain 'internalization'. It is probable that when one has to deal with most of the everyday contingencies of his environment that the internalizations and structures used closely correspond with the arrangement of stimuli in the environment. Consider, for example, a student who has just left an interview in an unfamiliar building and who is now making his way outside. On most occasions the set of responses learnt in such situations, and presumably associated in particular groupings, will be sufficient. In some situations, such a set of already available 'usual' responses will fail. The person will have to make new 'unusual' responses if he is to reach the front door. 'Problems' which one has to solve may thus be of two types— either congruent with the predominant or most used concepts which the person possesses, or non-congruent with these concepts. In the latter case, some reorganization of one's perceptions, or of the concept structure, appears to be necessary. This same dichotomy probably operates at all levels of concept development. If it does, it is now convenient to differentiate further the notion of intelligence. We use the terms 'structural intelligence' and 'problem intelligence' to distinguish between the two aspects. Structural intelligence is that which is immediately available for the performance of those tasks in which the stimulus arrangement bears a direct correspondence to the structure of the available responses. Problem intelligence is the facilitating process which brings about that reorganization which allows the application of structural intelligence in tasks where the stimulus arrangement is novel, that is, in problems.

We are now ready to construct the diagram promised at the beginning of this section.

Many of the relationships depicted in Figure 18.2 have already been suggested. The centrepiece is the *knowledge* possessed by the individual, which is here given the unusually broad meaning of the sum-total of all the 'cognitive' responses which the person is capable of making. The top part of the diagram indicates that this knowledge is derived from the environment, whether 'special' or 'common', with the aid of the inherited functions of the person. As a rough analogy, one might compare the situation here with that in a series of machines which, starting with the raw materials, finally manufacture a complex article such as an automobile engine. The machines have particular functions, corresponding to inherited characteristics, and the raw materials used have particular properties, corresponding with the environment. Change the raw materials or change the functions of the machinery and you do not get the expected products. The analogy falls far short of perfect, however, because, unlike the factory, the person may adapt to his environment. Unlike the factory, too, he is not born with all of his final processing functions. These also develop, and they develop in interaction with the environment. For this reason, the diagram shows a complex interaction between environment and heredity, an interaction whose precise nature is likely to be discovered in only the very far distant future.

FIGURE 18.2

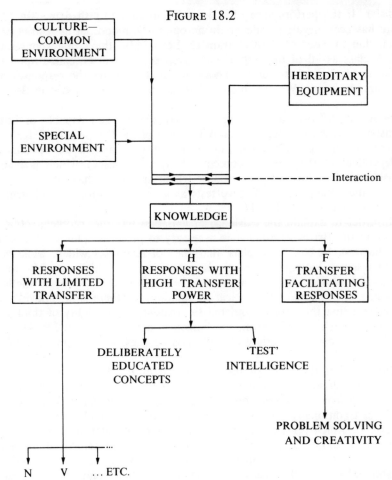

In the lower part of the diagram are the three types of responses described earlier. The division is made in terms of the 'transfer power' of the responses. What is meant by this is most readily seen by considering the learning task represented by the following pattern.

	First Task	Second Task
(1)	B	A
(2)		A

In case (1) the subject is required to perform task A, not ever having performed A before, but having previously learnt task B. In case (2) the subject is required to perform task A for the first time, without having previously learnt B. If the performance of A is improved by having previously learnt B, as compared with case (2), then there has been positive transfer. If the performance of A is worse in case (1) than in case (2) there has been negative transfer. In an optimistic mood, let us restrict our discussion to cases of positive transfer. Let us also think of responses in the A class as all of the responses a given person will be called upon to make in his immediate future. Those in the B class are the responses he has already learnt. We are interested in the transfer power of the B-type responses.

Some of the B-type knowledge is fairly specific and capable of little transfer. This is the category of box L. Some of the B-type knowledge has extremely high generality—so much that it may appear to be almost independent of the kind of content (A-type responses) which is being considered. It is this type of response which appears to have been sought out by the makers of intelligence tests as a good measure of intelligence. This is the category of box H.

In order to explain the existence of variables like the 'problem-solving' factor in the Brisbane study it is necessary to place an additional box in the diagram. In box F we place that class of responses which, while not in themselves having any particular place on the 'high-transfer—low-transfer' dimension, do facilitate transfer. How this occurs, or even whether it occurs, is of course a theoretical speculation, but there is much evidence to suggest that the ability is related to creativity or flexibility of thinking. Using Dunker's (1945) term, the person is able to broaden his 'search-field', or increase the variety of responses he tries, in attempting to solve the problem.

For each of the types of response in boxes L, H, F, there are wide ranges of individual differences. The top of the diagram reminds us that these arise from an interaction of heredity and environment. Intelligence, as it has traditionally been measured, is that part of box H, and sometimes of box L, which remains when the environmental determinants are held constant at those common to all of the people being compared. Finding this lowest common denominator for a homogeneous culture like 'urban Australian' or 'middle-class U.S.A.' has been difficult enough. It is much more difficult when different cultures are involved; as, for example, in the recent building of the 'Queensland Test' which is meant to measure the intelligence of Australian Aborigines and white Australians on the same scale.

These important points must be emphasized about the L, H, and F cells of the diagram. First, the distinctions between the types of responses are fairly arbitrary, and many responses will be marginal rather than clearly belonging to one category or another. Second, with any single response, there are likely to be both genetic determinants as well as environmental determinants of its nature and quality, and of whether or not the response exists at all.

For box H, a distinction is made between concepts arising from deliberate education or individual educational opportunities, and those arising from the kinds of learning opportunities open to everyone in a particular society, i.e., the intelligence commonly measured by tests. This distinction is clearly a matter of convenience for measurement rather than a basic one. Piaget's theory indicates that a given single person will tend to achieve the whole range of concepts which there is opportunity for *him* to acquire, each in much the same sequence, depending on the nature and complexity of the concept. For example, the concept of 'proportion' seems to emerge in a particular child at about the same time for a vast variety of situations. We might now extrapolate from Piaget's theory to argue that, given a number of children with precisely equal learning opportunities and experiences, that the rate of acquiring concepts or of passing through the Piaget stages is an individual parameter depending on biological or genetic intelligence only. Thus it is that in measuring intelligence, an attempt must be made to hold the environment, i.e., learning opportunities, constant, by restricting the test items to situations with which all members of the population for which the test is intended will have an equal environmental advantage.

The evidence supplied by such workers as Bloom (1964), suggests that these attempts may always be much less than successful. Inequalities in the environments of young children may have permanent, possibly irreversible, effects on measured or 'test' intelligence.

The question whether 'intelligence', as it has been operationally defined here, is a single variable, has been hotly debated. (*See, for example,* McNemar, 1964, Vernon, 1961, and Guilford, 1967.) It is certain, however, that there are a number of cognitive 'abilities' which do not correlate at all with the single general intelligence score provided by any one test, or with the general reasoning factor from various factor analyses. Such traits are illustrated by the verbal and numerical factors which have emerged from a great number of factor studies. Individual differences in these traits presumably also arise from an interaction of environment and inherited characteristics. It may be that the biological mechanisms which enable the person to acquire various types of skills are not all equally efficient. It may also be that children growing up not only meet environments of differing overall quality, but that within each child's experience there are differing opportunities for learning various types of skills. However they come about, individual levels in traits such as verbal comprehension and numerical facility seem to become crystallized in the primary school. It seems that there is very little change in status or level during adolescence. The same appears to be true of what we have termed 'problem intelligence', which grows less than 'structural intelligence', although for the latter there is little change in relative status.

Catering for Individual Differences

How to cater for individual differences among students has come to be accepted as one of the major problems to be faced in classroom teaching. How it is tackled is dependent on two things: first, whether the particular attribute has any importance in the achievement of educational goals, and, second, whether the amount of the attribute possessed by a particular student can be modified.

The action to be taken in the first case seems obvious, but there is a clear need to define the educational goals in such a way as to determine relevance. The results reported in the mathematics study, for example, suggest that ability in numerical computation over and above a certain minimum has little importance for performance in mathematics generally, but it may be important in other fields, and of vital importance in certain occupations.

The second condition is not so simple. If the trait is both relevant and unmodifiable, the appropriate educational procedure entails the offering of differentiated courses of study suitable to a student's level of ability, and streaming would be both justifiable and desirable as soon as the attribute can be reliably measured. If the trait is modifiable, a different course of action seems to be required. This would again entail differential teaching, but the objectives would be different, being more towards improvement in the trait. The evidence available from this study suggests some courses of action and several lines of research with respect to these questions. Two kinds of modification have been observed. The first is concerned with increase in score over time. For both those who left school at the end of the junior year and those continuing to the senior year in the Brisbane study, there were large annual mean increases in both the mathematics education factor and the general reasoning factor. For the number factor, there were small, but significant, increases between the first and second occasion for both groups. Only those who continued to senior showed any increases in the problem-solving factor, but in this case the increases were small and there were extensive overlaps with sex differences. Boys who left at the end of first year scored nearly as well in this factor as continuing students did in their final year.

The second kind of modification occurred mainly in the education factor scores. In this case the relative status of students changed from year to year.

This evidence suggests that the abilities underlying the mathematics education factor are both relevant and modifiable, and that teaching aimed at understanding of principles as well as technical proficiency is likely to have some success with all groups of students. There would still need to be ability grouping, but this would be on the basis of present performance in mathematics, and the differences in teaching methods based on type of presentation and rate of progress, not differences in behavioural aims.

The main difficulty with this argument is that it assumes mathematical performance to be a linear composite of the underlying abilities. Within the restricted range of ability shown by those who proceed to the senior year, or even to the junior year, this may be the case. It is likely, however, that real excellence at one extreme, and the ability to make any headway at the other, are more dependent on some kind of multiple cut-off model. That is to say, a minimum level on abilities such as those underlying the general reasoning and problem-solving factors is probably necessary. This cannot be shown from the present analysis in which a linear model is assumed. It points to a necessary line of research.

What are the prospects of modification in the general reasoning and problem-solving abilities, apart from the 'natural' increases that appear to be independent of teaching style? The first point to note is that problem-solving abilities do not seem to be exploited by teachers. This result is supported by work such as that of Getzels and Jackson (1962) and Torrance (1962). While there is again some risk in arguing from the linear model, the results of the present study suggest that, if students were given more opportunities to solve suitable problems as a means to the development of concepts, rather than as applications of inadequately conceptualized verbalizations, otherwise slow-learning children might have increased opportunities for success. Such participation and success would have clear importance for motivation, and, of course, there would be gains for the 'bright student' also.

The literature abounds with prescriptions for increasing problem-solving ability, but there are few reports of experimental studies under classroom conditions. Unfortunately, most of the new programmes in secondary mathematics have been conducted without control groups. Corman (1958), in reviewing the available research, was able to claim, at that time, that accurate experimentation and interpretation of results would have to wait for a clearer delineation of significant variables. This still seems to be the case. In a more recent review by Getzels (1964), reports of actual experiments were still few and the results conflicting.

Summary

In this chapter, an attempt has been made to define the relationship between environmental events and inherited traits so far as individual differences in the classroom are concerned. There has been no attempt to enter into the nature versus nurture argument. Rather, evidence and arguments have been presented to show what is meant by terms like ability and intelligence, and just what part the environment plays in their determination.

The model suggested supposes that, at any stage of his development, each secondary school student has some traits which have crystallized and others which are emerging. Our present state of knowledge constrains the author merely to emphasize this point in the hope that, being aware of it, the teacher may gain some advantage from the knowledge in ordering activities and experiences for his students.

The evidence suggests important lines of research. There is a need to locate the really important kinds of individual differences, to specify these as mental processes or operations. For each important trait we need evidence of the extent to which it can be varied by learning. The science of medicine has proceeded by either utilizing or 'getting round' natural law in order to overcome what seemed to be natural limitations. In education we have become so wedded to the idea of a 'natural' ceiling on student performances that we have barely bothered to investigate the alternatives.

We have been too much concerned with prediction and too little with achieving a desired effect or state. What are those skills which facilitate problem solving? Can they be improved by teaching? How dependent is this type of learning on the social interaction between pupil and teacher?

References

Bloom, B. S., 1964: *Stability and Change in Human Characteristics.* John Wiley & Sons, Inc., New York.

Corman, B. R., 1958: Learning II, Problem solving and related topics. *Review of Educational Research*, 28, 459.

Duncker, Karl, 1945: On problem solving. *Psychological Monographs*, 58 (whole no. 270).

Evans, G. T., 1967a: Factor analytical treatment of growth data. *Multivariate Behavioral Research*, 2, 109-134.

Evans, G. T., 1967b: Growth factor analysis of the Iowa tests of educational development. *Journal of Educational Measurement*, 4, 179-190.

Evans, G. T., 1967c: Patterns and development of the mathematical performance of secondary school students. *Australian Journal of Education*, 11, 235-250.

Flavell, J. H., 1963: *The Developmental Psychology of Jean Piaget.* D. Van Nostrand & Co. Inc., Princeton, N.J.

Getzels, J. W., 1964: Creative thinking, problem solving and instruction. In E. R. Hilgard (Ed.), *Theories of Learning and Instruction. NSSE Yearbook*, LXIII, Pt I, University of Chicago Press, Chicago, Ill.

Getzels, J. W. and Jackson, P. W., 1962: *Creativity and Intelligence: Explorations with Gifted Children.* John Wiley & Sons, Inc., New York.

Guilford, J. P., 1959: Three faces of intellect, *American Psychologist*, 14, 469-479.

Guilford, J. P., 1967: *The Nature of Human Intelligence.* The Macmillian Company, New York.

Hamley, H. R., 1934: Relational and functional thinking in mathematics. *9th Yearbook. National Council of Teachers of Mathematics.* Teachers College, Columbia University, New York.

Hebb, D. O., 1949: *The Organization of Behavior.* John Wiley & Sons, Inc., New York.

Inhelder, Barbel and Piaget, J., 1958: *The Growth of Logical Thinking.* Routledge and Kegan Paul, London.

Iowa Tests of Educational Development, 1963: *How to Use The Test Results.* Science Research Associates, Chicago, Ill.

McNemar, Q., 1964: Lost: Our Intelligence? Why? *American Psychologist*, 19, 871-882.

Peel, E. A., 1960: *The Pupil's Thinking.* Oldbourne, London.

Piaget, J., 1963: The genetic approach to the psychology of thought. *Journal of Educational Psychology*, 102, 195-201.

Thomson, G. H., 1951: *The Factorial Analysis of Human Ability* (5th edn). Houghton Mifflin Co., Boston, Mass.

Torrance, E. P., 1962: *Guiding Creative Talent.* Prentice-Hall Inc., Englewood Cliffs, N.J.

Vernon, P. E., 1961: *The Structure of Human Abilities* (2nd edn). Methuen, London.

19

Some Effects of Textbooks on Learning of Mathematics

K. F. Collis

Two of the most significant advances in education during the last decade have been the definition of objectives in behavioural terms and the development of curricula which, it is hoped, will contribute to the achievement of these objectives. The Taxonomies of Educational Objectives (Bloom *et al.*, 1956; Krathwohl *et al.*, 1964) are probably the best known examples of the first, and the curricula designed by the Physical Science Study Committee and the Biological Sciences Curriculum Study are outstanding examples of the second.

Both of these advances are very important, but in the absence of appropriate theories of learning and teaching they are in danger of nullification. The study reported here was undertaken in order to contribute to knowledge on how children learn and how teachers should teach to facilitate effective learning. It is focused upon the teaching of mathematics in grade 8 (first-year secondary) classes of Queensland and was made possible by the introduction in 1964 of a new mathematics syllabus aimed at broadening the educational experiences of the students and at developing the kind of cognitive objectives outlined by Bloom in the first of the Taxonomies. The introduction of this new syllabus was followed by the publication of two textbooks, both of which introduced students to the appropriate topics. However, while one was organized to facilitate 'logical' presentation of material, the other assumed that teaching would proceed on the principle of 'increasing differentiation'. The former was used by approximately two-thirds of grade 8 pupils in 1964 and 1965 (the period of this study), and the latter by the remaining one-third.

Although there was an element of chance in the selection of mathematics as the content area within which to study methods of teaching, mathematics is a discipline of considerable, and increasing, importance in modern living. As Dienes (1964) says, 'Every country in the world is finding itself short of scientists, technicians and other specialists needed to carry on a technological civilization. The basic skill underlying all scientific and technological skills is control of the tools of mathematics structures . . .'. In addition to what may be described as its economic value, mathematics could be justified on cultural grounds. Few writers on the subject during the last fifty years have omitted mention of the value of mathematics in a general education.

Probably because of this recognition of its twofold significance, mathematics has been the centre of considerable educational concern in recent years. In particular, concern has been expressed with the unfavourable attitude (Beberman, 1959; Biggs, 1962; Allendoerfer, 1965) that many students have for the subject, and with the failure of courses to develop an understanding of principles among the students. During the last fifteen years, a large number of experimental mathematics programmes have attempted to overcome these deficiencies. In the United States alone there are over a dozen major experimental programmes in operation. Some were begun in the early 1950s (e.g., University of Illinois Committee on School Mathematics, 1951; Boston College Mathematics Institute, 1953, at college level), many more towards the end of that decade (e.g., University of Maryland Mathematics Project, 1957; School Mathematics Study Group, 1958; The Greater Cleveland Mathematics Program, 1959), and several during the 1960s. In England, The School Mathematics Project (1962) and the Midlands Mathematical Experiment (1962), are two of the best known projects and both were begun in the 1960s. Considerable experimentation is occurring also in Russia, France and Belgium.

In general, the programmes mentioned have been developed by mathematicians and classroom teachers without much guidance from experts in psychological fields. The influence of the mathematicians can be seen in the emphasis placed on careful use of language, the slackening of interest in social applications, and the awareness of structure in mathematics. The teacher's expertness is reflected in the grading of programmes and in the methods of teaching suggested. This collaboration between mathematician and teacher has been very fruitful, but it lacks the expertise which can be contributed by the psychologist specializing in the areas of learning and teaching theory. This latter neglect has led to three rather serious consequences.

First, when the objectives of courses are stated at all, they are frequently expressed in general terms. Terms such as understanding, insight, imagination and basic skills, which are often used, require careful definition in behavioural terms before they become useful from the point of view of evaluation.

Second, current thinking and research concerned with classroom learning finds inadequate expression in the curricula. The theories implied in many of the new programmes are those that would be familiar to James or Dewey (Woodring, 1964); 'learning by doing' and 'discovery methods' have become clichés in the language of education.

The third consequence is that teaching theories have tended to be either ignored or assumed to be inferable from learning theories. The result has been that teachers tend to revert to previously learned patterns of teaching behaviour in a situation where a new approach is warranted (Williams, 1966). Learning theories give direction to the teacher by implication, but they view the educative process from the standpoint of the pupil, and many teachers see them as inadequate guides to specific teaching behaviour. Currently the outstanding advocate of the need for teaching theories is Gage, who writes: 'Too much of educational psychology makes the teacher *infer* what he needs to do from what he is told about learners and learning. Theories of teaching would make *explicit* how teachers behave, why they behave as they do, and with what effects. Hence, theories of teaching need to develop alongside, on a more equal basis with rather than by inference from, theories of learning' (Gage, 1964, p. 133).

The purpose of this study was to contribute to the development and evaluation of a teaching theory in relation to mathematics at the first-year secondary level.

According to Bruner (1963), 'The task of teaching a subject to a child at any particular age is one of representing the structure of that subject in terms of the child's way of viewing things.' The trouble is that very little is known about precisely what structure is appropriate to 'the child's way of viewing things'. It is sometimes assumed that nothing special is needed; all that a teacher need do is to present the subject in its logical structure. However, Ausubel (1963) fiercely denies this. He begins with the proposition that '. . . an individual's organisation of a particular subject-matter discipline in his own mind consists of a hierarchical structure in which the most inclusive concepts occupy a position at the apex of the structure and subsume progressively less inclusive and more highly-differentiated sub-concepts and factual data.' From this he argues that teachers should facilitate this naturally occuring 'subsumption' process by organizing the sequence of lessons along the same lines.

The study reported here was aimed at testing, in an exploratory way, and within a classroom situation, the theory advanced by Ausubel. Ideally, one would have set up a carefully controlled experiment with one group of teachers presenting subject matter strictly according to Ausubelian principles, and another according to traditional logical principles. As so often happens in educational research, particularly when classroom behaviour is involved, the ideal was not possible in this study. Instead of following through to the teacher behaviour we had to be content with 'experimenting' at what might be termed a contextual level, namely with the *textbooks* which the teachers would use. In some cases, of course, textbooks determine the teaching style and in others they reflect it. As Nelson (1965) says, 'The importance of the role of the text book in determining the content, organization, and model of presentation of school mathematics can hardly be over-emphasized.' In similar vein, Begle (1965) writes, 'From past attempts at reform, it has been shown that the only way to have a new curriculum put into practice is to write appropriate text books.' There is, then, some justification for experimenting at this level. Unfortunately, this study suffers from a further weakness associated with the texts: neither was deliberately written as a pure type of the contrasting approaches. However, as we shall attempt to illustrate in the next paragraphs, they seemed to be sufficiently different in approach, and sufficiently consistent with two contrasting theories of learning and teaching to justify the launching of a study to examine their effects upon pupils.

The Ausubelian-type text (henceforth called A-type) begins with a plea to regard arithmetic and algebra not as separate subjects but as a single discipline—mathematics. The first eight pages are devoted to relating mathematics to everyday experiences and to introducing basic principles, such as Commutative Laws, Associative Laws and Distributive Laws. Variables and functions are also introduced early in the text. Having established and reinforced the basic principles, this text proceeds to derivative and correlative ideas. Progressive differentiation of subject matter, and its integrative reconciliation with other experiences, characterize the whole book. Something of its flavour can be gained if we turn to the pages which deal with mensuration. The teachers are warned that many of the pupils will not have a clear understanding of length, area or volume, and they are advised to '. . . put before them a host of experiences from which they can abstract the concepts', without bothering, at this stage, about definitions. The topic is developed through a series of exercises which illustrate the following points: the arbitrary nature of units used in measuring; the additive nature of lengths and areas; the use of the distributive law; counting is involved in measurement of lengths and area; the importance of selecting *relevant* data from the situation; addition and multiplication will speed up counting; the convenience of a standard unit; and the principle of variation.

The traditional-type text (henceforth called T-type) is firmly divided into chapters, on the basis of topics, and the emphasis is upon giving the pupils techniques which will allow them to manipulate symbols in order to obtain correct answers. It appears to make two basic assumptions: (a) that the mathematics taught previously has been understood and merely requires revision exercises or more drill before extensions are introduced; and (b) that the presentation of model examples, followed by sets of exercises based on these models will result in the pupils 'learning mathematics'. Mensuration is isolated from other topics, and begins with diagrams of squares and rectangles, accompanied by rules such as these:

$$\text{Perimeter} = (\text{length} + \text{breadth}) \times 2 \qquad P = 2(l + b)$$

$$\text{Length} = \frac{\text{Perimeter}}{2} - \text{breadth} \qquad l = \frac{P}{2} - b$$

$$\text{Breadth} = \frac{\text{Perimeter}}{2} - \text{length} \qquad b = \frac{P}{2} - l$$

Then the students are required to attend closely to the working of two problems, one on carpeting and the other on painting, before proceeding to work on additional problems, of a similar kind, on their own.

At the beginning of 1965, a complete list of Brisbane secondary schools was obtained, and the schools were classified according to whether they used the A-type or T-type text. Using a table of random numbers, nine schools were chosen from each group and then one class from each school. This gave a total of 359 pupils in the A-type group, and 306 in the T-type. The proportion of boys in each group was .55, and there were no age differences (mean age 12.7 years in each case). During the first two weeks of the first term, all pupils in the study completed:

1. ACER Intermediate Test A (an intelligence test).
2. Mathematics Test I (an attainment test).
3. Mathematics Attitude Test.

At the end of the year, the Attitude Test was re-administered together with a Mathematics Test II.

Table 19.1 shows the data on reliability and validity of all the tests used, while Table 19.2 shows the degree of relationship among the variables.

TABLE 19.1

Reliability and Validity Coefficients

	Split-Half	*Test-Re-Test*	*Concurrent Validity*
IQ	.95	—	.83
Attitude	.91	.91	.74 to .77
Maths I	.86	.75	.79
Maths II	.93	.93	.70 to .80

TABLE 19.2

Intercorrelation of Variables

	Age	*IQ*	*Attitude (I)*	*Maths I*	*Attitude (F)*	*Maths II*
Age	1.000					
IQ	—0.1968	1.000				
Attitude (Initial)	—0.0621	0.1320	1.000			
Maths Test I	—0.1376	0.6645	0.2399	1.000		
Attitude (Final)	—0.0394	0.1947	0.4773	0.2749	1.000	
Maths Test II	—0.1567	0.6531	0.2697	0.7052	0.3747	1.000

Two hypotheses guided the analysis of the data:

1. The means of the scores on Mathematics Test II, adjusted for initial attainment and intelligence, will be the same irrespective of the textbook used.

TABLE 19.3

Achievement in Mathematics Test II (Criterion, Y) with Intelligence (X) and Initial Mathematics Score (Z) as Controls

Source of Variation	df	Σx^2	Σz^2	Σxz	Σxy	Σzy	Σy^2	$\Sigma y'^2$	df	ms'_y	F ratio
Treatments (A)	1	19.7917	0.0325	−0.8012	8.4083	−0.3427	3.6195	9.1631	1	9.1631	$\frac{9.1631}{6.084} = 1.507$
Groups within Treatments (GWA)	16	794.2161	73.8685	224.2673	561.7532	192.2742	589.8853	85.1360	14	6.0811	df 1 and 14
Total	17	814.0078	73.9010	223.4661	570.2170	191.9315	593.5048	94.2991	15		Non-significant

Null hypothesis stands

TABLE 19.4

Attitude to Mathematics after One Year (Criterion, Y) with Initial Attitude to Mathematics (X) as Control

Source of Variation	df	Σx^2	Σxy	Σy^2	$\Sigma y'^2$	df	ms'_y	F ratio
Treatments (A)	1	59.9031	−35.9829	21.6146	103.8023	1	103.8023	$\frac{103.8023}{15.5795} = 6.6627$
Groups within Treatments (GWA)	16	252.9612	218.3754	422.2121	233.6939	15	15.5795	df 1 and 15
Total	17	312.8643	182.3925	443.8267	337.4962			Significant beyond .03 level

Null hypothesis rejected

2. The means of the scores on the final attitude test, adjusted for initial attitude, will be the same irrespective of the textbook used.

Covariance analyses were undertaken to test these hypotheses, and the findings are shown in Tables 19.3 and 19.4.

In view of the rejection of the null hypothesis involving the attitude variable it is useful at this stage to make a closer examination of the distribution of the attitude means. This is done in Table 19.5.

From Table 19.5 it can be seen that the A-type schools maintained their measure of variance over the year and also their attitude towards mathematics. On the other hand, the variance in the T-type schools increased, and the attitude of the pupils became less favourable.

Previous research workers in this area of attitude-towards-mathematics (Poole, 1956; Ellingson, 1962) have shown that a deterioration in attitude can be expected in the early years of secondary school. Poole's findings are of particular interest since it was his test which was used in this study, and since he, too, was concerned with students in their first year at Queensland secondary schools. His findings of a deterioration, significant at the .01 level for both boys and girls, is consistent with the findings from the T-type schools in this study, but inconsistent with those from the A-type schools.

Discussion

The inconclusive results on the attainment variable are a little disappointing but not altogether unexpected. There are probably several factors which militate against positive results, and these are common to most 'methods' studies. First, the A-type text was written by a mathematician who was not deliberately following Ausubel's theory but who had an intuitive understanding of many of his principles. While the text seemed sufficiently close to justify inclusion in the study, it contained, inevitably, a number of inconsistencies and discrepancies. Clearly, the study would have been better if a new 'experimental' text could have been written. Second, the teachers using the A-type text were unfamiliar with its philosophy, but were, as former pupils, teacher-trainees and experienced classroom teachers, very familiar with the T-type approach. Undoubtedly, 'method-reversion' occurred in several instances. Third, the children in both groups had been educated in the conventional approach for seven years, and would have developed quite complex, even if, in many cases, inadequate, structures and strategies associated with mathematics. While the T-type students continued along familiar lines, with teachers versed in the method, those from schools using the A-type text were obliged to adopt a new approach and to restructure the mathematical knowledge that they had already mastered at the primary school level. Finally, as Bloom (1963) reminds us, '. . . [the research worker] should not expect to secure significant evidence . . . in a single study carried on over a one-year period'. A long-term project, extending over several years, with teachers trained in the suggested method and using a text carefully designed to represent Ausubelian principles, would probably be needed to secure conclusive results.

TABLE 19.5

Attitude Means showing Differences

School	Class Sex	A-Type			School	Class Sex	T-Type		
		Att. 1	Att. 2	Difference			Att. 1	Att. 2	Difference
01	B & G	73.0000	71.5429	−1.4571	15	B & G	75.2941	72.8529	−2.4412
02	G	66.4583	64.8333	−1.6250	16	B	73.6429	69.4286	−4.2143
03	B	66.3725	66.4902	+0.1177	17	B & G	76.1935	70.2581	−5.9354
04	G	65.7429	62.6000	−3.1429	18	B & G	70.6538	59.2692	−11.3846
05	G	73.9333	73.2889	−0.6444	20	G	73.9231	67.6154	−6.3077
06	B	81.0556	79.0278	−2.0278	21	B & G	75.0303	65.4848	−9.5455
07	B	67.4667	69.4444	+1.9777	22	B & G	71.9394	61.6061	−10.3333
08	B	64.8750	69.1250	+4.2500	23	B	71.0196	71.9020	+0.8824
09	B & G	69.3750	75.5312	+6.1562	24	G	73.4194	73.7419	+0.3225
Mean		69.8088	70.2093	+0.4005			73.4574	68.0177	−5.4397
Variance		24.8074	24.4162				3.2993	22.4961	

Viewed against the background of militating factors listed above, the significant difference in attitude, and the tendency (significant at .20 level) for the pupils being taught from an A-type text to do better in achievement, provide some support for the teaching principles advocated by Ausubel. It is possible, for example, that the significant difference in attitude is only beginning to make its influence felt in the achievement scores, and that a long-term study, even with all the existing handicaps, would provide clear evidence of the superiority of an A-type text.

References

Allendoerfer, C. B., 1965: The second revolution in mathematics. *The Mathematics Teacher*, 58, 690-695.

Ausubel, D. P., 1963: *The Psychology of Meaningful Verbal Learning*. Grune and Stratton Inc., New York.

Beberman, M., 1959: *An Emerging Program of Secondary School Mathematics*. Oxford University Press, New York.

Begle, E. G., 1965: School mathematics study group—Philosophy of curriculum development. *Mathematics in Secondary Schools—Report on Australian Unesco Seminar*.

Biggs, J. B., 1962: *Anxiety, Motivation and Primary School Mathematics*. NFER Occasional Publication No. 7.

Bloom, B. S., 1963: Testing cognitive ability and achievement. In N. L. Gage (Ed.), *Handbook of Research on Teaching*. Rand McNally and Co., Chicago, Ill.

Bloom, B. S., *et al.*, 1956: *Taxonomy of Educational Objectives: I Cognitive Domain*. Longmans Green & Co., London.

Bruner, J. S., 1963: *The Process of Education*. Harvard University Press, Cambridge, Mass.

Dienes, Z. P., 1964: *The Power of Mathematics*. Hutchinson, London.

Ellingson, J. B., 1962: Evaluation of attitudes of high school students toward mathematics. Unpublished thesis, University of Oregon.

Gage, N. L., 1964: In E. R. Hilgard (Ed.), *Theories of Learning and Instruction*. NSSE Yearbook, LXIII, Pt I, Chicago University Press, Chicago, Ill.

Krathwohl, D. R., *et al.*, 1964: *Taxonomy of Educational Objectives: II Affective Domain*. Longmans Green & Co., London.

Nelson, L. D., 1965: Text-book difficulty and mathematics achievement in junior high school. *The Mathematics Teacher*, 58, 724-729.

Poole, P. C., 1956: A study of students' attitudes towards science and mathematics. Unpublished BEd thesis, University of Queensland.

Williams, J. D., 1966: 'Method-reversion': The problem of sustaining changes in teacher behaviour. *Journal of Educational Research*, 8, 128-133.

Woodring, P., 1964: Reform movements from the point of view of psychological theory. In E. R. Hilgard (Ed.), *Theories of Learning and Instruction*. NSSE Yearbook, LXIII, Pt I, Chicago University Press, Chicago, Ill.

20

Some Effects of Affective Climate on the Achievement Motivation of Pupils*

W. J. Campbell

A CONSIDERABLE amount of attention has recently been given to the issue of achievement motivation among students, and the established findings may be briefly summarized as follows:

1. Despite uncertainty about the precise relationship between motivation and learning, a striving to excel appears to be an essential element in effective classroom learning (NSSE, 1964; Hilgard, 1963; Rethling-shafer, 1963).
2. This striving to excel, which is usually referred to as *need achievement*, or, more simply, *n Ach*, exists both as a motivational disposition and as an aroused motive (Sears & Hilgard, 1964; McClelland, 1949, 1951).
3. In its generalized form, need achievement is developed through the accompaniments of child-training experiences, particularly *warmth* and *achievement pressure*, and it is relatively stable after the child has reached the age of seven years (Winterbottom, 1958; Rosen & D'Andrade, 1959; McClelland & Friedman, 1952).
4. *Cultural attitudes* and *values* which the child encounters and accepts direct the generalized striving towards particular goals—in one case sport, in another school learning, and in another burglary (Rosen, 1959; Strodtbeck, 1958; Coleman, 1963).
5. Whether or not a disposition to strive for a standard of excellence will become an aroused motive within the classroom will depend upon such *situational elements* as: (a) prior satisfaction of more demanding needs, for example, affiliation and self-esteem (Maslow, 1954); (b) size of learning group (Barker & Gump, 1964); (c) the extent to which the curriculum and teaching methods stimulate problem solving rather than emphasize reception and recall (Torrance, 1962); (d) guidance towards and recognition of success (Atkinson & Reitman, 1956); and (e) the value of success (Atkinson, 1958).

*First published in *Australian Journal of Education*, 11, 1, 1-12.

6. Projective techniques, such as the Thematic Apperception Test (TAT), are the most effective means of measuring the extent of need achievement being displayed (Murray, *et al.*, 1938; McClelland, *et al.*, 1953, 1958).

It is generally agreed that there is a need for more research in this area and, in particular, for studies concerned with the teacher and school variables related to the arousal of strivings among pupils. The study reported here is aimed at clarifying the role of the teacher in the motivation of learners and, while there are links with investigations undertaken by other researchers, it differs from most in its method of distinguishing strivings for excellence from those concerned with the avoidance of failure.

The research was guided by two hypotheses:

(a) Teachers who vary in the measures of *striving for excellence* which they arouse within their students will differ with respect to the nurturance of their personalities and the warmth, challenge and dominance which characterize their classroom behaviour: those who arouse high measures of strivings for excellence will rate high in nurturance of personality, warmth and challenge, but low in dominance, while those who arouse low measures of these strivings will be correspondingly low in nurturance, warmth and challenge, and high in dominance.

(b) Teachers who vary in the measures of *striving for avoidance of failure* which they arouse within their students will differ with respect to the nurturance of their personalities and the warmth and dominance which characterize their classroom behaviour: those who arouse high measures of strivings for avoidance of failure will rate low in nurturance and warmth but high in dominance, while those who arouse low measures of these strivings will be correspondingly high in nurturance and warmth, and low in dominance.

In broad outline, the study involved rating a group of teachers according to their 'success' in arousing strivings for excellence and avoidance of failure among their students, predicting from these ratings the pattern of characteristics which would be found in each teacher, and testing the predictions by reference to scores on appropriate measures.

Twelve classes from three Brisbane state primary schools, situated within residential areas of similar socioeconomic status, were chosen for the study. All class teachers were males, school grades ranged from 5 to 7, and the ages of the children were between nine and twelve years. Class enrolments ranged from 33 to 45, and a total of 395 students were involved in the study.

As in most studies of need achievement, written responses to selected TAT pictures were used to assess the types and amounts of motivation being displayed. Class teachers were instructed to present three of the pictures to their students under standardized conditions but as though the exercise was a normal class one. The pictures were:

1   A young boy is sitting looking at a violin which rests on a table in front of him.

9BM An adolescent boy looks straight out of the picture. The barrel of a rifle is visible at one side, and in the background is the vague portrayal of a medical operation.

17BM A naked man is clinging to a rope. He is in the act of climbing up or down.

The student responses were scored by the author and three assistants according to whether the themes were: unrelated to achievement, or of a routine task nature (score value 0), strivings to excel (score value 3), and strivings to avoid failure (score value 3). An example of a response scored in each of the categories follows:

Unrelated to Achievement

My friend John had to practise the violin. He didn't like it at all. He just sat and looked at it. When he first got the violin John was thrilled. Then his mother told him he had to practise every day for three hours. John went round moping. He tried to think of some way to talk his mother into selling it. Finally, he had it. He asked his mother politely, and, you know what, she sold it, so John always says to be honest about everything. (Score 0)

Striving to Excel

This is a rope-climbing competition. Bill has been practising for a long time and he is sure that he is going to win the competition. He is already several seconds ahead of his nearest rival, but he wants to set a new record. He did do this, and he's probably wishing that he'll win again next year. I'm wishing that too. (Score 3—excel)

Avoidance of Failure

This is an operation in the olden days. The patient is seriously ill and the doctor is wondering if he can save his life. Everyone is fearful that the man will die, and the doctor is too. The little boy is very sad because the man is his father. The doctor is thinking, 'If only I can keep him alive'. He finished the operation and the man lived until they moved him to a proper hospital. (Score 3—failure)

The classes had been chosen so as to minimize the likelihood of pupils differing in achievement dispositions. However, as an additional safeguard, the author administered the same TAT pictures, one month later, under conditions that were strictly standardized and calculated to arouse optimal strivings for excellence among the children. It was assumed that the researcher behaved in the same way on the twelve occasions, and that variations from one class to another, under his administrations, would suggest that the classes were not strictly equivalent with respect to achievement dispositions. The mean score obtained by each class, under its teacher's administration, was expressed as a ratio of that obtained under the researcher's administration, to provide a common comparative measure of the teacher's ability to arouse the motives under examination.

Table 20.1 shows the mean pupil scores, obtained by each of the teachers, expressed as a ratio of those obtained by the researcher.

TABLE 20.1

TAT Mean Scores
(ratio of teacher to researcher)

Teacher No.	Mean 'Excel' Scores	Mean 'Failure' Scores
1	1.472	1.474
2	1.262	1.000
3	1.151	0.320
4	1.109	1.529
5	0.956	1.100
6	0.905	1.226
7	0.887	6.200
8	0.787	4.000
9	0.597	6.000
10	0.545	5.105
11	0.455	2.900
12	0.452	0.800

(Teachers 9, 10, 11 and 12 received scores for 'excellence' that were significantly lower (.01 level) than those of both the researcher and teachers 1, 2, 3 and 4. The researcher's scores varied little from class to class, except in the case of the class taught by teacher No. 8, from which particularly high scores were obtained.)

The rationale underlying the choice of instruments to measure the teacher variables is that since classroom interaction is the focus of concern and is mainly verbal in nature, an analysis of the statements made by the teacher to the pupils will be particularly helpful. Verbal exchanges provide a direct link between teacher and pupils, but they are superimposed upon, and enjoy varying degrees of compatibility with, a personality orientation of the teacher towards pupils and teaching. In many instances the verbal statements reflect the personality orientations, but, for a variety of reasons, a degree of incompatibility can exist. In such cases, if not in all, the pupils may respond in part to the underlying personality which they sense as well as to the more obvious verbal behaviours. Accordingly, it was decided to use both a measure of teacher personality associated with 'nurturance', and an analysis of teacher statements.

The Minnesota Teacher Attitude Inventory (MTAI) (Cook, Leeds & Callis, 1951) was an obvious choice for the assessment of the general personality quality, referred to here as nurturance. The inventory is widely used in research studies of this kind; it has been adequately validated and tested for reliability; it is simple to administer and it is not subject to easy faking. It aims to assess, through responses of an attitudinal kind, the likelihood of teachers being oriented towards and able to maintain: harmonious, affectionate, and sympathetic relations with pupils; an enjoyable workshop atmosphere; a minimum of status differentiations; and a climate characterized by freedom, mutual respect and group solidarity.

Among the 150 statements to which respondents are asked to indicate extent of agreement are:

13. The first lesson a child needs to learn is to obey the teacher without hesitation.
20. A teacher should not be expected to burden himself with a pupil's problems.
62. Most pupils are resourceful when left on their own.
71. Children should be allowed more freedom in their execution of learning activities.
95. Children should not expect to be allowed to talk when adults wish to speak.
132. Children just cannot be trusted.
133. Children should be given reasons for the restrictions placed upon them.

The scores ('rights' minus 'wrongs') obtained by the twelve teachers, together with their percentile ranks (U.S.A. norms) are shown in Table 20.2.

TABLE 20.2

MTAI Scores (Nurturance)

Teacher No.	Raw Score	Percentile Rank
1	–6	21
2	63	79
3	106	98
4	–31	6
5	13	35
6	–37	5
7	38	54
8	–13	15
9	–31	6
10	4	28
11	–9	18
12	–4	24

It would appear that, in terms of orientations towards children and teaching, these teachers differed considerably. Some (Nos 3 and 2) were highly nurturant, others (Nos 6, 4 and 9) were correspondingly low in this measure, while the majority, when compared with a similar group of teachers from the United States, would be placed in the bottom quartile.

The verbal behaviour of the teachers was examined by means of the Withall technique (Withall, 1951), whereby statements made by the teacher are classified into seven categories as follows:

1. *Learner Supportive*: These are statements which express agreement with the ideas, actions or opinions of the learner, or that commend or reassure the learner. The dominant intent is to praise, and encourage the learner. Examples: 'Good answer'; 'Right'; 'Well done'; etc.

2. *Acceptant or Clarifying*: In these the teacher accepts and restates the content of the learner's statements. The dominant intent is to help the learner gain insight into the issue. Thus: 'Yes, that seems to suggest . . .' 'Yes, what Billy has been saying is . . .'

3. *Problem Structuring*: These are frequently posed as questions seeking further information either to increase the teacher's understanding of what the learner said, or to challenge the learner to give further thought to the issue. The dominant intent is to foster problem-solving activities. Examples: 'I am not quite sure if I understand you correctly.' 'If that is so, what would you expect to happen to X?'

4. *Neutral*: These include statements in which the teacher questions himself aloud, repeats verbatim comments made by others,. uses a polite formality, or discusses some administrative detail. Thus: 'Good morning.' 'We will be meeting in room 16 for Biology.'

5. *Directive*: These are statements which advise the learner regarding a course of action or his future behaviour. They convey the impression that the teacher expects that the learner will follow his prompting. The dominant intent is to have the learner adopt a specified behaviour. For example: 'Grade 5, work quietly.' 'Please get on with your work.'

6. *Reproving, Disapproving or Disparaging*: By means of these statements the teacher admonishes the learner for unacceptable behaviour and aims to deter him from repeating it. He may impress upon the learner the fact that societal or school standards are not being met. Thus: 'This is very bad work.' 'You are just a young delinquent.'

7. *Teacher Supportive*: In these the teacher refers to his own qualifications or achievements in order to confirm his position or his ideas in the eyes of those around him. He may rigidly advocate an idea simply because it is his, and despite the call for a re-examination. For example, 'After all, I'm the teacher here.' 'It's right because I said so.'

It is claimed that a sample of 200 statements uttered by the teacher in the classroom provides a reliable pattern of his verbal behaviour there. In this study, 300 statements from each teacher were obtained before any analysis of student responses had been made. The number of statements suggesting 'warmth' (categories 1 and 2 combined), 'challenge' (category 3), and 'dominance' (category 6) was determined, and the findings are reported in Table 20.3.

Since the analysis of relationships is based upon ranks on the various measures, for convenience in discerning patterns these are collated in Table 20.4.

The interrelations among the six variables are shown in Table 20.5.

In general, the coefficients are of the order predicted. Warmth, challenge and lack of dominance in the teachers are each related significantly to strivings to excel among the students, and dominance is related significantly

TABLE 20.3

Number of Teacher Statements Concerned with Warmth, Challenge and Dominance

Teacher No.	Warmth	Challenge	Dominance
1	79	126	15
2	47	145	30
3	33	51	4
4	100	100	0
5	115	79	0
6	82	160	3
7	14	96	38
8	39	117	35
9	11	105	49
10	33	42	48
11	30	75	33
12	3	48	45

TABLE 20.4

Teacher Ranks on Student Motivations and Teacher Characteristics

Teacher Ranks

Teacher No.	Excel	Failure	Nurturance	Warmth	Challenge	Lack of Dominance
1	12	6	6	9	10	8
2	11	3	11	8	11	7
3	10	1	12	5.5	3	9
4	9	7	2.5	11	7	11.5
5	8	4	9	12	5	11.5
6	7	5	1	10	12	10
7	6	12	10	3	6	4
8	5	9	4	7	9	5
9	4	11	2.5	2	8	1
10	3	10	8	5.5	1	2
11	2	8	5	4	4	6
12	1	2	7	1	2	3

to avoidance-of-failure strivings. While the measure of nurturant teacher personality on its own is not a good predictor of student motivations, a distinct trend in line with the expectations is revealed. The coefficients throughout are sufficiently high to justify the calculation of multiple correlation coefficients, and these are shown in Table 20.6.

TABLE 20.5

Matrix of Correlation Coefficients

	Excel	Failure	Nurturance	Warmth	Challenge	Lack of Dominance
Excel		−.371	.271	.670*	.538**	.670*
Failure			−.348	−.267	.035	−.519**
Nurturance				−.133	−.400	−.012
Warmth					.456	.857*
Challenge						.309
Lack of Dominance						

* significant at .01 level; ** significant at .05 level (one-tailed test).

TABLE 20.6

Multiple Correlation Coefficients
($\overline{R}_c$—i.e., corrected for Inflation)

Striving to excel with warmth and challenge	$= +.640$
Striving to excel with warmth, challenge and lack of dominance	$= +.643$
Striving to excel with warmth, challenge, lack of dominance and nurturant personality (hypothesis 1)	$= +.825$
Striving to avoid failure with dominance and lack of warmth	$= +.502$
Striving to avoid failure with dominance, lack of warmth and a non-nurturant personality (hypothesis 2)	$= +.649$

Some readers may be surprised at the high order of the relationships established, but others may wonder why they have not approached even closer to perfection. There are several reasons why coefficients of +1.00 could not be expected in a study of this kind. *First*, concepts in the social sciences are relatively ill-defined, and the techniques for measuring them are, when compared with those in the physical sciences, rough-and-ready. The TAT, the MTAI and the Withall analyses are reputable instruments in this field, but they do not measure with complete validity and reliability. Moreover, additional errors arise from the human factor in observing, recording, interpreting and scoring. Precautionary measures aimed at avoiding errors of bias and scoring were applied, but 100 per cent accuracy is seldom achieved. *Second*, while there are good theoretical grounds for selecting the variables of nurturance, warmth, challenge and dominance, it would not be claimed that they exhaust the universe of potentially significant characteristics. Even in our present state of knowledge other variables suggest themselves and undoubtedly further advances will indicate still others that warrant inclusion. *Third*, no measure of the pupils' perceptions of the teachers was obtained, and it is to these, not to the researcher's observations, that student reactions occur. It has been implicitly assumed that the researcher's observations coincide with those of the pupils, but some discrepancies are bound to have occurred. *Finally*, in a study of this kind over-generalizations are made. Granted that nurturance, warmth, challenge and lack of dominance are, *in general*, teacher qualities that will foster strivings for excellence among pupils, it would be surprising if exceptions did not exist. In this study, even the coldest, the least challenging, and the most dominant teachers were clearly motivating a few students to strive for high standards. When all of these detracting influences are considered, the order of relationships established is particularly high.

For those who have difficulty in interpreting statistical findings, it may be useful at this stage to present pen-portraits of the contrasting types of teachers which this study has revealed.

Motivators towards Excellence (Teachers 1 and 2)

These teachers have friendly attitudes towards children, establish pleasant relationships with them and are willing to share and assist with the problems which are brought to them. Status differentiations are not highlighted within the classroom. However, they are not mere 'supporters'. Their classroom behaviour is characterized mainly by the encouragement which they give to problem solving, intellectual questioning, originality and creativity, and evaluative comments feature prominently in their verbal statements.

Motivators towards Avoidance of Failure (Teachers 7, 9 and 10)

The personality orientations of these teachers do not always differ greatly from those whose students strive for excellence, but they display much greater dominance and much less warmth in their relationships with pupils. They are more concerned with directing and supervising, and, when they evaluate, they tend to make disparaging and reproving statements rather than ones that are friendly, constructive and encouraging.

The findings of research can be highly significant statistically and quite insignificant in a nonstatistical sense. However, those reported here would seem to have a number of important implications for teachers and for those responsible for their training and subsequent guidance.

While one would not be justified in discounting the effects that the teacher's personality orientations have upon the motivation of his students, his overt style of teaching appears to be crucial, and, fortunately, this is something that is amenable to training and correction.

Most teachers will probably accept the conclusion that dominating tactics do not arouse the kind of motives that we seek in our students, but many seem unable to think of any alternative but that of a tender-hearted mental-health approach. This, the study suggests, will prevent pupils from dissipating their energies in striving to avoid failure, but it is ineffective in arousing them to strive for excellence. What is lacking in the latter approach is the element of challenge or demand, and the attendant sense of success when problems are mastered.

Many of the recent advances in curriculum planning are based upon excellent motivational principles. The work of the Biological Sciences Study Group (Glass, 1962) and of the Physical Sciences Study Group (Finlay, 1962) are outstanding examples of how content and method can be ultimately interwoven into highly motivating experiences. Perhaps less well known is the programme of inquiry training in the elementary school which Suchman has been conducting at the University of Illinois (Suchman, 1960, 1965). In this, short films of scientific demonstrations (such as the 'Ball and Ring' demonstration) pose problems of cause and effect, and the pupils learn to attack these problems with questions by which they gather data and perform imaginary experiments. The teacher provides the answers to the questions. A portion of a typical session would go something like this:

Pupil: Were the ball and ring at room temperature to begin with?
Teacher: Yes.
Pupil: And the ball would go through the ring at first?
Teacher: Yes.
Pupil: After the ball was held over the fire it did not go through the ring, right?
Teacher: Yes.
Pupil: If the ring had been heated instead of the ball, would the results have been the same?
Teacher: No.
Pupil: If both had been heated would the ball have gone through then?
Teacher: That all depends.

Television viewers who have been fascinated by the teaching technique of Professor Julius Sumner Miller, will recognize some elements which this has in common with the more structured programme being used by Suchman.

To come still closer to home, the new science and mathematics curricula recently introduced into Queensland schools are based very firmly upon a philosophy of problem solving, and, if implemented in the same spirit, are likely to affect the motivations of pupils for the better. However, it cannot be assumed that teachers who have been selected and trained as 'directors' and 'transmitters of the culture' can easily shed or reduce these roles in favour of the new one of expert 'stimulators'. What is required is a set of experiences deliberately designed and introduced to develop the characteristics of warmth, challenge and lack of dominance which seem to be closely related to strivings to excel among pupils. There are lessons here for our universities, our teachers' colleges, and for those responsible for in-service programmes.

References

Atkinson, J. W., 1958: Towards experimental analysis of human motivation in terms of motives, expectancies and incentives. In J. W. Atkinson (Ed.), *Motives in Fantasy, Action and Society.* D. Van Nostrand & Co. Inc., Princeton, N.J.

Atkinson, J. W., and Reitman, W. R., 1956: Performance as a function of motive, strength and expectancy of goal attainment. *Journal of Abn. and Soc. Psychol.,* 53, 361-366.

Barker, R. G., and Gump, P. V. (Eds), 1964: *Big School, Small School.* Stanford University Press, Stanford, Calif.

Coleman, J., 1963: The adolescent sub-culture and academic achievement. In W. W. Charters and N. L. Gage, *Readings in the Social Psychology of Education.* Allyn & Bacon, Boston, Mass.

Cook, W. W., Leeds, C. H., and Callis, R., 1951: *Minnesota Teacher Attitude Inventory.* The Psychological Corporation, 522 Fifth Avenue, New York.

Finlay, G. C., 1962: The psychical science study committee. *School Review,* 70, 63-81.

Glass, B., 1962: Renascent biology: A report of the AIBS biological curriculum study. *School Review,* 70, 16-43.

Hilgard, E. R., 1963: Motivation in learning theory. In S. Koch (Ed.), *Psychology: A Study of a Science,* Vol. V. McGraw-Hill Book Co., New York.

McClelland, D. C., 1951: *Personality.* Wm. Sloan Assoc., New York.

McClelland, D. C., 1958: Methods of measuring human motivation. In J. W. Atkinson (Ed.), *Motives in Fantasy, Action and Society.* D. Van Nostrand & Co. Inc., Princeton, N.J.

McClelland, D. C., *et al.,* 1949: The effect of the need for achievement in thematic apperception. *Journal of Experimental Psychology,* 37, 242-255.

McClelland, D. C., *et al.,* 1953: *The Achievement Motive.* Appleton-Century-Crofts, New York.

McClelland, D. C., and Friedman, G. A., 1952: A cross-cultural study of the relationship between child-training practices and achievement motivation appearing in folk tales. In G. E. Swanson, *et al., Readings in Social Psychology.* Holt, Rinehart and Winston, Inc., New York.

Maslow, A. H., 1954: *Motivation and Personality.* Harper Bros, New York.

Murray, H. A., *et al.,* 1938: *Explorations in Personality.* Oxford University Press, New York.

National Society for the Study of Education (NSSE), 1964: *Theories of Learning and Instruction,* LXIII, Pt I, University of Chicago Press, Chicago, Ill.

Rethlingshafer, D., 1963: *Motivation as Related to Personality.* McGraw-Hill Book Co., New York.

Rosen, B. C., 1959: Race, ethnicity, and the achievement syndrome. *American Sociological Review* 24, 47-60.

Rosen, B. C. and D'Andrade, R., 1959: The psychological origins of achievement motivation. *Sociometry,* 22, 3, 185-218.

Sears, P. S. and Hilgard, E. R., 1964: The teachers' role in the motivation of the learner. In E. R. Hilgard (Ed.), *Theories of Learning and Instruction. NSSE Yearbook,* LXIII, Pt I, Chicago University Press, Chicago, Ill.

Strodtbeck, F. L., 1958: Family interaction, values and achievement. In D. C. McClelland, *et al.* (Eds), *Talent and Society: New Perspectives in the Identification of Talent.* D. Van Nostrand & Co. Inc., Princeton, N.J.

Suchman, J. R., 1960: Inquiry training in the elementary school. *Science Teacher*, 27, 42-47.

Suchman, J. R., 1965: Inquiry and education. In J. J. Gallagher (Ed.), *Teaching Gifted Children*. Allyn & Bacon, Boston, Mass.

Torrance, E. P., 1962: *Guided Creative Talent*. Prentice-Hall Inc., Englewood Cliffs, N.J.

Winterbottom, M. R., 1958: The relation of need for achievement to learning experiences in independence and mastery. In J. W. Atkinson (Ed.), *Motives in Fantasy, Action and Society*. D. Van Nostrand & Co. Inc., Princeton, N.J.

Withall, J., 1951: The development of the climate index. *Journal of Educational Research*, 45, 93-100.

21

The Nature of Verbal Discourse in Classrooms

R. P. Tisher

Introduction

IT IS generally expected that cognitive growth will occur in pupils as a consequence of classroom experiences, and the teacher is usually viewed as the director or controller of these experiences. It is he who largely determines: the way in which pupils are brought into contact with the learning material; the demands made upon pupils' thinking and reasoning operations; and the extent to which pupils' reasoning capacities are challenged and developed. Primarily, the teacher appears to achieve his tasks through verbal activity, and it is for this reason that verbal behaviour is singled out for detailed study in many research projects. Unfortunately, the results of this type of study, when it goes on to investigate the effects of teacher behaviours on pupil development, are somewhat disappointing, although some associations between verbal behaviour and learning out-comes have been established.

One reason for the disappointing results may be associated with the nature of the behaviour categories studied. In the main the categories (e.g., 'inquiry' (Rutherford, 1964), use of advance organizers (Ausubel, 1960, 1963) and problem solving (Wittrock, 1967)) are 'molar' units, and each is composed of permutations and combinations of other behaviour units. Thus the behaviours 'use of advance organizers', or 'inquiry' include several, all, or some of the following activities: repeating a statement, stating a unit, classifying an object, describing an object, reporting an observation, drawing an inference, justifying a statement, and comparing objects or statements. Whether molecular units or different categories are the more appropriate for research on teaching is a critical issue and one that is only recently receiving attention.

In the study reported here, molecular categories were used to study verbal interaction in science classes and its association with pupils' under-standing in science. The basic aims were:

(a) to identify the nature, distribution and patterning of verbal discourse within some Queensland secondary-school classrooms; and
(b) to investigate, in an exploratory way, the relationship between these ecological data and growth in understanding in pupils.

This chapter deals with the findings associated with the first aim, and a subsequent one (Chapter 22) deals with the findings associated with the second.

Ecological Data

The ecological data were obtained in nine grade 8 science classes in two state high schools in Brisbane, and fifty-four (six per class) representative lessons were tape-recorded and transcribed. Complete details of the methodology and research design are presented elsewhere (Tisher, 1968). The methods of classifying verbal behaviour were based on techniques developed by Smith and Meux (1962), Nuthall and Lawrence (1965) and Withall (1951). The last of these techniques is described elsewhere in this book (Chapter 20) and only the findings obtained using this method will be reported here. The twelve *major* Smith and Meux categories which deal exclusively with cognitive interaction (Boyd & Vere de Vault, 1966), and the modification suggested by Nuthall and Lawrence (1965) will, however, be discussed. It is appropriate here to describe the modified Smith and Meux classificatory scheme. The data obtained using this technique appear later.

Smith and Meux Classification

Using transcripts of tape recordings of seventy class periods, Smith and Meux were able to break classroom discourse into a series of units called episodes and monologues. A monologue is the solo performance of a speaker addressing the class, and although it can be analysed from a number of points of view, its main limitation is its one-way, teacher-centred characteristic. During a monologue, 'there is no direct way of knowing how the pupils are reacting to the statements addressed to them. In it the teacher's general plan in handling his subject may be revealed, but it gives no information about his specific methods of stimulating and guiding pupil responses.' (Nuthall & Lawrence, 1965.) An episode, on the other hand, is a unit of verbal interactions or exchanges in which there is a completed verbal transaction between two or more speakers. It is characterized by an initiating or opening phase containing a remark or set of remarks (assertions, questions, invitations, directions) which initiate discussion, a continuing phase which contains claims, questions or comments resulting from the initiating remarks, and a closing, or terminal phase, which may contain remarks designed either to supplement preceding statements or to cut off the flow of discussion. The episode can also be analysed from a number of points of view including the nature of the questions and directions that begin classroom discussion, and the nature and adequacy of the pupils' responses.

Smith and Meux found that an initiating phase called for a certain type of operation to be performed by pupils, for example, a logical operation of proving, and they classified their twelve major categories in terms of these operations. The categories may be characterized and illustrated as follows (Nuthall & Lawrence, 1965; Smith & Meux, 1962; Meux & Smith, 1964):

Describing:

An account of something which has been mentioned or suggested is required; e.g., 'Where do scientists look for these fossils?' 'What can you tell us about the material which makes up these rocks?' 'What do you notice about these animals?'

Designating:

Something has to be identified by name—a word or symbol; e.g., 'What are the three states of matter?' 'What liquid was it that had the lively taste?' 'Give an example of a substance which dissolves in water.'

Stating:

Statements of issues, steps in a proof, rules, conclusions or a statement of affairs are required. Names, descriptions, etc., are not required. For example, the question 'What can you conclude from that?' asks for a statement of some sort: it can seldom be answered satisfactorily merely by naming. 'What is centripetal force?' 'What is the formula for the pressure given these quantities?' 'What answer did you get?'

Reporting:

A request is made for a report on information contained in some source such as a textbook, or for a review or summary of this or other information; e.g., 'Did the book say anything about chitons?' 'What was demonstrated in the school broadcast on erosion?'

Defining:

Implicitly or explicitly, the meaning of words or terms is demanded; e.g., 'If somebody asked you what science was, what answer would you give?' 'What is the meaning of "density of a substance"?' 'In H_2O, what does the H_2 mean?' 'What is a mollusc?'

Substituting:

Students are asked to perform symbolic operations, usually of a mathematical nature; e.g., 'I weigh 150 lbs and my shoes take up an area of 30 square inches. What is the pressure I exert per square inch on the floor?'

Evaluating:

An estimate of the worth, dependability, etc., of an object, person, expression, event, action or state of affairs is required; e.g., 'Are they useful wings?' 'Do you think that is a satisfactory way to measure friction?' 'Are these small holes in the body very important?'

Opining:

Students are required to express beliefs or opinions about what is possible, what might have been the case, what could be in the future, whether something is necessary, etc. The students make an inference from evidence rather than a report of a single fact; e.g., 'Do you think it (moth) will be able to eat the hard outer shell?' 'Can you burrow very far into the earth?' 'Does a fish have to live in water?'

Classifying:

Explicit reference is made to an instance or class (type, sort, group, set, kind) of things or both, and students are required to place a given instance in the class to which it belongs, or to place a given class in a larger class; e.g., 'To which phylum do earth worms belong?' 'Would this (granite) be metamorphic, sedimentary or igneous?'

Comparing and Contrasting:

Students are required to compare two or more things—actions, factors, objects, processes, etc. The initiating phase is usually marked by the presence of such words and expressions as 'difference between', 'differ from', 'be different', 'compare', 'like', 'correspond'; e.g., 'What are the differences between plants and animals?' 'Just look at that list (of characteristics) and tell me what the important thing is that they are lacking.' 'Is there any difference in the tongues of these two animals?'

Conditional Inferring:

A prior condition or antecedent is given and a consequence is asked for, or both the antecedent and consequent are given and the students are asked to affirm or deny the consequent; e.g., 'If we connected a wire from here to there and put a meter in between, what happens?' 'We've got this force acting downwards and this one acting upwards. What will the resultant be?' 'Is hydrogen produced if we place copper in dilute sulphuric acid?'

Explaining:

A particular consequent is given and students are required to supply an antecedent. 'To explain is to set forth an antecedent condition of which the particular event or process to be explained is taken as the effect, or else, to give the rules, definitions, or facts which are used to justify decisions, judgments, actions, etc. In the example "why did the light go out?" the consequent is "the light go out". The question asks the student to give a reason (reasons) to account for the fact that the light is out. The reason(s) is the antecedent.' (Smith & Meux, 1962, pp. 40-1.) Depending upon the type of antecedent used to account for the consequent, subcategories of explaining may be identified. They are mechanical, causal, sequent, procedural, teleological, and normative. Some examples are; 'Why does a suspended magnet point to the north?' 'How on earth would it breathe if it hasn't got a nose?' 'Why do they live in such shells?'

Many initiating phases have little or no logical significance. They are designed, not to evoke thought, but to keep the classroom functioning and to maintain classroom activities. The final Smith and Meux category, Directing and Managing the Classroom, accounts for these demands. The pupils are asked about reports, homework, or are directed to complete or undertake some task; e.g., 'Would you read?' 'Was this the question for homework?' 'Take this apparatus outside.' 'Take the reading on the scale.'

Examples of episodes appear in the following excerpt from a transcript.

Each episode is marked off with brackets [ ] and the category to which it was assigned is designated by a number. The legend appears in the first column of Table 21.1 (p. 374).

    Teacher: . . . [Which way will the body go?
    Pupil: Upwards.
1 Teacher: It will go up. In other words, what will the body do? It will—?
    Pupil: Float.
    Teacher: It will float. Righto.] [Now, we can show this force. There must be a force acting on the body because if I take a glass here and place it in there it floats. Well, let's push down on it. (Pause.)
12   Push down. I can feel something pushing back here. Up it comes again. Now I wonder what is pushing that glass up when I try to push it down?
    Pupil: The upthrust.
    Teacher: Or there's an upward force, isn't it? And seeing it's a thrust, well you've gone one step ahead and you're going to call it?—tell the class again.
    Pupil: The upthrust.
    Teacher: Right. The upthrust. (Pause.)] [Now, if I weighed this . . .

The Incident

An initial plan in the Brisbane study was to classify verbal behaviour using the Smith and Meux scheme in toto. This plan, however, was modified, as there appeared to be a more satisfactory unit of verbal interaction than the episode. This new unit, the incident, was suggested by Nuthall and Lawrence (1965). After using the Smith and Meux classification scheme in New Zealand they proposed the smaller unit which could be more easily identified and categorized. It consists of any question or demand by the teacher and all the subsequent verbal moves which occur up to, and including, the final response. Any introductory comments preceding the initial question, or terminal comments following the last response, are also included.

Following Nuthall and Lawrence (1965) the incident was adopted as the unit of verbal interaction and all transcripts were analysed into these. Each incident was classified on the basis of the demand made upon the pupils in the initiating or opining move. The Smith and Meux criteria for classification of episodes were used for the classification of incidents. Examples of incidents appear in the following excerpt from another lesson.

    Teacher: . . . [Now, can you give me any others that aren't on
2   the board. Snakes and lizards. Come on.
    Pupil: Water snakes.
    Teacher: Yes, all sorts of snakes.] [Give me some others that aren't
2   on the board. (Pause.) Come on. Yes?
    Pupil: Goannas, Sir.

	Teacher:	Yes, he's a type of lizard and crocodiles? Yes, all these things go in together.] [What do you think we could call them? What—you've probably heard of snakes called this
2		sometimes. We could give them a certain name.
	Pupil:	Reptiles.
	Teacher:	Yes, that's right and we'll call that class the reptiles. It also has a Latin name a bit like that. . . .] [Which ones
2		do you think should go with the dog? Come on.
	Pupil:	Horse.
	Teacher:	Alright. Well, we'll put a horse with him too.] [Well, let's start at the top of the list. What about whales? Should
8		they go with the dog?
	Pupils in chorus: No Sir!]	
	Teacher:	[Who thinks they should go somewhere else?
13		(Some pupils raise hands.)]
	Teacher:	[Who thinks they go with the dog?
13		(A few pupils only raise their hands.)] [Well, they're warm blooded animals and they . . .

Episodic analysis and classification was, however, undertaken, and thus a comparison can be made with Smith and Meux's findings.

Comparative Data

In Illinois, Smith and Meux analysed transcripts of seventy lessons in science, mathematics, social studies and English. Only twenty of their transcripts were records of science lessons. In New Zealand, Nuthall and Lawrence coded the transcripts of eighteen lessons: seven in arithmetic, seven in language, and four in spelling and social studies. There were no data for science lessons.

Although a comparison between science lessons in New Zealand and Australia cannot be made, a comparison between science lessons in Illinois and Brisbane is possible. Smith and Meux (1962) provide a table showing the frequency of various types of initiating phases in episodes for all science lessons. Their figures are reproduced in Table 21.1. This table also shows the distribution of the logical operations in initiating statements for all the American, New Zealand and Australian transcripts.

The figures in Table 21.1 indicate that there are similarities in the distribution of categories in the American, New Zealand and Australian transcripts. A comparison between the distributions for the Illinois and Brisbane science transcripts, for example, indicates a similar emphasis by American and Australian science teachers on explanation and conditional inference. Approximately twenty per cent of all episodes for both groups of science classes were classified into these two categories. One might have expected explanation to have occurred more frequently since at meetings of science teachers, in science teaching journals, and in science curricula, discovery, inquiry, observation and interpretation of observations are advocated as 'essential' and worthwhile behaviours to be

TABLE 21.1

Distribution of Operations in Initiating Statements
(Percentages)

Operation	Smith and Meux		Nuthall and Lawrence Transcripts	Brisbane Science Transcripts
	All Transcripts	Science Transcripts*		
1 Describing	25.3	31.4	20	27.2
2 Designating	14.8	17.0	11	26.2
3 Stating	6.8	3.2	15	11.6
4 Reporting	2.9	3.2	2	0.0
5 Defining	4.1	6.1	8	2.4
6 Substituting	0.3	0.4	2	0.3
7 Evaluating	4.6	2.4	2	0.5
8 Opining	5.3	2.2	2	1.0
9 Classifying	3.0	3.2	3	1.0
10 Comparing and Contrasting	3.3	4.6	4	2.8
11 Conditional Inferring	7.3	8.8	13	7.9
12 Explaining	12.9	12.1	11	12.2
13 Classroom Management	9.4	5.4	4	6.9
14 Unclassified	—	—	3	—
	100	100	100	100
Total Number of Statements	3,397	935	395	2,422

*These figures were obtained from an analysis of 20 transcripts from four science classes (5 transcripts per class). The distribution of classes was grade 10 (1), grade 11 (2) and grade 12 (1) (Smith & Meux, 1962).

fostered. The behaviours which did occur frequently in all classes were describing and designating ones. In forty-six (New Zealand) to sixty-five per cent (Australia) of all episodes teachers required their pupils merely to give an account of something, to identify something by a name, word or symbol, to state a conclusion, and to give a statement of issues, or steps in a proof.

Some of the differences between the distributions in Table 21.1 are also of interest. For example, a higher proportion of behaviours were classified as describing, designating and stating in the Australian transcripts (65 per cent) than in either the New Zealand (46 per cent) or American (52 per cent) ones.

The comparisons made here must be treated with caution; though they are of interest they are limited by the complexities of the classification procedures, the differences in educational setting between the countries, and the fact that teachers and classes were not matched.

Incident Analysis

When the incident was used as the unit of verbal interaction, the distribution of logical operations in initiating moves was as shown in Tables 21.2 and 21.3. In Table 21.2 a comparison is made between the distribution obtained by Nuthall and Lawrence (1965) when all questions in the transcripts were classified, and that obtained in this study when the initiating questions in the incidents were classified. Both procedures are almost identical, for the incidents in the Brisbane transcripts were usually very simple; they contained only a single question or demand.

TABLE 21.2

**Distribution of Operations for all Questions (New Zealand) and
Initiating Question in Incidents (Brisbane)
(Percentages)**

Operation	All Questions (New Zealand)	Initiating Questions (Brisbane)
1 Describing	26	27.9
2 Designating	11	32.5
3 Stating	12	10.7
4 Reporting	2	0.0
5 Defining	5	2.1
6 Substituting	2	0.3
7 Evaluating	4	0.4
8 Opining	2	0.7
9 Classifying	2	0.8
10 Comparing and Contrasting	2	2.4
11 Conditional Inferring	7	7.2
12 Explaining	11	10.4
13 Classroom Management	3	4.6
14 Unclassified	11	—
	100	100
Total Number Classified	997	4,487

Table 21.3 contains the distributions of logical operations in initiating moves for all the teachers in the study, and the last column in this table contains the distribution of the averages for the categories for all teachers. The figures in this last column differ from those in the right-hand column of Table 21.2 because, on reclassification, it seemed more appropriate to include the original procedural explaining incidents within the describing category.

TABLE 21.3

Distribution of Operations in
Initiating Moves: Incident Analysis for All Teachers
(Percentages)

Operation	Teacher									All Teachers
	1	2	3	4	5	6	7	8	9	
Describing*	19.3	40.7	29.9	37.5	30.3	26.0	33.7	30.1	22.2	29.7
Designating	40.7	24.5	39.6	28.6	26.1	23.8	37.2	32.8	36.5	32.5
Stating	8.7	11.9	7.2	5.4	15.6	12.6	8.2	8.5	15.4	10.7
Defining	1.8	2.3	3.1	2.9	1.4	4.0	1.8	0.7	1.8	2.1
Substituting	0.0	0.0	0.0	0.0	0.0	5.1	0.0	0.0	0.0	0.3
Evaluating	0.1	1.5	0.2	0.2	0.0	1.1	0.3	0.3	0.0	0.4
Opining	0.9	0.3	1.2	1.0	0.4	1.8	0.8	0.0	0.7	0.7
Classifying	1.2	0.2	1.2	1.5	0.0	0.3	0.3	0.3	1.3	0.8
Comparing and Contrasting	1.5	1.5	0.7	5.4	1.4	2.5	5.4	1.0	2.6	2.4
Conditional Inferring	10.8	7.5	3.3	3.4	11.9	4.0	2.8	8.2	7.8	7.2
Explaining*	8.7	4.7	9.8	10.3	9.4	9.4	7.7	10.6	8.5	8.6
Classroom Management	6.3	4.9	3.8	3.8	3.5	9.4	1.8	7.5	3.2	4.6
	100	100	100	100	100	100	100	100	100	100
Total Number Classified	678	653	419	523	571	277	391	293	682	4,487

*In this table the initiating moves classified originally as procedural explaining are included in the describing category.

The results in the final column of Table 21.3 also appear in graphical form in the histogram in Figure 21.1. The histogram and the table show that for all teachers in the study the prevalent behaviours are designating, describing and stating. These constitute seventy-three per cent of all the behaviours. Explaining and conditional inferring rank fourth and fifth among the most frequently occurring behaviours, but they constitute only sixteen per cent of all teacher behaviours.

Distribution of Operations in Initiating Moves (Incident Analysis)

If it is assumed that the twelve major Smith and Meux categories (i.e., classroom management excluded) may be divided into those which require

FIGURE 21.1

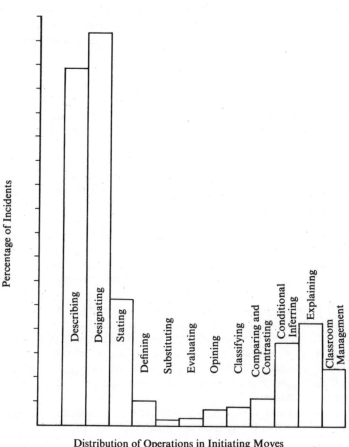

Distribution of Operations in Initiating Moves
(Incident Analysis)

pupils to engage in recall (e.g., describing, designating, stating and reporting) and into those which demand something more from the pupils (e.g., defining, substituting, etc.) the results in Table 21.3 also show that recall activities predominate in the science classes. In only twenty-three per cent of incidents did teachers demand more than recall of information from their pupils.

Table 21.3 reveals two other interesting facts. First, teachers differ in the number of questions they ask, or in the number of demands they make upon pupils. As the average duration of each lesson observed was thirty minutes, the results in Table 21.3 imply that the rate at which teachers ask questions ranges, on the average, from one in every thirty seconds to one in every fifteen seconds. The distribution of questions within each lesson, however, was irregular. This feature was gleaned from a study of the coded transcripts and from attempts to construct 'flow diagrams'.

The second fact of interest was the high degree of similarity in behaviours among teachers. This similarity became evident when rank intercorrelations between teachers were computed and when profiles were drawn for each teacher (Tisher, 1968).

Explaining Incidents

Explaining incidents were selected for closer study, not only because they ranked highest in frequency of occurrence of the 'higher-cognitive incidents' (Table 21.3), i.e., incidents which demand more than recall from pupils, but because explanation was assumed to play an important part in the scientific enterprise. The description here will be based on the elements, or moves, within explaining incidents. The moves are questions, replies and comments, and each explaining incident consists of a sequence of these. The purposes of this examination were, (a) to identify the types of replies pupils gave to questions demanding explanation, (b) to determine how frequently teachers, not pupils, supplied answers to the questions, and (c) to assess the extent to which teachers tolerate inadequate responses, i.e., responses which do not meet the demand of the question.

Nuthall and Lawrence (1965) studied explaining incidents in some detail and they developed categories for the classification of pupils' responses. Their categories were adopted here. The analysis of the explaining incidents, however, was not as detailed as that undertaken by the New Zealand researchers. Attention was focused on the pupils' responses to the 'explaining' question in the initiating move and the teacher's subsequent comments or questions.

Thirty-six transcripts (four per teacher) were selected for study and the incidents involving explanation identified. All the Smith and Meux types of explanation were found to occur. The incidents involving procedural explanation were then excluded from the analysis and it was noted that mechanical, causal and normative explanation accounted for ninety per cent of the remaining incidents. Sequential explanation accounted for only 1.8 per cent.

The types of pupils' responses were tallied and the results appear in column two of Table 21.4. Seven of the Nuthall and Lawrence (1965) response categories were used. They were:

1. *Aspect or Quality.* The response consists of a statement or description of a quality or aspect of the object, procedure or state of affairs to be explained.

2. *General Rule.* The response consists of a general rule or generalization which covers or includes the state of affairs to be explained.

3. *Causal Statement.* The response consists of a completed causal statement, or statement of conditional state of affairs.

4. *Action or Happening.* The response consists of a description of an action or procedure or something that has happened.

5. *Translation.* The response consists of translation of a state of affairs or word into another idiom or word or phrase with analogous meaning.

6. *Purpose or Aim.* The response consists of a description of the purpose or function of a procedure or action.

7. *Irrelevant Responses.* The response consists of a description of what the pupil has seen or done or heard of, or other general descriptive statements, which may provide relevant information but are not attempts at explanation (Nuthall & Lawrence, 1965, p. 42).

TABLE 21.4

Explaining Incidents.
Distribution of Type of Pupil Response**

Type of Response	*Number of Responses*	*Unacceptable Responses*	
		Question Repeated	*Answer Supplied*
Aspect	14 (11)	2	1
Rule	43 (41)	2	–
Causal	88 (74)	13	1
Action	26 (22)	4	–
Translation	4 (4)	–	–
Purpose	23 (21)	1	1
Irrelevant	39 (0)	31*	2*
Total	237 (173)	58	

*On six occasions the teacher asked a new question which did not require pupils to explain.
**Based on 36 transcripts.

The distribution obtained (column two, Table 21.4) indicates that the responses to the 'explaining' questions were heterogeneous.

Also, it was found that the teachers regarded 58 of the total responses as being unacceptable (see columns three and four, Table 21.4). On 53 of these occasions they indicated this by repeating the initial question. The repeated question was not preceded by any clarifying comment. On the other five 'unacceptable' occasions the teachers supplied the answer to the question. The distribution of the 173 acceptable responses is shown in parenthesis in column two of Table 21.4.

Forty-three per cent of the acceptable responses consisted of completed causal statements (74/173), but twenty-one per cent of the accepted responses were descriptions of actions or procedures, aspects or qualities of an object, or of a state of affairs. This indicates that teachers 'tolerated' replies that did not meet the demand of the question. Also, Aspect, Action and Irrelevant Responses formed a significant proportion (33 per cent) of the replies to all the questions demanding explanation.

Teacher Warmth or Learner-Supportiveness

The results from the administration of the Withall scale are summarized in Table 21.5. Three hundred statements per lesson were obtained from each teacher during two visits to the classroom, and three judges classified statements into the Withall categories. The inter-observer correlation co-efficient averaged 0.86 and the intra-lesson correlation coefficient averaged 0.79. Teacher-supportive statements did not appear in any of the lessons.

Table 21.5 contains the percentage of teachers' statements classified as either learner supportive, acceptant, clarifying, problem structuring, neutral, directive or reproving. The distribution of statements over categories is given for each teacher. Table 21.5 shows that the majority of statements for all teachers were classified as problem structuring and neutral. Sixty-five to eighty-five per cent of all statements were placed into these two categories. The problem structuring category accounted for all the questions asked, but, as was shown above, the most frequent demand made, or 'problem' set, was to require the pupils to recall names, or terms, or other factual information. The neutral category accounted for approximately

TABLE 21.5

Withall Scale.
Percentage of Statements in Each Category

Category	1	2	3	4	5	6	7	8	9	Average
					Teacher					
Learner Supportive	3	2	9	7	12	6	9	3	2	6
Acceptant	11	13	6	10	7	2	6	5	5	7
Clarifying	1	1	2	0	1	0	0	0	1	1
Problem Structuring	29	30	19	21	26	21	17	21	24	23
Neutral	36	40	37	51	36	57	54	57	59	47
Directive	12	9	17	8	9	12	9	10	4	10
Reproving	8	5	10	3	9	2	5	4	5	6

one-third to one-half (36–59 per cent) of all the teachers' statements. These neutral statements were neither teacher sustaining, nor learning sustaining, nor problem centred.

Withall (1949, 1951) assumed that the categories lie along a continuum from 'learner-centredness' to 'teacher-centredness', or high to low teacher warmth. If more of a teacher's statements were classified in the first four categories the classroom climate was said to be learner centred; if more were classified in the remaining three categories the climate was said to be teacher centred. The results in Table 21.5 show that, for all teachers, the majority of statements (54–71 per cent) were classified in the last three categories. Thus, the 'social-emotional climate' (Withall, 1949) in all the classrooms was teacher centred. Teachers did praise, encourage, or support the learner, but warmth or learner supportiveness was by no means prevalent in these science classrooms. The percentage of the teacher's statements classified as learner supportive, acceptant or clarifying ranged from eight to twenty per cent. It was shown too (Tisher, 1968) that a high degree of similarity existed among the teachers in their classroom behaviour as classified on the Withall Scale.

Conclusion

From the findings presented in the preceding paragraphs, a pen-picture of the science teacher and his classroom may be compiled.

Grade 8 science teachers exhibit a high degree of similarity in their behaviour patterns and, on the average, they ask from two to four questions per minute. The questions frequently require the pupils to recall names, terms and other factual material, and, less frequently, to engage in higher-cognitive behaviours such as classification, explanation and inference. When explanation is required, not only are a proportion of the pupils' responses irrelevant, but the teachers tolerate responses that do not meet the demands of the question. It is rare for students to ask questions of the teacher.

Within the classroom the social-emotional climate is teacher centred rather than learner centred, and, though on occasions the teacher is learner supportive, the majority of the statements he makes have no supportive intent.

Whether this picture applies to all grade 8 science teachers is an open question, and, perhaps, other research workers will test the conjecture that it does. Other projects will also show whether a high degree of similarity exists among teachers in their classroom behaviour. The finding, in this study, that they differed little from each other, was contrary to the judgement of senior officials in the schools who rated the teachers when the project began. The officials stated that there was considerable variability in teaching style within the sample.

The discussion in the preceding paragraphs indicates that considerable success was attained with the first aim of the Brisbane study. The modified Smith and Meux technique, for example, led to the presentation of a comprehensive 'map' of classroom verbal behaviour and of patterns within this. Data of this kind have high sociological value in much the same way as data from studies of families, peer groups and clubs do. Certainly, classrooms are important behavioural settings. With very few exceptions, human beings spend a large part of their formative years in them and on this ground alone a convincing case could be made for the more intensive and more sophisticated study of them. According to another viewpoint (Tisher, 1968), such data also have potential value in furthering our understanding of learning and teaching behaviours. Accepting this view, then, the study can be considered as a contribution to our understanding of the teaching process.

References

Ausubel, D. P., 1960: The use of advance organizers in the training and retention of meaningful verbal material. *Journal of Educational Psychology*, 51, 267-272.

Ausubel, D. P., 1963: *The Psychology of Meaningful Verbal Learning*. Grune and Stratton, Inc., New York.

Boyd, R. D. and Vere de Vault, M., 1966: The observation and recording of behavior. *Review of Educational Research*, 36, 529-551.

Meux, M. and Smith, B. O., 1964: Logical dimensions of teaching behavior. In B. J. Biddle and W. J. Ellena (Eds), *Contemporary Research on Teacher Effectiveness*. Holt, Rinehart and Winston, Inc., New York.

Nuthall, G. A. and Lawrence, P. J., 1965: *Thinking in the Classroom*. NZCER, Wellington.

Rutherford, F. J., 1964: The role of inquiry in science teaching. *Journal of Research in Science Teaching*, 2, 80-84.

Smith, B. O. and Meux, M., 1962: *A Study of the Logic of Teaching*. Co-operative Research Project No. 258, U.S. Department of Health, Education and Welfare, Office of Education, Bureau of Educational Research, University of Illinois, Urbana, Ill.

Tisher, R. P., 1968: A study of verbal interactions in science classes and its association with pupils' understanding in science. Unpublished PhD thesis, University of Queensland.

Withall, J., 1949: The development of a technique for the measurement of socio-emotional climate in classrooms. *Journal of Experimental Education*, 17, 347-361.

Withall, J., 1951: The development of the climate index. *Journal of Educational Research*, 45, 93-100.

Wittrock, M. C., 1967: Replacement and nonreplacement strategies in children's problem solving. *Journal of Educational Psychology*, 58, 69-74.

22

Association between Verbal Discourse and Pupils' Understanding in Science

R. P. Tisher

Introduction

IN THE previous chapter it was stated that molecular behaviour categories were used in an Australian study (Tisher, 1968) to investigate, in an exploratory way, the relationship between teacher behaviour and growth in understanding in pupils. The categories, which are based on a modified Smith and Meux scheme, were chosen because they describe the manner in which the teacher in interaction with his pupils shapes and charts what is said, and presumably thought, about subject matter.

The twelve major classificatory categories were divided into those teacher behaviours which would seem to require pupils to engage in *recall* (for example, designating, stating and reporting), and *higher cognitive behaviours* (for example, substituting, classifying, evaluating, explaining and conditional inferring). It was then postulated that, other things being equal, teachers who engage more frequently in higher cognitive behaviours will foster a greater understanding in pupils than teachers who less frequently engage in these behaviours. An attempt was made to examine this postulate.

The teacher, however, is not the only one exerting 'psychological force' (Gage, 1967) in the classroom. The pupils often contribute directly to their own cognitive growth through their purposive behaviour, and at other times they 'filter' the contribution of the teacher. The study makes use of both of these leading ideas and its theoretical basis (Tisher, 1968) could be described briefly in the following way:

Within a classroom the teacher's verbal behaviour is an important factor in helping to develop the pupils' understanding in a subject. The effect of the teacher's behaviour is modified, however, by various pupil variables. Depending on the effect of the interaction between the teacher and the pupil variables, the development of pupils' understandings will be enhanced or inhibited.

Pupil variables, which, according to the available research evidence, modify the effects of a teacher's behaviour, may be grouped into three categories. The first group contains those variables associated with *abilities* to classify, transform and store information, the second, those associated with *personal structures and stores of knowledge*, and the third, those associated with *personality orientations*. The variables selected for examination were taken from each of the three categories. Here, reference is made to three only of these variables—ability, prior-knowledge-in-science and achievement orientation; others selected included flexibility and attitude to science.

Intellectual Ability

An interaction between teacher behaviour and pupil ability was reported by Gallagher and Aschner (1963). Using twelve classes of pupils of high intellectual ability they attempted to relate the type of teacher questions to the production of divergent thinking on the part of pupils. They found, in general, that when the percentage of divergent questions was high, the percentage of divergent thinking produced was also high. Conversely, when the percentage of divergent questions was low, the divergent thinking produced was also low. In a study of fourth-grade science classes, Schantz (1963) reported on the effects of interactions between indirect and direct teaching and pupil ability. She found that high ability children exposed to indirect teacher influence scored significantly higher on a criterion science test than did the high ability children exposed to direct teacher influence. Sears and Hilgard (1964) also report the effect of interaction between pupil ability and various teacher behaviours. They indicate that for children of superior mental ability certain teacher behaviours seem to be effective in producing gains in achievement. These behaviours included the frequency with which the teacher emphasized the expanding and amplifying of ideas, giving alternatives and possibilities rather than straight statement of facts, and also the extent to which the teacher listened to the child.

The results from some studies on the effects of various methods of instruction indicate that the high ability pupils achieve equally well under each method, and that in each teaching situation their achievement is greater than that of low ability pupils (Doty, 1967; Geller, 1963; Oliver, 1965).

Cognitive Structure : Cognitive Store

Psychological theories and a number of research studies (Ausubel, 1963) have substantiated that the extent and organization of a pupil's existing store of knowledge of subject matter affect subsequent learning. Mallison (1964), for example, found that students whose achievement in science was low in the early years at secondary school tended to be low in achievement in science later in high school. He suggested that lack of knowledge in science in the earlier years inhibited subsequent development of understanding in the subject. Also, Ausubel and Fitzgerald (1961) have shown that there is a relationship between a pupil's existing degree of knowledge and the learning of unfamiliar material in the same subject-matter field. Ausubel (1963) says that general background knowledge probably facilitates learning and retention by increasing the familiarity of the new material, and hence the learner's confidence in coping with it.

Ausubel (1963) advocates certain teacher behaviours aimed at fostering greater understanding in a subject. These include cross linking of ideas in cognitive structure, classification of significant similarities and differences between new and established ideational content, and reconciliation of real or apparent inconsistencies between new and established ideas. Processes of exploration, classification and reconciliation, says Ausubel, influence cognitive structure by affecting the stability and clarity of knowledge in a particular subject-matter field. When cognitive structure is stable and clear, and also suitably organized, valid unambiguous meanings emerge. These meanings tend to remain discriminable from the ideational contents which subsume them.

Personality Orientations : Achievement Orientation

Differences in pupils' responses to particular styles of instruction have been shown to be associated with differences in personality orientations (Beach, 1960; Wispe, 1953). In particular, differences in achievement orientation have been shown to affect pupils' responses to particular styles of instruction. The studies by Bush (1954) and Della-Piana and Gage (1955), for example, indicate that many pupils who rate high in achievement orientation respond most favourably to teachers who emphasize mastery of information. Other pupils respond most favourably to friendly and considerate teachers.

On the basis of the findings and arguments in the preceding paragraphs it was assumed that, other things being equal, the development of understanding in science will be greatest for pupils high and low in ability, prior-knowledge-in-science and achievement orientation, when they are taught by teachers who frequently make higher-cognitive demands, and least when they are taught by teachers who less frequently make these demands. The results from the testing of these hypotheses are reported below.

However, the results of the research referred to above also suggest that behaviours other than those specified in the hypotheses are necessary to enhance the development of understanding. Teacher warmth, i.e., teacher behaviour which demonstrates friendliness, affection and support for pupils, also appears to be effective. Certainly when the variety of studies on teacher warmth are considered (e.g., Reed, 1961, 1962; Cogan, 1958), there appears to be an association between teacher warmth and pupil growth, but the evidence is not conclusive. Solomon (1966), in a study of 229 teachers of adult evening courses, identified ten bi-polar teacher-behaviour factors of which factor 5, 'warmth', or 'approval versus coldness', was one accounting for five per cent of the total variance. Though the factor was found to be significantly related to the course area (for example, social science teachers and humanities teachers exceeded chance frequencies in coldness and warmth respectively), there was no significant correlation between this factor and student gains on a criterion test (Solomon, Bezdek & Rosenberg, 1963, 1964). On the other hand, Christensen (1960), in a study involving fourth-grade pupils and their teachers, established that there was a significant relationship between teacher warmth and pupils' growth in achievement in vocabulary and arithmetic. Although this finding must be treated with some caution because the experimental sample was small and non-random, the result supports the general contention that teacher warmth is related to pupil outcomes.

From the Solomon and Christensen studies one might infer that teacher warmth is significantly related to the achievement of younger rather than older students. The results from other studies (Bush, 1954; Della-Piana & Gage, 1955; Ryans, 1961), however, indicate that a significant relationship may occur between teacher warmth and the productive behaviour and achievement of *some* older pupils. Ryans (1961), for example, established the existence of a low positive correlation between teacher warmth and the productive behaviour of secondary-school pupils. Also, the results from Bush's (1954) research suggest that a more effective educational relationship will be established between teachers and secondary pupils when pupils who are low in achievement and who seek acceptance and approval within the classroom setting are taught by 'warm' teachers. On the other hand, a more effective educational relationship will be established between teachers and secondary pupils when achievement-oriented pupils are taught by teachers who are primarily subject oriented.

On the basis of the preceding discussion it was assumed that, other things being equal, the development of understanding in science will be greatest for high achievement-oriented pupils when they are taught by teachers rated low in warmth, and least when they are taught by teachers high in warmth. The converse applies for pupils who are low in achievement orientation. The results from the testing of this hypothesis, too, are reported below.

Hypothesis Testing

The basic research design for the hypothesis testing phase of the study was a non-equivalent control group one (Campbell & Stanley, 1963). The project, however, was a naturalistic one (Baldwin, 1965) in the sense that variables were not manipulated by the research worker.

Using the ecological data (*see* Chapter 21) the teachers were classified as either high or low in warmth, and into three groups (high, medium and low) according to the frequency of their higher-cognitive demands. The hypotheses were tested using a two-way analysis of variance (ANOVA), and, as there were unequal cell frequencies, the least squares method (Winer, 1962) was used. For each analysis pupils were divided into high and low groups on the basis of their scores on the pupil variable under consideration. Pupils with scores above the median were classified as high, and those with scores below, as low. The remainder with scores equal to the median, were classified, alternately, as high and low.

A criterion science test, an attitude scale, a prior-knowledge-in-science test, Raven's Progressive Matrices and the California Psychological Inventory were administered to 338 grade 8 pupils in nine classes in Brisbane, and complete data were obtained from 168 (92 females, 76 males). The criterion test was administered as a pre-test (February) and post-test (November), and residual scores were calculated for each pupil using regression analysis. Control of variables was achieved by this technique (Tisher, 1968). The residual scores were interpreted as those parts of the final criterion score due to teacher behaviour and the pupil variable under consideration (e.g., pupils' prior knowledge in science). The residual scores used in each ANOVA were calculated from separate regression analyses. For example, when the interaction between ability and teacher behaviour was analysed, the residual scores were calculated using a regression analysis in which ability was not an independent variable.

As this part of the study was exploratory, rigid adherence to traditional procedures of reporting results was not maintained. There were two departures from tradition. First, although convention was followed by choosing the .05 level of significance for the hypothesis testing, the level was not regarded as sacred (Skipper, Guenther & Nass, 1967). For example, some values which fall slightly below the level are reported for the interest of readers. This procedure receives support from Labovitz (1968) and Skipper, Guenther and Nass (1967) who argue against the sacredness of .05. Nevertheless, findings were regarded as supporting the hypotheses only when they were significant at the .05 level. Second, although it is traditional to refrain from making t tests on differences between means when the corresponding F of the ANOVA is not significant, in several instances this procedure was not followed. The departure was considered to be justified where the theoretical basis suggested that directional differences should occur. Winer (1962) advocates a similar practice. He states (p. 208) that specific comparisons which are suggested by the theoretical basis for the experiment can and should be made individually, regardless of the outcome of the corresponding F test.

HYPOTHESIS I

The development of understanding will be greatest *for the able and less able* students when they are taught by teachers who frequently make higher-cognitive demands, and least when they are taught by teachers who less frequently make these demands.

The results relevant to this hypothesis appear in Tables 22.1 and 22.2. Table 22.1 summarizes the results for ANOVA with teacher behaviour and pupil ability, and Table 22.2 shows the mean residual scores and number of pupils (n) for each group. The measure of pupil ability used in this instance was based on the scores of pupils on the ACER Inter D (Clark, 1958).

The significance of the difference between pairs of group means in Table 22.2 was tested using the t statistic and the standard error of the mean of each cell was estimated from the mean square within cells (Lindquist, 1956). This technique assumes homogeneity of error variance which may not be met in all groupings in this study. However, the t test is robust with respect to moderate departures from the hypothesis of homogeneity of variance (Winer, 1962).

TABLE 22.1

ANOVA: Teacher Demands, Inter D
(Residual Scores)

Source of Variation	Sum of Squares	df	Mean Square	F Ratio	p
Teacher Demands					
(D)	213.70	2	106.85	3.22	$p < .05$
Inter D (I)	344.65	1	344.65	10.38	$p < .01$
D × I	192.92	2	96.46	2.91	$.10 > p > .05$
Error	5,377.93	162	33.20		

A convention has been adopted for specifying means in tables similar to Table 22.2. First, cells are numbered by columns from left to right and then row by row in each table. Second, 'M' with these numbers as subscripts is taken to refer to the mean of the cell. For example, in Table 22.2, M_I = mean for cell I in column 1 and row 1, and M_V = mean for cell V in column 2 and row 2.

Table 22.1 shows that teacher behaviour and intellectual ability affect pupils' development of understanding in science and that there is an interaction between teacher behaviour and ability.

TABLE 22.2

Cell Means for ANOVA: Teacher Demands, Inter D
(Residual Scores)

Pupil Group	Teacher Group : Higher-Cognitive Demands		
	High	Medium	Low
High	10.89	14.65	10.72
Inter D	($n = 20$) I	($n = 23$) II	($n = 41$) III
Low	6.87	8.98	10.03
Inter D	($n = 26$) IV	($n = 20$) V	($n = 38$) VI

For $M_{II} - M_I$, $t = 2.14$ ($p < .05$)
$M_{VI} - M_{IV}$, $t = 2.14$ ($p < .05$)
$M_{II} - M_{III}$, $t = 2.62$ ($p < .01$)
$M_I - M_{IV}$, $t = 2.34$ ($p < .02$)
$M_{II} - M_V$, $t = 3.22$ ($p < .01$)

The results in Table 22.2 show that several of the differences between pairs of means are in the predicted directions. Of these, the significant difference M_{III}— M_{II}, for example, suggests that gains in understanding will be greatest for the able pupils when they are taught by teachers rated medium rather than low in higher-cognitive demands. The results also show that the gains of the able pupils are greater than the gains of the less able when both are taught by teachers rated high and medium in higher-cognitive demands. Other significant differences (M_{II} — M_I and M_{VI} — M_{IV}, Table 22.2) are not in the expected direction. It appears, for example, that when the able pupils are taught by teachers who rate high in higher-cognitive demands, their development of understanding in science is *inhibited*. There is no clear explanation of this finding, but teachers rated high in higher-cognitive demands were particularly prone to accept irrelevant answers, or ones that did not meet the full demands of the question. It might be that the able pupils noted the inconsistencies between the teacher's demands and pupils' responses, became confused, and, consequently, were inhibited in their growth of understanding in science. Able pupils might be expected to reconcile the perceived inconsistencies by solving problems themselves, but the predominant classroom activity in this study was recall of information with relatively little time devoted to skills associated with problem solving, i.e., to evaluation, classification, inference and explanation. Problem-solving skills, would, therefore, be inadequately developed, and the pupils would be less able to reconcile perceived inconsistencies.

The findings provide some, though not unequivocal, support for hypothesis I.

HYPOTHESIS II

The development of understanding will be greatest *for pupils high and low in prior knowledge* in science when they are taught by teachers who frequently make higher-cognitive demands, and least when they are taught by teachers who less frequently make these demands.

TABLE 22.3

ANOVA: Teacher Demands, Prior Knowledge
(Residual Scores)

Source of Variation	Sum of Squares	df	Mean Square	F Ratio	p
Teacher Demands (D)	71.77	2	35.79	1.11	$p > .10$
Prior Knowledge (PK)	188.35	1	188.35	5.87	$p < .05$
D × PK	75.94	2	37.97	1.18	$p > .10$
Error	5,200.98	162	32.10		

Data and results relevant to this hypothesis appear in Tables 22.3 and 22.4. The results show that prior-knowledge-in-science affects development of understanding in science. The difference M_{II} — M_V (Table 22.4), which is significant at the .05 level (two-tailed t test) suggests that the effect of the medium teachers is greater with pupils whose prior-knowledge-in-science is high rather than low.

The results in Table 22.3 show also that teacher behaviour does not affect development of understanding in science and that there is no significant interaction between teacher behaviour and prior knowledge. These findings (Tables 22.3 and 22.4), which do not provide support for hypothesis II, suggest that pupils high *and* low in prior knowledge gain equally when taught by teachers who rate *high* or *low* in higher-cognitive demands.

TABLE 22.4

Cell Means for ANOVA: Teacher Demands, Prior Knowledge
(Residual Scores)

| Pupil Group | Teacher Group : Higher-Cognitive Demands | | |
	High	Medium	Low
High in	10.26	13.89	11.34
Prior Knowledge	$(n = 19)$ I	$(n = 23)$ II	$(n = 42)$ III
Low in	9.60	9.54	9.54
Prior Knowledge	$(n = 27)$ IV	$(n = 20)$ V	$(n = 37)$ VI

For $M_{II} - M_{V}$, $t = 2.51$ $(p < .05)$
  $M_{II} - M_{I}$, $t = 2.15$ $(p < .05)$

Probably there are several reasons for the failure to substantiate the theory. The most important of these is that although care was taken to choose teachers who were likely to differ in teaching style, the differences were, in fact, very small. In order to proceed with the hypothesis testing it was necessary to differentiate among the group of teachers, but the differentiation did not provide extreme groups. In addition to this lack of teacher variability there was another 'handicap' under which this hypothesis-testing exercise laboured. It was the failure of almost all teachers to capitalize on existing knowledge of pupils. It was found (Tisher, 1968) that teachers rarely used organizers or advance organizers, and also that, when they integrated ideas, they merely required pupils to relate present learning material to previously-learned ideas through the recall of factual information. This failure to capitalize on pupils' prior-knowledge-in-science may have affected the findings associated with hypothesis II.

HYPOTHESIS III

The development of understanding will be greatest *for high and low achievement-oriented pupils* when they are taught by teachers who frequently make higher-cognitive demands, and least when they are taught by teachers who less frequently make these demands.

Data and results of computations relevant to this hypothesis appear in Tables 22.5 and 22.6. Pupils were allotted to achievement-orientation groups on the basis of their scores on both Ac and Ai scales of the

California Psychological Inventory. Pupils high on Ac ('achievement via conformance') display factors of interest and motivation which facilitate achievement in any setting where conformance is a positive behaviour. Pupils high on Ai ('achievement via independence') display factors of interest and motivation which facilitate achievement in any setting where autonomy and independence are positive behaviours (Gough, 1964).

The results show that neither teacher behaviour nor pupil achievement-orientation affect the development of pupils' understanding in science and that there is no significant interaction between teacher behaviour and achievement orientation. With the exception of (M_{II} — M_I) and (M_V — M_{IV}) differences between pairs of means (Table 22.6) are in the predicted directions.

These findings do not provide support for hypothesis III.

TABLE 22.5

ANOVA: Teacher Demands, Achievement Orientation
(Residual Scores)

Source of Variation	Sum of Squares	df	Mean Square	F Ratio	p
Teacher Demands (D)	83.86	2	41.93	1.27	$p > .10$
Achievement Orientation (A)	55.63	1	55.63	1.69	$p > .10$
D × A	77.96	2	38.98	1.19	$p > .10$
Error	5,327.81	162	32.89		

TABLE 22.6

Cell Means for ANOVA: Teacher Demands, Achievement Orientation
(Residual Scores)

Pupil Group	Teacher Group : Higher-Cognitive Demands		
	High	Medium	Low
High Achievement Orientation	9.99 ($n = 22$) I	13.66 ($n = 20$) II	10.81 ($n = 42$) III
Low Achievement Orientation	9.77 ($n = 24$) IV	10.25 ($n = 23$) V	10.14 ($n = 37$) VI

For M_{II} — M_I , $t = 2.07$ ($p < .05$)
M_{II} — M_V , $t = 1.96$ ($p = .05$)
M_{II} — M_{III}, $t = 1.83$ ($.10 > p > .05$)

HYPOTHESIS IV

The development of understanding will be greatest for the high achievement-oriented pupils when they are taught by teachers rated low in warmth and least when they are taught by teachers high in warmth. The converse applies for pupils who are low in achievement orientation.

Data and results of computations relevant to this hypothesis appear in Tables 22.7 and 22.8. The results in Table 22.7 show that teacher warmth and pupil achievement orientation do not affect the development of pupils' understandings in science and that there is a significant interaction between warmth and achievement orientation. The directions of the differences between pairs of means in Table 22.8 are as predicted but only the differences between M_{III} and M_{IV}, and M_{II} and M_{IV} are significant at the .05 level. The results provide support for hypothesis IV. First, the development of understanding in science is greatest for the low achievement-oriented pupils when they are taught by teachers rated high in warmth and least when they are taught by teachers low in warmth. Second, the effect of the teachers who are low in warmth is greater with the high rather than the low achievement-oriented pupils.

TABLE 22.7

ANOVA: Warmth, Achievement Orientation (Residual Scores)

Source of Variation	Sum of Squares	df	Mean Square	F Ratio	p
Teacher Warmth (W)	10.20	1	10.20	0.32	$p > .10$
Achievement Orientation (A)	59.15	1	59.15	1.86	$p > .10$
W $\times$ A	259.99	1	259.99	8.18	$p < .01$
Error	5,211.94	164	31.78		

TABLE 22.8

Cell Means for ANOVA: Warmth, Achievement Orientation (Residual Scores)

Pupil Group	Teacher Group	
	High Warmth	Low Warmth
High Achievement Orientation	10.45 ($n = 50$) I	12.51 ($n = 34$) II
Low Achievement Orientation	11.44 ($n = 45$) III	8.47 ($n = 39$) IV

For $M_{III} - M_{IV}$ $t = 2.39$ $(p < .02)$
$M_{II} - M_{IV}$, $t = 3.08$ $(p < .01)$
$M_{II} - M_{I}$, $t = 1.66$ $(.05 < p < .10)$

The criterion test may be divided into two groups of items, recall and higher-cognitive (Tisher, 1968), and analyses of variance may be made using both residual recall and residual higher-cognitive scores. (The correlation between residual recall and residual higher-cognitive scores for two sets of regression analyses was of the order of .08.)

When residual recall and residual higher-cognitive scores were used in ANOVA, results similar to those shown in Tables 22.7 and 22.8 were obtained. These findings substantiated those reported above, and provide support for hypothesis IV.

Gough (1964) has reported that Ac, rather than Ai, was associated with successful achievement in high school. This was not so in the Brisbane study. Product moment correlations between Ac, Ai and pupils' scores on the criterion test were as follows:

for post-test score with Ac, $r = 0.11$
for post-test score with Ai, $r = 0.26$

For a one-tailed t test, values of $r \geqslant 0.18$ are significant at the .01 level, and values of $r \geqslant 0.12$ are significant at the .05 level.

To test whether Ac or Ai affected pupils' development of understanding in science, two-way analyses of variance were computed in which these measures were used to group pupils. The only significant result obtained was for the interaction between teacher warmth and Ac using residual recall scores. The results of this ANOVA are summarized elsewhere (Tisher, 1968). The findings, however, not only provide support for hypothesis IV, but allow the earlier findings to be qualified as follows: first, the development of understanding in science (*recall*) is greatest for the low Ac pupils when they are taught by teachers rated high in warmth and least when they are taught by teachers low in warmth. Second, the effect (*on gains in recall*) of the teachers who are low in warmth is greater with the high rather than the low Ac pupils.

Conclusion

The hypothesis-testing exercises proved to be interesting and worthwhile, although only a small number of hypotheses was confirmed. Several reasons for the failure to achieve complete success with the theoretical predictions were stated above. Given these, and possibly other handicaps, it would be unrealistic to expect that all the hypotheses would be unequivocally supported; perhaps the best that one could hope for would be 'trends' in line with the hypotheses. These trends appeared in almost all cases, and they justify the retention of the hypotheses, as hypotheses, when more carefully controlled *experimental* studies are undertaken.

Some significant and interpretable results were obtained. These included:

1. Gains in understanding are greatest for the able pupils when they are taught by teachers rated medium rather than low in higher-cognitive demands.

2. Gains in understanding of the able pupils are greater than the gains of the less able when both are taught by teachers rated high and medium in higher-cognitive demands.

3. The effect on gains in understanding of teachers who are medium in higher-cognitive demands is greater with pupils whose prior-knowledge-in-science is high rather than low.

4. The development of understanding in science is greatest for the low achievement-oriented pupils when they are taught by teachers rated high in warmth and least when they are taught by teachers low in warmth.

5. The gains of the high achievement-oriented pupils are greater than the gains of the low achievement-oriented pupils when both are taught by teachers low in warmth.

6. Recall gains are greatest for the low achieving-by-conforming pupils when they are taught by teachers rated high in warmth and least when they are taught by teachers low in warmth.

7. The effect on gains in recall of teachers who are low in warmth is greater with the high rather than the low achieving-by-conforming pupils.

In conclusion, two general comments on studies of this kind might be made. First, although there is a case for naturalistic, ecological studies they provide information only about teaching *as it is*. Any training programme which might eventuate in the future from such data would have, as the standard, the performance of the more effective teachers, and there would, among other things, be no guide to improvement for these. There is a need, therefore, to study the effects of *new* teacher behaviours. Gage (1966) and Meux (1967) suggest that one way of obtaining these 'new' behaviours is to use existing behaviours or strategies combined in ways not presently observed, and they believe that these combinations may result in teaching strategies which are far more effective than those presently used by our best teachers. However, care needs to be exercised lest the 'errors' of some experimental psychology (e.g., the artificial tying and untying of variables) be repeated. A slight variation of the Gage and Meux suggestion is to set up a model of the teaching process, design experiments to test the model, and train teachers to master the teaching model rather than model the master teacher. This approach to research in teaching and to the education of teachers is advocated by Stolurow (1965) and Campbell (1968).

The second general comment is that studies such as this one deal with only a small, albeit important, segment of teaching. The selected events and behaviours are taken from a complex of ongoing activities which is seldom studied in its entirety. Perhaps a glimpse at the 'hidden' elements of teaching may increase understanding of some of the more visible and well-known features of the process.

It has been said (Jackson, 1966) that 'our present knowledge of what goes on in the classroom resembles in many ways the traveller's impressions of a foreign country obtained by taking a one-hour bus ride through its major city' (p. 23). However, even the modest research currently being undertaken is making a contribution to our understanding of teaching, and the future looks brighter, if more challenging, than ever before.

References

Ausubel, D. P., 1963: *The Psychology of Meaningful Verbal Learning*. Grune and Stratton, Inc., New York.

Ausubel, D. P. and Fitzgerald, D., 1961: The role of discriminability in meaningful verbal learning and retention. *Journal of Educational Psychology*, 52, 266-274.

Baldwin, C. P., 1965: Naturalistic studies of classroom learning. *Review of Educational Research*, 35, 107-113.

Beach, L., 1960: Sociability and academic achievement in various types of learning situations. *Journal of Educational Psychology*, 51, 203-212.

Bush, R., 1954: *The Teacher-Pupil Relationship*. Prentice-Hall, Inc., Englewood Cliffs, N.J.

Campbell, D. J. and Stanley, J. C., 1963: Experimental and quasi-experimental designs for research on teaching. In N. L. Gage (Ed.), *Handbook of Research on Teaching*. Rand McNally & Co., Chicago, Ill.

Campbell, W. J., 1968: Towards making experimental psychology more useful to classroom practitioners. Paper read at the Annual Summer Seminar, Australian Psychological Society, Brisbane.

Christensen, C., 1960: Relationships between pupil achievement, pupil affect-need, teacher warmth and teacher permissiveness. *Journal of Educational Psychology*, 51, 169-174.

Clark, M., 1958: *Manual for the A.C.E.R. Intermediate Test D*. ACER, Melbourne.

Cogan, M., 1958: The behaviour of teachers and the productive behaviour of their pupils: I. Perception analysis. *Journal of Experimental Education*, 27, 89-105.

Della-Piana, G. and Gage, N. L., 1955: Pupils' values and the validity of the Minnesota Teacher Attitude Inventory. *Journal of Educational Psychology*, 46, 167-178.

Doty, B. A., 1967: Teaching method effectiveness in relation to certain student characteristics. *Journal of Educational Research*, 60, 363-365.

Gage, N. L., 1966: Research on cognitive aspects of teaching. In *The Way Teaching Is*. Report of the Seminar on Teaching, Association for Supervision and Curriculum Development, Washington, D.C.

Gage, N. L., 1967: Psychological conceptions of teaching. *Educational Sciences*, 1, 151-161.

Gallagher, J. and Aschner, M. J., 1963: A preliminary report: Analyses of classroom interaction. *Merrill-Palmer Quarterly*, 9, 183-194. Reported in E. Amidon and A. Simon, 1965: Teacher-pupil interaction. *Review of Educational Research*, 35, 131-139.

Geller, M., 1963: The measurement of the effectiveness of a teaching machine program in the organic area of first year college chemistry. *Journal of Research in Science Teaching*, 1, 154-161.

Gough, H., 1964: *Manual for the California Psychological Inventory*. Consulting Psychologists Press, Inc., Palo Alto.

Jackson, P., 1966: The way teaching is. In *The Way Teaching Is*. Report of the Seminar on Teaching, Association for Supervision and Curriculum Development, Washington, D.C.

Labovitz, S., 1968: Criteria for selecting a significance level: A note on the sacredness of .05. *The American Sociologist*, 3, 220-222.

Lindquist, E. F., 1956: *Design and Analysis of Experiments in Psychology and Education*. Houghton-Mifflin Company, Boston, Mass.

Mallison, G., 1964: *Final Report on Science Motivation Project 1 Cooperative Research Project 503. An Analysis of the Factors Related to the Motivation and Achievement of Students in Science Courses in the Junior and Senior High Schools*, School of Graduate Studies, Western Michigan University.

Meux, M., 1967: Studies of learning in the school setting. *Review of Educational Research*, 37, 539-562.

Oliver, M., 1965: The efficiency of three methods of teaching high school biology. *Journal of Experimental Education*, 33, 289-300.

Reed, H. B., 1961: Teacher variables of warmth, demand and utilization of intrinsic motivation related to pupils' science interests: A study illustrating several potentials of variance–covariance. *Journal of Experimental Education*, 29, 205-229.

Reed, H. B., 1962: Implications for science education of a teacher competence research. *Science Education*, 46, 474-486.

Ryans, D., 1961: Some relationships between pupil behaviour and certain teacher characteristics. *Journal of Educational Psychology*, 52, 82-90.

Schantz, B., 1963: An experimental study comparing the effects of verbal recall by children in direct and indirect teaching methods as a tool of measurement. Unpublished doctoral thesis, Pennsylvania State University. Reported in E. Amidon and A. Simon, 1965: Teacher-pupil interaction. *Review of Educational Research*, 35, 130-139.

Sears, P. and Hilgard, E. R., 1964: The teacher's role in the motivation of the learner. In E. R. Hilgard (Ed.), *Theories of Learning and Instruction. NSSE Yearbook*, LXIII, Pt I, Chicago University Press, Chicago, Ill.

Skipper, J. K., Guenther, A. L. and Nass, G., 1967: The sacredness of .05: A note concerning the uses of statistical levels of significance in social science. *The American Sociologist*, 2, 16-18.

Solomon, D., 1966: Teacher behaviour dimension, course characteristics, and student evaluations of teachers. *American Educational Research Journal*, 3, 35-47.

Solomon, D., Bezdek, W. and Rosenberg, L., 1963: *Teaching Styles and Learning*. Center for the Study of Liberal Education for Adults, Chicago, Ill.

Solomon, D., Bezdek, W. and Rosenberg, L., 1964: Teacher behavior and student learning. *Journal of Educational Psychology*, 55, 23-30.

Stolurow, L. M., 1965: Model the master teacher or master the teaching model. In J. D. Krumboltz (Ed.), *Learning and the Educational Process*. Rand McNally & Co., Chicago, Ill.

Tisher, R. P., 1968: A study of verbal interaction in science classes and its association with pupils' understanding in science. Unpublished PhD. thesis, University of Queensland.

Winer, B. J., 1962: *Statistical Principles in Experimental Design*. McGraw-Hill Book Co., New York.

Wispe, L., 1953: Teaching methods research. *American Psychologist*, 8, 147-150.

Indexes

Subject Index

DATE DUE

MAR 2 9			
MAY 1 9 1994			

261-2500

Printed in USA